THE WORLD'S WORST

MURDERS

CHANCELLOR
❧ PRESS ❧

This 2001 edition published by
Chancellor Press, an imprint of Bounty Books
a division of Octopus Publishing Group Ltd,
2–4 Heron Quays, London E14 4JP

The material in this book has previously appeared in:
The World's Most Infamous Murders
(Hamlyn, Octopus Publishing Group Ltd, 1994)
The World's Greatest Crimes of Passion
(Hamlyn, Octopus Publishing Group Ltd, 1990)
The World's Worst Atrocities
(Bounty, Octopus Publishing Group Ltd, 1999)
The World's Greatest Serial Killers
(Bounty, Octopus Publishing Group Ltd, 1999)

ISBN 0 7537 0424 2

Printed in Great Britain by Mackays of Chatham

Reprinted 2001, 2002

Front cover picture acknowledgments:
Clyde Barrow and Ted Bundy (Bettmann./Corbis)
Myra Hindley (Hulton Getty Picture Collection)

Contents

Infamous Murders

The Glamorous Lovers
Bonnie Parker and Clyde Barrow

Despite the popular image of Bonnie and Clyde as glamorous, rather hard-done-by bank robbers, the reality was very different; they were extremely vicious thieves and murderers.

Handsome Clyde was born on 24 March 1909 to a poor Texas farmer. Even as a young child he displayed sadistic tendencies, taking great delight in torturing farm animals.

Bonnie Parker born in 1911 came from a devout Baptist family. Her father died when she was four and the family then moved to Cement City, Texas. She was a pretty, petite girl with blue eyes and fair hair. Bonnie had married a Dallas tearaway named Roy Thornton when she was only 16 but the marriage had ended when he was sentenced to 99 years' jail for murder. Her mother was delighted when she met Clyde Barrow because she felt he would help Bonnie to get over her broken marriage. Bonnie was then nineteen-years-old and Clyde twenty-one.

Their relationship did not get off to a good start. The first night that Clyde visited Bonnie's house he was arrested on seven accounts of burglary and car theft. He was given a sentence of two years, but escaped when Bonnie smuggled a gun into the jail. He was recaptured after robbing a railway office at gunpoint, only a few days after his escape. Clyde Barrow was sentenced to prison for fourteen years.

Life in Texas prisons was brutal and extremely tough. Desperate to get out, Clyde persuaded another prisoner to cut off two of his toes with an axe. He was released on crutches and headed straight back to Bonnie.

To please Bonnie's mother he took a job in

3

Massachusetts in an attempt to make an honest living. However, he could not bear being so far from home and was soon back in West Dallas. Bonnie left home just three days later, to embark on a life of robbery and murder. The couple were joined by a friend of Clyde's called Ray Hamilton, and two other men.

The first murder was committed in April 1932 for the paltry sum of $40 when they shot a jeweller named John W. Bucher in Hillsboro, Texas. Bonnie was in jail at the time on suspicion of having stolen a car, but she was released three months later without any charges having been made. During that time Clyde and his associates brutally gunned down a Sheriff and a Deputy-Sheriff outside a dancehall.

The gang's biggest ever haul was $3,500, stolen from a filling station at Grand Prairie. Bonnie and Clyde decided to celebrate with a motoring holiday around Missouri, Kansas and Michigan, staying at top hotels and eating at expensive restaurants.

Not surprisingly, the money did not last long. They reverted to petty crime, murdering for surprisingly small amounts of money. Bonnie coolly shot a Texas butcher three times in the stomach before robbing him, and William Jones, a 16-year-old member of the Barrow gang, shot dead the son of the owner of a car they were caught stealing. Shooting to kill was now an automatic reflex.

In March 1933 the gang was joined in Missouri by Clyde's brother, Buck, and Blanche, Buck's wife. They narrowly escaped arrest from the apartment they were all staying in and shot dead two policemen in their escape bid.

It was now no longer safe for the fugitives to stay anywhere and they fled from town to town, robbing and killing as they went. They were both very aware that they would not remain at liberty for much longer and, indeed, Bonnie predicted their deaths in her poem, *The Story of*

Bonnie and Clyde. Their greatest fear seemed to be that they would not see their parents again, to whom they were both deeply attached.

Near Wellington, Texas, their car plunged to the bottom of a gorge. Clyde and Jones were thrown clear but Bonnie was trapped and seriously burned when it caught fire. She was rescued, with the help of a local farmer. The gang were sheltered for a few days by the farmer and his family who soon became suspicious and called the police. Once again, the fugitives escaped at gunpoint, and were rejoined by Buck and Blanche. Bonnie was still seriously ill.

In July the gang decided to rest at a tourist camp in Missouri. Again, the police surrounded them. Although they shot their way to freedom Buck had been hit through the temple and Blanche was blinded by glass. Desperately hungry, with the two women seriously ill and Buck dying, they stopped to buy food. Within minutes the police were upon them and Buck was shot in the hip, shoulders and back. The police had found him, after the shoot-out, with his wife crouched over him, sobbing. Buck died in hospital six days later and Blanche was given a 10-year prison sentence.

Bonnie and Clyde spent the following three months desperately running from the police, but their luck could not hold out. On 23 May 1934 their Ford V-8 sedan was ambushed by six police officers. Their car was pumped full with 87 bullets and they died immediately, their bodies bloody and broken. Clyde was 25 and Bonnie just 23.

Incredibly, the glamorous legend of the two ruthless lovers had already begun. Vast crowds flocked to their funeral in Dallas, snatching flowers from the coffins as souvenirs. Time has done nothing to erase their memory, and despite their callous, cruel deeds, they are remembered by many as folk heroes.

The Voyage of Terror
Thomas Bram

On the stormy night of 13 July, 1896, Lester Monks, a passenger on the sailing ship *Herbert Fuller*, unlocked his door and stepped warily into the captain's cabin with a loaded revolver in his hand. He had been roused from sleep by what sounded like the scream of wind through the halyards. But wider awake, he knew it was more than that – a woman had been screaming.

The captain's cot had been toppled to its side and the skipper, Captain Charles Nash, lay dying in a pool of blood. His wife, Laura was on her bunk. Like Nash she had literally been chopped to death, her skull smashed in front and back and both jaws broken.

Monks staggered up the forward companion way to find the first mate, Thomas Bram, pacing the deck. And from the moment that he heard the news, Bram's conduct was bizarre. He refused to alert the second mate, August Blomberg, because he thought the man was inciting the crew against him. And in the end, incredibly, he slumped to the deck and hugged the passenger's legs, begging for protection.

At dawn they roused steward Jonathon Spencer and the three went to Blomberg's cabin. There they found the door wide open and the second mate hacked to death in his bunk, two of his severed fingers on the floor.

Surprisingly, Bram, who had by now assumed command of the ship, was able to lead them to the murder weapon on deck – a new axe sticky with blood and flesh. Still more strangely, the big man gave a throaty shriek and hurled the weapon overboard.

At a meeting of crew and passengers, Bram urged that

6

the three bodies be thrown into the sea – an idea vetoed by all. He tried to blame the killings on the dead Blomberg, insisting that the second mate must have died of his own wounds. And he wanted to take the murder ship to French Guiana in South America.

An air of terror filled the big square-rigger, which had left Boston on 3 July bound for Argentina with a cargo of timber. In the six days that it took to return to port, no one aboard slept easily in his berth.

Bram managed to convince the crew that one of their members, Charley Brown, was acting suspiciously. If anything, the silent Brown looked relieved when they manacled him in a cabin. There were reasons why. Just before the ship reached Halifax. Brown told other crewmen he had seen the captain slain. As he had stood at the helm on that bloody night, the scene in the chartroom had been visible to him through a small window in front of the wheel. Brown said, he had heard Laura Nash screaming.

But he had kept the knowledge to himself because he was afraid of the maniac with the axe – their commander, First Mate Bram.

Bram's trial began in Boston on 14 December, 1896. Former shipmates testified that he had often approached them with the idea of killing ship's officers and selling the stolen cargo. Bram himself boasted of looting two other vessels.

Sentenced to the gallows, he won a new trial on technical grounds and was committed to the U.S. penitentiary in Atlanta. He would have stayed there except for one thing – the strange intervention of mystery writer Mary Roberts Rinehart, author of *The Bat, The Cat and The Canary,* and other thrillers.

Mrs Rinehart had managed to convince herself that Bram was an abused innocent who had been framed by his shipmates. She wove the notion into a sensational novel, *The After House*, and managed to convince President Woodrow Wilson that she was right.

Thomas Bram was pardoned in 1919.

The 'Monster in Human Shape' Mary Ann Cotton

Welfare worker Thomas Riley walked briskly through the early morning summer sunshine. It was 06.00 and he was on his way to another day's duties at the village workhouse in West Auckland. Times were hard for the people of County Durham, and Riley was kept busy trying to care for those who could not cope. As he turned into Front Street, he recalled the widow at No. 13. She had come to him only six days earlier, asking if he had room in the workhouse for her seven-year-old stepson, Charles Edward. 'It is hard to keep him when he is not my own, and he is stopping me from taking in a respectable lodger,' she said. Riley joked about the identity of the lodger. Was it the excise officer village gossips said she wanted to marry?' 'It may be so,' the woman had replied, 'but the boy is in the way.'

Now, as he walked to work, Riley noticed the widow in the doorway of her three-room stone cottage. She was clearly upset, and he crossed the road to ask why. He could not believe his ears at what she told him: 'My boy is dead.'

Riley went straight to the police and the local doctor. What he told them was the first step in an investigation that was to brand the widow, Mary Ann Cotton, the worst mass murderer Britain had ever seen.

Riley was suspicious about the death because the lad had seemed in perfect health when he saw him six days earlier. Dr Kilburn was also surprised to hear of the tragedy. He and his assistant Dr Chambers had seen the boy five times that week for what they thought were symptoms of gastro-enteritis, but they never thought the illness could be fatal. Dr Kilburn decided to withhold a death certificate and asked for permission to carry out a post-mortem examination. The coroner agreed to the request, and arranged an inquest for the following after-noon, Saturday, 13 July, 1872.

The pressures of their practice meant the two doctors could not start their post-mortem until an hour before the hearing. After a cursory examination, Dr Kilburn told the jury in the Rose and Crown Inn, next to Cotton's house: 'I have found nothing to suggest poisoning. Death could have been from natural causes, possibly gastro-enteritis.' The jury returned a verdict of natural death, and Charles Edward was buried in a pauper's grave.

But Dr Kilburn had taken the precaution of preserving the contents of the boy's stomach in a bottle. On the fol-lowing Wednesday he at last had time to put them to proper chemical tests. He went straight back to the police with the results. There were distinct traces of arsenic. Next morning, widow Cotton was arrested and charged with murder. The boy's body was dug up and sent to Leeds School of Medicine, where Dr Thomas Scattergood, lec-turer in forensic medicine and toxicology, discovered more arsenic, in the bowels, liver, lungs, heart and kidneys.

Meanwhile, Thomas Riley was pointing out to the authorities that the death of Charles Edward was not the first in the family. In fact, there had been four in the two years since Mary Ann Cotton, a former nurse, had arrived in West Auckland. Her fourth husband, coal miner Frederick Cotton, died from 'gastric fever' on 19 September, 1871, two days after their first wedding anniversary. He was 39. Then, between 10 March and 1 April, 1872 10-year-old Frederick, Cotton's son by a previ-ous marriage, Robert, Mary Ann's 14-month-old son, and

Mary Ann's former lover, Joseph Nattrass, who had moved in with her again, all died. Gastric fever was again the cause of death on their certificates, except for the baby, who died from 'teething convulsions.'

Those three bodies were exhumed while Mary Ann waited for her trial in Durham Jail, and Dr Scattergood found traces of arsenic in all of them. Newspapers began looking more closely at the life of the miner's daughter from the Durham pit village of Low Moorsley. They unearthed a horrifying dossier of an apparently kind, good-natured and devout Methodist who seemed to spread death wherever she went.

In 1852, aged 20, she had married a labourer called William Mowbray, and moved to Devon. She had five children there, but four died. The couple returned to the north-east, moving from house to house in the Sunderland area, while Mary Ann worked at the town's infirmary. They had three more children. All died. Then Mowbray died. Mary Ann married again. Her husband, an engineer called George Wood, died in October 1866, 14 months after the wedding.

A month later, Mary Ann moved in as housekeeper to widower James Robinson and his three children. She soon became pregnant and married Robinson. But within weeks of her arrival in the household, Robinson's 10-month-old son John was dead. On 21 April, 1867, Robinson's son James, six, went to his grave. Five days later, his sister Elizabeth, followed him. And on 2 May, nine-year-old Isabella, the only survivor of Mary Ann's marriage to Mowbray, lost her life.

Mary Ann had two daughters by Robinson. The first died within days of birth. The second was given away to a friend when the marriage broke up. Robinson survived, possibly because he resisted his wife's pleas to take out insurance on his life. But others who knew Mary Ann were not so lucky. She went to visit her mother because she feared she 'might be about to die'. No-one else was worried about the apparently sprightly 54-year-old, but within nine days she was dead. Mary Ann moved on, laden with clothes and bed linen.

She met and became friends with Margaret Cotton, and was introduced to her brother Frederick. Mary Ann quickly became pregnant, and married her new lover bigamously – her third husband, Robinson, was still alive. The wedding was slightly marred by the unexpected death of Margaret, whose £60 bank account went to the newlyweds.

In all, 21 people close to Mary Ann lost their lives in less than 20 years. She had given birth to 11 children, yet only one survived – the girl she gave away. Small wonder, then, that on the morning of her trial, a local newspaper, unfettered by today's laws of libel and contempt, ran the headline: 'The Great Poisoning Case At West Auckland – Horrible Revelations'. But when she stepped into the courtroom at Durham Assizes shortly before 10.00 on 5 March, 1873, she was charged only with one killing, that of her stepson, Charles Edward.

The prosecution, led by Sir Charles Russell, later to become Lord Chief Justice, alleged the 40-year-old widow had poisoned the boy because there was a Prudential Insurance policy on his life worth £8, and because he was an impediment to her marriage to her excise officer lover, a man called Quick-Manning, by whom she was already pregnant. 'She was badly off and Charles Edward was a tie and burden to her,' said Sir Charles.

Mary Ann Dodds, a former neighbour of the accused, told the court she had bought a mixer of arsenic and soft soap from one of the village's chemist's shops in May 1872, two months before the boy's death. The mixture was needed to remove bugs from a bed in Mary Ann's home.' she said. 'I rubbed most of it into the joints of the bed and the iron crosspieces underneath.'

Chemist John Townsend said the mixture would have contained about a course of arsenic – about 480 grams. Three grains were enough to kill an adult. He also thought it significant that his shop was not the closest chemist to widow Cotton's home.

Thomas Riley gave his evidence about Mary Ann's eagerness to get the boy off her hands, and Dr Kilburn explained the medical steps he had taken. It was then that controversy entered the trial. The prosecutions wanted to introduce evidence of earlier deaths in the family. Defence lawyer Thomas Campbell Foster, appointed only two days before the trial because Cotton could not afford her own legal representation, protested that his client was charged with only one death, which he maintained was an accident caused by arsenic impregnation of some green floral wallpaper. To discuss the earlier deaths would prejudice a fair trial, he said.

But Judge Sir Thomas Archibald ruled against him, citing legal precedent. From that moment on, the verdict was a foregone conclusion. The defence introduced no witnesses, and at 18.50 on the third day of the trial, the jury returned after only an hour's deliberations to pronounce Mary Ann Cotton guilty of murder.

The judge donned his black cap to sentence her to death, saying: 'You seem to have given way to that most awful of all delusions, which sometimes takes possession of persons wanting in proper moral and religious sense, that you could carry out your wicked designs without detection. But while murder by poison is the most detestable of all crimes, and one at which human nature shudders, it is one the nature of which, in the order of God's providence, always leaves behind it complete and incontestable traces of guilt. Poisoning, as it were, in the very act of crime writes an indelible record of guilt.'

They were fine words, but not strictly true. The state of medical knowledge in the 1870s was a common killer, and overworked doctors could not examine every corpse without strong reasons. Though the final tolls of deaths in Mary Ann's circle was high, she avoided suspicion by moving house frequently, and always calling in local doctors when her victims began complaining of stomach pains. The fact that she had once been a nurse, and was well known for caring for sick neighbours, also made people trust her.

No-one will ever know how many of the 21 unlucky people around her were poisoned either for insurance money, possessions, or because they stood in the way of a new marriage. Most people put the number of murders at 14 or 15. But despite the horror at what the *Newcastle Journal* newspaper described as 'a monster in human shape', many people had misgivings about her death sentence. There were doubts about hanging a woman, doubts about the way her defence in court had been organized, doubts about whether evidence of earlier deaths should have been allowed, doubts about the lack of any witness for the defence.

The *Newcastle Journal* admitted:
'Perhaps the most astounding thought of all is that a woman could act thus without becoming horrible and repulsive. Mary Ann Cotton, on the contrary, seems to have possessed the faculty of getting a new husband whenever she wanted one. To her other children and her lodger, even when she was deliberately poisoning them, she is said to have maintained a rather kindly manner.' The paper felt instinctively that the earth should be rid of her, but added: 'Pity cannot be withheld, though it must be mingled with horror.'

Mary Ann spent her last few days in jail trying to win support for a petition for a reprieve. She gave birth to Quick-Manning's daughter, Margaret, and arranged for her to go to a married couple who could not have children. Five days before her execution, the baby was forcibly taken from her. On 24 March, 1873, still maintaining her innocence, she went to the scaffold at Durham. It was three minutes before the convulsions of her body stopped.

Within eight days, a stage play, *The Life and Death of Mary Ann Cotton,* was being performed in theatres, labelled 'a great moral drama'. Mothers threatened recalcitrant children with the prospect of a visit from the West Auckland widow, and youngsters made up a skipping rhyme which began: 'Mary Ann Cotton, she's dead and rotten.' But she remains today one of the most enigmatic figures in the gallery of killers – a simple-minded mass murderer who evoked revulsion and sympathy in equal measures.

The Strychnine Specialist
Neill Cream

Neill Cream had a surprise for the hangman when he mounted the scaffold on 15 November, 1892. He unexpectedly confessed that he was Jack the Ripper. But the authorities knew better. They realized it was just another attempt by the pathetic psychopath to glamorize his career as a killer. Cream described by one acquaintance as 'a degenerate with filthy desires and practices'. certainly killed the same targets, in the same area, as the Ripper, but he did so in a style that was even more loathsome than that of London's most notorious murderer.

Cream was a pitiless sadist who revelled in drawing attention to his exploits. He committed the worst of his murders after being released from a life sentence in jail. Cream was born in Glasgow in 1850, but his parents emigrated to Canada when he was only four, and were prosperous enough to send him to Montreal's McGill College, where he qualified as a doctor in 1876.

But it was taking life, not saving it, that interested him most. He became an abortionist, a profitable though illegal trade in those days. Cream was doing well, until the father of Flora Brooks, a girl to whom he gave an abortion after making her pregnant, forced him at gun-point to marry her. The honeymoon lasted one day, before Cream left to continue his medical studies in London. The reluctant bridegroom returned after a year to find his wife died of consumption. He again worked as an abortionist, he moved south to the United States, to try his luck in Chicago. By 1880 he was known to the police. He was arrested for murder after Julia Faulkner, a girl whose pregnancy he aborted, died. He was, however, tried and cleared. Later two of few legitimate patients died, the first a spinster who was going to Cream for medicine, the second an epileptic railway worker, Daniel Stott, whose wife collected pills for him, and enjoyed Cream's sexual favours, at the clinic.

The police were not suspicious about either death, until Cream went out of his way to attract their attention. He wrote to the coroner saying the chemist must have put too much strychnine in Stott's pills, and asking for the body to be exhumed. When it was, it soon became clear that the chemist was not responsible for doctoring the pills Cream, who had eloped with Stott's widow, was arrested, and jailed for life for second degree murder. But in July 1891, after less than ten years, the governor of Illinois commuted the sentence, and Cream was released. His father had died, leaving him $16,000, and powerful friends of the family pulled strings to set him free to enjoy his new riches. Cream returned to Canada, but not for long. He soon sailed for England and the gas-lit streets of Lambeth where he had wandered as a student.

Cream had studied the career of Jack the Ripper, and was proud to walk where his hero had struck. He also had a penchant for prostitutes, boasting to acquaintances that he sometimes took on two at a time, or visited three in one night. But sex was not his only pleasure. He gave some girls pills which he said would cure the spots on their faces. In fact, they contained strychinine, the most agonizing of all poisons. And as the girls trustingly took them after he left, Cream got his kicks from imagining the excruciating pain of the victims as they writhed violently before death.

Late in 1891, two young prostitutes, Elizabeth Masters and Elizabeth May, were watching for Cream from their window in Hercules Road, Lambeth. But as he walked towards their room, he was accosted by another lady of the night, Matilda Clover, aged 26, and followed her to her lodgings in Lambeth Road. Ten days later, on 20 October she died there in terrible pain, blurting that she had been poisoned by pills given to her by a man named Fred. But Matilda's doctor, who was treating her for alcoholism, wrote 'Natural Causes' on the death certificate.

Seven days earlier, on 13 October, Ellen Donworth, a 19-year-old prostitute, had been found in dreadful agony in Waterloo Road. Before she died on the way to hospital, she told of a tall man with cross-eyes and gold spectacles who had given her a bottle containing white fluid to drink. The man also wore a silk hat and had bushy whiskers. A post-mortem examination revealed that Ellen had been killed by strychnine.

Cream followed up his two murders with the curious correspondence that the British police only later realized was his trademark. He wrote in false names to Lord Russell and a Dr William Broadbent, accusing them both of killing Matilda. He demanded £2,500 from the doctor, under threat of exposing him. Broadbent went to the police, but the blackmailer never turned up as arranged. Cream also wrote to the coroner who was to hear the Ellen Donworth case, saying he had information about the murderer which he was prepared to sell for £300,000. Police consigned the letter, signed G. O'Brian, detective, to their idiot file.

What Cream's purpose was in writing the letters has never been discovered. Some experts in psychology say he wanted to keep his crimes in the public mind, inventing sensational sums of money merely to make the murders more newsworthy. Certainly he was never interested in collecting the sums he demanded. Others say he had a death wish, almost wanting to be arrested so he could bask in what he imagined to be the glory of public recognition. Perhaps also he remembered that Jack the Ripper had taunted his pursuers through the mail.

Cream sailed home to Canada in January 1892, after getting engaged to Laura Sabbatini, and whiled away the hours on board by bragging to fellow passengers about his sex life, the poisons he used to 'get women out of the family way' and the false whiskers he wore to make sure he was not recognized. Back in Canada, for no apparent reason, he had 500 posters printed. They read: 'Ellen Donworth's Death. To the guests of the Metropole Hotel: Ladies and Gentlemen, I hereby notify you that the person who poisoned Ellen Donsworth on the 13th last October is today in the employ of the Metropole and that your lives are in danger as long as you remain in this hotel'. He signed the posters, 'Yours respectfully, W. H. Murray,' and datelined them 'London, April, 1892.' But why he picked on the Metropole Hotel was never explained. And, in fact, the posters were never distributed there.

Cream left New York for Liverpool on 23 March, and was back in Lambeth by 11 April, when he enjoyed a three-in-a-bed romp with 18-year-old Emma Shrivell and 21-year-old Alice Marsh. He left at 02.00, giving each girl three pills for her complexion. The two prostitutes died horribly that night, gasping to companions that the pills had come from a man called Fred.

The inquest verdict caused a sensation in a city still not certain that it had heard the last of Jack the Ripper. The two girls had been killed by strychnine. But again Cream could not leave well alone. And this time, it was to lead to the hangman's noose.

He wrote to a Dr Harper, accusing his son Walter, a medical student who lodged near Cream in Lambeth Palace Road, of causing the deaths of Alice and Emma. This time the price for suppressing the information was £1,500. Harper had nothing to fear, so he went to the police. They compared the handwriting with a letter Cream himself had given them. It was allegedly sent to Alice and Emma, warning them to beware of Dr Harper, who had killed Matilda and a certain Lou Harvey. The writing matched, and Cream was charged with attempted blackmail and false pretense. Meanwhile, police exhumed Matilda Clover's body from her pauper's grave in Tooting. She too had died from strychnine, despite her doctor's diagnosis of natural causes.

Cream had made a fatal mistake – only Matilda's killer would have known that she had been murdered. By accusing another man, he had convicted himself. Elizabeth Masters and Elizabeth May were prepared to testify that they had seen Cream with her before her death. The police knew they had a cast iron case. Only one thing troubled them. Who was Lou Harvey? They arrested Cream on 3 June, charged him with murder, and set about finding out.

Lou Harvey, when discovered in Brighton, turned out to be the one girl who had cheated Cream's murderous plans. She had met him the previous October in London's Soho and spent the night with him at a hotel. Before he left next morning, he gave her some pills to clear up acne on her forehead, and arranged to meet her that evening near Charing Cross. Lou – short for Louisa – never took the pills. The man who lived on her earnings did not like the look of them, and forced her to throw them away. And when she kept the evening date, he was watching from a distance.

Cream bought the girl a drink and presented her with roses. He then gave her two more pills to take, but she managed to throw them away surreptitiously, and he seemed satisfied when he asked to see her hands, and they were empty. Cream left to enjoy his death agony fantasies – and seemed astonished, a month later, to see her alive and apparently well in Piccadilly.

Lou's story was added to the dossier against Cream, and on 17 October, 1892, the heartless poisoner went on trial at the Old Bailey. He had no credible evidence to offer against the accusations of Louisa and the two Elizabeths. A chemist testified that Cream had bought nux vomica, a vegetable product from which strychnine is extracted, and gelatin capsules. Police revealed that seven bottles of strychnine were found in Cream's lodgings. The jury took only 12 minutes to find him guilty. Nobody mourned when the rope put an end to his miserable life less than a month later.

Two curious claims kept Cream's name before the public for a while longer. In an extraordinary letter to *The Times*, his optician claimed that his moral degeneracy might have been avoided if his cross-eye defect had been corrected at an early age. And Sir Edward Marshall Hall, one of the most renowned advocates in British legal history, said he once successfully defended Cream against a charge of bigamy by claiming he was in prison in Sydney, Australia, at the time. The governor of the jail there confirmed that a man answering Cream's description had indeed been in his custody.

When Marshall Hall later learned that Cream had never been to Australia, he became convinced that the poisoner had a double in the underworld, and that the two look-alikes supplied alibis for each other when necessary. Some writers have even argued that the double may have been Jack the Ripper. But despite his claim on the scaffold, Cream could not have been the Ripper. For he had an unshakable alibi at the time of the Ripper's reign of terror in 1888 – he was serving a life sentence in Chicago's Joliet Prison.

Caught By A New Invention
Dr Crippen

No name in the annals of murder is more notorious that that of Dr Hawley Harvey Crippen. Yet Crippen killed only once and, but for three fatal errors, might have got away with it. He was a quiet, inoffensive little man, intelligent, courteous and kind with a touch of nobility about his actions. Perhaps that only served to enhance the horror of his ghastly crime.

Born in Coldwater, Michigan, in 1862, he studied long and hard for his medical degrees in Cleveland, Ohio, London and New York. He practised in several big American cities, and was already a widower when, at 31, he became assistant to a doctor in Brooklyn, New York. Among the patients there was a 17-year-old girl who called herself Cora Turner. Attractive and lively, she was the mistress of a stove manufacturer by whom she was pregnant. She miscarried.

Despite her circumstances, Crippen fell in love with her, and began trying to win her affections. He found that her real name was Kunigunde Mackamotzki, that her father was a Russian Pole and her mother a German, and that the girl wanted to be an opera singer. Crippen paid for singing lessons, though he must have known her dreams were bigger than her talent. They married in 1893.

In 1900, Crippen, now consultant physician to Munyon's, a company selling mail-order medicines, was transferred to England as manager of the head office in London. Later that year Cora joined him, and decided to switch her singing aspirations to music hall performances. She changed her name to Belle Elmore, and Crippen too took a new name. He dropped Hawley Harvey and called himself Peter.

Cora cultivated a large circle of Bohemian friends, dressing gaudily, bleaching her hair, and acquiring false blonde curls. She was extrovert and popular, particularly with men, and for a time her insignificant husband, small, slight and with an over-sized sandy moustache, was happy to observe her gay social whirl through his gold-rimmed spectacles, occasionally buying her furs or jewellery which he loved to present in front of her friends. The finery contrasted with the squalor of their home – neither had much inclination for household chores, and both were content to live in a dingy back kitchen, surrounded by dirty crockery, piles of clothes, and two cats that were never let out.

Any bliss that there had been in this marriage of apparent opposites vanished while Crippen was away on the company's business in Philadelphia. He returned after several months to be told by Cora that she had been seeing an American music hall singer called Bruce Miller, and that they were fond of each other.

In September, 1905, the Crippens moved to 39 Hilldrop Crescent, off Camden Road, in north London. It was a leafy street of large Victoria houses, enjoying its heyday as a good address, and cost £52 50p (£52 10s) rent a year – a large slice out of Crippen's £3 a week salary. But the new home did nothing to heal the growing rift between husband and wife. Crippen was to recall: 'Although we apparently lived very happily together, there were very frequent occasions when she got into the most violent tempers and often threatened she would leave me, saying she had a man she would go to and she would end it all. She went in and out just as she liked and did as she liked. I was rather a lonely man and rather miserable.' Soon they were sleeping in separate rooms.

Cora threw herself into working for the Music Hall Ladies Guild, pretending to be a big star helping the less lucky members of her profession via the charity organization. She also took a succession of lovers, some of whom gave her gifts and money. Crippen found consolation too, in the form of Ethel Le Neve, a secretary at Munyon's offices in New Oxford Street. She could not have been less like Cora. Quiet, lady-like, she craved respectability, and the doctor had to use all his powers of persuasion before she at last agreed to accompany him to a discreet hotel room for the first time. Thoughts of her kept Crippen's spirits up as life at home became even worse. His wife began taking in 'paying guests', and when he returned from work, he was expected to clean their boots, bring in their coal, and help with cleaning.

By 1909, Crippen was also a paying partner in a dental clinic, and his expenses, with two women to support, were strained. That November, he lost his job as Munyon's manager, and was paid only a commission for sales. The following month, Cora gave their bank 12 months notice that she was withdrawing the £600 in their joint deposit account. She did not need her husband's consent for that. Cora had also learnt of Crippen's affair with Ethel, and told friends she would leave him if he did not give the girl up.

On 17 January, 1910, Crippen ordered five grains of hyoscine from a chemist's shop near his office. The drug, a powerful narcotic used as a depressant in cases of mental or physical suffering, was then virtually unknown in Britain, and the chemist had none in stock. He delivered it to the doctor two days later.

On 31 January, the Crippens entertained two retired music hall friends to dinner and whist. It was, according to one of the guests, Clara Martinetti, 'quite a nice evening and Belle was very jolly.' Clara and her husband Paul left at 01.30. Then, according to Crippen's later statements, Cora exploded with fury, threatening to leave home next day because he, Crippen, had failed to accompany elderly Mr Martinetti to the upstairs lavatory.

Cora Crippen was never seen alive again. On 2 February her husband pawned some of her rings for £80 and had Ethel Le Neve deliver a letter to the Music Hall Ladies Guild, saying that Cora, by now treasurer, would miss their next few meetings. She had rushed to America because a relative was seriously ill. On 9 February Crippen pawned more of his wife's gems, receiving £115. And soon her friends noticed still more of her jewels and clothes – being worn by Ethel Le Neve. She even went to the Guild's benevolent ball with Crippen, and wore one of Cora's brooches.

Inquiring friends started to get increasingly bad news about Belle Elmore from her husband. First she was uncontactable, 'right up in the wilds of the mountains of California.' Then she was seriously ill with pneumonia. And on 24 March, Crippen sent Mrs Martinetti a telegram just before he and Ethel left for a five-day Easter trip to Dieppe. It read: 'Belle died yesterday at six o'clock.' Two days later, notice of the death appeared in *The Era* magazine. Her body, according to Crippen, had been cremated in America.

Meanwhile, Ethel Le Neve had moved into 39 Hilldrop Crescent as housekeeper, bringing a French maid with her. She told her own landlady that Crippen's wife had gone to America. Clearly she was not likely to come back – Ethel left her wardrobe behind, expecting to use Cora's clothes.

Crippen had given his own landlord notice of quitting,

but he grew more confident as the constant questions about Cora tailed off, and so extended his lease until September. Then, on 28 June, came the first of what would prove fatal blows. A couple called Nash arrived back from touring American theatres, and told Crippen they had heard nothing of Cora's death while in California. Unhappy with his answers, they spoke to a highly-placed friend of theirs in Scotland Yard.

On Friday 8 July, Chief Inspector Walter Dew and a sergeant called at Crippen's office, and asked to know more about Cora. Did her husband have a death certificate? Crippen admitted that the story of her death was a lie, designed to protect her reputation. She had, in fact, run off to America to join another man, probably her old flame Bruce Miller. The doctor dictated a long statement over five hours, broken only for amicable lunch with the policemen at a nearby restaurant. He readily agreed to accompany the officers back to Hilldrop Crescent for a search of the house. Dew was mildly puzzled that Mrs Crippen had left behind all her finest dresses, but he left satisfied nothing was amiss.

Crippen did not know that, however. He panicked, and made what would prove to be his biggest mistake. Overnight, he persuaded Ethel to leave with him for a new life in America. Early next morning, he asked his dental assistant to clear up his business and domestic affairs, then sent him out to buy some boy's clothes. That afternoon Crippen and Ethel left for Europe.

On the following Monday, Chief Inspector Dew returned to ask Crippen to clarify a few minor points in the statement, and discovered what had happened. Alarmed, he instantly ordered a more thorough search of Crippen's house and garden. At the end of the second day, Dew himself discovered a loose stone in the floor of the coal-cellar. Under it he found rotting human flesh, skin and hair, but no bones.

A team of top pathologists from St Mary's hospital, Paddington, painstakingly examined the remains, and decided they were of a plump female who bleached her hair. Part of the skin came from the lower abdomen, and included an old surgical scar in a position where Mrs Crippen was known to have one. The remains also contained huge traces of hyoscine, which kills within 12 hours if taken in excess. On 16 July, warrants for the arrest of Crippen and Ethel were issued. They were wanted for murder and mutilation.

Crippen had made two errors. He had carved out the bones of the body, and presumably burned them in the kitchen stove. But he had treated the fleshy remains with wet quicklime, a corrosive substance only effective when dry. And he had wrapped them before burial in a pyjama jacket with the label 'Shirtmakers, Jones Brothers, Holloway.' All might still have been well but for his third error, fleeing.

The discovery of the body aroused horrified indignation in the British press, but the two runaways, staying in Rotterdam and Brussels, did not realize the storm had broken. On 20 July, they left Antwerp in the liner *SS Montrose*, bound for Quebec. Crippen had shaved off his moustache and discarded his glasses, and was posing as John Philo Robinson, while Ethel, dressed in the boy's clothes Crippen's assistant had bought, pretended to be his 16-year-old son, John. But if they thought they were safe, they were wrong.

The ship's commander, Captain Kendall, had read all about the gruesome findings at Hilldrop Crescent, and was aware that the *Daily Mail* had offered £100 for information about the couple the police were hunting. Kendall noticed an inordinate amount of hand-touching between Mr Robinson and his son. The boy's suit fitted badly, and he seemed almost lady-like when eating meals, when his father would crack nuts for him or offer him half his salad.

Kendall surreptiously collected up all the English-language papers on board so as not to alarm the couple. He checked Crippen's late of reaction when he called him Robinson, and invited the couple to dine at his table. After two days at sea, he sent a message to the ship's owners over the newly-installed wireless telegraph, reporting his suspicions. On 23 July, Chief Inspector Dew and his sergeant set sail from Liverpool in the *Laurentic*, a faster trans-atlantic liner, which would overtake the *Montrose* just before it reached Quebec.

Then followed eight bizarre days. Crippen sat on deck, admiring the 'wonderful invention' of the wireless telegraph, not realizing that he was the subject of the crackling messages. Kendall's daily reports were avidly printed by the *Daily Mail*, whose readers relished every word as the net closed in on the unsuspecting doctor.

It was 08.30 on 31 July when Dew, accompanied by a Canadian policeman, boarded the *Montrose* disguised as a pilot. The ship was in the St Lawrence, and only 16 hours from Quebec. After reporting to Captain Kendall, Dew walked down to the deck and approached his suspect. 'Good morning, Mr Crippen.' he said. 'I am Chief Inspector Dew,' Crippen said only: 'Good morning, Mr Dew.' Ethel, reading in her cabin, screamed, then fainted, when a similar introduction was made. Crippen said later: 'I am not sorry, the anxiety has been too much. It is only fair to say that she knows nothing about it. I never told her anything.' He described Ethel as 'my only comfort for these three years.'

Extradition formalities took less than three weeks, and on 20 August, Dew set sail for England with his celebrated prisoners aboard the liner *SS Megantic*. Dew, who was travelling as Mr Doyle, kept Crippen, now known as Mr Neild, apart from Ethel, though on one evening he did allow the two to gaze silently at each other from their cabin doors, after a request from Crippen. Huge, angry crowds greeted the two at every stage of their rail journey from Liverpool to London. And public feeling was still at fever pitch when their trials began. Crippen was charged with murder, Ethel being an accessory, and wisely they elected to be tried separately.

The doctor refused to plead guilty, even though he knew he had no credible defence. Seven days before his hearing began, at the Old Bailey on 10 October, the remains found at Hilldrop Crescent were buried at Finchley as those of Cora Crippen. Yet her husband claimed in court that they could have been there when he bought the house in 1905. That argument fell when a buyer for Jones Brothers swore that the pyjama material in which the remains were wrapped was not available until 1908. Two suits in it had been delivered to Crippen in January, 1909.

Crippen had no answer to questions about why he had made no effort to search for his wife after she vanished on 1 February, why no-one had seen her leave the house, why he had then pawned her possessions or given them to Ethel. Bruce Miller, now married and an estate agent in Chicago, said he last saw Cora in 1904, and denied ever having an affair with her.

On the fifth day of the trial, the jury found Crippen guilty after a 27-minute retirement, and Lord Chief Justice Alverstone, who had been scrupulously fair throughout the proceedings, sentenced him to death. Crippen, who had stood up remarkably well to cross-examination, declared: 'I still protest my innocence.'

A curious story, that Crippen had rejected a suggested defence because it would compromise Ethel, began circulating. The line, allegedly suggested by eminent barrister Edward Marshall Hall, was that the doctor had given his nymphomaniac wife hyoscine to calm her demands on him, because he was also making love to Ethel, and that Cora had died through an accidental overdose. Crippen

27

was wise to reject the story, if he did so. For if death was accidental, why go to so much trouble to chop up the body, remove the bones, and to hide the flesh?

All along, he had been anxious to clear Ethel Le Neve's name, and on 25 October the Old Bailey did so after a one-day trial dominated by a brilliant speech by her defence lawyer, F.E. Smith, later Lord Birkenhead. He asked the jury if they could really believe that Crippen would take such care to hid all the traces of the murder, then risk the 'aversion, revulsion and disgust' of a young, nervous woman by telling her. 'This is how I treated the woman who last shared my home, and I invite you to come and share it with me now.' Ethel was found not guilty and discharged.

But she did not desert her lover, and as he waited for execution, he thought only of her, continually proclaiming her innocence, kissing her photograph, and writing touching love letters to her. He also wrote in a statement: 'As I face eternity, I say that Ethel Le Neve had loved me as few women love men . . . surely such love as hers for me will be rewarded.'

The man whose name has become synonymous with murder was hanged in Pentonville Prison on 23 November, 1910, still protesting that he had murdered no-one. His last request was that Ethel's letters and photograph be buried with him. They were. A curious kind of sympathy had grown for the quiet, considerate little man, both among prison staff and those who came into contact with him. F.E. Smith called him 'a brave man and a true lover.' And there were many who agreed with Max Beerbohm Tree's verdict on the day of execution: 'Poor old Crippen.'

Ethel Le Neve slipped quickly into obscurity. Some say she emigrated to Australia, and died there in 1950, others that she went to Canada or America. Another report was that, for 45 years, she ran a tea-room near Bournemouth under an assumed name. And there have been rumours that she wrote her version of the Crippen affair, to be published after her death. But all the theories could be as wide of the mark as the wild legends that have turned her mild-mannered lover into the most monstrous murderer the world has even seen.

The Lonely Hearts Killers
Raymond Fernandez
and Martha Beck

Raymond Fernandez and Martha Beck were two social misfits whose crimes outraged the society that had scorned them. Both had at one stage led almost normal, useful lives, but fate had played cruel tricks on them. After they teamed up in 1947, it was they who played the cruel tricks. And they paid for them with their lives.

Fernandez, born in Hawaii of Spanish parents, moved to Spain in the 1930s and married a Spanish woman. After serving in Franco's forces during the Civil War, and gaining the reputation of a war hero, he worked with distinction for British intelligence in the Gilbraltar docks. In 1945, he sailed for America, working his passage on an oil tanker. During the voyage, a hatch cover fell on his head. He recovered in hospital at Curaçao, but his personality had changed radically. He became a cunning, ruthless swindler, convinced that he had supernatural powers over women, and determined to use them to the utmost.

He began advertising in lonely hearts magazines, and fleecing the gullible people who answered his pleas. By 1947 he had claimed more than 100 victims. He was just back from Spain, where his latest dupe had died mysteriously during their holiday, when he decided to follow up an intriguing letter from a woman in Florida with a personal visit.

Martha Beck's name had been forwarded to the lonely hearts club as a joke by one of her friends. Martha was an outsize woman of 280lb whose bulk and sexuality constantly made her a figure of fun to others. At 13 she had been raped by her own brother, who continued the incestuous relationship until she complained to her mother. For reasons which Martha never understood, she was blamed for the sordid affair, and forced to live a cloistered existence which deprived her of normal relationships as a teenager.

She became a nurse, moving to California and an army hospital. But the scandals of her nymphomaniac sex life forced her to return east, where she became superintendent of a home for crippled children at Pensacola, Florida. There she met Fernandez, who was using his business name, Charles Martin.

A torrid affair quickly began, Fernandez introducing Martha to new perversions which satisfied her sexually for the first time in her life. She gave up her job and left behind her two children, one illegitimate, the other the product of a disastrous marriage, to follow Fernandez. When he explained his line of business, she agreed to become his accomplice, posing as his sister. But she loved him too much to allow him a free hand. He could woo and wed women – but she would not allow him to consummate the marriages.

Such jealously hampered the romantic con-man. The first joint effort resulted in the victim claiming back her car and $500, and refusing to sign over her insurance policies. The ill-starred lovers moved on to Cook County, Illinois, and Fernandez married Myrtle Young in August 1948. But again there were violent rows when the bride expected to sleep alone with her husband, and Martha refused to allow it. Myrtle was given an overdose of barbiturates, and put on a bus to Little Rock, Arkansas. She collapsed and died there. Fernandez and Beck made $4,000 and gained a car.

In Albany, New York, that December, Fernandez charmed a naive widow, Janet Fay, 66, into signing over all her assets and her $6,000 insurance policy to him. Then she was strangled and battered to death with a hammer. The body was stuffed into a trunk, and the couple took it with them to New York City, where they rented a house in Queens, and buried the makeshift coffin under cement in the cellar.

The following year Fernandez and Beck were in Grand Rapids, Michigan, trying to fleece a 28-year-old widow called Delphine Downing. Once again, Martha reacted angrily when Fernandez started sleeping with her. Then Delphine saw her husband without his toupe, and threaten to leave him, taking her daughter Rainelle. Before she could go however, both Delphine and Rainelle were killed and their bodies were cemented into the cellar floor. Curious neighbours were told that Delphine and her daughter were away on holiday.

But suspicious relatives called the police. They searched the house while Fernandez and Beck were out at the cinema, found the two bodies, and arrested the couple on their return. A curious tug-of-war between two states now began. Michigan did not have the death penalty, but New York did. The murder of Janet Fay had been discovered, and New York asked for the couple to be sent there for trial. Public fury at the couple's evil exploits played some part in New York getting its way.

Fernandez and Beck were charged with three murders, and suspected of 17 more, including that of Mythle Young. The trial began in July 1949, and lasted 44 days. Press coverage of the proceedings was unprecedented in its hatred and intolerance, and every intimate detail of the sordid sex life of the couple created sensational headlines. Crowds flocked to the courtroom to catch a glimpse of the 'monster' and his 'overweight ogress'.

The verdict was never in doubt. Fernandez and Beck were found guilty of first-degree murder, and sentenced to death on 29 August. Their appeals were dismissed and on 8 March, 1951, they went to the electric chair at Sing-Sing Prison.

Two hours before the execution, Fernandez sent Martha a message of love. She said: 'Now that I know Raymond loves me, I can go to my death bursting with joy.' But there was nothing joyful about the death. Newspapers gleefully reported the struggle to fit her huge bulk into the chair, and the prolonged writhing as the electric shocks struggled to have an impact through her flabby body. Such was public distaste for the Lonely Hearts Killers that more people laughed at that last ordeal than felt pity for its victim.

The Killer Clown
John Wayne Gacy

When they christened him with the name of their favourite film star, John Wayne Gacy's parents had high hopes that their little boy would one day become famous. In a way they saw their dreams realized – although not quite as wished.

John Wayne Gacy today is a name that conjures up revulsion among millions of Americans. He is one of the country's most sadistic and prolific mass murderers, and known as the Killer Clown. When he was finally tracked down and tackled by the Chicago police in 1978, Gacy readily admitted to murdering no fewer than 33 young men and boys. Before strangling and stabbing them to death, he had brutally raped them.

Gacy was a fat, lonely homosexual with an insatiable

sexual appetite. He longed to be loved by the neighbours who regarded him as 'a weirdo'. And he had aspirations of becoming somebody in local politics. To that end, he began a deliberate campaign to win over the local populace in the Chicago suburb of Norwood Park Township. A friend with connections in the Democratic Party showed him how: he would have to become a local benefactor with particular emphasis on the neighbourhood children.

Gacy set about this task with gusto. He designed three clown outfits himself, then set about creating a character. Very soon he was a local celebrity as Pogo the Clown, performing in the streets, at children's parties and other functions. He was so successful that President Carter's wife Rosalynn posed with him for a photograph, then sent him an autographed copy. He treasured that.

But while 38-year-old Gacy clowned for the kids and posed for posterity, the Chicago police were baffled by the mysterious disappearance of a number of local youths. On their files were also several missing persons from other states.

It took the police six years to nail Gacy. When they did, they met with a torrent of abuse from residents of Northwood Park for the appalling record of overlooked clues and bungled detective work. Had they been more efficient, people argued, at least some of the Killer Clown's victims might have lived. In fact, on four occasions between 1972 and 1978, Gracy's name had appeared on police files as a suspect in the missing persons cases. He had also been convicted twice for sex assaults on young men.

Interviewed at police headquarters, Gacy drew a detailed map of his property, pinpointing the location of 28 of the bodies. After raping and killing his victims, he had methodically buried them in the extensive, landscaped garden of his neat and modern ranch house. The bodies of five other boys had been thrown into the Des Plaines river, near his home.

Gacy had been heavily influenced by his mother since childhood. His older sister also seemed to dominate him. He was a weak-willed man who carried his resentment towards women with him through later life. Nevertheless, he was determined to succeed in business. And that much he did. From humble beginnings, he built up a construction business that flourished.

Gacy took advantage of the rising unemployment in Chicago and offered jobs to young unskilled men who stood the least chance of finding employment. His local lads were all under 20 and receiving unemployment benefit. Others he picked up from the Greyhound Bus station in Chicago: these were often drifters heading for California hoping to find their pot of gold. Instead they found death.

'I wanted to give these young people a chance' he told police during questioning. 'Young people always get a raw deal. But if you give them responsibility they rise to the occasion. They're hard workers and proud of their work.'

Gacy's teenage workforce were well-paid and happy. As the contracts continued to pour in, he needed more labourers. At the end of a hard day – for he put in many hours himself – Gacy would get into his Oldsmobile and head for the Greyhound Station, looking for more employees among the itinerants. He always found somebody.

He had been married in 1967 and again five years after that. His first wife, who divorced him in 1969, bore him two children. She said of him. 'He was a likeable salesman who could charm anything right out of you.' Wife number two, Carole Hoff, said her husband 'started bringing home a lot of pictures of naked men' just before they separated. They were divorced in 1976. Both his wives described him as 'mysterious' and said he had been a normal husband for the first few months of marriage, but then began staying out at night in his car. He beat his wives.

Where did Gacy go? Later it emerged that he would frequent 'Bughouse Square', a notorious corner of Chicago populated at night by legions of young homosexuals and male prostitutes. He picked up young men and they, like the itinerants and the local boys who worked for his building company, were among the dead found later by police.

All this time, Gacy was winning friends and influencing people with his Pogo The Clown antics. He made hefty contributions to the Democrative Party, which he supported wholeheartedly. In the three years before his capture, Gacy funded and organized an annual political summer fete with beer, hamburgers and music and attended by five hundred local dignitaries and business bigwigs. The proceeds went to President Carter's re-election fund, and for his efforts he was lauded by the White House.

A pure coincidence led to his arrest. One of Gacy's political contacts during this time had known one of the victims, and harried police into mounting an extraordinarily intensive search for the missing youngster. Once again, as had happened on several occasions years before, the trail seemed to lead to Gacy. Police raided his luxury ranch house in December 1978. They placed Gacy under arrest and a team of forensic experts moved in, combing the place for clues.

As the horrified neighbours watched, police systematically dug up the garden. By the third day, the remains of 28 different bodies had been unearthed. Gacy had at first denied murdering anyone, but gradually admitted the first few, then finally drew a detailed map of his garden for police. The five remaining corpses were fished out of the Des Plaines river by police frogmen in a massive dredging operation.

Details of Gacy's *modus operandi* emerged over the ensuing months. Since boyhood, he had had a fixation for police matters. He loved to play policeman, and owned guns and other paraphernalia, including handcuffs. When he got a young man back to his house he would show the unsuspecting fellow the 'handcuff trick', assuring him that he would be released after only a few seconds. Instead, of course, once the victim was in Gacy's power, he would become the subject of a wild homosexual rape. Instead of learning, as Gacy had promised, how to get free from the handcuffs, the victim would hear Gacy say: 'The way to get out of these handcuffs is to have the key. That's the real trick.'

The handcuff trick was quickly followed by the 'rope trick' and this always spelled the end for the victim. Gacy would throw a piece of cord around the victim's neck, and tie two knots in it. Then he would push a piece of wood through the loop and slowly turn. Within seconds the victim was unconscious; a few seconds more and he was dead.

At his trial in 1979, Chicago District Attorney William Kunkle described him as a sick man who methodically planned and executed his many murders. Kunkle asked for the death penalty; the State of Illinois was then debating whether to reintroduce execution for certain types of murder.

Defence attorney Sam Amirante pleaded that Gacy was insane at the time he committed the murders. But there had been so many, and over such a long period of time that Gacy was convicted and given life imprisonment.

The Vampire Killer
John Haigh

Donald McSwann entered a den of death when he followed his friend John Haigh into his basement workshop. McSwann operated a pinball arcade in London where Haigh sometimes worked as a mechanic. Haigh boasted about his workshop and it was, indeed, a basement to be proud of. There was equipment for every kind of craftsman . . . for the carpenter, the welder, the sheet metal worker – and the murderer.

McSwann stared at the 40-gallon vat of sulphuric acid in one corner. His curiosity drove him to ask about the need for such a strange array of equipment. His questions were never answered. Crouching behind him. Haigh viciously swung a hammer in a deadly arc . . . and he had slaughtered his first victim.

According to Haigh, when he later confessed to the crime, he drank some of McSwann's blood. Then he spent the night methodically dismembering his body and feeding it into the vat. The sulphuric acid bubbled and smoked, occasionally forcing him to escape outdoors for a breath of fresh air. By the next afternoon, McSwann's remains had dissolved into a mass of sludge. Haigh disposed of it, bucket by bucket, sloshing the ghastly residue into a basement manhole connected to the sewer system.

It was September 1944 and no one thought anything of McSwann's disappearance. Haigh's murder-for-profit scheme was succeeding to perfection.

He assured McSwann's aging parents that their son was hiding out in Scotland until the end of the war. Haigh even went to Scotland once a week to post a letter to them signing McSwann's name.

In between the trips, he ran the pinball arcade business that had belonged to his victim. Wartime crowds poured into the arcade and Haigh was taking in money hand over fist. But it was still not enough to buy the lifestyle he wanted, and greed drove him to his next murder for profit.

His victims were to be McSwann's parents. He wrote to them, again forging their son's name, and begged them to meet him at the home of his dear friend, John Haigh.

One the night of 10 July, 1945, Haigh bludgeoned them to death in his workshop. Afterwards he dissolved their bodies in the vat of acid and poured the reeking sludge down the drain.

Using forged documents Haigh helped himself to the entire estate – five houses and a fortune in securities and later transferred it to his own name.

Because of his inveterate gambling, self-indulgence and a string of bad investments, he was broke again by February 1948. He decided to invite a young married couple, Rosalie and Dr Archie Henderson, to look at his new workshop at Crawley, south of London. Both went into the acid bath.

Although the Henderson's estate had been profitably disposed of in 1949 Haigh found that he needed one more victim. Still convinced he was living a charmed life, he chose this one with little caution.

She was Mrs Olive Durand-Deacon, a 69-year-old widow whose husband had left her £40,000. She lived at the same London residential hotel as Haigh, who had not paid his bills for months and who was desperate for money.

Mrs Durand-Deacon believed that, apart from having a private income, Haigh had made money by patenting inventions She put to him an idea for false plastic fingernails. Haigh showed interest, invited her to visit his Crawley workshop and in February 1949 drove her down there.

What happened next was described by Haigh in a statement he made to police and which was read at his trial:

> She was inveigled by me into going to Crawley in view of her interest in artificial fingernails. Having taken her into the storeroom, I shot her through the back of the head while she was examining some materials.
>
> Then I went out to the car and fetched a drinking glass and made an incision – I think with a penknife

– in the side of her throat. I collected a glass of blood, which I drank.

I removed her coat and jewellery (ring, necklace, earrings and crucifix) and put her in a 45-gallon tank.

Before I put her handbag in the tank, I took from it about 30 shillings and a fountain pen. I then filled the tank with sulphuric acid, by means of a stirrup-pump. I then left it to react.

As an afterthought, Haigh added: 'I should have said that, in between having her in the tank and pumping in the acid, I went round to the Ancient Prior's [a local teashop] for a cup of tea.'

It took some days and two further trips to Crawley to check on the acid tank before Mrs Durand-Deacon's body appeared to be entirely dissolved. Meantime, the police had questioned her fellow guests at the hotel, including Haigh.

The killer's glib, over-helpful manner made one detective particularly suspicious and he checked on the 39-year-old suspect's background. He unearthed a prison record for minor frauds and arrested Haigh. The murdered confessed, but claimed that he could never be proven guilty because police could never find any of his victims' remains.

He was wrong. Forensic scientists examined the foul sludge that had been emptied from the tank onto the ground in the yard of the Crawley workshop. They were able to identify a gallstone, part of a foot, remains of a handbag and an almost complete set of false teeth. These were shown to Mrs Durand-Deacon's dentist, who confirmed that they had belonged to the trusting widow.

In court Haigh's lawyers claimed that the killer was insane. They pointed to a strict and unhappy childhood – his parents belonged to the Plymouth Brethren – and to his claimed habit of drinking his victims' blood. But although the British press labelled him The Vampire Killer, the judge and jury failed to accept this bloody trait as evidence of insanity. After a trial of only two days, he was found guilty of murdering Mrs Durand-Deacon and sentenced to death. Asked if he had anything to say, Haigh replied airily: 'Nothing at all.'

On 6 August, 1949 he was hanged at Wandsworth Prison.

The A6 Lay-By Murder
James Hanratty

The A6 murder has led to more controversy than almost any other killing in Britain. An illiterate, feeble-minded petty criminal called James Hanratty was hanged for it after the longest murder trial in English legal history. Ever since, an extensive and distinguished lobby of authors has campaigned to persuade the public that British justice executed the wrong man.

At dusk on 22 August, 1961, two scientific workers at the Road Research Laboratory in Slough, Buckinghamshire, were cuddling in the front seat of a grey Morris Minor saloon in a cornfield at Dorney Reach, beside the river Thames between Windsor and Maidenhead. Michael Gregsten was 38, a married man with two children. Valerie Storie was an attractive, single 23-year-old who had been his mistress for three years.

They were interrupted by a tap on the driver's side window. Gregsten wound down the window, and the man standing there pointed a gun at him. The terrified couple thought it was a hold-up. They offered the man their money, watches, even the car. He sat in the back seat, warning them not to look at him, toying with the gun. He told them he was on the run, and that every policeman in

Britain was on the look-out for him. But he seemed undecided about what he was going to do.

Finally, at about 23.30, he ordered Gregsten to start driving. There followed a bizarre 30-mile drive through the northern suburbs of London, Slough, Hayes and Stanmore, broken only he stops to buy petrol and cigarettes. Gregsten, nervous already, was put further on edge by the back-seat driving of his captor, issuing instructions about the route and urging care at blackspots. They turned on to the A5 towards St Albans, Gresten occasionally flashing his reversing lights to try to attract attentions, and keeping an eye out for policemen, so he could stage a crash. He saw none.

On the A6, between St Albans and Luton, the gunman ordered Gresten to pull into a lay-by. He said he wanted 'a kip', and made an attempt to tie Miss Storie to a door handle. He asked Gregsten to hand him a duffle bag, but as the driver reached for it, he was shot twice in the head. 'He moved too quick, he frightened me,' the gunman said as the girl screamed: 'You bastard.'

As blood flowed from her lover's wounds, Miss Storie was forced into the back seat, ordered to remove some of her clothes, then raped. The man then made Miss Storie pull Gregsten's body from the car to the edge of the concrete lay-by. She sat beside the body, too stunned to cry, while the man continued to dither about what to do next.

Eventually, Miss Storie gave him a £1 note if he would leave quickly. He took it, and seemed to be going. But as he approached the car, he unexpectedly turned, and pumped five bullets at the girl. One pierced her neck, close to the spinal cord. She lay still, pretending to be dead, as he strode over to inspect his work. Convinced he had elminated the only witness to his earlier killing, he drove off.

Passing drivers failed to hear Miss Storie's screams. She took off and waved her petticoat, but no-one saw it in the dark. At last she passed out, and was found at around 06.30 by a teenager arriving for a traffic census. She recovered consciousness in hospital, and began giving waiting police officers extremely detailed description of all that had happened. Her wounds had paralyzed her, consigning her to life in a wheelchair, but her mind was unaffected.

Two identikit pictures were issued, based on her descriptions , and those of witnesses who saw Gregsten's car being driven before it was abandoned in Ilford, Essex. Police were following a confusing trail of clues. At first they suspected Peter Louis Alphon. Two .38 bullets were found in the hotel room at the Vienna Hotel, Maida Vale, where he spent the night after the murder. Ballistics expert matched them with those that had killed Gregsten. But when Alphon was put in an identity parade. Valerie Storie failed to pick him out. She selected one of the stooges who could not possibly have been the murderer. Alphon did not match the identikit descriptions, nor did James Hanratty. And the police did not suspect him because he was known to them only as a petty and non-too-successful villain. But then he seemed to go out of his way to attract attention.

Police were already puzzled by anonymous calls to the hospital where Valerie Storie was recovering, threatening her life. They moved her to a fresh bed every night, and reinforced the guard on her. Then Hanratty phoned Detective Superintendent Acott, the man in charge of the hunt, saying he was anxious about being suspected for the A6 murder, and denying his involvement. Since the call was completely unsolicited, Hanratty immediately became a prime suspect.

Police discovered that he had asked an associate, Charles France, whether the back seat of a London bus was a good place to hide a gun. Hanratty was known to have acquired a .38 Enfield revolver earlier in the year. A similar gun was found behind the rear seat on the top deck of a No 36 bus. Police also discovered that Hanratty had booked into the Vienna Hotel the night before Alphon, staying in the same room as J. Ryan. And Gregsten's widow named him as the likely killer of her husband, though many wondered how she could possibly know.

Hanratty was arrested in Blackpool on 9 October and put in an identity parade. Valerie Storie again failed to pick him out, though she had now mentioned piercing blue eyes in her description of the killer. Hanratty had such eyes. She then asked each of the line-up to say the words the murderer had used several times: 'Be quiet, will you. I am thinking.' Hanratty always pronounced the last words 'finking'. And it was then that Miss Storie identified him.

The trail began on 22 January, 1962. The police were given a hard time by the defence, who accused them of concentrating on implicating Hanratty instead of hunting down the truth. Much was also made of Miss Storie's identity parade failures, and the changes in her description of the killer.

But the defence was not helped by Hanratty himself. Though he pleaded not guilty, he was cocky and insolent throughout. A fellow prisoner who had been in custody with Hanratty swore that he had confessed to the killing and gave details of it known only to police and Miss Storie. Hanratty claimed that at the time of the murder he was in Liverpool with friends. But he refused to name them , saying to do so would break their trust to him. Then, inexplicably, he changed his alibi, and said he was in Rhyl, North Wales. Again he could not prove it.

There were enough doubts about both the prosecution and defence cases to keep the jury out for nine-and-a-half hours on 11 February. Once they returned for guidance from the judge. Then they filed back to court to return a verdict of guilty. He said only: 'I an innocent.' Every appeal was rejected. Hanratty, aged 25, was hanged at Bedford Prison on 4 April, 1962.

But even today, there are those who say there was too much 'reasonable doubt' about the affair to condemn any man. Peter Alphon made a series of sensational confessions to newspapers, saying Hanratty's conviction was contrived. Later, however, he withdraw them all. Charles France, Hanratty's friend, who had given evidence about the gun against him in court, hanged himself, leaving a note about the case. But it was not read at the inquest on the grounds that it was not in the public interest. Witnesses then came forward to claim that they had seen Hanratty in Rhyl on the night of the murder.

Books by Louis Blom-Cooper, Paul Foot and Ludovic Kennedy all helped to make Hanratty the greatest *cause célèbre* since Timothy Evans was condemned by Christie's evil lies, and was posthumously pardoned, Hanratty had virtually condemned himself by changing his alibi in court. And for everyone who claimed he was unjustly hanged, there were others who agreed with Detective-Superintendent Acott that Hanratty was 'one of the worst types of killers in recent years.'

The Mass-Murderer of Hanover Fritz Haarmann

Wild terror, more akin to the Middle Ages than the 20th century, swept the north German town of Hanover in the spring of 1924. In winding alleys beneath the gabled roofs of the old quarter, people whispered that a werewolf was at large, devouring anyone foolish enough to venture out after dark. Some said children were being butchered in cellars. Police doctors were inundated with strange-tasting meat brought in by housewives who feared it was human flesh. The authorities dismissed the alarm as 'mass hysteria'. And they blamed a prank of medical students when children found the first of many human skulls beside the river Leine on 17 May.

The authorities were as wrong as the panic-stricken public. But the truth, when it emerged later that year, was just as macabre as the people's wildest fears. It ended in execution for a 45-year-old mass murderer called Fritz Haarmann, the jailing of his 25-year-old partner in crime – and a national scandal.

Haarmann had been a wandering vagrant, hawker and pilferer for most of his life. He worshipped his mother – an invalid after his birth in Hanover on 25 October, 1879 – and hated his father, a morose, miserly locomotive stoker known to all as Sulky Olle. When Fritz's bitterness spilled into violence, his father tried to get him committed to an asylum. But doctors decided that, though the boy was incurably feeble-minded, there were no grounds to commit him.

He roamed the country, a popular figure with the underworld and the police of many cities. Fellow petty crooks regarded him as fat and stupid, but kind, always ready to offer help, money and advice to those worse off than himself. The police liked him because he always came quietly when arrested, laughing and joking with them. He was always a model prisoner, accepting and even enjoying jail discipline. He served time for picking pockets, petty thieving and indecent behaviour with small children.

In 1918, Haarmann emerged from a five-year sentence for theft and fraud to find post-war Germany in chaos. Law and order had broken down, and profiteers, swindlers and crooks reigned supreme in the anarchy. These were the people Haarmann understood. He returned to Hanover, spending most of his time among the con-men and dubious traders at the straggling markets outside the central railway station. He became obsessed with the people inside the station – refugees from all over Germany, human flotsam without jobs or money, homes or hopes, who cowered round stoves by day, and huddled on platform benches at night.

Haarmann knew he could make a living in this twilight world, but, as he grew more and more accustomed to it, he realized there were other opportunities for him. Among the down-and-outs were many teenage boys, some no more than 12 years old. They had run away from home, often unable to cope with life there once their stern fathers returned from the war after years away. Haarmann turned on his charm with them, listening to their grievances, offering them advice, winning their confidence. In a country where everyone was carefully documented, he had discovered a constant flow of people nobody could trace. They would disappear for ever, and their parents and the police would be none the wiser.

Haarmann took lodging at 27 Cellarstrasse, and set up in business as a meat-hawker and seller of secondhand clothes. He could haggle with the best of the market traders, and his business soon prospered. Housewives quickly learned that his prices were lower than anyone else's, and that his stock was always plentiful and varied. But he still spent his evenings with the boys at the station, laughing and joking with them, handing round chocolates and cigarettes, greeting hungry, forlorn new arrivals with the cheery offer of a meal and a mattress for the night.

Within weeks, Haarmann was such a familiar face there that welfare workers considered him almost as one of them. And the police decided to use his services, too. They needed spies in the underworld to try to stem the growing crime and corruption, and rewarded their 'narks' by turning a blind eye to their activities, legal and otherwise. Haarmann was delighted to help. Using the intimate knowledge of crooks he had gained over the years, he quickly earned the nickname of 'Detective' by reporting crimes, hiding places and plots. In return, the police did not pry into his business. And they were loathe to inquire too closely in September, 1918, when the parents of 17-year-old Friedel Rothe reported him missing after he was seen with Haarmann in a billiards room. It took the threat of force to persuade the officers to visit Haarmann's rooms, and their search was merely cursory.

Six years later, Haarmann was to brag at his trial: 'When the police examined my room, the head of the boy Friedel was lying wrapped in newspaper behind the oven.' For the truth was that the 'Detective' was not the bluff, genial do-gooder he seemed. The wretched youngsters he befriended were taken to his home for a good meal, often sexually assaulted, then killed in the most savage fashion – a bite at the throat. The bodies were then dismembered, the meat being sold, the skull and bones being disposed of in the river Leine.

That narrow escape in 1918 did not make Haarmann more cautious. If anything, he became bolder as the police relied more and more on his information. And in September 1919 he met the accomplice who was to incite him to more murders. Hans Grans was then 20, and himself a runaway from home. Slim, graceful, cynical and emotionless, the librarian's son soon established ascendancy over his social inferior, taunting him with insults and sarcasm. And he began to order the killing of selected victims, often merely because he coveted their clothing.

The two men moved to rooms in Neuestrasse, then into an alley called Rothe Reihe (Red Row), almost on the banks of the Leine. Neighbours noted that a constant stream of young boys went into the apartment, but that none ever seemed to come out. They overheard sounds of chopping and splashing. Occasionally police brought the grief-sicken parents of missing boys to the rooms. They had heard that their sons had last been seen with the

'Detective'. Somehow, they always left satisfied that Haarmann had nothing to do with the disappearances.

One morning, a neighbour met Haarmann on the stairs. As he stopped to gossip and joke with her, a paper covering the bucket he was carrying slipped slightly, and she saw that the bucket was full of blood. But she said nothing to the authorities. After all, Haarmann had to hack carcasses of meat as part of his trade. Another neighbour once heard him chopping in his room, and asked: 'Am I going to get a bit.' He chuckled: 'No, next time.' She also saw a young boy lying very still on Haarmann's bed, but was told: 'Don't wake him, he's asleep.' A customer took a piece of meat from Haarmann to the police doctor because she was suspicious of its taste. She was told it was pork.

By 1923, Haarmann had made himself indispensible to the police. Not only was he still informing on criminals, he had set up a detective agency in partnership with a highly-placed police official, and was also recruiting for the Black *Reichswehr*, a secret organization working against French occupation of the Ruhr. He was so sure of police protection that he was taking enormous risks, selling the clothes of victims only a day or two after murdering them. One woman bought a pair of socks from him for her son, and found two spots of blood on them. She threw them away. A man spotted Grans wearing a suit that, days earlier, had belonged to boy at the railway station.

But pressure was building up on the police. Newspapers had noted that large numbers of youths from all over north Germany had arrived in Hanover, then vanished. One paper claimed that 600 had disappeared in just one year. Hanover was acquiring a sinister reputation. The published fears brought out into the open suspicions many had been prepared to keep to themselves. The discovery of the skull by the river Leine in May 1924 was the final straw.

Now the police had to deal not with the occasional distraught parent, but with outraged public opinion. Another skull was discovered by the river on 29 May – a small skull, about the size of a young boy. Two more were unearthed on 13 June. A police spokesman claimed they could have been swept down-river from Alfeld, where hurried burials were taking place due to a typhus outbreak. But the explanation was not accepted by the frightened public. They believed a monster was preying on their town – and many were convinced that he lived in Rothe Reihe. Faced with a mounting tide of witnesses pointing the finger at Haarmann, the chief of the police decided to act.

Haarmann still had powerful friends, impressed by the help he was giving the authorities. So the police chief moved cautiously. He brought in two detectives from Berlin, instructing them to watch Haarmann's movements at the station. On the evening of 22 June, 1924, he approached a boy called Fromm who objected to his attentions. They began to quarrel, then fight, and the detectives moved in to arrest them both.

With Haarmann safe at headquarters, a police squad swooped on his rooms. The walls were splashed with blood, and there were heaps of clothing and personal possession. Haarmann protested that since he was both a meat trader and a clothes salesman, such findings were not unexpected. Then the mother of a missing boy recognized his coat – being worn by the son of Haarmann's landlady.

The game was up, and Haarmann knew it. He broke down and confessed to several murders, accusing Grans of instigating and assisting in many of them. Grans was immediately arrested. Meanwhile, more and more human remains were being discovered beside the River Leine. Boys playing in a meadow found a sack packed with them on 24 July. When dredgers probed the black ooze of the riverbed, watched by thousands lining the banks, they brought to the surface 500 bones.

Haarmann and Grans were tried at Hanover Assizes on 4 December, accused of killing 27 boys aged between 12 and 18. Haarmann was allowed to interrupt the proceedings almost as he pleased, and his grisly attempts at humour only added to the horror as the full story of his butchery unfolded.

'You're doing fine.' he shouted when the prosecution finished their opening speech. When one witness took his time pondering a question. Haarmann yelled: 'Come on, old chap. You must tell us all you know. We are here to get the truth.' Impatient when a distressed mother broke down while giving evidence about her lost son, the killer asked the judges if he could smoke a cigar – and was granted permission. And one morning, he protested that there were too many women in court, saying: 'This is a case for men to discuss.'

The names of boys were read to him, and he was asked if he had killed them. 'Yes, that might well be,' he said of 13-year-old Ernest Ehrenberg. 'I'm not sure about that one,' he replied about Paul Bronischewski. And he turned angrily on the anguished father of Hermann Wolf when shown a photograph of the boy.

'I should never have looked twice at such an ugly youngster as, according to his photography, your son must have been.' he sneered. 'You say your boy had not even a shirt to his name and that his socks were tied on to his feet with string. Deuce take it, you should have been ashamed to let him go about like that. There's plenty of rubbish like him around. Think what you're saying man. Such a fellow would have been far beneath my notice.'

Newspaper reporters in court could not disguise their disgust for the killer, or their sympathy for the relatives of his victims. One journalist wrote:

> 'Nearly 200 witnesses had to appear in the box, mostly parents of the unfortunate youths. There

were scenes of painful intensity as a poor father or mother would recognize some fragment or other of the clothing or belonging of their murdered son. Here it was a handkerchief, there a pair of braces, and again a greasy coat, soiled almost beyond recognition, that was shown to the relatives and to Haarmann. And with the quivering nostrils of a hound snuffling his prey, as if he were scenting rather than seeing the things displayed, did he admit at once that he knew them.'

Twice a shudder ran through the court. 'How many victims did you kill altogether?' asked the prosecution. Haarmann replied: 'It might be 30, it might be 40. I really can't remember the exact number.' The prosecution asked: 'How did you kill your victims?' Haarmann replied coldly: 'I bit them through their throats.'

Only when Gran's part in the murders was in doubt did Haarmann lose his composure. 'Grans should tell you how shabbily he has treated me,' he shouted. 'I did the murders, for that work he is too young.' He claimed Grans incited him to kill some victims because he had taken a fancy to the boy's trousers or coat. Grans left him alone overnight to do the murder, returning in the morning for the clothes. Once, though, he was too impatient. Haarmann told the court: 'I had just cut up the body when there was a knock at the door. I shoved the body under the bed and opened the door. It was Grans. His first question was, "Where is the suit." I sat down on the bed and buried my face in my hands . . . Grans tried to console me, and said: "Don't let a little thing like a corpse upset you."

The cold-hearted cynicism of Grans aroused more horror in court than the unsophisticated blundering of Haarmann. The younger man denied every accusation, but there was never any doubt that both would be convicted. Haarmann knew that, and his main concern throughout was that he was not found insane. Early in the

trial he shouted: 'Behead me, don't send me to an asylum.'
And after two psychiatrists declared him mentally sound,
the court decided he should have his wish.

Twelve armed policemen faced the public gallery on
the day of judgment, 19 December, 1924, after anonymous
threats that Haarmann would be shot in revenge for his
monstrous crimes. The courtroom was packed as sentence
of death was pronounced on him. Grans was jailed for life,
later commuted to 12 years.

Haarmann remained resolute to the end. On the last day
he screamed:

'Do you think I enjoy killing people? I was ill for
eight days after the first time. Condemn me to
death. I only ask for justice. I am not mad. It is true
I often get into a state when I do not know what I am
doing, but that is not madness. Make it short, make
it soon. Deliver me from this life, which is a torment.
I will not petition for mercy, nor will I appeal. I want
to pass just one more merry evening in my cell, with
coffee, cheese and cigars, after which I will curse my
father, and go to my execution as if it were a wedding.'

Next morning, Haarmann was beheaded, and the town
of Hanover was at last free from the curse of the worst
mass-murderer in modern history. No-one will ever know
exactly how many teenage boys he and Grans massacred
– but one police source guessed that, during their final 16
months, they were killing two every week.

The Sadistic Romeo
Neville Heath

Neville George Clevely Heath had the looks that boys' comic heroes are made of. His wide, blue eyes and fair, wavy hair set off a fresh-complexioned face which had women swooning. And his suave charm around the clubs and restaurants of London ensured that he was never short of a pretty companion when the evening ended. Girls fell for his impeccable manners, and his tales of der-ring-do in the war that had just finished. But Heath's handsome face hid a terrible secret. Possibly bored with the conventional sex that was so readily available to him, he began pandering to a sadistic streak. And in the summer of 1946, that perversion turned him into a ladykiller in every sense of the word.

Heath was then 29, and well known to both the police and the armed forces. He had served time in civilian jails for theft, fraud and false pretences. He had been court-martialled by the British RAF in 1937 (absent without leave, escaping while under arrest and stealing a car), the British Army in 1941 (issuing dishonoured cheques and going absent without leave) and the South African Air Force in 1945 (undisciplined conduct and wearing unauthorized decorations). In April 1946, he was fined £10 by magistrates by Wimbledon, London, for wearing medals and a uniform to which he was not entitled. By then, unknown to the authorities, he was also indulging in much more sinister fantasies.

A month earlier, the house detective at a hotel in London's Strand burst into a locked room after other guests reported hearing screams. He found Heath standing over a naked girl who was bound hand and foot, and being savagely whipped. Neither she nor the hotel wanted any publicity, and Heath was allowed to slink away, but in May he was at it again. This time he had a more willing victim, a 32-year-old masochist called Ocelot Margie to doormen at the clubs where she turned up in an ocelot fur coat, looking for men prepared to satisfy her craving for bondage and flagellation. Heath was more than ready to oblige, but when he took her to the Pembridge Court Hotel in Notting Hill Gate the hotel detective again intervened after hearing the sound of flesh being thrashed.

Ocelot Margie did not learn from her escape. When Heath phoned her a few weeks later, she agreed to meet him on Thursday, 20 June. After drinks at one of Heath's favourite haunts, the Panama Club in South Kensington, they took a taxi back to the Pembridge Court, where Heath had booked in four days earlier with another girl who had since left. It was after midnight when they arrived. Guests in adjoining rooms heard nothing to disturb their slumbers that night.

At 14.00 next day, a chambermaid entered Room 4 on the first floor of the 19-bedroom hotel and recoiled with horror when she drew back the curtains. The two single beds were bloodied and disordered. And in one of them lay the lifeless body of Ocelot Margie. She was naked, her ankles bound tightly together with a handkerchief. Her face and chin were bruised, as if someone had used intense force to hold her mouth closed. There were 17 criss-cross slash marks on her face, front and back. Her breasts had been badly bitten. And she had been bleeding profusely from the vagina.

Police forensic experts quickly built up a grisly picture of the indignities inflicted on the woman before her death from suffocation. Her wrists also showed signs of being tied together, though the bond had been removed and was missing. The killer had washed the face of the corpse, but left dried blood in the nostrils and eyelashes.

On Saturday, Heath was in Worthing, Sussex, wining and dining the girl with whom he had first occupied the room in Notting Hill. She was Yvonne Symonds, 19-year-old who had met the chilling charmer at a dance in Chelsea seven days earlier, and only consented to spend the following night with him after accepting his whirl-wind proposal of marriage. Now she was back at her parents' home. Heath booked into the nearby Ocean Hotel, and took her for dinner at a club at Angmering.

There he told her his version of the murder in the room they had shared. He said he met the victim on the evening of 20 June, and she asked to borrow his room to entertain another man, since they had nowhere else to go. Heath claimed he slept elsewhere, and was taken to the room by an Inspector Barratt next day and shown the body. It was, he told Yvonne, 'a very gruesome sight.' He added that the killer must be 'a sexual maniac.'

Both Yvonne and her parents were puzzled next morning to read in the Sunday papers that police were looking for Neville George Clevely Heath. Surely they had already seen him? Yvonne rang Heath at the Ocean Hotel, and he told her he was going back to London to clear up what must be a misunderstanding. He did indeed leave Worthing – but not for London. He went further down the south coast, to Bournemouth, where he booked in at the Tollard Royal Hotel as Group Captain Rupert Brooke.

Before he left Worthing, he posted a letter to Inspector Barratt at Scotland Yard. The two had never met, but Heath, who signed the letter with his real name, said he felt duty to report what he knew of the murder in his room. He again said Margery Gardner asked for his keys, but said she was obliged to sleep with the other man for mainly financial reasons. She hinted that, if Heath arrived back at 02.00 she would spend the rest of the night with him. He arrived at the appointed time, found her 'in the condition of which you are aware', then panicked and fled because of his 'invidious position'.

Heath gave a fictitious description of the other man – a slim, dark-haired character called Jack – and curiously added: 'I have the instrument with which Mrs Gardner was beaten and am forwarding this to you today. You will find my fingerprints on it, but you should also find others as well.'

The instrument never arrived, though Inspector Barratt was not surprised by that. Yet despite his suspicions, increased by the letter, Scotland Yard did not issue a photograph of the wanted man. Heath was thus able to enjoy himself in Bournemouth for 13 days, drinking freely, going to shows, and chatting up holiday-making girls at dances. On 3 July, he invited the friend of one of his dancing partners to tea, and they got on so well that a dinner date was fixed for that night at his hotel. Just after midnight, Heath left to walk her home along the promenade. He was asleep in his own bed at 04.30 when the night porter checked, not having seen him return.

Two days later, the manager of the nearby Norfolk Hotel reported one of his guests missing. Miss Doreen Marshall, a 21-year-old from Pinner, Middlesex, had last been seen leaving for dinner at the Tollard Royal. The manager there asked 'Group Captain Brooke' about his guest, and suggested he contact the police. Heath duly called at the station, identified the girl from photographs, and consoled her anguished father and sister.

But an alert detective constable thought the handsome six-footer fitted a description Scotland Yard had sent them. Heath was asked if he was the man wanted for questioning about a murder in London. He denied it, but was delayed long enough for other officers to take a good look at him. When he complained of feeling cold as the evening drew in, an inspector went to the Tollard Royal to collect Heath's jacket. And in the pockets was all the evidence the police needed.

As well as a single artificial pearl and the return half of a first class rail ticket from London to Bournemouth, there was a left-luggage ticket issued at Bournemouth West station on 23 June. It was for a suitcase which contained clothes labelled Heath, a bloodstained neckerchief, a scarf with human female hairs stuck to it, and a vicious-looking leather-bound riding crop, with a criss-cross weave. The end had worn away, and there was blood on the exposed wires.

Heath was taken to London and charged with the murder of Margery Gardner. On the same evening, 8 July, the body of his second victim was discovered. A woman walking her dog in a deep, wooded valley called Branksome Chine, a mile west of the Tollard Roayal, noticed swarms of flies around a rhododendron bush. She called the police, having read of the missing girl. And officers found a sickening sight.

Doreen Marshall was naked except for one shoe. Her battered body had been covered with her underwear, her inside-out black dress and yellow jacket. Her ripped stockings, broken pearl necklace and powder compact were discarded close by. Her wrists were tied and the inside of her hands ripped, as if she had been trying to avert the blade of a knife. One of her ribs was broken and sticking into her lung, as if someone had knelt on her. And her flesh had been mutilated – mercifully, as forensic experts later proved, after she had been killed with two deep cuts to the throat.

Heath told the police that he left Doreen near Bournemouth pier, and watched her walk towards her hotel through some public gardens. He then returned to his own hotel at around 00.30, and because he knew the night porter would be waiting for him, decided to play a practical joke on him, climbing to his room via a builder's ladder left outside. He described it as a 'small deception.' The police dismissed the whole statement as a great deception. And on Thursday 24 September, Heath was charged at the Old Bailey, London, with the murder of Margery Gardner.

His guilt was easily proved. And because he had subsequently killed again, Heath was unable to use what might have been a plausible defence – that Ocelot Margie willingly submitted to whipping and beating, and died accidentally when things got out of hand. Heath knew the game was up, and wanted to plead guilty and accept his punishment coolly and calmly. But his defence counsel persuaded him, against his better judgement, to plead insanity. The attempts of a psychiatrist called on his behalf to try to prove that insanity provided the only memorable moments of the two-day trial.

Dr William Henry de Bargue Hubert, a former psychotherapist at Wormwood scrubs jail, and one of the leading practising psychiatrists of the day., was utterly discredited by the prosecution cross-examination. A year later, he committed suicide.

Under close questionning from Mr Anthony Hawke for the prosecution, Dr Hubert claimed Heath knew what he was doing when he tied up and lashed Mrs Gardner, but did not consider or know it to be wrong. Did he then think it was right, Dr Hubert was asked. Yes came the reply. 'Are you saying, with your responsibility, that a person in that frame of mind is free from criminal responsibility if what he does causes grievous bodily harm or death?' asked the astounded Hawke. Hubert said he was, because sexual perverts often showed no regret or remorse.

Hawke then asked: 'Would it be your view that a person who finds it convenient at the moment to forge a cheque in order to free himself from financial responsibility is entitled to say that he thought it was right, and therefore he is free from the responsibility of what he does?' Hubert: 'He may think so, yes.'

Hawke: 'With great respect, I did not ask you what he

thought. I asked whether you thought he was entitled to claim exemption from responsibility on the grounds of insanity.' Hubert: 'Yes, I do.'

Hawke: 'You are saying that a person who does a thing he wants to do, because it suits him at the moment to do it, is entitled, if that thing is a crime, to claim that he is insane and therefore free from responsibility?' Hubert: 'If the crime and the circumstances are so abnormal to the ordinary people, I do.'

It was an extraordinary thing to claim, and even Heath knew the doctor was harming, not helping, his case. He passed anguished notes to his own counsel, urging him to drop the insanity ploy.

In 1946 the dividing line between the noose and being confined in a mental hospital was the difference between psychopath and psychotic. Psychopaths were considered able to control their evil urges, psychotics were not. In Heath's case, two Home Office prison doctors said he was certainly abnormal, a sadistic sex pervert, but as a psychopath, he was not insane.

The jury of 11 men and one woman found him guilty after only an hour's consideration, and Heath was sentenced to death. He did not bother to appeal, expressed no remorse or sympathy for the families of his victims, and refused to discuss his life or beliefs with any of the experts sent to examine him. He spent most of his last days writing letters, one of which was to his parents: 'My only regret at leaving the world is that I have been damned unworthy of you both.'

He was hanged at Pentonville Prison in London on 26 October, 1946.

The Heartless Husband
Johann Hoch

Johann Otto Hoch had never believed in very long courtships or in long marriages. He had at least 24 wives in 15 years – and he brutally murdered all of them. The diabolical 'Bluebeard' even proposed to his sister-in-law over the deathbed of his wife, who was dying from a massive dose of arsenic. She accepted. 'Life is for the living.' Hoch told her. 'The dead are for the dead.'

Throughout Hoch's bizarre years of marriage and murder in the United States between 1892 and 1905, a tough Chicago cop named George Shippy stalked him relentlessly. Shippy knew Hoch was cutting a bloody trail of murder but was never able to prove it.

Born Johann Schmidt in 1862, Hoch had emigrated from Germany at 25 leaving his wife and three children behind. A big, jovial man with a sweeping handlebar moustache, he found work in the country as an itinerant bartender.

From 1887 to 1895 it was anybody's guess how many women he murdered. In April 1895 he found a woman in a saloon in Wheeling, West Virginia. Using the name Jacob Huff, he married her and then killed her three months later.

As with his other murders, the doctor thought the woman died of kidney disease for which there was no cure. But the lady's pastor knew better and Hoch fled from the town after converting his wife's estate to cash. Leaving his clothes and a suicide note behind, he walked naked into the River Ohio. A hundred yards up he had anchored a boat with new clothing in it. He clambered aboard and rowed to the Ohio side.

In 1898, using the name Martin Dotz, the murderer ran foul of Inspector George Shippy. The killer was arrested in Chicago on a minor swindling charge. But the Wheeling preacher saw a newspaper photo, recognized Jacob Huff and contacted Shippy.

Hoch breezed through a year in the Cook County jail while Shippy backtracked the man's elusive trail and investigated dozens of unsolved cases of murdered women. The determined cop went to Wheeling and had the body of Hoch's ex-wife exhumed, only to find that Hoch had removed many of the woman's vital organs.

After serving his sentence. Hoch married and murdered another 15 women between 1900 and 1905. His weapon was always arsenic, which was easily available in any drugstore. The victims were always lonely but wealthy women overwhelmed by Hoch's animal charm. And slipshod doctors were always too quick with the wrong diagnoses.

By now Hoch was acting like a man possessed. He slipped like a ghost from city to city, murdering in record time. Frequently he married and murdered in less than a week.

In 1904 he buried his last victim, Marie Walcker, and promptly married her sister. He fled with his new wife's savings account and the enraged woman contacted Shippy. Her sister's body was exhumed and this time the medical examiner found enough arsenic to kill a dozen women.

Shippy then made his long-awaited arrest.

Throughout the trial Hoch maintained an air of boyish innocence. Even after the guilty verdict, Hoch was confident he would never swing from the gallows.

As guards led him to the scaffold on 23 February, 1906, the killer joked and said: 'You see, boys, I don't look like a monster, now do I?' Nobody answered the question as Hoch's massive hulk fell through the trapdoor.

The One Who Got Away
Bela Kiss

If the term 'kiss of death' had not already existed, headline writers would have invented it to describe Bela Kiss. For the well-to-do, middle-aged Hungarian murdered at least 23 people before 'dying' on a battlefield during World War One, and escaping to freedom in America. He is one of the few mass murderers to evade justice.

Kiss was 40 when he arrived in the Hungarian village of Czinkota in 1913 with his beautiful, 25 year-old bride Maria. He had bought a large house and taken on servants, and the locals soon warmed to the man who collected stamps, grew roses, and did a little writing, especially on astrology. From time to time he would drive to Budapest on business in his smart red car, and the village policeman, Adolph Trauber, readily agreed to keep an eye on the home of the man with whom he had struck up a close friendship.

War was clearly only months away, and Constable Trauber was not surprised when his friend started returning from Budapest with oil drums. Kiss explained they were full of petrol so that he could continue his business trips when fuel became scarce. Trauber decided to keep quiet about the fact that, while Kiss was away, his wife was entertaining a young artist called Paul Bihari. But the affair was common knowledge among villagers and servants at the house. And they sympathized when, after another trip to Budapest the distraught husband emerged from his empty home to show them a note, saying the couple had eloped together.

For several months, Kiss shut himself away, refusing to see anyone, even Trauber. But in the spring of 1914, the constable persuaded him to rejoin the world, and found him an elderly widow to act as housekeeper. Kiss resumed his journeys to the Hungarian capital, returning each time with more oil drums. He told Trauber that the petrol was in payment of a debt owed to him by a Budapest garage owner. But Kiss brought other things from Budapest – women, not young like Maria, but sometimes even older than himself. Several times his housekeeper stormed out when her kitchen was invaded, only to return when Kiss told her the offending female had left.

Kiss and Constable Trauber spent many evenings together in conversation, and during one of their chats, the policeman mentioned the disappearance of two widows in Budapest. They had vanished after answering a lonely hearts advertisements in a newspaper, placed by man named Hofmann. Both had drawn heavily on their savings after meeting him. Kiss joked that he too had had some unsuccessful affairs with middle-aged widows, and both men laughed.

War broke out that August, but Kiss was not among the first to be called up. He continued his trips to Budapest, returning with more oil drums and more women. When he was eventually conscripted, he left the house and his petrol stockpile in Trauber's care. And the constable continued to look after them after May 1916, when news arrived that Bela Kiss had been killed in action.

Later that summer, soldiers arrived in Czinkota looking for petrol. Trauber remembered the oil drums, and led the way to where they were stood. But a horrific discovery awaited him. Instead of petrol, each of the seven drums in the house contained alcohol. And each contained the doubled-up body of a naked woman.

Detectives called in from Budapest combed the gardens, and dug up yet more drums, each containing a grisly secret. In all, there were 23 tin-can coffins. The victims, who included faithless Maria and her lover, had all been garotted. Letters found in the house made it clear that Kiss and lonely-heart Hofmann were the same person, and that he had taken money or possession from each of his fatal conquests. But there was nothing police could do. Their quarry had died at the front. The file was closed.

Then, in 1919, a friend of one of the victims recognized Bela Kiss crossing Margaret Bridge in Budapest, and reported the sighting to police. Shocked detectives discovered that Kiss had exchanged identities with a fallen colleague during the war, but before they could find him, he vanished again.

In 1924, a deserter from the French Foreign Legion told French police of a colleague called Hofmann, who had boasted of garotting exploits. But by then Hofmann, too, had deserted. It was ten years before he was again recognized, in Times Square, New York. And in 1936, he was reportedly working as a janitor at a Sixth Avenue apartment block. Fellow Hungarians there described him as a small, plain, inoffensive man in his middle sixties, a man with a bleak future. Bela Kiss did not talk about his even bleaker past.

The Vampire of Düsseldorf
Peter Kurten

He is the king of sexual delinquents . . . he unites nearly all perversions in one person . . . he killed men, women, children and animals, killed anything he found.' Those were the chilling words used to describe Peter Kurten, the Vampire of Düsseldorf, at his trial in 1930. They came not from the judge, nor the prosecution, but from defending counsel, pleading for a verdict of insanity. But Kurten, 47, did not escape the execution his reign of terror so richly deserved, because the court agreed with the verdict of one of the top psychiatrists called to examine the callous killer: brutal sadist Kurten 'was at the same time a clever man and quite a nice one.'

Psychopaths ran in the Kurten family, and young Peter, the fifth child in a family of 13, saw the exploits of one at first hand in his home at Cologne-Mulheim. His father would arrive home drunk, beat the children, and sexually violate his unwilling wife in front of them. He also committed incest with his 13-year-old daughter, and Kurten followed his father's example with her. From the age of nine, he also had another teacher. The local dog catcher initiated him to torturing animals. Kurten was enthusiastic pupil, and progressed from dogs to sheep, pigs, goats, geese, and swans. What excited and aroused him most was the sight of their blood. He frequently cut the heads off swans and drank the blood that spurted out.

Soon Kurten switched his attentions to human victims. As a boy he had drowned two playmates while all three swam around a raft in the Rhine. By the age of 16, he was living with a masochistic woman who enjoyed being beaten and half-strangled. She had a daughter of 16, and all three enjoyed a sordid co-existence, interrupted only when Kurten's attempts at theft and fraud landed him in prison. He was later to claim that the inhumanity and injustice of his treatment in jail led to his blood-soaked career as a killer. In fact prison provided him with another outlet for sadism. He deliberately broke prison rules to gain solitary confinement, where he indulged his erotic reveries.

'I thought of myself causing accidents affecting thousands of people,' he was to recall in court. 'I invented a number of crazy fantasies such as smashing bridges and boring through bridge piers. Then I spun a number of fantasies with regard to bacilli which I might be able to introduce into drinking water and so cause a great calamity. I imagined myself using schools and orphanages for the purpose, where I could carry out murders by giving away chocolate samples containing arsenic. I derived the sort of pleasure from these visions that other people would get from thinking about a naked woman.'

When he was freed from prison, Kurten began to turn his daydreams into nightmare reality. He became an arsonist – 'the sight of the flames delighted me, but above all it was the excitement of the attempts to extinguish the fire and the agitation of those who saw their property being destroyed.' And he began to attack defenceless women and children.

His first attempt at murder was unsuccessful. He admitted leaving a girl for dead after assaulting her during intercourse in Düsseldorf's Grafenburg Woods. But no body was ever found. It was assumed that the girl recovered enough to crawl away, too ashamed or scared to report the incident. Eight-year-old Christine Klein was not so lucky. She was found in bed, raped and with her throat cut. Her uncles was arrested and tried, and though aquitted for lack of evidence, the shame of the charge stuck to him until he died during World War One. Kurten must have enjoyed that. His own trial was shocked by the detailed, fussy, matter-of-fact way he related what had really happened, 17 years earlier.

'It was on 25 May, 1913,' he recalled in the clipped, precise tone that only made his deeds seem more ghastly. 'I had been stealing, specializing in public bars or inns where the owners lived on the floor above. In a room above an inn at Cologne-Mulheim, I discovered a child asleep. Her head was facing the window. I seized it with my left hand and strangled her for about a minute and a half. The child woke up and struggled but lost consciousness.

'I had a small but sharp pocketknife with me and I held the child's head and cut her throat. I heard the blood spurt and drip on the mat beside the bed . . . The whole thing lasted about three minutes, then I locked the door again and went to Düsseldorf. Next day I went back to Mulheim. 'There is a cafe opposite the Klein's place and I sat there and drank a glass of beer, and read all about the murder in the papers. People were talking about it all around me. All this amount of horror and indignation did me good.'

Kurten was not prepared to use his sadism on the Kaiser's behalf when war broke out. He deserted a day after call-up, and spent the rest of the hostilities in jail, for that and other minor crimes. Released in 1921, he decided to marry, and chose a prostitute at Altenburg as his bride, overcoming her reluctance by threatening to kill her. He gave up petty crime and went to work in a factory as a moulder. He became an active trade unionist, and a respected pillar of society, quiet, charming, carefully dressed and meticulous about his appearance – even a little vain. Those who knew he was having affairs with other women did not tell his wife. And the women were not prepared to confide that Kurten was a rough lover, who enjoyed beating and half-choking them.

But once Kurten and his wife moved to Düsseldorf in 1925, blood lust again got the better of him. Though his relations with Frau Kurten remained normal, his assaults on his mistresses became more vicious. Soon he was attacking innocent strangers with scissors or knives, aroused by the sight of their blood. As he escaped detection, he stepped up the rate of attacks, varying his style to cover his tracks. By the summer of 1929, the town of Düsseldorf was in the grip of terror. Police had pinned 46 perverted crimes, including four killings, down to someone who seemed to have vampire tendencies. But they had no clues as to the monster's identity.

On the evening of 23 August, two sisters left the throng at the annual fair in the suburb of Flehe to walk home through nearby allotments. Louis Lenzen, 14, and five-year-old Gertrude stopped when a gentle voice sounded behind them. 'Oh dear, I've forgotten to buy cigarettes,' the man said to Louise. 'Look, would you be very kind and go to one of the booths and get some for me? I'll look after the little girl.' Louise took his money and ran back to the fair. Kurten quietly picked up her sister, and carried her into the darkness behind a stand of beanpoles, and efficiently slaughtered her, strangling her and cutting her throat with a Bavarian clasp knife. When Louise returned, he pocketed the cigarettes, accepted his change – and did the same to her.

Twelve hours later, a servant girl called Gertrude Schulte was stopped by a man who offered to take her to a fair at nearby Neuss. As they strolled through woods, he attempted to rape her, but she fought him off. He produced a knife, and began stabbing her in a frenzy, piercing her neck, shoulder and back. When he threw her to the ground, the knife snapped, leaving the blade in her back.

Gertrude was lucky – her screams alerted a passer-by, and she was rushed to hospital. But Kurten had escaped again. The newspapers continued to report his exploits with mounting hysteria. In one half hour, the 'Vampire' attacked and wounded a girl of 18, a man of 30 and a woman of 37. Later he bludgeoned serving girls Ida Reuter and Elizabeth Dorrier to death. And on 27 November he slashed five-year-old Gertrude Albermann with a thin blade, inflicting 36 wounds on her tiny body.

Gertrude was the last victim to die, but the attempted murders and vicious attacks continued through the winter and early spring, attracting headlines across Germany. Maria Budlick, a 21-year-old maid, had read the stories while working in Cologne, 30 kilometres away, but when she lost her job, she boarded a train for Düsseldorf, her desperation for employment out weighing any fears about the vampire.

It was 14 May, 1930, when she stepped on to the platform at Düsseldorf, and was soon approached by a man who offered to show her the way to a girls' hostel. She accompanied him happily through the streets, but when he turned into the trees of Volksgarten Park, she drew back. The man assured her she had nothing to fear, but she refused to be placated. As they argued, another man emerged from the shadows and asked: 'Is everything all right?' Maria's escort left, and she was left alone with her rescuer – Peter Kurten.

Convinced that he had saved her from a fate worse than death, or death itself, Maria agreed to go with him to his home for a meal. Kurten gave her a glass of milk and a ham sandwich, then offered to take her to the hostel. They boarded a tram – but for the second time in less than an hour, poor Maria was being misled. Her rescuer led her straight into Grafenburg Woods, on the northern edge of town, then lunged at her, gripping her throat and attempting to rape her against a tree. Maria struggled, but the man was too strong for her. Then, as she was about to pass out, he let go of her, and asked: 'Do you remember where I live, in case you ever need my help again?' Maria gasped: 'No.' Kurten escorted her out of the woods, and left her.

Maria had remembered where he lived, but surprisingly she did not go to the police. Instead, she wrote about her ordeal to a friend in Cologne. The letter was incorrectly addressed, and opened at the post office to be returned to the sender. An alert official realized the implications of its contents and contacted the authorities. Next day, plain clothes detectives took Maria back to the street she remembered, Mettmannerstrásse, and she identified Number 71 as the home of her assailant. She also saw Kurten, but he vanished before she could tip off her police escort.

Kurten had also seen Maria, and realized that the net was closing in on him. He went to the restaurant where his wife worked, and confessed everything to her. He had never felt guilt for his crimes, and even admitting them now did not affect his appetite. He ate not only his own meal, but the one his shocked wife could not touch. On the morning of 24 May, Frau Kurten went to the police, and told them she had arranged to meet her husband outside a certain church at 15.00. Armed officers surrounded the area, and when Kurten arrived four rushed at him, revolvers pointing at his chest. He smiled and offered no resistance, saying: 'There is no need to be afraid.'

The trial, when it opened in a converted drill-hall at Düsseldorf's police headquarters on 13 April, 1931, was almost a foregone conclusion. Thousands surrounded the building to try to catch a glimpse of the man who had admitted 68 crimes, apart from those for which he had already served time, while being questioned. He was charged with nine murders and seven attempted murders, and the prosecution hardly needed to produce any evidence to gain a conviction – Kurten admitted everything coldly, calmly, and in astonishing detail. Sleek and immaculate, he confessed to being a sex maniac, a rapist, a vampire, a sadist, an arsonist. He gave chapter and verse about his bestiality, his jail fantasies, and how he had strangled, stabbed and clubbed women and children to death. He admitted drinking blood from one woman's cut throat, from a wound on a man's forehead, from the hand of another victim. He described how he had enjoyed reading about Jack the Ripper, and how he had visited a wax works Chamber of Horrors, and promised himself: 'I'll be here one day.'

A shoulder-high cage had been built round the accused man's stand to prevent him escaping. Behind him were the exhibits – the knives and scissors he had used to kill, the matches he had used to burn property, the spade he had used to bury one woman, the skulls of the innocent strangers he had butchered for the sake of an orgasm. The judge treated him gently, guiding him carefully through the catalogue of appalling crimes. There was no need to be tough, Kurten was as mild-mannered and courteous as his unsuspecting neighbours had always known him. But by the time it came to the prisoner's final speech, even the hardened judge was sickened.

Incredibly, Kurten, who had blamed his childhood and prison for turning him into a killer, now began preaching puritanically about the behaviour of others. He said:

'My actions as I see them today are so terrible and horrible that I do not even make an attempt to excuse them. But one bitter thing remains in my mind. When I think of the two Socialist doctors accused recently of abortions performed on working class mothers who sought their advice, when I think of the 500 murders they have committed, then I cannot help feeling bitter.

The real reason for my conviction is that there comes a time in the life of every criminal when he can go no further, and this spiritual collapse is what I experienced. But I do feel that I must make one statement: some of my victims made things very easy for me. Man-hunting on the part of women to day has taken on such forms that ...'

The judge could stand no more unctuous rhetoric, and angrily banged his desk for silence.

The jury took 90 minutes to find Kurten guilty on all accounts, and he was sentenced to death nine times. On 1 July, 1932, he chose veal, fried potatoes and white wine for the traditional last meal, and enjoyed it so much that he asked for second helpings. At 06.00 next morning he marched to the guillotine in Cologne's Koingelputz prison, and was beheaded after declining the attorney general's offer of a last wish.

But the twisted mind of Kurten had had one final wish. He asked the prison psychiatrist, minutes before he left his cell for that last walk, 'After my head has been chopped off, will I still be able to hear, at least for a moment, the sound of my own blood gushing from the stump of my neck?' As the appalled official sat stunned in silence, Kurten smiled and said: 'That would be the pleasure to end all pleasures.'

The Killer Who Kept Quiet
Henri Desire Landru

Few murder trials in history have aroused so much controversy, as that of Henri Desire Landru at Paris in November 1921. He was accused of 11 murders, but the prosecution could produce no bodies, no proof of how he killed his victims, and no proof of how he disposed of them. The jury convicted him on circumstantial evidence, then petitioned for mercy. Eventually Landru went to the guillotine still protesting his innocence – and even today, there are those who believe him.

The court proceedings themselves degenerated into farce. France was demob-happy after World War One, and hungry for entertainment. The French government was happy to divert attention from the peace talks at Versailles which were going badly. A nation that still holds romancers in high esteem could not resist the small, thin, bald, strange-looking man with deep-set, flickering black eyes who was said to have made the acquaintance of 283 ladies in five years. In court, men roared and cheered as this curious Casanova baffled his frustrated accusers by resolutely refusing to discuss his amours. Women blew him kisses and made blatant gestures of sexual invitation. When one woman arrived late in the packed courtroom, Landru earned applause by gallantly getting to his feet, and offering her his seat in the dock.

The facts of the case, alas, were less romantic. Henri

Desire Landru was a small-time thief and swindler well-known to the police since his first arrest in 1900. He had progressed from petty pilfering to conning widows and lonely spinsters out of their savings via lonely-heart matrimonial advertisements in the Paris newspapers. But he was not very good at it. As soon as his dupes realized he was only interested in their money, many went to the police. Landru was in and out of prison until 1914. His father, a respectable ironworker who had retired to the Dordogne, committed suicide in 1912 when he came to visit his son, only to find him in jail for fraud.

By July 1914, the French judicial system had had enough of Landru. He was convicted, in his absence, of a motor cycling business swindle, and sentenced to four years, with a recommendation that he be banished to the penal establishment in New Caledonia as a habitual criminal. Landru, who had a wife and four children, was on the run, knowing that one mistake would mean transportation and exile. Yet he needed money to live. His answer, according to the prosecution at his trial, was chillingly simple. He continued to seduce willing ladies for profit, but ensured that they would not complain to the authorities by murdering them.

Had the French police not been undermanned and fully stretched because of the war, Landru could never been survived for so long. He had a distinctive, disproportionately big red beard, which later earned him the inevitable nickname 'Bluebeard', and he continued to visit this old haunts around Paris, particularly the garages where he hoarded stolen goods. It was at one of them, in February 1914, that he had met Madame Jeanne Cuchet.

She was 39, a widow working in a Paris store, and was accompanying her son Andre, 18, who had applied to Landru for a job. She quickly became infatuated with the smooth-talking man who called himself M. Diard, said he was a well-to-do engineer, and wore an impressive violet ribbon, an 'Order' he had invented and bestowed upon himself. Madame Cuchet's married sister was suspicious of Diard, however, and went so far so to break into his villa at Chantilly, discovering letters from several women addressed to a variety of differently-named men. But Madame Cuchet was not be deterred.

She agreed to her lover's suggestion of renting a villa called The Lodge at Vernouillet, on the outskirts of Paris, and happily paid six months rent. They moved in on 8 December, 1914, and the woman and her son were last seen alive in the garden the following 4 January. By that time Madam Cuchet's family had washed their hands of her, and though she was later reported missing, the inquiries into her whereabouts were almost non-existent.

Encouraged by this success, which netted him about 15,000 francs in jewels, furniture and securities, Landru embarked on another conquest. Madame Therese Laborde-Line was 47, a widow with little money and no relatives in France – she came from Buenos Aires, Argentina. Recklessly using the name Cuchet, Landru wooed her and won what she possessed. He took her to Vernouillet in June 1915, and she too vanished there.

This was convenient for Landru, for on 11 May, he had placed this advertisement in the Paris morning paper, *Le Journal:* 'Widower with two children, aged 43, with comfortable income, affectionate, serious and moving in good society, desires to meet widow with a view to matrimony.' Three of the women who answered the advertisement that May were to disappear before the year was out.

Madame Désiree Guillin was 51, a former governess with a legacy of 22,000 francs. She was delighted at the prospect of going to Australia as the wife of 'diplomat M. Petit', and happily went to The Lodge with him on 4 August. She was never seen again. Landru sold her furniture and forged her signature to get at her bank balance. The bank should have spotted that, but again the war was the excuse.

Landru decided to leave The Lodge for somewhere more secluded. He picked the Villa Ermitage, a large, sparsely-furnished house in a little-used side road near the village of Gambasis in the department of the Seine. It was close to the forest of Rambouillet just outside Paris, with several lakes and ponds nearby. One of the few improvements Landru made was to install a small stove. Then he was ready to entertain guests.

The first was Madame Heon, a 55-year-old widow who replied to the May advertisement, and fell for 'M. Petit', now head traveller for a large South American company. She was last seen alive at Gambais in December, which left Landru free to pursue his wooing of the third likely candidate from his advertisement, Madame Anna Collomb.

She was 44 – though she discreetly put her age at 29 in her letter to him – and a widow. Landru had at first told her he was M. Cuchet, a war refugee from Rocroi who had a factory at Montmartre, and she fell for him, she told her mother, 'because he is a real gentleman and says such beautiful things to me.' The infatuated woman moved in with him at a flat in the Rue Chateaudun, and gave him her furniture to put in store. When she visited Gambais with him, she found he was known there as M. Fremyet. Landru explained to her suspicious mother that he used two names to secure a double war indemnity, a fact that confirmed her opinion of him as a crook. But Anna's love was unshakeable. On Christmas Eve, she invited her sister Madame Pelat to Gambais, and Landru spoke warmly of his plans to marry Anna and move to Nice. Madame Collomb was not seen again after 27 December.

Landru was 8,000 francs richer when he met his next lover, a 19-year-old serving girl, on the Paris Métro in January. Though she was penniless, Andree Babelay was pretty, and he dallied with her for nearly four months. She was last seen on 12 April at Gambais, after which Landru renewed his acquaintance with 44-year-old Madame

Celestine Buisson, another widow who agreed to trust him with her furniture and securities. She disappeared on 17 August.

Three more ladies were to take a one-way trip to Gambais: Madame Louise Jaume, 38, a devout Catholic separated from her husband, who vanished only hours after she and Landru knelt in prayer at a church in November, 1917; Madame Anne-Marie Pascal, 33, a divorcée, who seemingly bequeathed Landru her false teeth and umbrella when she disappeared in April, 1918 – he sold them or 30 francs – and Madame Marie-Therese Marchadier, 37, a lodging housekeeper with a luride past who was seen no more after 13 January, 1919. Landru then cleared everything from her Paris apartment.

But by then the web of deceit Landru had woven was slowly being unravelled. Madame Pelat, sister of Anna Collomb, was puzzled when she received no replies to letters she sent to the Villa Ermitage. She wrote to the mayor of Gambais, asking if he knew the whereabouts of M. Cuchet-Fremyet. Shortly before, the mayor had had another letter, from Mademoiselle Lacoste, the sister of Madame Buisson, inquiring about the man she had called on at the villa, M. Dupont. The mayor wrote to both women, suggesting that they contact each other. When they met, it did not take long to discover that Cuchet-Fremyet and Dupont were one and the same man.

The two men went to the police, and the name Cuchet rang a bell. Madame Cuchet and her son were still listed as missing after going away with a man named Diard. The coincidence seemed too strong to be ignored. And the description of the wanted man – small, bald, with a big red beard – also fitted an engineer named Guillet, suspected of fraud and theft. On to April, 1919, an arrest warrant was issued.

Just one day later, the search was over. Mlle Lacoste was walking in the Rue de Rivoli when she spotted the man she knew as Dupont strolling arm-in-arm with a smartly-dressed young woman. She followed them into a shop, and heard them order a white china dinner service. Mlle Lacoste lost the couple in the crowds, but went straight to the police, who discovered that the china had been ordered in the name of Lucien Guillet. Early next morning, they swooped on the address he had given, No 76 Rue de Rochechouart.

Landru at first protested that he was Guillet, born at Rocroi in 1874. But when he was searched, he tried to throw a small, loose-leaved black book out of the window. That book was to send him to the guillotine. For Landru had been insanely meticulous about keeping details of his affairs. He had listed each reply to his lonely hearts advertisements under seven headings – to be answered *poste restante;* without money; without furniture; no reply; to be answered to initials *poste restante;* possible fortune; to be investigated. He had noted every expense, even down to the two sous he put in the collection box when he went to church with Madame Jaume. More seriously, he had described the tickets bought for his trips to Gambais – a return one for himself, a single ticket for his ladies.

On the front cover of the book he had written in pencil: Cuchet, J. *idem,* Bresil, Crozatier, Havre, Buisson, A. Collomb, Babelay, Jaume, Pascal, Marchadier. The police knew only three names on the list at that stage, but they were enough for them to arrest Landru for murder. Painstaking investigations revealed that women answering to the names Babelay, Jaume, Pascal and Marchadier had also vanished, that Bresil denoted Madame Laborde-Line (Landru may have muddled Argentina and Brazil), that Madame Guillin lived in the Rue Crozatier, and that Madame Heon came from Havre.

Police searched the Villa Ermitage on 9 April but found nothing. After the arrest, they raided all Landru's properties, and discovered intimate papers and identity cards for all the missing women, plus clothes and personal trinkets belonging to them. They also found two wax cords, of the type sometimes used to strangle people. On 29 April, they returned for a thorough search of the villa at Gambais. Sifting through ashes beside the stove, they came across 295 fragments of bone, as well as fastenings from parts of buttons and other remains of women's clothing.

The French judicial system involves a preliminary interrogation by an examining magistrate, with wide-ranging powers to prepare the ground for a trial. An able inquisitor called Bonin was assigned to Landru. Aided by witnesses and the best advice from crime experts, he questioned the little man for two-and-a-half years, going over and over the evidence in the black book, warning him that forensic experts had identified the bone fragments as being from three human bodies, asking him about each missing woman in turn. Landru took refuge in his right, under the law, to remain silent.

To most questions, he replied: 'I have nothing to say.' Occasionally he would tell Bonin: 'I am a gallant man. I cannot allow you to ask me questions concerning the ladies. If they have disappeared, it is nothing to do with me. I know nothing of what became of them. Discover proofs, bring them to me, and then I will discuss them with you.' Another time, Bonin said: 'You are a murderer.' Landru replied: 'You say so. Prove it. Look, investigate, imagine, but prove it if you can.'

Asked about Madame Cuchet, he said: 'Her hiding place is a secret between herself and me. I am a man of honour, and though I understand the accusation you have brought, I will not reveal it. I have given my word.' When Bonin pointed out that she had broken off contact with her closest friends, Landru replied stonily: 'Madame Cuchet was heartbroken by the hypocrisy of the world, as I am.'

It was a remarkable feat of endurance by Landru, particularly as he was weakened by attacks of gastritis. The authorities had evidence that black, acrid smoke had been seen coming from the chimney at Gambais, and that a man answering Landru's description had been seen throwing a package into a lake near the Villa Ermitage. The bones of Madame Marchadier's two griffon dogs had been dug up in the grounds. But there was still no concrete proof of murder, and no bodies. Nonetheless, in France, unlike Britain, a man was guilty until proved innocent.

In September 1921, M. Bonin sent the result of his examinations – 7,000 documents – to the Department of Criminal Prosecution. The trial began at the Versailles Palais de Justice on 7 November. Landru was only 52, but his illness and prison pallor made him look like a weary old man. It took three hours for the clerk to read the indictment – an astonishing catalogue of seduction, swindling, forgery and multiple murder. Landru seemed indifferent, reacting only when the phrase 'exploitation of women' was read out.

On the second day of the trial, the court president questioned the prisoner who disputed some facts in his statement, saying: 'The police are often inefficient.' When asked why he had not co-operated with M. Bonin, Landru said: 'It is not my business to guide the police. Have they not been accusing me for the past three years of deeds which the women who disappeared never for one moment reproached me with?' The president stifled a burst of laughter in court with the words: 'It is you who have made it impossible for these women to complain.'

Landru claimed the names in his book were all business clients. He bought their furniture, ready to sell it back to them once the Germans had left France. When the prosecution pointed out that, on one day, he had met six or seven women, Landru replied: 'That proves well that I was not concerned with any affairs.' He claimed the matrimonial advertisements were an innocent business ruse, 'to flatter their conceit'. But again he refused to discuss details of his dealings with the women, saying they were 'private matters'.

Landru parried some questions with black humour. Asked what had become of Madam Guillin, he said: 'It is not for me to say, it is for the police to find out. They took six years to find me. Perhaps they will end up finding Madame Guillin.' To the prosecutor, he said: 'I fully recognize, sir, that you are after my head. I regret that I have not more than one head to offer you.'

But on one occasion, a witness wiped the smile from his face. Madame Friedmann, sister of Jeanne Cuchet, shouted at Landru: 'My sister loved you so much that she would not have left you to be condemned if she had been living.' Then, in hushed tones, she told of a dream in which her sister had appeared before her, and told her that Landru had slit her throat while she slept. Madame Friedmann's sobbing, and the emotional response of the public galleries, forced the session to be adjourned. No court of law could accept dreams as proof of murder. Yet no jury could forget such a powerful moment.

Though no-one had proved that Landru burned any bodies, lengthy testimony from a medical jurist on the effects of burning human remains was allowed. It made grisly listening. 'A right foot disappears in 50 minutes,' the jury was told, 'half a skull with the brains taken out in 36 minutes, a whole skull in 1 hour and ten minutes.'

Civil lawyers representing relatives of the missing women were also allowed to make dramatic accusation against the prisoner, denouncing him as a murderer who chopped up bodies, without a shred of conclusive factual justification.

Faced with a mounting tide of circumstantial evidence against his client, defence attorney Moro-Giafferi one of the most distinguished lawyers in France, put up a brave fight. He produced the girl Landru was with when he was arrested, Fernande Segret, who made the most of her big moment in a sealskin coat and picture hat. She described herself as a 'lyric artist', and no singer could expect a more enthusiastic welcome than she got from the men in the court. When order was restored, she declared that Landru was a good lover, strongly passionate, and that he made her very happy. She said she had cooked for him on the stove at Gambais, where Landru was alleged to have burned the bodies, and had cleared the cinders afterwards without noticing any skulls or bones.

Moro-Giafferi then made an emotionally brilliant speech, saying that under civil law, none of the missing women would have been presumed dead for several years. Why assume they were now, when a man's life depended on it. He claimed that Landru was a white slave trader, who had dispatched the women to brothels in Brazil, and that that was the real reason for the word Brazil appearing in the little black book. But the jury were not prepared to believe that Brazilians had a penchant for middle-aged widows.

There was uproar in court when Landru was convicted. Photographic flashlights exploded, men cheered, women fainted. Moro-Giafferi was shattered. He was convinced his man was not guilty, and immediately drew up a petition for mercy, which the jury signed. Landru, under the sentence of death, found himself in the bizarre position of consoling his crestfallen counsel.

Moro-Giafferi was there on the morning of 25 February, 1922, when Landru went to the guillotine. The prisoner refused offers of Mass and confession, and waved aside a tot of rum and a cigarette. Asked if he had anything to say, he retorted: 'Sir, to ask such a question at such a time is an insult. I have nothing to say.' But he turned to Moro-Giafferi, shook his hand, and said: '*Maître*, I thank you. You have had a desperate and difficult task to conduct. It is not the first time that an innocent man has been condemned.'

Landru begged them not to cut off the bushy red beard

of which he was so proud. They merely trimmed it. Followed by his lawyer and the rejected priest, he walked out into the cold dawn air, shivering slightly with the cold, and muttering: 'I will be brave.'

His death solved none of the still unanswered questions. Had he killed all the women? If so, how? And how had he disposed so expertly of them, the murder weapons, and any other tell-tale clues? If he killed for money, why did he kill a penniless serving girl and the impecunious Madame Pascal? Was it because they discovered papers relating to the other women? Those questions will probably never be answered, despite an alleged confession printed by newspapers in 1968. The reports claimed that a framed picture given to a defence lawyer had the words, 'I did it, I burned their bodies in my kitchen oven' scribbled on the back.

The intriguing Landru story has two other odd postscripts. On the night before his execution, he wrote a letter to the man who had prosecuted him, the Advocate General *Mâitre* Godefroy, which was said to have greatly distressed the man. It read:

'Why could you not meet my gaze when I was brought back to court to hear my sentence? Why did you so indignantly rebuke the crowd for its unseemly behaviour? Why today are you still seeking for the vanished women, if you are so certain that I killed them?

It was all over. Sentence had been pronounced. I was calm. You were upset. Is there a conscience that troubles uncertain judges as it ought to trouble criminals? Farewell, *Monsieur*. Our common history will doubtless die tomorrow. I die with an innocent and quiet mind. I hope respectfully that you may do the same.'

Nearly 50 years after the execution, a film called *Landru*, scripted by novelist Françoise Sagan, was released. To the film-makers' astonishment, Landru's last mistress, Fernandez Segret, turned up and sued them for 200,000 francs damages. She got 10,000. Since nothing had been heard of her for years, she had been presumed dead. In fact, she had been working as a governess in the Lebanon. After winning her case, she retired to an old people's home in Normandy. But the money did not buy her peace. She drowned herself, because she was tired of being pointed out as 'the woman in the Landru case.'

The Monster of the Andes
Pedro Lopez

The guards fingered their pistols and watched nervously as the steel door to cell 14 was unlocked. There, in Ambato Jail, high up in the Andes mountain in Ecuador, was the man who held the world's most horrible distinction.

Inside, cowering in a corner of his cell in the women's section of the prison, was Pedro Alonzo Lopez. He was petrified that he might be burned alive, or castrated, by the other inmates or the guards themselves. Lopez, known in South America as 'the Monster of the Andes' had admitted to murdering 300 young girls. Lopez had been credited with being the world's worst mass sex killer, with the highest ever tally of victims.

Like most mass killers, Lopez' motive was sex. Before the 300 were strangled, they were first raped. Lopez did away with girls in this fashion at the rate of two a week for the three years he was on the rampage.

In Ambato alone, nestling 3,000 metres up in the Andes, the killer took police to the secret graves of the bodies of the 53 girls all aged between 8 and 12. At 28 other sites he described to police, bodies could not be found because the graves had been robbed by prowling animals. Some of the girls' bodies were buried at construction sites, and police have had to assume that they are now encased in concrete, perhaps never to resurface. Others are under roads.

In his confession, Lopez admitted to killing 110 girls in Ecuador, another 100 in neighbouring Colombia and 'many more than 100' in Peru. Retired Major of Police, Victor Hugo Lascano, director of Ambato prison, said: 'We may never know exactly how many young girls Lopez killed. I believe his estimate of 300 is very low, because in the beginning he co-operated and took us each day to three or four hidden corpses. But then he tired, changed his mind and stopped helping.'

Lopez was eventually charged with 53 of the murders but another charge listed 110 more bodies named in his confession. Major Lascano said: 'If someone confesses to 53 you find, and hundreds more that you don't, you tend to believe what he says. What can he possibly invent that will save him from the law?'

In his cell in the women's section of Ambato Prison, Lopez was kept out of immediate danger from enraged guards and male prisoners. The women prisoners were considered to be in no danger themselves 'because his sex drive was geared only to young children.'

This mass child-killer was born the seventh son in a family of 13 children. His mother was a prostitute in the small Colombian town of Tolima, who threw him out onto the street when he was eight for sexually fondling one of his younger sisters. A stranger found the boy crying and hungry, took him in his arms and promised to be his new father and care for him. Instead, the stranger took young Pedro to a deserted building and raped him. For the rest of his life, Lopez would be afraid to sleep indoors.

'I slept on the stairs of market places and plazas', he told police. 'I would look up and if I could see a star, I knew I was under the protection of God.'

In Bogota, an American family fed and clothed the street urchin, and enrolled him in a Colombian day school of orphans. When he was 12 he stole money from the school and ran away with a middle-aged woman teacher who wanted to have sex with him.

At 18 he stole a car and drove across Columbia. He was caught and jailed. On his second day in prison he was raped in his cell by four male prisoners. Lopez made himself a crude knife. Within two weeks, according to the story he told police, he had murdered three of the men; the fourth stumbled across their bodies and ran screaming through the prison. Lopez was given an additional two-year sentence for the killings, which were deemed self-defence.

Released from jail, Lopez found himself excited by pornographic magazines and movies. But he was afraid of women and therefore unable to communicate with them. 'I lost my innocence at the age of eight', he told police, 'so I decided to do the same to as many young girls as I could.'

By 1978, Lopez had killed more than 100 Peruvian girls, many of them belonging to indian tribes.

His crimes first came to light when he was caught by Ayacucho indians in the northern sector of Peru as he carried off a nine-year-old girl. They stripped and tortured him, then put him in a deep hole . . . they were going to bury him alive.

An American woman missionary saved his life. She convinced the indians that they should not commit murder. She took Lopez in her jeep to the police outpost. Within days he had been deported; the police did not want to bother with dead indian girls at that time. Only later, when the full story emerged, was a proper investigation begun.

Across the border in Ecuador the real killing spree then began. 'I like the girls in Ecuador' Lopez told police. 'They are more gentle and trusting, and more innocent. They are not as suspicious of strangers as Colombian girls.'

Lopez would walk through market squares seeking out his victims. He said he deliberately sought out young girls with 'a certain look of innocence'. In graphic detail he told police how he would first introduce the children to sex, then strangle them.

'I would become very excited watching them die. I would stare into their eyes until I saw the light in them go out. The girls never really struggled – they didn't have time. I would bury a girl, then go out immediately and look for another one. I never killed any of them at night, because I wanted to watch them die by daylight.'

Police in the three countries were by now collating information, but they still did not realize they were looking for a mass killer. Their main theory was that an organization had been kidnapping the girls and transporting them to work as maids and prostitutes in large cities.

In April 1980, a rain-swollen river overflowed its banks near Ambato and horrified townspeople discovered the remains of four missing girls. Police launched a manhunt, but it was unsuccessful.

Days later, Carlina Raman Poveda, working in the Plaza Rosa market, discovered her 12-year-old daughter Maria was missing. Frantically, she ran through the plaza, calling for her. She saw her walking out of the market, holding a stranger's hand.

Carlina followed her daughter and the tall man to the edge of town and then called for help. A dozen local indians jumped on Lopez and pulled him to the ground. They held him until the police arrived.

In jail awaiting trial, Lopez was tricked by police into making a confession. A priest, Pastor Cordoba Gudino, masqueraded as a fellow prisoner. For a month he stayed locked in the same cell as Lopez, and developed a behind-bars friendship with him. For the information he gave Gudino, the Ecuadoran people were able to extract a full confession from Lopez. Subsequent liaisons with the police forces of Colombia and Peru substantiated Lopez's story.

Convicted of the murders in Ecuador, Lopez received a life sentence, which, in that country, means a maximum of 16 years, with good behaviour he could be a free man by 1990. Had he been convicted in Colombia, Lopez would be dead. There, the penalty for murder is death by firing squad.

The Murderous 'Family'
Charles Manson

Charles Manson preached bloody revolution and ruled a satanic cult who killed at his bidding. He was sentenced to die in the gas chamber, but with the death sentence now abolished in California he is serving nine life sentences for nine murders. On his orders, his followers slaughtered the actress Sharon Tate, the wife of film producer Roman Polanski, and three friends at her Hollywood home in August, 1969.

Two nights later he sent his followers into action again to butcher close neighbours of the Polanskis, supermarket owner Leno la Bianca and his wife Rosemary. He was also found guilty of beheading stuntman Donald Shea and of ordering the execution of musician Gary Hinman.

Manson, 48, is the illegitimate son of a prostitute. When he was young his mother and brother were jailed for beating and robbing men she picked up.

At 11, Manson fell foul of the law and was sent to reform school. He spent the next 21 years in penal institutions, emerging at 32 never having slept with a woman or drunk a glass of beer. Confused by freedom, he caught a long-distance bus chosen at random and alighted at San Francisco's Haight-Ashbury district, centre of the world hippie movement.

It was 1967, the height of the peace-and-love flower-power era. Manson grew his hair long, wore a beard and played the guitar. Soon he had a circle of admirers. Girls came to kneel at his feet. One said: 'The first time I heard him sing, it was like an angel. He was magnetic.' Another, Lynette 'Squeaky' Fromme, said: 'With Charlie, I was riding on the wind. Making love with Charlie was guiltless, like a baby.'

But Manson had little respect for women. At the commune he set up in the Hollywood hills, they outnumbered men four-to-one. One of the rules of his 'family' was that the gods had to be fed before the women. Girls had to submit instantly to the men Manson named. He banned contraceptives, alcohol and the wearing of spectacles. Questions by the girls were forbidden and they could not use the word 'Why?' But they worshipped him as a god.

Women would travel miles to ask him to sleep with them. A film actress who begged for his favours was told to first climb a nearby mountain. Another woman brought along her 15-year-old daughter. Manson told the mother to go because she was too old, and to leave her daughter. She obeyed.

Manson's incredible magnetism gave him an entry to the wilder fringe of the Hollywood party circuit. It is almost certain he and some of his followers had been entertained by the Polanskis before the night Sharon and her friends died.

The slaughter was the culmination of months of testing to which Manson had subjected his disciples. Bored with their simple adoration of him, he started to organize law-breaking exercises. He made them steal cars, commit petty thefts and prowl round people's homes in 'creepy-crawling' black clothes. Then he ordered them to Sharon Tate's house to terrorize a man whom he said had broken several promises to him.

Polanski was in Europe making a film, and he asked an old friend, Voytek Frykowski and his girlfriend Abigail Folger, to move in with Sharon to keep her company.

On the evening of 8 August, Jay Sebring, Sharon's ex-lover and now a friend, had dropped in too. They and an 18-year-old youth visiting Frykowski, were to die horribly that night at the hands of three girls and an ex-football star, trusted members of Manson's inner circle. Sharon, who was eight months pregnant, was stabbed 16 times. The word 'Pig' was written in her blood on the front door.

Today the man whose reign of bloody terror stunned the world is serving out his sentence as caretaker of the prison chapel at Vacaville, in southern California. He is unrepentant about the past, claiming to feel no guilt for the bestial crimes committed at his command. He told he British photographer Albert Foster: 'I am not ashamed or sorry. If it takes fear and violence to open the eyes of the dollar-conscious society, the name Charles Manson can be that fear.'

Bad But Not Mad
Peter Manuel

Sentencing Peter Thomas Anthony Manuel to death at Glasgow in May, 1958, the judge Lord Cameron said: 'A man may be very bad without being mad.' Manual, who callously killed at least nine people, certainly qualified as very bad. But does a sane man pick victims at random, murder for no apparent reason, attempt to extort money from a man he has made a widower, then eagerly offer the evidence that will lead him to the gallows?

Manuel was certainly no fool. Halfway through his

trial, he dismissed his lawyers and conducted his own defence so well that Lord Cameron congratulated him on his performance. He used legal knowledge studied during his frequent prison sentences for burglary, theft, indecent assault, rape and violence. But he forgot one vital fact: in Scotland, a multi-murderer is charged with every killing. In England, on the other hand, he would have been charged with only one of them, on the grounds that evidence of other crimes might prejudice a jury unfairly.

Manuel's astonishing record as a killer reads like that of a gangster in Chicago, and he would have been proud of the comparison. He was, in fact, born in America. His parents left Scotland for New York in the 1920s, and Peter was born there in 1927. But the Depression forced them back to Britain, and their misfit son was soon in trouble. By the time he was 16, a senior probation officer said he had the worst record he had ever known in a boy. In January 1956, Manuel added murder to that record.

Anne Kneilands was just 17 years old. She was waiting for her boyfriend in an East Kilbride street when Manuel met her. He had rugged, Teddy Boy good looks, and she agreed to go to a nearby cafe with him. But as he walked her home later, he suddenly dragged her into a wood, and smashed her to death, beating her skull with a piece of iron. Police were baffled by the seemingly motiveless attack. They interviewed all the possible suspects on their books, including Manuel, but put the scratches on his face down to Hogmanay excesses. Manuel had had enough police interviews in his life to know exactly what to say.

During that summer Manuel, the rebel without a cause, decided he needed a gun. His criminal ego was growing. He had killed once and got away with it. He could do it again.

On 16 September, 1956, he and two other men and a woman went on a robbery expedition to the wealthy area of High Burnside, a few miles south of Glasgow. They plundered one empty house, and even started a drinking party there. Manuel pointed out another home nearby, but the others were reluctant to stage a second break-in. Manuel went alone.

Getting in on the ground floor, he went straight upstairs, and saw two women asleep in one room. He opened another bedroom door, and saw 16-year-old Vivienne Watt. She was awake, and sat up in fear when she spotted him. Manuel bounded across the room, knocked her out and tied her up. Then he returned to the other room. Mrs Marion Watt, a semi-invalid and Vivienne's mother, was still asleep. So was her sister, Mrs Margaret Brown. Manuel calmly drew his gun and shot them both at close range. Then he walked back to Vivienne, who had come round and was struggling with her bonds. Holding her roughly down on the bed, he shot her through the left eye.

Manuel interfered with the night-dresses of all three women but, again, did not touch them. Expert witnesses later declared that he got sexual satisfaction from killing without the need for contact. It was 03.00 when he rejoined his pals in the first house, and about 05.00 when they went back to Glasgow.

But Manuel's shot had not killed Vivienne instantly. Her body was still warm when the family's daily help arrived next morning. And if that gave Manuel added satisfaction, the next development delighted his twisted mind. Police arrested Mrs Watt's husband, William, and accused him of the three murders.

Mr Watt, a baker, had been staying at a hotel in Lochgilphead, Argyll, 80 miles away, on the night of the killings. Witnesses had seen him there at midnight and 08.00. But police proved it was possible for him to have driven to his home and back comfortably in those eight hours. And they had witnesses who swore they had seen Mr Watt in his car on the Renfrew Ferry at 03.00

The unfortunate man spent two months in prison before he was set free. The police could find no reason why a prosperous, loving father would kill his happy family. But Mr Watt's ordeal was not over. For Peter Manuel, who had equally little reason for killing his loved ones, now tried to extort money from the bereaved man. First he told Watt's solicitor he could name the Burnside murderer for a price. Then he met Mr Watt, and offered to remove lingering suspicions by killing the Burnside murderer, and making it look like suicide. It would only cost £120. The baker declined.

Manuel was playing with fire, but amazingly he got away with it. And he was also continuing to kill. On 8 December, 1957, he took a train to Newcastle upon Tyne, south of the border. He then took a taxi and ordered Sidney Dunn, the driver, to a deserted moorland road near Edmondbyers, then shot and stabbed him. Just after Christmas, he met 17-year-old Isabelle Cooke on the outskirts of Glasgow, dragged her into a field, tore off most of her clothes, and strangled her. He then buried the girl he had never seen before in a shallow grave.

While the rest of Scotland was sleeping off Hogmanay, Manuel broke into the Glasgow bungalow of Peter Smart on New Year's Day, 1958. He found £25 in a wallet, and could have left undetected because Mr Smart, his wife Doris and their son Michael had not heard a thing. Instead, Manuel went into their bedrooms and shot all three dead. Then he calmly fed two tins of salmon to the family cat.

But at last Manuel had made a mistake. Under routine surveillance as he was after every major crime, he was seen passing some new blue £5 notes – notes of the type Peter Smart had drawn from the bank before his death. The home Manuel shared with his parents was searched, and after discovering house-breaking equipment, the police arrested both Manuel and his father. Manuel then agreed to make a statement on condition his father was released.

What he told them was an emotionless, detailed story of his murders. The cold-blooded confession stunned hardened officers, who reported that, when he led them to Isabelle Cooke's grave, he said almost light-heartedly: 'This is the place. In fact, I think I'm standing on her now.'

Manuel craved the limelight, and longed to be feared as a big man. But neither the police, nor the court, were awed by his exploits. After listening to 250 witnesses and a three-hour closing speech from Manuel himself, the jury found him guilty of seven of the eight murders with which he was charged – the Newcastle killing was outside Scottish jurisdiction, and the killing of Anne Kneilands was not proven for lack of evidence.

Peter Manuel, a particularly vicious and wanton murderer, was hanged at Glasgow's Barlinnie Prison on 11 July, 1958.

The Prince of Poisoners
William Palmer

William Palmer has gone down in history as the Prince of Poisoners, a murderer so notorious that the town where he practised his evil arts applied to the prime minister for permission to change its name. Palmer's trial has been hailed as the most sensational of the nineteenth century. What made it so was not that he was the first prisoner to use strychnine, but the incredible story of debauchery and lust that unfolded. For Palmer and his wretched relatives were leftovers from an earlier age. And an England trying to get used to the puritanism of Queen Victoria lapped up each lurid detail of Palmer's Regency lifestyle – sex, gambling, drinking, scandal . . . and murder.

Palmer was born in Rugeley, Staffordshire, in 1824, the second son of a sawyer who had swindled his employer, the Marquess of Anglesey, out of £70,000 by selling his timber, and a woman whose uncle had fathered an incestuous granddaughter by his own illegitimate daughter. Such a heritage need not have brought out the worst in young William – four of his brothers and sisters led perfectly normal lives. But his eldest sister, Mary Ann, turned to promiscuity, taking after her mother; his brother Walter became an alcoholic; and William himself turned to a life of wine, women and gambling – funded by theft and fraud.

His father died when he was 12, but any hopes William had of enjoying a life of leisure on his legacy were dashed when he received only a £7,000 share of the ill-gotten fortune. When Palmer left school, he was apprenticed to a Liverpool firm of chemists, Evans and Evans, but the demands of his heavy flutters on the horses, entertaining the ladies, and keeping up with the rich, idle circle of friends he formed soon exhausted his allowance. Palmer began stealing money sent with orders he collected for the firm from the Post Office. He was soon discovered and sacked.

His mother settled the bill for the missing cash and sent him to work for a surgeon, Edward Tylecote. Though outwardly industrious and ambitious, Palmer was more intent on profit and profligacy than medicine. He stole from his employer and took advantage of his position to seduce his patients. It is estimated that he fathered 14 illegitimate children during the five years he worked for Tylecote. Eventually the surgeon lost patience with his troublesome assistant, and enrolled him as a 'walking pupil' at Stafford Infirmary. Palmer quickly found that this in no way lessened his opportunities for sex and stealing, and he also grabbed the chance to indulge a new passion – poisons. The hospital authorities were so alarmed by his activities that they barred him from the dispensary, but Palmer was not so easily rebuffed.

In 1846, an inquest was held at Stafford into the death of a man called Abley. He had been unwise enough to accept a challenge to a drinking bout from Palmer, who was having an affair with his wife. After only two tumblers of brandy, Abley was violently sick, and died within minutes. Though the authorities were suspicious, nothing could be proved against Palmer, who left shortly after the death to continue his studies at St Bartholomew's Hospital in London. In retrospect, most experts believe Abley was the poisoner's first victim in what may have been a toxicological experiment.

Palmer squandered more than £2,000 during a riotous year in London – an enormous sum in those days – and only just managed to qualify as a doctor. But in one subject he was top of his class. The only note he made in one of his textbooks was: 'Strychnine kills by causing tetanic fixing of the respiratory muscles.'

In August 1846, Palmer was back in Rugeley, setting up his practice in a large house opposite the Talbot Arms Inn. The lascivious reputation of both his widowed mother and himself made the locals far from eager to put their lives in his hands, and Palmer had few patients to keep him away from his first love, the race track. But already he was tumbling into debt, and was anxious to cut his expenditure in other directions. One day he asked to see the illegitimate daughter he had fathered by a maid he had known when working for Dr Tylecote. She died shortly after returning to her mother the same evening. Soon other illegitimate offspring unaccountably suffered fatal convulsions after licking the honey their fond father spread on his finger.

In 1847, Palmer took himself a wife. Ann Brookes was herself illegitimate. Her father, an Indian Army colonel, had committed suicide, and her mother, the colonel's former housekeeper, had taken refuge in drink. Both were well provided for, the widow inheriting property worth £12,000, the daughter living on the interest of £8,000 capital as a ward of court. One of her two guardians was a cousin of Palmer's former employer, Dr Tylecote, and was opposed to the marriage, but Palmer successfully asked the courts for permission to wed their charge. From all accounts, the two were very much in love, and their happiness was clouded only by the way their children kept dying. Four were killed by mysterious convulsions when only days or weeks old between 1851 and 1854. Only the eldest boy, Willy, survived.

Several of Palmer's relatives and racing companion were not so lucky. He called on his uncle, Joseph Bentley, a drunken degenerate, and suggested a trial of drinking strength. Again, sharing brandy with Palmer proved a sickening experience. The uncle died three days later, leaving his nephew a few hundred pounds. In 1848, Palmer invited his mother-in-law to stay at Rugeley. Though an alcoholic, she still had enough of her wits about her to detest her daughter's husband. She confided to a friend before the journey to Rugeley: 'I know I shan't live a fortnight.' She died ten days after arriving.

That nobody found anything suspicious in the deaths of those around Palmer was due in large measures to his performance as an actor. To the community, he was a respected, church-going, unctious man, charming, pious, kind and generous. His wife believed he was doing his best to save her mother when he gave her medication and personally prepared her food.

Palmer also allayed suspicion by calling in a second opinion, a good-hearted, doddering local doctor named Bamford, who was over 80 and prepared to agree with his young friend's diagnoses. When Palmer told him death was due to apoplexy or English cholera. Bamford obligingly signed death certificates to that effect.

The death of Palmer's mother-in-law was not as profitable as he expected. Her property was tied up, and what little money accrued to the grieving newly-weds was only a drop in the ocean of the doctor's gambling debts. Already he owed thousands of pounds to a dubious Mayfair lawyer, Thomas Pratt, and lesser sums to Midlands' moneylenders called Padwick and Wright. His attempts to remove his own relatives continued, but when the wife of another uncle became ill while paying him a visit, she refused to take the pills he proferred, throwing them out of a window instead. Palmer managed to explain away the fact that chickens who pecked at the pills were dead next morning.

He turned his attentions to his racing companions. He owed a man called Leonard Bladen £800 after a run of back luck. He invited him to Rugeley, and after a convivial evening, the guest took to his bed with a stomach upset. Within a week he was dead. Bladen's wife, who heart about the illness from a third party, arrived just before the end, but was upset at not being allowed to see the body. She was also perturbed to be told that her husband had only £15 on him, and that Palmer expected £59 from the man's estate to settle a gambling debt. Her friends urged her to go to the police, but she refused, out of consideration for Mrs Palmer. Another gambler called Bly also learned how lethal it could be to win money from Palmer. Mrs Palmer was becoming upset at the string of deaths in the house. 'My mother died here last year, now these men.' she wailed, 'What will people say?'

Towards the end of 1853, Palmer's finances were in a more hopeless state than ever. He backed one of his own horses, Nettle, to win £10,000 in the Oaks. It lost. Twice he was declared a defaulter on bets, and barred from Tattersalls, the Mecca of the racing establishment. Pratt, Padwick and Wright were all becoming increasingly strident in their demands for payment – and interest on his gambling debts was now running into thousands of pounds. Palmer needed money desperately – desperately enough to kill the wife he loved.

In January 1854, the month he poisoned his fourth child, he took out three insurance policies on Mrs Palmer, for a total of £13,000. They were arranged with the help of Pratt and a local attorney, Jeremiah Smith. Smith was having an affair with Palmer's mother, now aged over 60, but was not anxious for the news to be broadcast. Palmer knew of the liaison, and had used it to pressure Smith into helping him forge his mother's signature on guarantees for his own debts. Now Smith helped to fix up the three life policies – two, with Norwich Union and Sun Insurance, for £5,000 each, one, with the Prince of Wales company, for £3,000. The premium was a total of £760 a year, and apparently none of the companies bothered to ask how a country doctor with little income and a penchant for betting could afford to pay so much. In fact, Palmer borrowed the money from Pratt.

Palmer managed to tide himself over during the summer, but a fresh cash crisis hit him in September. As luck would have it, his wife returned from visiting relatives in Liverpool with a chill. She took to her bed, and Palmer's devoted care soon turned a minor ailment into chronic antimony poisoning.

This time, he took the precautions of calling in not only Dr Bamford, but also his wife's former guardian, the once-suspicious Dr Knight. He too was now an octogenarian, and, like Bamford, was prepared to concur with Palmer's diagnosis. All three signed a death certificate citing English cholera. Palmer seemed distraught at the death, weeping and sobbing inconsolably. But he still managed to spend that night with his maid, Eliza Tharm, who gave birth to a child exactly nine months later.

At first the insurance companies were reluctant to settle the policies Palmer had taken out such a short time before. They were suspicious at such a sudden death in a seemingly healthy woman of 27. But faced with the verdicts of two doctors of good repute, they decided not to call for an inquest, and Palmer was given his money. He immediately gave £8,000 to Pratt and £5,000 to Wright. But Padwick stepped up his demands, and Pratt was soon insisting on further efforts to settle Palmer's account. Shrugging off the suspicions of the insurance companies, Palmer decided they were the best policy for saving him from ruin.

With Pratt's help, he devised a scheme to cover the life of his brother Walter, a bankrupt dipsomaniac, for an astonishing £82,000. The total was split between six companies, and Palmer persuaded Walter to co-operate by promising to lend him £400, and by offering to provide him with the drinks that Walter's wife was rationing.

The insurance companies, once bitten, were shy about dealing with the Palmer family again. Walter's doctor, a man called Waddell, signed one application form, declaring that his patient was 'healthy, robust and temperate'. But he added in a covering note: 'Most confidential. His life has been rejected in two offices. I am told he drinks. His brother insured his late wife's life for many thousands, and after the first payment she died. Be cautious.'

Palmer finally secured policies to a total of £13,000, invited his brother to Rugeley, and for five months plied him with gin. It has been estimated that Walter drank 19 gallons of the spirit before leaving for home in July, 1855. Palmer arranged to meet his brother at Wolverhampton races on 14 August, and prepared for the encounter by buying some prussic acid. Again Walter embarked on a gin binge, but this time the drinks were laced. Two days later he was dead of an apoplectic fit. By the time his widow learned of his demise, the body was already in its coffin.

Palmer instantly applied for the life insurance policies

to be paid up, but the companies delayed settlement until they had investigated further. Palmer would have been wise to wait, but Pratt, who had been assigned the policy on Walter as security for loans of £11,500 would not let him. In September, he demanded a £6,000 payment. Palmer desperately tried to take out new insurance policies on George Bate, whom he described as a 'gentleman farmer'. When the companies investigated, they found they were being asked to take a £25,000 risk on a penniless undergroom at Palmer's stables.

Palmer was told there would be no policy on Bate's life – and no payment on the insurance for Walter. If he went to court to claim his £13,000, they said, they would counter claim with a charge of murder. Palmer was now in desperate straits. Pratt was threatening to sue for his money by issuing writs against Palmer's mother, the unwitting guarantor. Palmer knew that the penalty for forging signatures was transportation. He also had a new problem to contend with. Some years earlier he had arranged an abortion for a Stafford girl, Jane Burgess, whom he had made pregnant. He unwisely sent her passionate love letters, described by one author who read them as 'too coarse to print'. Palmer had urged the girl to burn them, but she was not that foolish. Now she wrote to him, threatening blackmail.

On 13 November, 1855, Palmer went to Shrewsbury races with his pal John Parsons Cook, a 27-year-old rake who had squandered a £12,000 legacy from his father, but aimed to recoup some of it on his horse Polestar in the Shewsbury Handicap. To the delight of both men, Polestar won. Cook collected £800 in cash from bets on the course, and unwisely showed Palmer a betting slip from Tattersalls for a further of £1,200.

Cook, like Palmer, was generous in sharing his successes. He and a party of friends celebrated the victory with a slap-up champagne supper at the Raven Hotel in

Shrewsbury. But after accepting a glass of brandy from Palmer, he was violently ill. He handed over his cash winnings to another man, saying: 'I believe that damned Palmer has dosed me.' Yet he agreed to Palmer's suggestion next morning that he come back to Rugeley for medical treatment.

Cook took rooms in the Talbot Arms, where Palmer, living just across the road, could keep a careful eye on him. On Friday, 16 November, Cook dined with Palmer and Jeremiah Smith. Next morning, he was again violently sick. Palmer kept popping in with medicines, and on the Sunday sent some broth across to the inn. A chambermaid who tasted it while heating it retched for the next five hours, but nobody blamed the broth, and Palmer was allowed to take a bowl up to his friend. Dr Bamford had already been called in for consultations, and by the Monday Cook was feeling a little better. This could have been because Palmer had gone up to London to cash Cook's betting slip at Tattersalls, and pay £450 of it to Pratt.

There could now be no turning back for Palmer. He returned to Rugeley at 22.00, and bought three grains of strychnine from the local surgeon's assistant on his way to the Talbot Arms. That night, Cook went through agony. Chambermaid Elizabeth Mills was with him. She said later: 'He was sitting up beating the bedclothes with his hands. His body, his hands and his neck were moving then – a sort of jumping or jerking. Sometimes he would throw himself back on the pillow and then raise himself up again He screamed three or four times and called out "Murder" '.

Next day, Cook refused to take any more medication. But Palmer had summoned Cook's own physician, Dr William Jones, from Lutterworth, and he, Bamford and Palmer persuaded the patient to take some pills made up by Dr Bamford. He agreed, not realizing that Bamford had given the pills to Palmer, who had bought more strychnine that morning, along with some prussic acid.

Cook's long ordeal was almost over. At midnight on Tuesday, the jangling bell in his room sent Elizabeth and her fellow chambermaid Lavinia Barnes hurrying upstairs. The patient was arched in excruciatingly painful contortions, resting only on his head and heels, as Dr Jones massaged his neck. Curiously, Cook was screaming for Palmer. One of the girls ran to the doctor's house, and found him fully dressed and ready. He forced two more pills through Cook's clenched teeth, and the poor man writhed in new agonies before slumping lifeless, on the bed. The two chambermaids had watched the death scene in the eerie candlelight with terrified awe. Now Elizabeth was amazed to see Palmer going through the dead man's pockets.

Desperation had forced the maniacal medic to throw all caution to the wind, he had already persuaded the Rugeley postmaster, Samuel Cheshire, to help him forge a cheque for £350 from Cook to Palmer. Now he asked him to witness a document saying Cook owed him another £4,000. Cheshire refused.

More trouble was in store for Palmer. On Friday, 23 November, Cook's stepfather, William Stevens, arrived in Rugeley. The appearance of the body, the haste with which it had been given to an undertaker, the search of Cook's pockets, and the claim for money from Cook's estate all made him suspicious. Unhappy with the stated cause of death, apoplexy, he ordered that the room where the body lay be locked, and left for London to see a solicitor, and demand a post-mortem.

It was held at the Talbot Arms on the following Monday morning, under the direction of a Dr Harland. Both Palmer and Bamford were present – one of the rare occasions a murderer has taken part in the search for clues to his murder. Palmer did all he could to obstruct that search. As the medical students cutting the body lifted out the stomach, Palmer brushed against them, and much of the vital contents spilled irretrievably back into the abdomen. Harland reprimanded Palmer, assuming the doctor was playing a joke, and Palmer whispered to Bamford: 'They won't hang us yet.'

The stomach and intestines were sealed into a bottle, to be sent for analysis in London. Then the bottle disappeared. Harland angrily demanded to know where it was, and Palmer produced it from behind his back. There were two cuts in the air-proof lid. Still Palmer would not admit defeat. He offered the post-boy £10 if he would upset the carriage taking Stevens and the bottle to Stafford to catch the London train. The boy refused.

Palmer waited impatiently for the results of the London autopsy. He learned them before anyone else. Postmaster Cheshire was in the habit of allowing his friend to read any mail that interested him, and Palmer was delighted to intercept the report from the analyst. No poison had been found, apart from slight traces of antimony.

Palmer now took leave of his senses. He wrote two letters to the coroner, saying he was confident of a 'death by natural causes' verdict at the inquest – and enclosing the gift of some game and a £5 note. The coroner handed both letters and gifts to the police and recorded a verdict of wilful murder. Palmer, already in the custody of the sheriff's officer because of his debts, was arrested and taken to Stafford jail.

The bodies of his wife Ann and brother Walter were exhumed for post-mortems, and soon all England was talking of the Rugeley poisoner, attributing him with even more grisly deeds that those that were suspected. A special Act of Parliament, still known as 'Palmer's Law', had to be passed to transfer the trial from Stafford to the Old Bailey in London. Local prejudice was the given reason –

and according to one of Palmer's defence team, Edward Kenealy, it was the fear that a local jury would never convict him. Kenealy wrote in his memoirs: 'Palmer was a such a general favourite and had so many personal friends and acquaintances that no verdict of guilty could have been obtained.'

The Crown had no such problems at the Old Bailey. The trial, which began on 14 May, 1856, attracted intense attention from high society. The courtroom was packed each day, and outside throngs of spectators blocked the pavements to watch the protagonists arrive and leave. Bound volumes of verbatim evidence sold in their thousands, even though much of it was conflicting technical jargon from medical men.

The prosecution, led by Attorney-General Sir Alexander Cockburn made problems for itself by specifying that Cook was murdered by strychnine. Though Palmer was known to have bought it, no traces were found in Cook's corpse. Both sides brought in batteries of experts to try to explain this. Palmer's attorney, Serjeant Shee, berated one doctor for cruelty to animals after he spoke of the effects of strychnine on rabbits. Another man said the state of Cock's stomach when it reached London would have made establishing cause of death virtually impossible, 'if I had not been informed that there was a considerable quantity of strychnine present.'

Medical science knew little about the relatively new poison, or how to detect it, and some experts were prepared to swear that Palmer had found ways of disguising it. If so, he was not about to share the secret. There was little doubt that Palmer was guilty of poisoning Cook, and the jury and three judges were happy to go along with the Attorney-General's convenient theory: that Cook had been softened up with other poisons, then finished off by strychnine in an almost imperceptible dose. On 27 May, having listened to a masterly closing oration from Sir

Alexander Cockburn, and a strong recommendation to convict from Lord Chief Justice Campbell, the jury took one hour to find Palmer guilty of murder.

He accepted sentence of death philosophically, and was taken back to Stafford under strong escort. He showed little sign of conscience or depression in prison, except when news that the Home Secretary had rejected his appeal came through, and to the end refused to make any confession, beyond saying, ambiguously: 'I am innocent of poisoning Cook by strychnine.'

Nearly 30,000 people were outside Stafford Jail on the morning of 14 June, 1856. Packed trains arrived in the town from the early hours, and spectators paid up to a guinea to take their places on the 23 platforms erected to give them a better view. When Palmer arrived, apparently indifferent to and amused by his fate, police had trouble controlling the mob as it surged forward. The sensational details of his sordid life had enthralled the nation, but there was nothing exceptional above his death at the end of the rope.

Few murderers have rivalled William Palmer for cold-hearted, premeditated callousness and cruelty. Though convicted and hanged for only one killing, he was suspected of at least 15 more, many of the victims being innocent children he fathered through debauched lechery. But even his horrific story has two wry postscripts. The moneylenders who hounded him received nothing after his death, because his mother refused to honour forged guarantees. And when the town of Rugeley, shamed by the notoriety brought on it by its infamous son, applied to change its name, the prime minister is alleged to have replied: 'By all means, provided you name your town after me.' His name was Lord Palmerston.

The Murderous Musician
Charles Peace

What kind of man could sit calmly in a court's public gallery and watch another condemned to die for a murder he had committed? Charles Peace could: and it was only after his arrest, two years later, for another murder, that he made a full confession to a chaplain and saved the innocent prisoner's life. For stony-hearted Peace lived his criminal life by the maxim, 'If I make up my mind to a thing, I am bound to have it.' And for 20 years, he had made up his mind to be one of England's most cunning crooks.

Peace was a small, wiry man who walked with a limp and used an artifical hook arm to conceal the loss of two fingers in a childhood accident. He played the violin well enough to be billed at local concerts as 'The Modern Paganini'. But at night, he turned into an expert cat-burglar, carrying his tools in a violin case and using his monkey-like agility and phenomenal strength to plunder from the rooftops. For many years he wandered from town to town, until 1872, when he returned to his native Sheffield with his wife Hannah and their son Willie, and set up shop as a picture framer and bric-a-brac dealer in Darnall.

He was then 40, an ugly man whose tongue seemed too big for his mis-shaped mouth. Yet he seems to have had a way with certain women. He began an illicit affair with Mrs Katherine Dyson, the buxom wife of one of his neighbours in Britannia Road, visiting pubs to satify her craving for drink, then going to the attic of a nearby empty house to satisfy his own cravings. Soon Peace grew less cautious, calling on the Dysons whenever the fancy took him, and eventually Katherine's husband Arthur, a giant of over 2 metres in height, banned him from the house.

But Peace could not stand rebuffs. Mrs Dyson recalled later: 'I can hardly describe all that he did to annoy us . . . he would come and stand outside the window at night and look in, leering all the while. He had a way of creeping and crawling about, and of coming on you suddenly unawares.' The Dysons went to the police after their persecutor made threats at gunpoint in July 1876, but he fled to Hull to escape the arrest warrant that was issued. The Dysons decided to move home, to Banner Cross Terrace, Ecclesall Road, but when they arrived at what they thought would be their haven, Peace walked out of the front door, declaring: 'I am here to annoy you and I will annoy you wherever you go.'

On the evening of 29 November, Mrs Dyson left the house to visit the outside WC. Peace was waiting in the shadows holding a gun. Her shriek brought her husband running from the parlour, and he chased Peace down the alleyway that ran behind the terraced houses. When they reached the street, two shots were heard in rapid succession, and Dyson fell dying, a bullet in his head. Peace fled, dropping as he went a bundle of notes Mrs Dyson had written him. And though a reward of £100 was put on his head by police, he evaded capture, burgling his way from town to town until he reached London, and set up home in Evelina Road, Peckham.

It was a strange household. His wife Hannah and their son lived in the basement, while Peace and his mistress masqueraded as Mr and Mrs Thompson on the floor above, throwing musical parties for new friends and neighbours, and attending church every Sunday. Eventually the 'Thompsons' had a baby boy.

Peace cultivated a respectable image quite deliberately, saying: 'The police never think of suspecting anyone who wears good clothes.' He dyed his grey hair black, shaved off his beard. By day he drove his cart round south London, ostensibly collecting other people's unwanted

possessions. At night he went out and stole the possessions they were not so keen to lose. Though his exploits
made the newspapers, police had no idea who the daring
raider was, and Peace made the most of their ignorance.
He delighted in chatting to policemen he met on trains,
and even shared lodgings with an officer while staying
briefly in Bristol.

But on 10 October, 1878, his luck ran out. Police were
waiting in force outside a house in Blackheath when Peace
emerged at 02.00 carrying a silver flask, a letter case and a
cheque book. The cornered villain threatened them with a
gun, and fired four shots, but the officers ignored him. The
fifth shot struck PC Edward Robinson in the arm, but he
still managed to overpower the gunman with colleagues,
inflicting quite a beating-up in the process.

Peace was tried under the false name he gave, John
Ward, for attempted murder, and the Old Bailey jury took
four minutes to find him guilty. Despite a whining personal plea for mercy from the 'most wretched, miserable
man,' he was jailed for life. Then his mistress revealed his
true identity so she could collect the £100 murder reward
still on offer at Sheffield. Police brought Mrs Dyson from
her native America, where she had gone after the death of
her husband, and charged Peace.

On 22 January, 1879, two wardens accompanied the
handcuffed prisoner on to the 05.00 express from London
to Sheffield. He proved troublesome throughout the journey, and when the train reached Yorkshire, he flung himself out of a window. The wardens stopped the train and
ran back a mile to find him unconscious in the snow, having landed on his head. Committal proceedings were held
outside his cell in Sheffield, and Peace was sent for trial at
Leeds.

The jury took 12 minutes to find Peace guilty, and he
was condemned to death. He spent the days before the
execution writing moralistic letters and praying. And he

also revealed to the chaplain, the Rev. J. H. Littlewood, that four months before the death of Dyson he had shot and killed a policeman who disturbed him during a robbery at Whalley Range, Manchester.

Even more chillingly, he confessed that he had sat in the gallery at Manchester Assizes when two Irish brothers were charged with the death, and had watched 18-year-old William Habron be sentenced to death on 28 November just 24 hours before he shot Dyson. 'What man would have done otherwise in my position?' he said when asked why he had remained silent at such a blatant miscarriage of justice.

Harbron was pardoned and given £800 compensation, and at 08.00 on 25 February, 1879, aged 46, Charles Peace took his place on the scaffold at Armley Jail, Leeds, after complaining bitterly about the 'bloody rotten bacon' he was served for his last breakfast. Though he pretended contrition and trust in God in an odious final speech, he confessed to the chaplain: 'My great mistake, sir, has been this: in all my career I have used ball cartridge; I ought to have used blank.' His last words before Marwood the executioner pulled the trapdoor lever were: 'I should like a drink; have you a drink to give me?' And he left his own epitaph in his cell. He was executed, he wrote, 'for what I done but never intended.'

The Triangular Chamber of Death
Dr Marcel Petiot

Few mass killers have cashed in on the chaos of war as profitably as Dr Marcel Petiot. When the guillotine sliced his scheming head from his body on the morning of 26 May, 1946, he had made more than a million pounds from murder. And but for foolish pride, the 49-year-old doctor, might have escaped to enjoy his ill-gotten gains.

The medical profession was a natural choice of career for a man who showed sadistic tendencies even as a boy in his native Auxerre, where he relished cruelty to animals and smaller children. He spent Word War One in a casualty clearing station at Dijon, peddling stolen morphia to drug addicts, before entering an asylum, where he studied medicine. By 1921 he had qualified as a doctor, and set up a practice in Villeneuve-sur-Yonne.

Flouting the Hippocratic oath, Petiot quickly prescribed a life of luxury for himself. He overcharged the rich while treating the poor for free. And villagers soon realized that Petiot was the man to see if they wanted drugs or illegal abortions. The mysterious disappearance of his young and pretty housekeeper when she became pregnant, and strange cries of pain from the good doctor's house, caused no more than idle gossip, and Petiot was soon sufficiently well-regarded to be elected Mayor.

But by 1930 life at Villeneuve had become too hot for him. One of his patients, a local shopkeeper, was robbed and killed, and Petiot was suspected, though nothing could be proved. Another patient persisted in accusing the doctor while continuing to visit him for treatment for his rheumatism. When he died suddenly, Petiot wrote 'natural causes' on the death certificate, and headed for Paris.

Again his readiness to supply addictive drugs and terminate unwanted pregnancies soon earned him plenty of loyal patients. Quickly his practice at 60 Rue Caumartin became one of the most lucrative in the city. Petiot kept up the pretence of the good citizen – model husband and father, attending church each Sunday. His outward respectability helped him survive a fine for drug offences and the disappearance of a woman who unwisely accused him of turning her daughter into a junkie. Then, in 1940, the Nazi army marched into Paris. And Petiot seized the chance to set up a sinister sideline that satisfied both his passion for profits and his sadistic perversions.

Gestapo activity had turned the French capital into a city of fear. Jews disappeared to concentration camp gas chambers, able-bodied Frenchmen were rounded up for labour camps, and those left behind soon learned that it did not pay to ask too many questions about friends who vanished. The situation was ideal for what Petiot had in mind.

He bought a disused mansion at 21 Rue Lesueur for half a million francs, then set about modifying it for his purposes. The house included a sound-proof triangular room with no windows and only one door. Petiot installed peepholes, telling the builders the room was for his mental patients. He installed a furnace in the cellar under the garage. Shortly before Christmas, 1941, everything was ready.

Petiot now spread the word that he was in touch with the French Resistance, and could smuggle people hunted by the Gestapo to safety in Spain or Cuba. The desperate refugees who contacted him were told that their escape would be costly, and that they would need innoculations before being allowed into their new lands. Such was their state of fear that they readily agreed, selling up all their possessions to meet the bills, or giving them to Petiot. One of the first customers, a Polish-born tailor, paid two million francs to get himself and is family out of France. One by one, they crept surreptiously to Rue Lesueur, bared their arms for the necessary injections, and were ushered into the hidden triangular room. None of them left it alive.

When the doctor was satisfied, via his peepholes, that his deadly serum had done its work, he dragged the bodies to the cellar, where he treated them in quicklime – bought in bulk from his brother Maurice at Auxerre – before stuffing them into his grisly furnace. Then he scrupulously noted the details of each transaction – the money, jewellery, furs, gold and silver each victim had handed over.

111

As word spread, more and more customers queued at Petiot's door – Jews, people who had fallen foul of the Gestapo, rich families who were not prepared to wait until France was free of the Nazi terror. Petiot even dispatched a friend of his, Dr Paul Braumberger, a drug addict whose prostitute companion was appropriated by German troops, making it impossible for her earn the money to satisfy his cravings.

For 18 months, Petiot was able to combine curing patients at Rue Caumartin with killing them at Rue Lesueur. Though his wife noted how tired he was becoming, she never suspected the evil nature of his extra work.

But in the late spring of 1943, Petiot hit a snag. The Gestapo had been puzzled by the disappearance of several Jews they were seeking. When their investigations revealed that all had had links with Petiot they suspected he was what he pretended to be – a Resistance agent smuggling refugees to freedom. They sent a Gestapo man to Petiot, pleading to be sent abroad. Petiot had no reason to believe he was any different from his usual clients, and promptly killed him.

The Nazis arrested the doctor, and held him for several months before releasing him early in 1944. The suspicion was that Petiot had earned his freedom with one of the most bizarre defences ever – that he was only doing what the Germans were doing, killing Jews and anti-Nazis. However he had achieved it, he returned to his factory of death, and was soon busy burning bodies again.

Now, however, he had no way of treating them before throwing them into the flames. During his enforced absence, his brother Maurice had visited Paris, and called at the Rue Lesueur premises. Family loyalty and loathing for the Germans persuaded him to keep what he found there a grim secret, but he was no longer prepared to act as an accessory to disposing of human flesh, and cut off his supplies of quicklime.

112

Incinerating untreated remains made the smoke belching from Petiot's chimney even blacker and more acrid, and soon the doctor's neighbours, never happy about the pollution found it intolerable. On 11 March, 1944, the owner of 20 Rue Lesueur called both the police and fire brigade, saying the fumes were a fire danger. Petiot was not in, and a card on the door directed inquiries to his practice in Rue Caumartin. The gendarmes set off there while firemen broke in. They soon located the furnace, but what they found around it horrified them. Dismembered corpses littered the floor. Limbs, heads and torsos were scattered in grisly disarray. The firemen refused to do anything until the police returned.

Forensic experts later pieced together the bones and made a total of 27 human bodies. But when Petiot arrived, he blithely informed the gendarmes that all were Nazi collaborators who had betrayed the French maquis, and deserved the execution he had carried out. Amazingly, the police were prepared to give him at least some benefit of their doubt. Though still under the control of the Germans, they were Frenchmen who hoped the Allies would soon free them from Nazi oppression. They returned to HQ without Petiot.

The doctor was intelligent enough to know that the game was up. Once his story was checked, it would be obvious that he had lied. He fled Paris and for months laid low in the countryside. Meanwhile, senior police officers visited 21 Rue Lesueur, and discovered the cache of treasures, and Petiot's meticulous records. They showed that 63 people had entered the triangular room, never to leave it alive. And it was soon clear that none of them were traitors to France.

Far from being a patriot, Petiot was suspected of being a Gestapo agent. The front-page story of his horrific exploits stunned even a nation accustomed to Nazi atrocities. Yet the doctor declined to take his chance of disappearing in the confusion of the German retreat as the Allied armies reconquered France. He had talked his way out of so many awkward corners that he doubtless thought he could do it again. He wrote to the newspaper *Resistance*, claiming the Nazis had framed him by dumping bodies round the furnace while he was under arrest. Then he had the effrontery to enlist in the Free French forces under a false name.

As life returned to normal after the liberation, police began tidying up the loose ends of law and order. Petiot's case was a priority. Detectives guessed they had not seen the last of him, and they were right. When General de Gaulle led his army in a victory parade down the Champs Elysees, there was Petiot, marching proudly in rank with phoney medals on his chest. He had grown a beard, but he was wanted too badly to escape recognition.

Petiot insisted throughout his 18-month interrogation by a magistrate that he had killed only Germans and collaborators. But when he was brought to trial, the jury were not so gullible. They were shown 47 suitcases packed with more than 1,500 items of clothing, almost all without identity tags. They visited Petiot's triangular room, saw his cellar of death, and heard that he had plundered more than one million pounds from those he butchered.

When the verdict was announced, Petiot could not hear it above the excited babble of the court. He had to ask whether he had been found guilty or not. And when sentenced to death, he screamed: 'I will be avenged.' But he went to the guillotine quietly enough, leaving behind him an ironic epitaph to a blood-soaked life. He asked a companion on that final walk whether he could relieve himself. Permission was refused. Petiot was alleged to have joked: 'When one sets out on a voyage, one takes all one's luggage with one.' It was a luxury he did not allow any of his 63 victims.

The Teenage Monster
Jesse Pomeroy

Horrified vacationers stumbled across the body of four-year-old Horace Millen on the beach on Dorchester Bay, near Boston, in April 1874. The child's throat has been cut and he had been stabbed no fewer than 15 times. Before he died, the boy had been savagely beaten. It was the work of a monster , and police immediately launched a full scale hunt for the killer.

They were looking for a grown man, but some cross-referencing in the official files produced the name Jesse Harding Pomeroy: a lad of 14 who has been reprimanded and sent to a special reform school two years earlier for beating up young children. Fights among youngsters were commonplace, but the name of young Pomeroy, only just out of primary school, had been remembered by the authorities because of the extraordinary amounts of unnecessary force he had used.

When police called on Jesse Pomeroy, his answers to questioning immediately aroused suspicion. He was arrested, brought to court and convicted. But Pomeroy's was one of the most remarkable murder cases ever. For, though sentenced to die, he was to live for another 58 years and the first 40 years – until he was 55 – were spent in solitary confinement.

The American public refused to take a chance on some-one who had already displayed the most vicious cruelty. When arrested, he had been at liberty only 60 days after spending 18 months in the Westboro Reformatory. The magistrate who sent him there remarked on the savagery of the beatings he had handied out to children younger than himself and a short while after his trial for the Millen

115

killing, it was established that just five weeks earlier he had killed nine-year-old Katie Curran. He had buried her body in the cellar of a shop.

At the Millen trial, Jesse Pomeroy pleaded innocence by way of insanity but it did him no good. He was convicted and sentenced to death. There were those who, because of his age, urged that his death sentence commuted to life imprisonment but they were shouted down by the masses who demanded a swift execution. As it turned out, Pomeroy's life was spared only due to the legal complexities governing death sentences in the state of Massachusetts.

Although a judge had passed a sentence of death on him, the law required that the state governor of Massachusetts set the date of execution and sign the death warrant. Governor Gaston, in office at the time, refused possibly for political reasons to do anything at all: he would neither sign the death warrant nor commute young Pomeroy's sentence. He compromised with an order, signed and sealed, that Pomeroy must spend the rest of his natural days in solitary confinement. That order stood until long after Governor Gaston had passed away himself.

It was 1916, when Pomeroy was 54, before he was finally released from solitary and allowed to mix with the other prisoners at Charlestown Prison. He had survived what must have been a superhuman ordeal by burying himself in studies. He read an immense number of books, and he wrote a lot himself.

If he had been mad at the time of the beatings, there was no longer any sign of it in his writings in these later years. One of the manuscripts he spawned was an autobiography which chronicled his early life, the crimes of which he had been convicted and an attempt he made to break out of jail.

Pomeroy died in the prison in which he had spent all his life, on 29 September, 1932. He was 73 and spent more than 60 of those years behind bars.

116

The Suicide Murders
Rouse, Tetzner, Saffran and Kipnik

Over the years, many people have tried to evade their problems and responsibilities by disappearing, but three Europeans devised more fiendish means of vanishing. The men had never met, but within 12 months, each tried similar ways of escaping the mess they had made of their own lives – by taking the lives of complete strangers.

Alfred Arthur Rouse was known to his neighbours in Buxted Road, Finchley, London, as a cheery, chatty, charming chap. He and his wife Lily May had built a comfortable little home on the proceeds of his job as a commercial traveller for a Leicester company. Rouse loved his work. He was obsessed with cars, and had the gift of the gab when it came to selling.

Then, on 6 November, 1930, two plain clothes policemen called on Mrs Rouse. Her husband's Morris Minor car, registration number MU 1468, had been found burnt out in Hardingstone Lane, just off the London road near Northampton. A charred body had been found inside. Would she go with them to Northampton to try to identify some of the few personal effects left undamaged?

Mrs Rouse inspected some braces buckles and items of clothing, and thought they may have belonged to her husband. She was not allowed to see the corpse, which was virtually unidentifiable, but she was satisfied enough to start thinking of the £1,000 life insurance her husband had taken out on himself.

The police, however, were not so sure. Two young cousins, one of them the son of the village policeman at Hardingstone, had reported a strange encounter as they walked home from a 5 November Bonfire Night Party in

Northampton. At 02.00 a car had flashed past them bound for London, and as they watched it, they saw a man scrambled out of a roadside ditch. He was agitated and breathless, carrying an attache case and wearing a light raincoat, but no hat. As they wondered what he could be doing, they noticed a bright ball of flame 200 yards down Hardingstone Lane. The man said: 'It looks as if someone has had a bonfire.' But he went off in the opposite direction when the boys ran towards the blazing car.

That was enough to arouse police suspicions. What was a respectably-dressed man doing crawling about in a ditch at 02.00? Why did he not share the alarm of the youngsters, and try to see if he could help fight the fire? They issued a nationwide alert for a man of between 30 and 35, about 2 metres (5ft 10in to 6ft) tall, with a round face and black curly hair. And at 21.20 on 7 November, they found him. Rouse was met by Scotland Yard detectives as he stepped from the Cardiff to London coach. And slowly they pieced together an amazing story of deception and callous cruelty.

Far from being a happily married suburban husband, Rouse was a bigamist. He had discovered that his good looks and amiable chat worked wonders with women, and he began to pick up waitresses and shop assistants on his travels.

In 1920, he made a 14-year-old Edinburgh girl pregnant. The child died after only five weeks, but Rouse persisted in the relationship, posing as a single man, and in 1924 went through a marriage ceremony with her at St Mary's Church, Islington, North London. A second child was born, and Rouse somehow persuaded her to let his real wife look after the boy from time to time in Buxted Road. In 1925, Rouse met a 17-year-old maid servant from Hendon, London, and was soon taking her with him on trips, and promising to marry her when trade picked up. She had a child by him in 1928, and gave birth to a second

girl in October 1930 – seven days before he burnt his car.
At the same time, a girl in the Monmouthshire village of
Gellygaer was lying ill in her parents home. She too was
pregnant by Rouse, and believed she was married to him.
Rouse had promised her parents he had bought and furnished a house for him and his 'wife' at Kingston, and
they would move there when the baby was born.

But the commercial traveller was earning only £10 a
week. The new baby and the imminent one only added to
his problems, which also included an illegitimate child in
Paris and another in England. Rouse decided there was
only one thing to do. He had to disappear, and start a new
life, unfettered by responsibilities. A few days before the
fateful 5 November, he met an unemployed man outside a
public house in Whetstone, London. The man told him of
his desperate hitch-hiking round the country in search of
work, and added: 'I have no relations.' A fiendish idea
came to Rouse as he noted that the man was about his
own height and build.

On 5 November, Rouse visited the girl who had borne
his daughter seven days earlier. She noticed that he
seemed pre-occupied, constantly glancing at his watch.
He left, muttering about bills he had to pay, and shortly
after 20.00 met the unemployed man by arrangements in
Whetstone High Road. He had promised to drive him to
Leicester in search of a job.

Rouse was a teetotaller, but he brought along a bottle of
whisky for his new friend, and the man drank from it lib-
erally. Near St Albans, the inebriate switched off the car
lights by mistake, and they were stopped by a policeman,
but allowed to drive on after a warning. What happened
next was told with chillingly clinical efficiency in a confession Rouse wrote just before his execution.

'He was the sort of man no-one would miss,
and I thought he would suit the plan I had in mind,'
he wrote. 'He drank the whisky neat from the bottle

and was getting quite fuzzled. We talked a lot, but he did not tell me who he actually was. I did not care.

I turned into Hardingstone Lane because it was quiet and near a main road where I could get a lift from a lorry afterwards. I pulled the car up. The man was half-dozing – the effect of the whisky. I gripped him by the throat with my right hand. I pressed his head against the back of the seat. He slid down, his hat falling off. I saw he had a bald patch on the crown of his head.

He just gurgled. I pressed his throat hard. The man did not realize what was happening. I pushed his face back. After making a peculiar noise, the man was silent. I got out of the car, taking my attache case, a can of petrol and a mallet. I walked about eight metres (ten yards) in front of the car and opened the can, using the mallet to do so. I threw the mallet away and made a trail of petrol to the car. Also I poured petrol over the man and loosened the petrol union joint and took the top off the carburettor. I put the petrol can in the back of the car.

I ran to the beginning of the petrol trail and put a match to it. The flame rushed to the car, which caught fire at once. Petrol was leaking from the bottom of the car. That was the petrol I had poured over the man and the petrol that was dripping from the union joint and carburettor. The first was very quick and the whole thing was a mass of flames in a few seconds. I ran away.'

In fact Rouse had planned the killing flawlessly. The left leg of the unconscious man was doubled up under the leaking union joint, so that the constant drip would send intense heat into the victim's face, making it unrecognizable. The man's right arm was stretched towards the can in the back seat, and soaked to produce another source of flames to the head and shoulders. And though he had tampered with the engine, the damage was consistent with what might be expected in an accidental blaze.

But the calculating killer had not reckoned on meeting two witnesses as he ran away. And it was that which proved his undoing. Knowing he had been seen, he panicked. Instead of escaping to a new life, he hitched a lift home to Finchley in a lorry, arriving at 06.20. He stayed only to change his clothes, then took a coach to Cardiff and Gellygaer. All the way, he unnecessarily told people his car had been stolen, but changed the details each time. To his amazement, the story of the burned-out car was on the front page of every newspaper. People who knew him in Gellygaer kept asking if it was his car. He denied it, and decided to return to London. Waiting for the coach in Cardiff, he again told conflicting tales about how his car had gone missing. He seemed almost relieved to be met at Hammersmith by the police.

But his horrific confession was still many months away. He first claimed that he had picked the man up as a hitch-hiker near St Albans, then lost his way. When the engine started to spit, he stopped to relieve himself, and told the passenger to fill the tank from his petrol can. The man asked for a cigarette. Next thing, Rouse claimed, he turned and saw a ball of flame. He ran back to the car, but could not get near it because of the heat. Then he had 'lost his head' after coming over 'all of a shake', and had fled, feeling vaguely responsible but not knowing what to do.

It was a plausible story, and though Rouse changed certain details in subsequent re-tellings of it, he still arrived at Northampton Assizes with a jaunty, self-assured air on 26 January, 1931. The prosecution, led by Norman Birkett, had a tricky task to prove murder, and Rouse knew it.

Unfortunately for him, his confidence was his undoing. Rouse had been invalided out of World War One with head wounds after a shell exploded close to where he was standing in the trenches at Givenchy, northern France. A medical report on him in September 1918 said: 'The man is easily excited and talkative.' That, as much as the chance meeting in the country lane, was to condemn him to the nose.

When Birkett suggested Rouse had thrown the man into the car carelessly, face down, Rouse was foolish enough to argue that he had more brains than to do that. Another witness, an expert on car fires, noticed that Rouse seemed unperturbed, even amused, while the court discussed whether the carburettor top might have melted or fallen off. Rouse was also too keen to offer technical explanations about what might have happened inside the blazing engine. He was too clever by half.

The most damning evidence was produced by the eminent pathologists Sir Bernard Spilsbury and Dr Eric Shaw. They testified that the victim had been unconscious but alive when the fire began, and that a tiny scrap of unburnt clothing from the crotch of his trousers was soaked in petrol. Other expert witnesses contended that the man could have spilled petrol over himself, but they did not carry much weight with a jury who looked on appalled at an accused man who coldly discussed leaving his 'good wife' because she never made a fuss of him, inexplicably made no real effort to rescue the man in his car, and, worst of all, never showed the slightest compassion or concern for the unknown wretch who had died.

On 31 January, 1931, Mr Justice Talbot sentenced Alfred Arthur Rouse, one of the most ingenious yet most loathsome murderers in British criminal history, to death. His appeal against sentence was dismissed 23 days later, and on 10 March Rouse was hanged at Bedford.

A week later, Kurt Erich Tetzner, also a young commercial traveller, stepped into the dock at Ratisbon, Germany, accused of burning to death in his car an unknown man with intent to defraud insurance companies by passing the body off as his own.

Tetzner had been in custody for 14 months, having been arrested ten days after his burned-out car was found on the outskirts of Etterhausen, Bavaria, on 25 November, 1929. The charred body at the wheel was buried in lavish style by a weeping Frau Tetzner, who had identified it as her husband, but police were alerted by insurance companies who stood to pay out nearly £7,500. They watched the widow take two telephone calls at a neighbour's house from a Herr Stranelli in Strasbourg, Alsace, and soon discovered that Stranelli and Tetzner were the same man.

Tetzner was worse than Rouse at explaining his crime. He admitted the insurance fraud, and at first confessed to murdering the passenger. But five months after his arrest, he changed his story, saying the man in the car was a pedestrian he had run over who had died as he took him to hospital.

The court found it inconceivable that anyone would confess to murder to try to cover up a case of manslaughter. And it doubted the second story after Tetzner made another admission. Once he had advertised for a travelling companion, but the man who answered dropped out. The second time, he had attacked his passenger, a motor mechanic called Alois Ortner, with a hammer and a pad of ether, after first giving him money to make himself look respectable by having a shave and buying a collar. But Ortner had proved too strong for him and escaped into a nearby forest. Ortner was called as a prosecution witness, and revealed that he had gone to police after the attack – but they refused to believe his 'fantastic' story.

Tetzner was condemned to death, and the sentence was carried out on 2 May, 1931. Shortly before, the young murderer at last confessed the truth. He had picked up an unknown young man in thin clothes who complained of being cold. Tetzner wrapped a rug around him, trapping his arms, then strangled him with rope. He then crashed the car into a tree, made a petrol trail and set fire to it.

The public prosecutor at Ratisbon referred to Rouse as 'just a pupil of Tetzner.' It is not known whether Rouse had heard of the German case before he hatched his own scheme. But the third man who tried to disappear by substituting another man's body for his own certainly had.

Fritz Saffran was young, good-looking and successful. He had made such a good job of running the Platz Furniture Store in Rastenburg, eastern Prussia, that the owner of the shop, whose daughter he married, felt able to retire early, and leave things to his 30-year-old son-in-law.

Then, on 15 September 1930, an explosion rocked the store, and flames quickly destroyed it. Thirty workers escaped, but one did not. Chief clerk Erich Kipnik claimed Saffran had dashed into the blazing building to try to save the ledgers. Sure enough, firemen sifting the debris found the charred body. It wore the remains of one of Saffran's suits, had two of his rings on its fingers, and his monogrammed watch in an inside pocket.

Saffran had been popular with all his staff and customers, but one employee in particular was inconsolable at his death. It was known that Ella Augustin had been in love with him for years, but he had publicly refused to respond to her flirting. He was, after all, a happily married man.

Two days after the fire, Ella called at several garages in the town to try to hire a car to take her mother, who was seriously ill, to Konigsberg. The chauffeur who accepted the task was surprised to be asked to arrive at her house at 03.00. He was even more amazed when the ailing mother turned out to be Saffran.

The man drove to the village of Gerdauen; but refused to go further. He had worked for the Platz firm before, and was reluctant to go to the police. But he told a friend about the secret journey, and was arrested – though later cleared – for aiding Saffran's escape. The friend alerted the police, who quickly discovered that all was not what it seemed at the prosperous Platz store. Saffran had burdened the business with huge debts after hire purchase buyers defaulted on payments. He had also raised money fraudulently on fake hire purchase deals and falsified the ledgers. Ella Augustin had helped him do this, and was his secret lover.

She was arrested, and tried to smuggle a note out to Saffran. It told the police that he was staying with one of her relatives in Berlin. Saffran somehow learned that police in the German capital were looking for him. Seven weeks after his getaway he stole the relative's identity papers, took a local train to the suburb of Spandau, and boarded the 01.00 train to Hamburg, where he hoped to get a ship to Brazil. But a fluke thwarted his clever plans. The rail official at Spandau had lived in Rastenburg several years earlier, and recognised the fugitive. Police were waiting when the train pulled into Wittenburg, the next station down the line.

Dental records helped detectives identify the body in the Platz store as Friedrich Dahl, 25, a dairyman from Wermsdorf, near Konigsberg. And on 23 March, 1931, Saffran and Kipnik, arrested when he was implicated in the conspiracy, went on trial at Bartenstein charged with Dahl's murder, attempted murder, arson, forgery, bribery and insurance frauds. Ella Augustin was accused of incitement to murder and complicity in frauds.

It quickly became clear that all three were more than anxious to blame each other for the murder. And what emerged was a chilling story of cold, calculated killing. Ella claimed that Saffran started it, brandishing a newspaper and saying: 'Have you read the report about this man Tetzner? That is how I will do our job too.'

Saffran claimed he took out an insurance policy for £7,000 so his wife would be well provided for. It was his intention to commit suicide, but Ella argued him out of it. Kipnik then suggested securing a body and burning it. They considered digging up a corpse from a grave, but dismissed the idea as impractical for their purposes.

The court was hushed as Saffran continued: 'We established a murder camp in the Nikolai Forest. The girl stayed there while Kipnik and I, each in his own car, roved the countryside for miles around, looking for a likely victim, then reported to the camp at evening. After a while we all three began to go out on these manhunts together.'

Several countrymen had lucky escapes. Once, near the village of Sorquitten, a man accepted a lift. Saffran said he speeded up, then jammed on the brakes, and Kipnik was supposed to smash the victim's skull as it jolted back. But Ella lost her nerve, clutched Kipnik's arm, and the man got away.

Kipnik claimed that, on another occasion, they picked up a pedestrian and were about to kill him when he revealed that he had six children. Sometimes they hid in woods or behind hedges, waiting for a likely victim to come along. The search went on night after night. Finally, on 12 September, 1930, Kipnik and Saffran met a man near Luisenhof just about midnight. It was Dahl.

Both men accused the other of firing the fatal three shots into his head, and both made exaggerated claims of contrition when the victim's widow took the stand. The public prosecutor had to tell them sternly to stop play-acting. But both continued to speak in terms more suited to a playhouse than a courtroom. 'Gentlemen of the jury, think of my terrible position,' Saffran pleaded, arms outstretched. 'I was leading a double life. At home I had to appear cheerful and contented while my heart was breaking. At night I was forced to go out hunting for men to murder.' Later Kipnik shouted: 'Saffran has ruined my life. I place my fate in the hands of the court. I wish I could prove to them that I am really a decent man.'

The jury believed neither story, and both men were sentenced to death. Accomplice Ella was jailed for five years. But Saffran and Kipnik were luckier than Rouse and Tetzner. The Prussian government commuted their sentences to life imprisonment. Many Germans wondered why two such callous killer should be spared the fate they had so cold-bloodedly meted out to an innocent stranger.

The Rat Poisoner
Lydia Sherman

Whenever Lydia Sherman went she found buildings infested with rats. Or at least that was the story she told the neighbourhood druggist from whom she bought her poison.

The arsenic soon eliminated the rats and, as it turned out, some of the human beings she considered a nuisance, too. As many as 42 people were believed to have died by Lydia's hand.

Married to patrolman Edward Struck of the New York Police Department, the sturdy but attractive housewife kept a low profile until 1864. Then Struck was sacked by the police for a shabby display of cowardice and promptly turned into unemployed drunk. Lydia put him to bed one evening with a lethal snack of oatmeal gruel and rat poison.

Puzzled as to the manner of his death, the doctor blamed it on 'consumption' but made up his mind to ask for an official investigation. But Lydia had ensured her husband had a quick burial and the authorities saw no reason to intrude on her 'grief'.

One by one Lydia's children died – Mary Ann, Edward, William, George, Ann Eliza, and finally the widow's namesake, tiny toddler Lydia. In every case she shrewdly called in a different doctor, all of whom obligingly took her word for the cause of death.

An ex-brother-in-law went to the authorities swearing

Lydia was 'full of black evil' and demanding that the bodies be exhumed. But the bored bureaucrats refused to budge.

Lydia moved from one job to another. In 1868 she married an aging and rich widower named Dennis Hurlbut. With rat poison available at 10 cents package, he was soon out of the way.

That left her free to marry Nelson Sherman, who took her with him to his Connecticut home. There she had problems, including a suspicious mother-in-law and the four Sherman children by a previous marriage.

Two of the children she disposed of at once. Mourning the death of his 14-year-old daughter, Addie, Nelson Sherman turned to alcohol and thus signed his own death warrant.

'I just wanted to lure him of the liquor habit.' Lydia said. A Connecticut doctor was suspicious and insisted that his stomach and liver be analyzed. Toxicologists found enough arsenic to kill an army. The vital organs of the two children were also permeated with poison.

Pleading that she had murdered out of human compassion – 'all those people were sick, after all' – the fashionably dressed widow cut an impressive figure at her trial in New Haven, Connecticut. And in a way, her luck held. Amazingly gentle with the not so gentle murderess, Judge Park instructed the jury to consider only charges of second-degree murder.

Sentenced to life in Weathersfield Prison, she vowed she would never die in jail. But there her luck did end – she was still behind bars when she died in 1878.

The Lethal Romeo
George Smith

Many men have made a living by playing with the affections of plain, naive, lovelorn spinsters, then abandoning them once they have handed over their savings. The public often find the foolish victims of such romantic con-men comic rather than tragic figures, and found reasons for amusement even at the trial of Henri Landru, who was accused of killing ten such dupes. But nobody found anything remotely funny about the exploits of another wicked womaniser, George Joseph Smith.

Smith was born in London's Bethnal Green in 1872, and was soon the despair of his parents. His mother predicted he would 'die with his boots on', and she was hardly surprised when, at the age of only nine, he was sentenced to eight years in a Gravesend reformatory. But the sentence merely helped train him for a life of crime, and, apart from three years as a soldier in the Northamptonshire Regiment, he became a full-time thief, constantly in and out of prison.

Smith was cunning. He realized he was having little success stealing for himself, so he decided to get others to do it for him. Though his bony face was not really attractive, he had small, dark mesmerising eyes that seemed to have an extraordinary magnetic power for some women. 'They were little eyes that seemed to rob you of your will.' one of his victims told police later.

Smith found it easy to persuade women to work with him, and not to implicate him if they were caught. Using the proceeds of one woman's raids, he opened a baker's shop in Russell Square, Leicester, in 1897, and a year later married an 18-year-old bootmaker's daughter, Caroline

Beatrice Thornhill, despite her family's disapproval. He was 26 and calling himself George Love.

They moved to London, and Smith found his wife employment as a servant with a succession of wealthy families in Brighton, Hove and Hastings. She had no trouble getting work. She had impeccable references from a past employer – Smith. But late in 1899 she was arrested trying to pawn the loot from one theft, some silver spoons, and was jailed for a year. Smith abandoned her, which increased her bitterness, and after her release, she spotted him by chance in London, and alerted the police. In January 1901, he was jailed for two years for receiving stolen goods. Revenge was in his mind, too, once the sentence ended. He travelled to Leicester, bent on killing his wife. But her family beat him up, and Caroline later emigrated to safety in Canada.

Smith had already discovered a new way of making women work for his living. In 1899 he had bigamously married a middle-aged boarding-house keeper, milking her of what money she had while living rent free at her lodgings. Now he began to tour the south coast, particularly seaside resorts, wooing, wedding and walking out on his brides, who were often too humiliated to reveal the truth to police or their friends and relations.

He did it all in the cheapest way possible – third-class rail travel, meagre lodgings, outings to places of free entertainment. In that way, he made the maximum of profit from each of them. In June 1908 he met Florence Wilson, a Worthing widow with £30 in her Post Office savings account. They married in London after a whirlwind three-week affair. On 3 July, he took her to the White City exhibition and left her there, claiming he was going out to buy a newspaper. In fact he dashed back to their rooms in Camden Town and sold all her belongings.

In October 1909, calling himself George Rose, Smith married Southampton spinster Sarah Freeman and they set up home in Clapham, South London. Smith played the charming gent, in smart frock coat and top hat, and his bride did not demur when he said he needed money to set up an antiques business. She withdrew her savings, and sold her Government stocks. On 5 November he took her to the National Gallery, excused himself to go to the lavatory, and scuttled back to their rooms, clearing out everything, and leaving his deserted bride destitute. In less than a month he had made a £400, four times the average annual wage.

In between these two coups, Smith had taken another wife, Edith Mabel Pegler. Dark-haired, round-faced and plump, she was 28 when she answered his advertisement for a housekeeper in a local newspaper at Bristol, where he had opened a shop in Gloucester Road. But for once Smith, who used his own name this time, was not after money. What he took from others, he gave to Edith. And though he left her from time to time, claiming he was travelling in search of antiques, he always returned after his matrimonial adventures.

Those adventures now took a more sinister turn. In August 1910, he met 33-year spinster Beatrice Constance Anne Mundy while strolling in Clifton, a resort near Bristol. The ardent wooer could hardly believe his luck when she told him of the £2,500 in securities her father, a Wiltshire bank manager, had left her when he died. The legacy, managed by a trust of relatives, paid her £8 a month. Smith, now going under the name of Henry Williams, whisked her off to Weymouth, where they set up home in Rodwell Avenue. They married on 26 August and began to flood the relatives with reassuring letters.

But the relatives had more sense than bride Bessie. They did not like the look of Wiliams, suspecting that he was a fortune hunter, and it was December before they finally sent £134 owed in interest. Smith, despairing of collecting the capital, abandoned Bessie on 13 December in an especially heartless way. He left her a letter claiming she had 'blighted all my bright hopes of a happy future' by infecting him with venereal disease, and accusing her of not being 'morally clean.' He was off to London to be cured, 'which will cost me a great deal of money.' So he took the £134, advising her to tell her relatives it was stolen while she was asleep on the beach.

Poor Bessie resumed her spinster life, telling friends, on Smith's advice, that her husband had gone to France. Smith went back to Edith Pegler, moving to Southend, then London, and back to Bristol again. The VD accusation had only been an excuse, though it must have upset a woman who was far from worldly-wise.

That she missed her adoring husband was only too clear when, 18 months later, they met again by sheer chance in Weston-super-Mare. Bessie, staying with a friend, popped out to buy daffodils one morning in March 1912, and spotted Smith on the seafront. The smooth-talking Casanova had an explanation for his note, his long absence, and the fact that he had spent all her money, and by mid-afternoon the besotted girl was ready to ignore her friend's pleas and leave with her husband, taking none of her belongings.

They travelled across country, and in May set up a modest home at 80 High Street, Herne Bay, Kent. Smith had been asking expert advice on how he could get at Bessie's £2,500 nest-egg, and in July a lawyer told him that it was only possible if she left it to him in her will. The wily bigamist wasted no time – and seemingly had no qualms about turning to murder to feather his nest. On 8 July the couple signed wills, leaving their worldly possessions to each other should they die. On 9 July, Smith bought a tapless zinc bath, haggling half-a-crown off the ironmonger's price of £2.

On 10 July, he took Bessie to a young, inexperienced doctor, claiming she had had a fit. Two days later the doctor called at their home after another fit was reported. He found Bessie in bed, flushed but seemingly well, and left a prescription for sedatives. That night, Bessie wrote to her uncle, telling him of her attacks, of how her husband was looking after her well, and of how they had both made their wills.

At 08.00 next morning, Saturday 13 July, the doctor received a note saying: 'Can you come at once? I am afraid my wife is dead.' He arrived to find Bessie submerged in the bath. She was naked and lying on her back, a bar of soap clasped in her right hand, Smith said his wife had filled the bath herself, making 20 trips downstairs to the kitchen to fetch water for it. He had gone out to buy some fish, and returned to find her dead. The police were called, but saw no reason to think the death was suspicious. Smith wept throughout the inquest on the following Monday, and was offered words of comfort by the coroner, who recorded a verdict of misadventure.

No-one asked why Bessie had drowned in a bath far shorter than her full height, or why Smith had left her lying under the water until the doctor arrived, instead of trying to resuscitate her. Nor was it found suspicious that she had just made a will, a point Smith was foolish enough to mention to the estate agent when he cancelled the letting of their home.

He had been careful to time the murder for a Saturday. Although he wired news of the death to Bessie's uncle, saying a letter would follow, there was no time for relatives to get to the inquest, or the economy-version funeral which followed just 24 hours later. Trustees of Bessie's legacy asked in vain for a post-mortem examination, and tried to stop Smith getting her money. But he had been too clever for them, and reluctantly they handed over £2,591 13s 6d.

Smith had one last piece of business to attend to. He took the bath back to the ironmonger to avoid having to pay for it. Then he left for Margate, and summoned Edith Pegler to join him. He told her he had made a nice profit selling antiques in Canada, but lost his temper when she revealed that she had been looking for him in Woolwich and Ramsgate. 'He said he did not believe in women knowing his business,' she was to recall. 'He remarked that if I interfered I should never have another happy day.'

Smith was one of the few big-time bigamists not to squander his earnings. He bought eight houses in Bristol with Bessie's money and opened a shop, and also invested in an annuity for himself. By October 1913, he was anxious for more cash, and there seemed no reason why a once-successful scheme should not work again.

Alice Burnham was short, plump and 25, a private nurse to an elderly invalid, when she met a tall, charming stranger at Southsea. Her father, a Buckinghamshire fruit-grower, took an instant dislike to the man, but that did not stop her marrying him at Portsmouth on 4 November, one day after he took out a £500 insurance policy on her life. Nor did it stop Smith writing immediately to her father, demanding £104 he was holding for his daughter, and withdrawing £27 from his bride's savings account.

Then he decided to take his new wife on holiday. It was Wednesday, 10 December when they arrived in breezy Blackpool for their bracing, out-of-season break. They called first at a boarding house in Adelaide Street, but Smith rejected the offered rooms – there was no bath. Mrs Crossley at 16 Regent Road had one, however, and the couple booked in there for ten shillings a week. A local doctor was consulted about Mrs Smith's headaches, and the dutiful wife wrote to her father, saying she had 'the best husband in the world.'

On the Friday evening, the couple asked for a bath to be prepared for Mrs Smith while they went for a walk. At 20.15 the Crossleys were having a meal downstairs when they noticed water staining at the ceiling. They were about to investigate when a dishevelled Smith appeared at the door carrying two eggs which he said he had just bought for next day's breakfast. Then he went upstairs, and shouted down: 'Fetch the doctor, my wife cannot speak to me.'

Alice had gone the same way as Bessie, and though Smith was asked at the inquest next day why he had not lifted her from the bath, or pulled the plug out of it, an accidental verdict was recorded. Again Smith wept copiously throughout the hearing, but at least one person was not impressed by his tears. Mrs Crossley was so appalled at his seeming indifference to his wife's death that she refused to let him sleep in her house that Friday night. She also noted that, while waiting for the inquest on the Saturday afternoon, he played the piano in her front room and drank a bottle of whisky.

Even worse was to come. Smith refused to have an expensive coffin for the burial, which took place at noon on Monday. He said: 'When they are dead, they are done with.' He left by train for Southsea – to clear out and sell all Alice's belongings – immediately after the funeral, and Mrs Crossley shouted 'Crippen' at him as he left the house. She also wrote on the address card he gave her: 'Wife died in bath. We shall see him again.' She could not know how prophetic those words were.

Smith rejoined the faithful Edith Pegler at Bristol in time for Christmas and used the £500 insurance money to increase his annuity. By August they were in Bournemouth, via London, Cheltenham and Torquay. Smith announced he was going up to London again, alone, for a few days. He had met and wooed a maid called Alice Reavil while listening to a band on the seafront. They married at Woolwich on 17 September, but Smith did not stay long. He was back in Bristol with the girl's £80 savings and some of her clothes – a gift for Edith – by late autumn.

The callous truth was that Alice was so poor she was not worth killing. Smith abandoned her in some public gardens after a long tram ride. But he already had a third murder victim in mind. He had met Miss Margaret Lofty, a 38-year-old clergyman's daughter, in Bath the previous June. She worked as a lady's companion, living between jobs with her elderly widowed mother. And she was ripe for exploitation – she had discovered earlier in the year that her 'fiancé' was a married man.

Smith was now calling himself John Lloyd and posing as an estate agent. He took her out to tea on 15 December and two days later they were married in secret. Smith had taken the precaution of persuading his beloved to insure her life for £700 and had even generously paid the first premium. They moved to London, taking rooms at 14 Bismarck Road, Highgate. Naturally they had a bath. But Smith seemed to have grown over-confident after the success of his two previous killings. This time he was amazingly impatient.

He took Margaret to see a local doctor on their evening of arrival, 17 December. Next morning, he took her to a solicitor to make her will – leaving everything to him. Then she wrote to her mother, describing her husband as 'a thorough Christian man.' By 20.00 on 18 December, she was having a bath. Her landlady, ironing downstairs, later recalled a splashing sound, and a noise 'as of someone putting wet hands or arms on the side of the bath.' Then there was a sigh, followed by the strains of the hymn Nearer My God Go To Thee on the harmonium in the front room. Ten minutes later the landlady answered the door-bell and found 'Mr Lloyd' standing outside, saying he had forgotten his key after popping out to buy tomatoes for his wife's supper. Sadly, Mrs Lloyd was not alive to eat them.

Though Margaret was buried on the following Monday morning, the inquest was held over until after Christmas. Smith hurried home to Bristol again, and even had the cheek to tell Edith to beware of taking a bath, adding: 'It is known that women have often lost their lives through weak hearts and fainting in the bath.' That had been the coroner's verdict on Alice Burnham, and the Highgate coroner saw no reason to think differently when he considered the death of Margaret 'Lloyd' on 1 January, 1915.

But it was to be no happy new year for George Joseph Smith. His impatience to get rid of Margaret proved his undoing. The previous deaths had not attracted too much press attention. But this one had all the ingredients of a front page story. 'Found death in bath,' said the headline in the *News Of The World*. A second headline read: 'Bride's Tragic Fate On Day After Wedding.'

Two readers, miles apart, noticed the story and thought it was too much of a coincidence. In Buckinghamshire, Alice Burnham's father contacted his solicitor, who went to the police. And in Blackpool, landlady Mrs Crossley also passed on her fears to the authorities. They began investigating possible connections between John Lloyd, estate agent, and George Smith, bachelor of independent means, and pieced together the incredible story of Smith's bigamous philanderings. On 1 February, a detective inspector and two sergeants arrested the deadly bridegroom as he left his solicitor's office, where he was making arrangements to collect the £700 insurance on his third victim.

Though the bodies of all three women were exhumed, and examined by famous pathologist Sir Bernard Spilsbury, there were no obvious signs of how they had drowned. And though Smith was charged with all three murders, he could only be tried, under English law, with one, that of Bessie Mundy. Smith denied strenuously that he had murdered anyone. He described the deaths of three brides in the same way as a 'phenomenal coincidence.' Any jury might have been prepared to accept that one such death was just an unfortunate accident. The prosecution therefore had to apply for permission to produce evidence about all three killings to show proof of a 'system'. Smith's attorney, Sir Edward Marshall Hall, protested, realizing that his only hope of a successful defence would be destroyed. But Mr Justice Scrutton agreed to consider all three deaths.

Marshall Hall, who believed privately that Smith used hypnotic powers to persuade all three wives to kill themselves, had another setback before the trial. Some newspapers had agreed to foot the defence bill in return for Smith's exclusive life story. But the Home Office vetoed the plan, and since all Smith's money was tied up in annuities, Marshall Hall received only a paltry fee under the Poor Persons Defence Act.

He received no help at all from his client. Smith repeatedly soured opinions, both at committals and at his trial, which began at the Old Bailey on 22 June, 1915, with bad-tempered outbursts at witnesses, his own lawyers and the judge. At one stage he screamed: 'It's a disgrace to a Christian country, this is. I'm not a murderer, though I may be a bit peculiar.'

The irony of the timing of the trial during World War One was not lost on Mr Justice Scrutton. A month before it, 1,198 lives were lost when a German submarine torpedoed the *Lusitania*. On the morning the trial began, *The Times* listed 3,100 men killed in the trenches. 'And yet,' said the judge in his summing-up, 'while this wholesale destruction of human life is going on, for some days all the apparatus of justice in England has been considering whether the prosecution are right in saying that one man should die.'

It took the jury only 22 minutes on 1 July to decide that he should. They had heard pathologist Spilsbury explain how Smith could have lifted his brides' legs with his left arm while pushing their heads under water with his right. And they had watched a dramatic reconstruction of such a possibility, carried out by a detective and a nurse in a bathing costume in an ante-room of the court. Even though the nurse knew what was about to happen, she still needed artificial respiration after her ordeal.

Smith was taken from Pentonville Jail to Maidstone Prison, still protesting his innocence. He remained unrepentant, though he turned to religion and was confirmed by the Bishop of Croydon, who was said to be impressed with his sincerity. On the eve of his execution, Smith wrote to Edith Pegler, who had wept for him outside the Old Bailey, saying: 'May an old age, serene and bright, and as lovely as a Lapland night, lead thee to thy grave. Now, my true love, goodbye until we meet again.'

Edith alone mourned on Friday, 13 August, when Smith was led to his execution. One day later, his first and only legal wife, Caroline Thornhill, took advantage of her widowhood to marry a Canadian soldier in Leicester.

Atlanta's Streets of Fear
Wayne Williams

The 'Missing and Murdered Children' file in the Atlanta Police headquarters had 26 unsolved cases by late spring of 1981. Through-out the two previous years black children had been snatched from the streets or simply disappeared in this town in America's deep south and it was sometimes months before their bodies were discovered hidden in undergrowth or dumped in a river. Murder had reached epidemic proportions in Atlanta. The victims were always coloured and often too young to have had any chance to defend themselves. Death was usually due to strangulation. Forensic experts believed the children, one of whom was aged only seven, were being attacked from behind by a man who squeezed the life out of them by locking his arm around their necks.

A shroud of fear fell over the town while the homicidal maniac stalked the streets. At night the roads and the pavements were deserted. Parents too scared to let their children out of their sight for more than a few seconds were locking their doors to keep them inside. Vigilante parent patrols were formed. Fathers often armed themselves with baseball bats. And over everything hung suspicion. Was a white man carrying out his own macabre mission against blacks or was a crazy cult killer on the loose?

The two-year search for the killer had broken the health of many senior police officers, stretched the resources of the whole town and even caused the State Justice Department to set up a special unit to join in the hunt. Every time another child went missing the efforts were intensified. But despite millions of dollars spent, the murders continued.

FBI officers had to be drafted in to Atlanta to help police chief Lee Brown who was under universal attack from the townspeople. And hordes of cranks arrived in town eager to pick up the $100,000 reward for information leading to the arrest of the killer. It was a frightening and macabre mystery – made the worse by the fact that the police believed the killer was taunting them.

After November, 1980, when the eleventh killing occurred, children were being murdered at intervals of about three and a half weeks. The bodies, instead of being hidden, were left conspicuously in parks. And despite all precautions the parents were taking, the killer was still finding victims.

As he stepped up his campaign of deaths, a grisly pattern was beginning to emerge. All the children had been aged between 7 and 14 years and all but two were boys. Yet despite fears of a crazed pervert being on the loose, there was no evidence that any of the children had been sexually assaulted. Worse, the police were worried that if just one person was responsible for all the deaths then other psychopaths may be encouraged by the apparent ease and lack of detection. The desperate hunt for the killer was one of the biggest police operations ever launched in the United States. Twenty-thousand citizens were interviewed by officers, another 150,000 were questioned over the telephone. Tens of thousands of children were spoken to because the police believed that at some-time the killer could have tried to abduct a child unsuccessfully. Thirty-five FBI agents were permanently stationed in Atlanta and had been told they would stay there until the investigation was over.

Then one night in May 1981 there was a dramatic breakthrough. Two police officers and two FBI agents were huddled in a corner under the arches of the four-lane South Drive Bridge. They were one of dozens of teams which undertook around-the-clock vigils in the city. Ironically they were not watching the river on that misty night. They were merely covering the bridge because it formed one of the main routes to and from the town and they could quickly be on the road to join in any chase or stop any suspect leaving Atlanta. But as they chatted in whispers they were startled by something splashing into the water only a metre or so away. Two of the men went into the water to try to help whoever had gone in, and two sprinted up to the road and were there within a few seconds. They radioed ahead and a patrol car arrived almost instantly at the end of the bridge and stopped the traffic coming off it. Drivers were questioned briefly and then allowed to go on their ways.

Two days later police frogmen fished out of the river the body of Nathaniel Cater a 27-year-old negro. Strangulation was given as the cause of death.

If the same killer had struck again, the he had broken his pattern. The victim was black and had died from stran-

gulation . . . but he was an adult. There were enough sim-
ilarities for the police to suspect that Cater was number 27
in the chain of killings. The 'Missing and Murdered
Children' file was renamed 'Missing and Murdered
People'.

A few days later the body of a second victim, 21-year-
old Ray Payne, also a negro, was recovered from the river.
He had been thrown in at the same time as Cater and had
also died from strangulation. Knowing that four of the
child victims had previously been recovered from the
river, the investigation team went back to the drivers they
had stopped on the night the surveillance team had been
under the bridge.

One of the men they questioned was Wayne Bertram
Williams a 23-year-old black who lived quietly with his
parents, both retired school-teachers, in a modest single-
storey house in north-west Atlanta. He was taken to the
city police headquarters and held overnight but was
released despite the police discovery that he lived a
bizarre lifestyle and considered himself a genius. Williams
was a a self-described 'media groupie'. He used to sit
around in his car with a short-wave radio and tune in to
police and fire services listening out for crimes or fires.
Then, equipped with a camera, he would rush to the
scene, usually arriving ahead of reporters and television
crews and sell his exclusive pictures to the highest bidder.
At the age of 14 he had started broadcasting on his own
small pirate radio station in Atlanta. An only and lonely
child, he had been convicted at 18 of impersonating a
police officer. All his friends were shocked and surprised
when they learnt that he was a police suspect.

On 3 June he was again taken in for questioning by
police and given a 12-hour grilling. The next day, he rang
newspapers and TV stations and held a press conference.
Professing his innocence, he claimed the police had told
him he was the prime suspect in some of the slayings. He

said: 'One cop told me "You killed Nathaniel Cater. It's just a matter of time before we get you." I never killed anybody and I never threw anything from the bridge.'

For the next two and a half weeks Williams was under constant surveillance. And then the results of tests on fibres taken from his car came from the laboratory. The fibres matched those on clothing of murder victims Cater and Payne. Williams was arrested and indicted on the charge of murdering Cater. The Payne charge was added later.

The police then faced up to the real problem of trying to get Williams convicted. Their evidence was not good. They had no witnesses either to the killings or the dumping of the bodies. All their hopes were pinned on the wizardry of the forensic scientists.

Their fears were justified as the nine-week trial got under way. Firstly, there was no motive, though prosecution lawyers suggested that Williams was 'a frustrated man driven by a desire to purify the black race by murdering poor young blacks'. Defending the accused man was Alvin Binder a well-known Mississippi trial lawyer, who was clearly scoring points as he tore the prosecution's evidence into shreds. Then the trial took a remarkable turn when the judge made a surprise ruling after a plea from the prosecution. With their case literally hanging by threads, the lawyers persuaded him to allow them to introduce evidence linking Williams to the deaths of ten other victims. The assistant District Attorney, Joseph Drolet, said: 'He has not been formally charged with the killings but the cases will reveal a pattern and bent of mind.'

The evidence brought to life a case that had slipped into a repetition of complicated forsenic evidence. A boy aged 15 said he had been fondled by Williams who he later saw with 14-year-old Lubie Geter whose decomposed body was found clad only in underpants. Other witnesses said they had spotted him with more of the victims. One music business contact of Williams' said the accused man had one passed him a note which said: 'I could be a mayor – I could even be a killer.'

When Williams took the stand he denied everything. No, he had not stopped his car on the bridge, nor even slowed down. No, he had not thrown Cater's body over nor did he believe he would have had the strength to lift it. No, he was not a homosexual. Yes, all the witnesses and even the police had lied. He told the jury: 'I never met any of the victims. I feel just as sorry for them as anybody else in the world. I am 23 years old and I could have been one of the people killed out there.'

Later, under persistent cross-examination, he accused the prosecutor of being a fool and he described two FBI men who had interviewed him as 'goons'.

Finally the jury of eight blacks and four whites retired. They deliberated for 12 hours before returning a verdict of 'Guilty'.

As he was being led away to start two consecutive life terms Williams turned with tears streaming down his face, and protested his innocence 'from my heart'. His father, Homer Williams, cried out: 'It's impossible to find a young man like this guilty.' But guilty he was found and he went to jail knowing that it would be 14 years before he could be eligible for parole.

His lawyers immediately made plans to appeal – a process which many expected to take years.

The Case of the Lethal 'Cuppa' Graham Young

He was the most charming and efficient tea boy. His coffee was good, too. But a price had to be paid for it. It cost two people their lives. In April 1971, 23-year-old Londoner Graham Young, who was on a government training course at Slough, Berkshire, answered a 'help wanted' advertisement in a local paper. It said that John Hadland, manufacturers of specialist, highspeed optical and photographic instruments, needed a storeman at their small factory in the Hertfordshire village of Bovingdon.

Young said on his application form that he had 'previously studied chemistry, organic and inorganic, pharmacology and toxicology over the past 10 years and had 'some knowledge of chemicals'.

He told the managing director, Mr Godfrey Foster, that before going to the training centre he had a nervous breakdown after his mother's death and had had mental treatment. Mr Foster was sent the report of a psychiatrist who had treated Young. It said that Young had made 'an extremely full recovery' from a 'deep-going personality disorder' and would 'do extremely well training as a storekeeper'. It also said Young was of above-average intelligence and 'would fit in well and not draw any attention to himself in any community'.

The report was hopelessly wrong on all counts – as Young's workmates were to find out. They did their best to make him feel at home, and he was befriended in particular by the head storeman, Bob Egle, 59, Frederick Biggs, 61, head of the works-in-progress department, and storeman-driver Ronald Hewitt, 41. Rob and Frederick would often lend him cigarettes and money, and Young offered to get tea and coffee for everybody who was kind to him.

Then a strange illness which was nicknamed the 'Bovingdon Bug' began to hit the staff at Hadland's. About 70 members of the staff went down with the illness. Symptoms include diarrhoea, stomach pains, loss of hair and numbness in the legs. Some said their tea tasted bitter, and a medical team was called in to find out if the chemicals used at the factory were responsible. The 'bug' killed

145

two members of the staff – the kindly Bob Egle and Frederick Biggs. Bob died first. He became ill less than month after Young joined the firm. His condition deteriorated rapidly and he was admitted to hospital. His heart stopped twice while he was in intensive care unit and he died, paralyzed, on 7 July. Young appeared to be very concerned at Egle's death and attended the funeral. Then, in September 1972, Frederick was taken ill with stomach pains and vomiting. He died three weeks later in a London hospital.

When he heard about it Young is reported to have said: 'Poor old Fred. I wonder what went wrong? He shouldn't have died. I was very fond of old Fred.'

With Biggs' death, panic set in at the factory and several employees threatened to resign. Iain Anderson, the firm's medical officer, became suspicious when Young boasted about his knowledge of medicine and poisons. Detective Chief Inspector John Kirkland, of Hemel Hempstead police, was called in and asked Scotland Yard to check Young's background. When the answer came back, Young was arrested on suspicion of murder.

Police found that his bedsitter was full of bottles containing various chemicals and poisons, and the walls plastered with photography of his heroes – Hitler and other Nazi leaders. A bottle of thallium, a deadly poison, tasteless and odourless, was found on Young when he was arrested.

Young went on trial at St Albans in July 1972. It took the jury less than an hour to find him guilty of two murders, two attempted murders and two charges of administering poison.

He was jailed for life and placed in a top security hospital. But it was only there that his background came to light. The hospital in which he had been treated for his breakdown turned out to be Broadmoor. In 1962 he had pleaded guilty at the Old Bailey to poisoning his father, his sister and a friend. Young was, in fact, a compulsive poisoner before he was 15.

Mr Justice Melford Stevenson had committed Young to Broadmoor with a recommendation that he should not be released for 15 years. He was discharged nine years later as having made 'an extremely full recovery', and the result was that two kindly innocent men died.

Jill Dando

On the 26 April 1999 the well known and much loved television presenter Jill Dando was cruelly murdered on the doorstep of her own home in Gowan Avenue, Fulham, south-west London. Nationwide shock resulted at the outrage of the news that this could happen to such a vibrant and undeserving person.

Jill was born in Weston-Super-Mare, Avon, in 1961. She began her career by securing a job as a trainee reporter at the *Weston Mercury* newspaper but became interested in broadcasting. She moved to Radio Devon where she presented the *Breakfast News*, progressing to presenting South West regional news programmes. She later moved to London to present BBC's *Breakfast Time*, from which she became a household name, and she then was catapulted to peak time television in the form of BBC's *Holiday* programme series. Her career had gone from strength to strength as she presented a wide range of programmes including *Crimewatch UK*, *Songs of Praise* and *6 O'clock News*.

Jill became known as the 'Golden Girl of Television' due to her blonde hair and good looks. She had a talent for broadcasting which allowed her to present news, light entertainment and travel programmes. She was popular with both men and women alike, men were attracted by her good looks and women admired and respected her. Part of Jill's appeal was the fact that she seemed approachable and because she combined a head girl quality with that of a girl next door.

Jill was just about to start a new series and had recently altered her image by posing in leather to promote the series *Antiques Inspectors*. It was not just her career which was blooming, in fact she had begun to scale down her television activities as she had recently become engaged. She was planning to marry Alan Farthing, a gynaecologist, in the autumn of 1999.

Her career was cut short on the 26 April 1999 when she was shot outside her Fulham home. Emergency treatment both at the scene and at Charing Cross Hospital could not save her and Jill was pronounced dead at 13:03. A huge police operation was launched. It emerged that Miss Dando was killed by a shot to the head at very close range from a 9mm semi-automatic pistol. The bullet used was later found to be modified, this was suggested to be a trademark or because powder had been removed in order to make the explosion quieter.

The murder occurred in broad daylight in front of the star's own home, as she was returning home from a morning shopping trip in the Kings Mall shopping centre at Hammersmith. There were several initial leads from sightings made by the public. A smartly dressed man carrying a mobile phone was seen walking briskly from the scene. There were several sightings of this suspect, it is thought that he used heavy black-framed glasses in order to disguise himself. On the 30 April the police released an E-fit of the prime suspect and CCTV footage showing a metallic blue Range Rover on Fulham Palace Road shortly after the killing. On the 5 May the police disclosed that the prime suspect had made his getaway on a number 74 bus.

In a cruel twist of fate Jill's own murder was reconstructed on *Crimewatch*, the very programme she used to present. The showing of this programme on 18 May was very sad and emotional but received a great response with over 500 calls from the public being made. The two main theories to the killing were that Miss Dando was shot by an obsessive fan or a contract killer. Jill received a large amount of unwelcome attention during her lifetime and by hosting a programme like *Crimewatch*, she was further exposing herself to unpleasant attention. Due to Jill's popularity, many websites featured her and she was frequently on television, an easy target for some unsavoury obsessions. The fact that Jill had recently become engaged may have caused an obsessive fan to go over the edge.

On 28 May, a man was released who was arrested in connection with the enquiry. On the 100th day of the police investigation *The Sun* newspaper offered a £100,000 reward to help catch the murderer. This brings the total reward on offer to £250,000, with the other money being pledged by the *Daily Mail* newspaper and *Crimestoppers*. By putting up the reward it was thought that someone with a vital piece of information may come forward.

Despite the large scale police operation and numerous appeals no-one yet has been charged for the murder of Jill Dando and the inquiry continues. Everybody close to Jill remains optimistic that the crime will be solved.

Kenneth Noye

Kenneth Noye has been described as one of Britain's most wanted men, having been held responsible for the road rage murder of Stephen Cameron on May 19, 1996.

Noye was well-known to the British police many years before the road rage crime was committed. He had been arrested and charged with handling stolen goods in the aftermath of the Brinks-Mat gold bullion robbery in 1983.

Noye's involvement in the robbery led to a fourteen year prison sentence of which he served nine years and four months.

The road rage incident occurred on the Swanley interchange of the M25 on May 19, 1996. From evidence pieced together in the courtroom and witness statements, most of the details of the event have been collated to form a coherent and true account of what happened that evening.

Noye claimed the incident began with a case of mistaken identity. He saw two people in a red van driving along the same stretch of road: the two people in the van were Danielle Cable and her fiance, Stephen Cameron. Noye claimed that he believed Cable was a girl friend of one of his mates, Mickey Taylor; she was, in fact, a total stranger. Noye proceeded to cut the red van up, irritating Cable and her fiance so much that the couple flashed their headlights at Noye's Land Rover Discovery at the next set of traffic lights. Cameron got out of the van and approached Noye's Land Rover, in an apparently confrontational manner.

The two men argued and swore at each other accusingly. Both punched, kicked and lashed out at one another. Then, fatally, Noye produced a four-inch lock knife from his jeans. He proceeded to stab Stephen Cameron, lunging into his heart and liver. As Cable's fiance lay fatally wounded on the road, Noye fled. Danielle, helpless, had witnessed the brutal stabbing of her husband-to-be.

Noye drove straight home to his wife, Brenda, who had already heard about the incident on the news. Cameron was dead; both knew Noye could not remain in the country. Later that evening, Kenneth Noye fled the UK in a quick, but carefully contrived plan with the help of a close friend, who, to this day, Noye has not named. Police were later able to track Noye's escape through a series of mobile telephone calls that he made in the process of leaving the UK. Noye fled to Spain to escape capture from the police, but also to escape the English prosecution system, who, he claimed, would not have given him a fair trial after his previous criminal history. British police, convinced of Noye's presence at the murder scene, had to undergo extradition proceedings to return Noye to the UK.

This was not the first time Noye had stood in a court accused of murder. In 1985, he stood trial for the murder of undercover policeman DC John Fordham in his own back garden. The detective, staking out Noye's property, was stabbed by Noye 'in self defence'. That time, the jury believed Noye and he was acquitted. This was, claimed Noye, the reason for carrying the knife with him. Ever since the Brinks-Mat robbery, Noye persistently claimed that his life was under threat and in constant danger from people who believed he still had access to great wealth (amounting to millions) from the gold haul. Noye stated he lived in constant fear of being attacked for the money.

The jury, though, in 1996 did not acquit Noye. They found him guilty of cold-blooded murder by a jury majority of 11 to 1. In one of the first trials in a British court as a result of road rage, Noye was given a life sentence. The attack on Stephen Cameron occurred on a busy stretch of road, and there were plenty of witnesses, in addition to Danielle Cable, to positively identify Noye as the murderer. But some evidence is still missing. The acquaintance of Noye's who aided his escape to Spain, was also responsible for disposing of Noye's car and the murder weapon, the knife, after the incident. Neither have been found by the police.

Murders of
Passion

'I'll Kill Him!'

When 23-year-old Kittie Byron stabbed her lover to death on the steps of a London post office, the charge really had to be murder. And murder in 1902 was a hanging offence. It made no difference that, when the flood of her fury was spent, she collapsed sobbing on his crumpled body, calling pitifully: 'Reggie . . . Dear Reggie . . . Let me kiss my Reggie . . .'

The crime was committed in broad daylight before a dozen witnesses. She had stabbed him twice: once through the back and once through the breast. The second blow was probably the one that killed him. He died almost instantly.

Yet everyone's sympathy was with the frail, dark-haired girl who had wielded the knife. The coroner's jury, for example, brought in a verdict of manslaughter. The officials were incredulous, and the coroner himself asked: 'Do you mean unlawful killing without malice?'

'Yes,' insisted the foreman, 'killing on the impulse of the moment. We do not believe she went there with the intention of killing him.'

In fact, all the evidence suggested that Kittie Byron went there with precisely that intention. And when she was brought for trial the following month, it was on a charge of murder.

For some months before the fatal episode, Kittie Byron has been living with Arthur Reginald Baker in rooms at 18 Duke Street, off Oxford Street, in the West End. Baker was a married man and a member of the Stock Exchange. But that did not prevent him from presenting himself and his mistress to the landlady as 'Mr and Mrs Baker'. He drank heavily, often knocked Kittie about, and on one occasion half strangled her. But Kittie was loyal. She never touched liquor herself, and tried to shield her lover from the consequences of his actions.

Events came to a head on the night of Friday 7 November 1902, when the landlady heard a furious row erupt in the bed-sitting room. She went up and entered; bed-clothes had been thrown all about and lay in chaos on the floor; to one corner was a hat which had been ripped into shreds. The landlady confronted the drunken Baker, but Kittie interceded. 'Oh, there's nothing the matter,' she said, 'We've been playing milliner.'

Not long after the landlady left the room, the quarrel broke out again. It went on all evening, and at 01.15 the householder went back again to try and stop it. She found Kittie in the corridor, shivering in her nightdress. She was plainly terrified – yet still she insisted that nothing was the matter.

The next morning the landlady gave the couple notice to leave the premises. A weekend of calm followed, and on Monday morning Baker even took Kittie a cup of tea before leaving for the office. She kissed him goodbye – a domestic scene – nothing hinted at the coming drama. The date was 10 November 1902, the day of the fatal stabbing.

The whole sequence of events emerged clearly at the trial. Just before he left the house, Baker asked the landlady for a private word. He requested that they be allowed to stay in the house after all. The landlady, however, insisted that they must leave. It was then that Baker informed her that Kittie was not his wife. The girl was the cause of the trouble, he said. She was 'no class' and would leave tomorrow.

The conversation was overhead by a housemaid who immediately told Kittie that Baker was going to cast her aside. 'Will he?' fumed the enraged girl. 'I'll kill him before the day is out!' She made her own preparations for going out, and confessed to the landlady about the phoney marriage. 'Then why don't you leave him?' asked the landlady, who had assumed that only wedlock kept the couple together. 'I can't,' said Kittie, 'because I love him so.'

She went to a shop in Oxford Street and asked a cutler for a long , sharp knife. He showed her a large item with a sprung blade that fitted into the hasp. She seemed too slight a girl to handle it, and the cutler suggested alternatives. No, said Kittie, she had a strong grip, and she proved it by operating the spring action several times. Having bought the knife she slipped it into her muff and made her way to a post office in Lombard Street. The building stood in the heart of the City where Baker worked. It was Lord Mayor's Day. The crowds were out in the streets.

From the post office, Kittie sent Baker an express letter bearing the words: 'Dear Reg. Want you immediate importantly, Kittie.' But the messenger boy could not reach Baker at the Stock Exchange and returned to Lombard Street with the note. Kittie insisted that he go back again. The boy did so – and this time located Baker who returned with him to the post office.

Staff at the post office had noticed the girl's excited state. And they also noticed an absurdly trivial dispute which arose when Baker arrived. An extra charge of two pence had to be paid for the messenger boy's time. Baker flatly refused to hand the sum over; Kittie insisted that it be paid and offered her lover a florin. Somehow, the incident speaks volumes about the relative characters of the couple. Baker was still refusing to pay as he left the post office, with Kittie rushing after him. The staff noticed something flash in her hand as she made her exit.

She caught him on the steps. The two blows were swift, and bystanders noticed no blood. In fact, the several witnesses at first thought she was striking him with her muff. Baker may well have been dead before a workman grabbed Kittie's hand and the knife fell with a clatter to the pavement. The trance of her fury was shattered, and it was then that Kittie fell sobbing on her lover's body: 'Let me kiss my Reggie . . . Let me kiss my husband. . .'

Kittie Byron made two different statements to the police shortly after her arrest. In the first she said: 'I killed him wilfully, and he deserved it, and the sooner I am killed the better.' In the second: 'I bought the knife to hit him; I didn't know I was killing him.' At the trial which followed she only managed to whisper: 'Not Guilty' as her plea to the indictment.

She made a pitiable figure in the dock, a pale and delicate girl whose dark eyes wandered dazedly around the court. She wore a blue serge suit and a shirt whose white linen collar was high about her throat, fastened with a black tie. The court heard that her real name was Emma Byron, but it was not hard to see why she had earned the diminutive of 'Kittie'. Sir Travers Humphreys, then a junior brief for her defence, later recalled how she clung to the wardress who brought her into the dock: 'It seemed as if she would break down at the very outset.'

Some twenty witnesses were called by the prosecution, and Kittie did break down. It happened as a surgeon was indicating on his own body the position of her lover's stab wounds. A stifled wail was heard. All eyes turned to the dock where Kittie was racked with violent sobs.

The defence called no witnesses – not even Kittie herself. Her counsel was Henry ('Harry') Dickens, son of the great Victorian novelist, and a man who had inherited his father's genius for stirring the emotions. Dickens tried to make out a case for Kittie having intended to commit suicide rather than murder. It was an improbable thesis which ran contrary to the evidence. He was on safer ground in pointing to the plight and character of the injured girl, and in touching the hearts of the jurors.

The judge, in his summing-up, was candid about his own emotions: 'Gentlemen of the jury, if I had consulted my own feelings I should probably have stopped this case at the outset.' But he was equally candid in dismissing manslaughter as an appropriate verdict. The jury was out for ten minutes. They found her guilty of murder – but with a strong recommendation for mercy.

The form had to be observed. The black cap was brought forth, and the dread sentence was passed. Kittie, weakly professing herself innocent of wilful murder, was to hang by the neck until dead. But she never did. Great waves of public sympathy had gone out to the frail and mistreated girl. A huge petition was quickly raised asking for a reprieve and no fewer than 15,000 signatures were obtained in a single morning. Three thousand signatures were raised from among the clerks at the Stock Exchange itself. In the event, the petition was never formally presented to the authorities, for the Home Secretary granted the reprieve before receiving the document.

Kittie Byron's sentence was commuted to penal servitude for life. In 1907, her sentence was reduced, and she was released the following year.

Death of a Minister

Pierre Chevallier's public career had been a story of brilliant success. He came from a family of well-to-do doctors and served as a medical officer during the early months of World War Two. As a result of his bravery in tending wounded soldiers under fire he was decorated. When the Germans occupied his native city of Orléans, Chevallier continued to practise medicine by day, but by night he headed the local Resistance. Before the Allies arrived to liberate the city, Pierre Chevallier had bravely led the attack which drove the Germans out.

Elected mayor of Orléans at the age of only 30, Chevallier threw himself into the task of postwar rebuilding. So masterfully did he manage the work that Orléans was officially cited as the best reconstructed city in France. Chevallier became parliamentary representative for Orléans. And on 11 August 1951, he won an even greater honour. Aged 41, he was given ministerial rank in the new government of René Pleven.

The following day, Pierre Chevallier returned from Paris to Orléans as Under Secretary of State for Technical Education. He was driven down in a big, black limousine decorated with the official tricolor cockade. He only really came for a change of clothes – there were ceremonies to attend. His wife Yvonne was waiting at their home, and told their younger son Mathieu to run and greet him with the words, *'Bonjour, Monsieur le Ministre'* (Good day, Minister).

The child ran to the doorway with his greeting. Chevallier was delighted with the reception, and tenderly hugged his son. There were, however, no joyous greetings for his wife.

Chevallier went upstairs to change clothes in the bedroom. Yvonne followed him up. There was a quarrel – and she shot him four times with a 7.65 mm Mab automatic.

Downstairs, little Mathieu heard the shots and started crying. Yvonne went down to comfort him and hand him for care to a maid. Then she returned to the bedroom. A fifth shot was heard – and a fifth bullet drilled into her husband's corpse.

He had been a minister for precisely one day. Soon, the whole of France was to learn that behind the glittering façade of Pierre Chevallier's life lay a story of failure – the failure of a marriage.

Pierre and Yvonne had married before the war. She was a nurse of peasant background who worshipped the dynamic young doctor. From the outset, Pierre's family considered the marriage a mistake, never really accepting it. And their judgement seemed to the confirmed as

Pierre's fortunes rose. Yvonne lacked the social graces, becoming tongue-tied at dinners and receptions. When the smart talk started she would fall silent. A dull girl, his colleagues would say afterwards, a bit of a liability.

In fact, she loved her husband passionately, and none of her failings need have mattered if Pierre had returned her affection. But he did not. Bit by bit, Yvonne become distanced from her husband's career and concerns. The abyss opened when one of their two sons grew ill. The child's little bed was brought into the couple's bedroom while the sickness lasted. Pierre took to sleeping in his study. And when the boy recovered, Pierre continued to sleep in his own room. He never returned to the marriage bed.

The seed of suspicion was planted in Yvonne's mind. One day, searching through his pockets, she found a love letter to Pierre signed by someone called 'Jeanette'. She strongly suspected that it was written by a mutual friend, Jeanne Perreau, who was 15 years younger than herself. After a clumsy attempt to get a sample of her handwriting, Yvonne went round and accused her rival to her face. Jeanne denied that a liaison existed and back at home, Pierre told his wife to shut up and mind her own business.

But the suspicion did not die. Jeanne Perreau was the wife of a wealthy department store owner. She was a beautiful woman with luxuriant red hair and a very opulent figure. Above all, she was witty and sophisticated, shining at precisely those functions which for Yvonne were an ordeal. In June 1951, Pierre won his parliamentary seat and gave a lavish reception. His wife saw him there flirting openly with Jeanne Perreau. Yet when Yvonne herself tried to embrace her husband, he rebuffed her in front of everybody.

There was a terrible row that night. Yvonne demanded an explanation; he begged Pierre to return to their marriage bed. He replied cruelly that not only did he not want to make love to her – he did not even think himself capable of it. She had disgraced him at the reception: 'Can you really see yourself at the big banquets in Paris?' he taunted.

Pierre said that he wanted a divorce. Failing that she should take a lover. Yvonne was outraged and refused to countenance a separation. She loved him too much for that.

Tensions were building up now to the point where something had to give. Yvonne had, for sometime, been taking drugs: tranquillisers to make sleep possible, stimulants to nerve her for the day. She drank coffee in great quantities and smoked incessantly. And it was in this state of dangerous disorientation that she took the children off for a seaside holiday. From the coast she wrote a passionate letter to her husband saying that she would try to improve herself as a wife. Pierre did not reply. And when she came back, Yvonne took poison in an attempt to end her life.

She only just failed, and was desperately ill afterwards. Every attempt to get through to her husband met with cold scorn on his part. Yvonne followed Pierre to Paris and tried to see him at the Chamber of Deputies, She was told, through an official, that he was too busy. Then she ransacked his flat in the city, seeking evidence of his betrayal. She found it in the form of a railway timetable. He had ticked off the times for Châtelguyon trains – Jeanne Perreau was holidaying there.

Yvonne returned in a rage to Orléans and confronted the husband of her rival. M. Perreau at first tried to soothe her fears. But after a second visit he admitted that he knew Jeanne was having an affair with Pierre. Léon Perreau was not the least distressed about it either, he was one of those curious characters beloved in French farce – *a mari complaisant* or compliant husband who simply did not mind being cuckolded.

But Yvonne was no compliant wife. Pierre had found out about her trip to Paris and phoned her to called her a 'cow' and tell her to stop ruining his life. It was after this call, and Perreau's admission, that Yvonne went out and obtained a firearms licence.

There was no problem in getting the certificate; her husband was now an important political figure and she claimed he had dangerous enemies. Armed with the certificate, Yvonne went to a gun-shop where she asked for a weapon that was guaranteed to kill. They sold her the Mab automatic

Killing was clearly in her mind – but killing whom? On 11 August Yvonne heard over the radio that Pierre had been appointed a minister. Immediately, she sent a warm telegram of congratulation. Then she contacted a nun who was a close friend and told her that she was going to commit suicide.

The nun, of course, advised her against the act. Pierre phoned later from Paris saying that he would be coming back the next day to pick up some clothes. He did not thank her for the telegram. Perhaps it was his curt and disdainful manner that mingled thoughts of murder with those of suicide.

She spent a terrible night. The next morning, Pierre's name was blazoned across every newspaper. Chevallier a Minister! – no mention, as customarily, of the loving wife. That must have rankled. Still, she mustered up enthusiasm to get little Mathieu to say his party piece – 'Bonjour, Monsieur le Ministre.'

Having kissed his son, Chevallier went upstairs with no word of kindness for his wife. He stripped to his trunks in the bedroom, and asked her to hand him clean linen. Yvonne demanded an explanation for his liaison with Jeanne. Chevallier replied with obscenities. He was going to marry Jeanne, he said, 'and you can remain in your own filth!' Amid the curses for his wife, he gloated over his appointment' 'I'm a minister!' he kept shouting.

Pierre remained unmoved when Yvonne fell sobbing to her knees and pleaded for a reconciliation. He called her worthless, he told her she stank, he piled insult upon insult. Finally, as she reached out pleading towards him, her hand brushed against his leg.

This was the catalyst. She had dared to *touch* the Under Secretary of State. Chevallier hurled a peculiarly foul-mouthed insult at his wife and made an especially obscene gesture.

Yvonne stiffened. She warned that if he went off with Jeanne she would kill herself. 'Go ahead,' he replied. 'It will be the first sensible thing you've done in your life.'

'I'm serious,' she cried, producing the automatic. 'I will kill myself.'

'Well, for God's sake kill yourself, but wait until I've gone.'

They were the last words Pierre Chevallier ever spoke. Yvonne came towards him firing as she walked: he was hit in leg, chin, chest and forehead. Having rushed downstairs to calm the crying Mathieu, she returned to the body in the bedroom. What happened next remains something of a mystery. By Yvonne's own account, she stooped over his body intending suicide. But thoughts of her children stayed her hand. As she rose from the corpse, the gun went off by accident and a fifth bullet lodged in his back.

France was outraged by the shooting. The war hero – the dynamic young mayor with his ministerial career just opening – had been cut down by what the newspapers presented as a nagging wife. Feeling ran so high in Orléans itself that the trial was held in Rheims, far from the passions of the populace.

But when the case came to court, the mood changed. In part it was due to Yvonne and the tragic figure she made in the dock. Her face was a mask of suffering, the eyes dark and sunken from evident nights of anguish and remorse. Mechanically, she knotted and unknotted a handkerchief as the defence told of the humiliations she had endured. In contrast, the *soignée* elegance of Jeanne

Perreau seemed almost an insult. Hissing was heard from the public benches as she gave evidence in the box. And Jeanne's husband, Léon Perreau, made a quite ridiculous impression as the *mari complaisant* in the case. It emerged that Jeanne had told him on the very first night that she had slept with Pierre. The affair had lasted 5 years, and throughout M. Perreau had been quite acquiescent. He had even been rather flattered to be cuckolded by the up-and-coming mayor. There were positive advantages too: Perreau's brother had been decorated with the Légion d'Honneur – on Chevallier's recommendation.

What a cosy arrangement for all concerned – except poor, suffering Yvonne. Public sympathy went out strongly to the deceived wife, and the prosecution sensed the climate of opinion. For example, the prisoner was not questioned about the mysterious fifth shot fired into the corpse. This could have been exploited at length as a possible act of malice and sacrilege. Nor did the prosecution make a ritual demand for the death penalty (as in the cases of Pauline Dubuisson and Léone Bouvier). It pressed instead for a short prison sentence, suggesting two years as an appropriate penalty.

The jury was out for less than an hour, one member asking for a point of clarification. The juror wanted to know precisely what was the obscene gesture that provoked Yvonne into reaching for the gun. The accused woman had broken into hysterical sobs when the question was asked during the trial; she had not been pressed at the time. Now, the authorities privately submitted an explicit description. It must have been thoroughly outrageous, for when the jury returned it acquitted Yvonne Chevallier of every charge against her. She left the court a free woman, cheered by a large crowd outside.

Although fully exonerated for her tragic action, Yvonne Chevallier selected a punishment for herself. A few months after the trial, she took herself and her two sons off to the benighted settlement at St Laurent du Maroni. This had been the site of one of France's notorious penal colonies in the mosquito swamps of French Guiana. The prison was closed, but a ramshackle community of natives and French settlers still lived there.

Banishing herself to that tropical hell, Yvonne Chevallier took up the post of a sister in charge of the maternity wing of the hospital. She was trained for the job. Yvonne had been a midwife before meeting Pierre and participating in his brilliant career.

Tess and the Wessex Hanging

She is the most moving of all Thomas Hardy's doomed heroines. Bright-eyed, peony-mouthed Tess of the d'urbervilles is an innocent dairy maid seduced by a young man of means. Later, caught in a love triangle from which she sees no issue, Tess muders her seducer to liberate herself. Tried and condemned to death without reprieve she dies on the scaffold, a tragic sport of the gods.

Hardy drew on the country girls of his native Wessex when he painted her portrait; there was no one model for Tess. But a macabre event from his childhood provided the emotional inspiration for the novel, perhaps darkening the whole of his work. On 9 August 1856, young Thomas Hardy saw a woman hanged. Her name was Martha Brown and, like Tess, she was a victim of the eternal triangle.

Hardy was only 16 at the time. But the impression was to stay with him for the rest of his life. In 1925, when in his eighties, the novelist was to write of the execution: 'I remember what a fine figure she showed against the sky as she hung in the misty rain, and how the tight black silk gown set off her shape as she wheeled half-round and back.'

There is more than a trace of morbid sensuality in the

passage; we can only guess what effect the experience may have had on the adolescent's awakening sexual impulse. The condemned woman's face had been hooded but the material, wet with rain, permitted her face to be seen quite clearly. This evidently haunted the novelist. He wrote: 'I saw – they had put a cloth over her face – how, as the cloth got wet, her features came through it. That was *extraordinary.*'

Tess, of course, has been made the subject of films, plays – and even an Italian opera by d'Erlanger. Martha Brown's story is not so well known. And yet it caused quite a sensation in its day.

Elizabeth Martha Brown was a handsome woman who lived at Birdsmoorgate, near Beaminster in Dorset. She was some 20 years older than her husband John Brown, a carrier by trade. He, it was whispered, had only married her for her money and he certainly had a roving eye. For one day in 1856, Martha caught him making love to another woman. Late that night the couple had a furious row at their home. John Brown struck his wife with his carrier's whip, and she responded by seizing an axe. The blow proved fatal.

In France, Martha Brown might have gone to trial confident of securing an acquittal. It was a classic domestic *crime passionnel,* in which sympathy for the outraged wife would surely have won leniency. But a sterner morality prevailed in Victorian Dorset. And the accused woman made matters very much worse by trying to conceal the crime. She claimed that her husband had been killed by a kick from his horse – a falsehood in which she persisted throughout her trial. It was only at the end that she confessed to having wielded the axe herself.

By then it was too late. She was condemned to death and despite immense public interest, the Home Secretary refused to grant a reprieve.

A crowd of some three or four thousand gathered at

Dorchester Gaol to attend the hanging. Rain was falling, and a certain nervousness seems to have afflicted the officials. No woman had been hung there for some time, and the prison chaplain was too overcome with emotion to accompany Martha to the scaffold. A young clergyman was brought in to deputize (his name was Henry Moule and he was, as it happened, a friend of the Hardy family).

The public executioner, a man named Calcraft, was supposed to tie the condemned woman's dress around her so that it did not ride up to expose her as she dropped. being out of practice, he forgot this item of procedure. Having made his way down to operate the trap, he had to climb the scaffold again.

Through all the grim preparations, Martha Brown remained calm and dignified. She had shaken hands firmly with the prison authorities before being led up the steps. And she waited in silence for the ordeal.

Young Thomas Hardy saw it all. He was apprenticed, at the time, to a Dorchester architect, and obtained a very close view of the gallows by climbing a tree close to the gaol's entrance. His second wife was to suggest that the episode tinged his life's work with bitterness and gloom. But Hardy's own reference to it betray a ghoulish relish rather than melancholy. It was, no doubt, the same relish that had drawn the other thousands to the scene. In old age he professed to being ashamed of attending the hanging, 'my only excuse being that I was but a youth.'

Certainly the case fascinated him, and there is no question that the image of the condemned woman was with him as he planned his Tess. For in his personal scrapbook he kept a newspaper cutting in which a friend discussed the influence of the event on his most famous novel. Hardy pencilled in some corrections to minor points of detail (the text said that Martha had used a knife, for example). But he let the claims regarding Tess stand. And he also left the following:

He never forgot the rustle of the thin black gown the woman was wearing as she was led forth by the wardens. A penetrating rain was falling; the white cap was no sooner over the woman's head than it clung to her features, and the noose was put round the neck of what looked like a marble statue.

Hardy looked at the scene with the strange illusion of its being unreal, and was brought to his complete senses when the drop fell with a thud and his companion on a lower branch of the tree fell fainting to the ground. Hardy's boyhood companion was not alone in feeling the horror of the event. The execution provoked a leading article in the *Dorset County Chronicle*, which called for an end to the death penalty. And though it was over a hundred years before capital punishment was finally abolished in Britain, local sensitivities had clearly been aroused. For after the hanging of Martha Brown, there were no more public executions in Dorchester.

Delayed Action

Postwar France had no sympathy for collaborators. Most of the population had submitted to the German invaders, and resistance – at least until the last months of the war – was much more limited than is often supposed. Nevertheless, people who had actively assisted the Germans learned to tremble after the D-Day landings. They lived in terror of the midnight knock, of strangers at their door – of the fatal shots.

For girls who had gone out with German soldiers, a ritual humiliation was reserved. They had their heads shaved and were paraded through the streets to face the kicks, spittle and jeers of the populace. Pauline Dubuisson knew the ordeal; her head too had been shaved.

Her father was a successful engineer who lived in Dunkirk, scene of the famous beach evacuation. An admirer of Nietzsche's philosophy and of the authoritarian Nazi regime, he willingly undertook building contracts for the Germans. He brought Pauline up in a hard school. She was taught to think much and to feel little.

Pauline was only 13 when France fell, but soon she was flirting with enemy soldiers. At 17 she was mistress to a 55-year-old German colonel, and was listed by the Resistance as a collaborator. The price was paid after the Allied landings. Pauline was dragged into the main square and forced onto a stool while the men sheered off her long black hair.

Still, she had her whole life ahead of her. In 1946, the year after all hostilities ended, Pauline enrolled as a medical student at the University of Lille. Her first year report described her as intelligent, even brilliant at times, 'but she is not a steady worker. She is well balanced but haughty, provoking and a flirt. Her conduct is mediocre.'

It was at Lille that Pauline first met a handsome and athletic young student named Félix Bailly, who came from St Omer. They had a tempestuous three-year affair in which Pauline repeatedly cuckolded her lover, sleeping with other students and members of the faculty. Félix offered to marry her; it was Pauline who refused. she continued to behave promiscuously, even keeping a notebook in which she recorded details of her different lovers' performances. In the end, Félix decided to break with her. He left Lille and went to Paris to continue his medical course there.

What happened – or rather, what didn't happen – next, played a key part in the coming controversy. For some 18 months the couple saw nothing of each other. Félix settled down to his work as a diligent, well-liked student. And he also became engaged to a beautiful fair-haired young woman named Monique Lombard. Back in Lille, meanwhile, Pauline was as promiscuous as ever. She even arranged a summer holiday in Germany where she resumed her friendship with the former German colonel. She made no attempt to contact Félix. Not until 1951.

Early in March of that year, a mutual friend who had been to Paris learned of Félix's marriage plans. Back in Lille Pauline heard all about the beautiful blonde and the happy future which beckoned Félix. She immediately went to Paris to meet her former lover, and try to rekindle his affections, but it didn't work. Something must have snapped then. On 10 March Pauline went back to Dunkirk to celebrate her birthday. Her father gave her 5,000 francs and with it, having acquired a fire-arms licence, she went out and bought a little .25 calibre automatic.

Pauline did not head straight for Paris. She first returned to Lille where she penned a note declaring her intention of killing both Félix and herself. The landlady had noticed the gun in her handbag, and after Pauline took the Paris train, she also discovered the threatening note. Realising the terrible danger Félix was in, the land-lady telephoned Félix's father and sent a warning telegram to Félix himself.

It was less than a fortnight before his wedding was due. Félix recognised the peril, and on the night of 15 March he stayed away from his small apartment on the Left Bank, preferring to stop over at the flat of a friend, Georges Gaudel. The next night he did return to his apartment, but with Gaudel with him to act as a guardian. They were having breakfast together there on the morning of 17 March when a knock was heard at the door. It was Pauline.

She said that she wanted to see Félix alone; impossible, he replied, he had a friend with him. She persisted: 'I want to be alone with you, just for a moment ...'

'Why alone?'

'Because I'm afraid of crying.'

Félix refused to admit her. But he did cautiously agree to a meeting in a public place, as long as Gaudel was present. They chose the Place Cambronne as a suitable site and arranged to meet there in three-quarters of an hour. Pauline left, and so in due course did Félix with Gaudel at his side.

However anguished Pauline may have been – with jealously, despair or pure malice – there is no question that her brain now calculated with the utmost coolness and clarity. She never went to the Place Cambronne at all. Instead, she found a vantage point in a café opposite Félix's flat. There she sat and she waited, watching as the two men left, with a drink before her on the table.

Félix and Gaudel spent a nervous hour at the Place Cambronne, expecting Pauline at any moment. Eventually, though, Félix considered the danger over and decided to return to his flat. Gaudel, he said, could make his own arrangements for the day. But the companion was not so reassured. He insisted they phone another friend Bernard Mougeot to take over the role of guardian.

The call was made and Mougeot agreed to go to Félix's flat immediately. It seemed that they had covered every possible peril and Félix returned to the flat.

He was expecting Mougeot to be there already. But fate had determined otherwise. There was a transport strike in Paris that day, and the hurrying friend's taxi got stuck in a traffic jam. Pauline watched as her ex-lover returned alone to the apartment block. She paid for her coffee and followed him to the seventh floor where his flat was situated.

It is not certain how she gained admittance; probably, Félix heard a knock and assumed that Mougeot had arrived. What is beyond doubt is that Pauline shot her ex-lover three times. Any of the wounds could have killed him. The third bullet was apparently a cool *coup de grâce* delivered behind the right ear.

Pauline then tried to shoot herself too, but the gun

jammed on the fourth bullet. Instead, she disconnected the pipe in the kitchen which led to the gas stove. Placing the free end in her mouth, she lay down and prepared for death.

It was some time before Bernard Mougeot arrived. He could smell the gas in the corridor and hurried in to find his friend weltering in blood on the living-room floor. Pauline, in the kitchen, was unconscious. Mougeot pulled the pipe from her mouth and summoned the fire brigade. They arrived quickly and managed to revive her with oxygen cylinders.

Pauline recovered in hospital. But the case was to claim another victim before it came to court. In Dunkirk, Pauline's father discovered what had happened. While the family discussed which lawyer to hire, he came to a decision of his own. Declaring the shame to be unendurable, he wrote a letter expressing grief and commiseration to Félix's parents. Then, having taken a dose of poison for good measure. He gassed himself in the kitchen. M. Dubuisson's will triumphed where Pauline's had failed. He was dead when they found him there.

It was many months before Pauline's trial came up in Paris. The date was set for 28 October 1952, but on that morning she was discovered unconscious in her cell, bleeding from her wrist. She had managed to open a vein with a needle and a splinter of glass. A suicide note, apparently written in the dark after her wrist was cut, expressed both regret for the crime and disdain for the coming trial: 'I think my family is accursed and myself also. I only hurt those whom I love most in the world. I have lost over a litre of blood but I am still all right . . .'

Again revived, she was brought to trial a month later amid intense public interest. The *crime passionnel* is, of course, something of a French speciality. But the case of Pauline Dubuisson did not fit the classic pattern. The problem for the jurors and the fascinated public alike revolved around the time span involved. Could jealous love really be quickened 18 months after the liaison was over? Or had Pauline acted purely out of malice: indifferent to Félix while she possessed him, wrathful when he sought happiness elsewhere?

The stigma of her wartime past inevitably weighed against her. She could scarcely be represented as an injured lover. If there was a woman in court to be pitied it was surely the beautiful Monique Lombard, bereaved fiancée of the murder victim. She appeared pitifully in the witness box, and the prosecutor at one point compared her innocent love with the malevolence of (pointing dramatically at Pauline) 'this bitch!'

The prosecution called for the death penalty, and pursued its case savagely. Even Pauline's suicide attempts were scorned. How convenient, it was insinuated, that the gun jammed before Pauline could shoot herself. Had she really tried to gas herself? Or did she turn the tap only when she heard the sound of someone arriving at the door? Remarkable, was it not, that she should have failed yet again when she cut her wrist. 'You are more efficient when it comes to murder', taunted the prosecutor.

The thrusts were vicious – and surely unfair. The murder weapon was found jammed on the fourth shot. Firemen testified that Pauline had second-degree asphyxiation when they arrived: she was foaming at the lips. And she had lost over a litre of blood when discovered in her cell.

But Pauline's character was such that things looked very black for her. Extracts from the notebook in which she described her lovers' performances were read out in court. The passages concerning Félix and her other lovers too were cold and acid in tone. In the dock she remained largely unmoved by others' grief – everyone noted the 'mask of pride' that she wore. To win an acquittal, the defence had to prove the case to be a *crime passionnel*.

What did Pauline Dubuisson know of love?

Might she even go to the guillotine? No woman had been executed in France during peacetime since 1887. On that occasion, a writhing female victim had to be dragged under the blade by her hair. The episode was so sickening that the public executioner threatened to resign if any more women were brought before him. A convention had since developed, whereby even if a woman was sentenced to death, she would always be granted a reprieve.

If Pauline were found guilty of murder, would the convention hold? Perhaps there was a trace of doubt in the jury's mind, for they brought in a verdict of murder – but without premeditation. She was sentenced to penal servitude for life.

A curious verdict. Her behaviour for days before the shooting suggested that she had murder very much in mind. A curious sentence, too. For a more orthodox *crime passionnel* she might have expected much more lenient treatment.

Clearly this was a killing with an extenuating circumstance. It is hard to know how to define it, – unless you called it delayed-action love.

A Tale of Two Sisters

Chronic alcoholism is a deep-rooted problem in the French countryside. Wine is cheap and the hard routines of farming life can be monotonous. To escape them, many a working man daily stupefies his senses with the bottle. M. Bouvier of Saint-Macaire came from a long line of hereditary alcoholics. His special drink was not wine, as it happens, but a crude cider alcohol distilled in the region of western France where he lived. Bouvier used to get violently drunk and regularly threatened to murder his wife and two daughters. From an early age, the girls learned to help their mother with the almost nightly ordeal of strapping him down to the bed. Someone would then run for the doctor. The doctor would give him the injections that brought a fragile calm to the household.

This is the story of those two sisters. Georgette, the older one, plays only a peripheral role in the drama. Yet it was to be intensely significant in the life of Léone, the younger girl.

The village of Saint-Macaire lies near the town of Cholet in the Maine-et-Loire department. And at the local school, Georgette showed considerable intelligence. At the age of 18 she managed to escape the household by entering a convent at Angers. Forsaking the hell of her family life, she submitted to the pious disciplines of a nun's existence and there, for a while, we must leave her.

Léone Bouvier, two years younger, cried for a week when her sister abandoned the household. She was alone now with the wreck of her father and a mother who had also taken to drinking. Léone was not bright; in fact, her school years had left her practically illiterate. The meagre salary she earned at a local shoe factory was absorbed by the family's needs. But her mother showed no gratitude. She mocked Léone for being worthless and dull-witted. And, rejected by all those closest to her, Léone looked for love elsewhere. She turned, in particular, to men.

She was not a pretty girl. Her eyes were wide-set, her nose was large and a ragged shank of dark hair fell across her low brow. A generous heart only made her an easier prey for the local lads.

Léone lost her virginity to a fellow factory worker at a hurried coupling in the corner of a field. She saw him the next day, laughing about the episode with his mates in the factory yard. Other sad encounters were to follow until she struck up with a decent-hearted young man in the Air Force. Fate never gave Léone a break, though; not long after they arranged to be married, the youth was killed in an accident.

It was in the bleak period following the incident that Léone met Emile-Clenet, a 22-year-old garage mechanic from Nantes. Their first brief encounter was at a dance in Cholet, and they made a rendezvous for the following afternoon. Misfortune was Léone's constant companion, and while cycling to the meeting she had to stop to fix a puncture. By the time she arrived, he was gone.

Six months later, however, they met again at the Lent carnival in Cholet. 'You're six months late,' joked Emile. 'But never mind, we've found each other again.' They enjoyed all the fun of the fair together and afterwards, Emile took her to a hotel room. She had never been treated to clean sheets before. She learned to love him then.

The couple fell into a set pattern of meetings. To reverse the lyrics of the popular song, it was 'Only on a Sunday' for Emile and Léone. He was a hard worker and reserved only the seventh day for his pleasures. Every Sunday, Léone would cycle to a particular spot near Cholet, and Emile would pick her up on his motorbike. After picnicing and perhaps some evening dancing, they would retire to a cheap hotel.

There was talk of marriage, and Emile took her home to meet his parents, who rather liked their son's strange little girlfriend. It is hard to determine exactly what went wrong. Perhaps Emile never seriously intended marriage. Once, there was an accident with his motorbike and Léone took a knock on the head. She suffered headaches and bouts of depression after that.

Emile could be cruel, too. Once, snapped by a street photographer, the couple went to pick up the picture. Emile took one look and said he didn't want it. When Léone asked why, he said: 'Just look at that face and you'll understand.' She hurried off to cry alone. Since meeting Emile, Léone had been taking care of her appearance, indulging in all the feminine vanities. Words like those must have wounded deeply.

The real blow came when she found she was pregnant and Emile told her to get rid of the unborn child. She did so – but the headaches and depressions grew worse after that. Then, in January 1952, she lost her job. There was a furious row in her home that night: her mother raged at her and her drunken father tried to give her a thrashing. Léone fled the household. It took her all night to cycle the 30-odd miles to Nantes where Emile worked. But when she got there in the morning, Emile was annoyed. Their arrangement was only for Sundays, he said. It was a weekday. She must leave.

Utterly abandoned, Léone spent two weeks as an outcast in Nantes, wandering the cold, winter streets. A second attempt to see Emile resulted in another rebuff. He said he was too busy to see her for the next couple of Sundays. Her money ran out. She had nowhere to sleep. And though she was never very clear about what happened during that blank fortnight, it seems she slipped into prostitution.

During the days, Léone took to standing outside gun-shop windows, gazing dazedly in at the gleaming butts and barrels. Later, she was to say that she did not quite know why she did so, perhaps suicide had been in her mind. But she remembered one incident very clearly. As she stood there, shivering in the rain, a strange young man had appeared at her side. 'Don't', said the figure, 'He is too young. He has the right to live.' Then he disappeared.

Hallucination? Léone had been a victim all her life, and perhaps her conscious mind was moving towards thoughts of self-destruction. But perhaps, too, some last instinct to survive and strike outward was prompting from within. The impulse was to murder her lover. And to redress the balance, her conscience invented the phantasmagoric young man who seemed to know her thoughts.

Whatever the truth, that voice seems to have earned Emile a reprieve. For she did not yet buy a gun. Instead, physically and emotionally exhausted, she returned to her village. Nothing had changed there. On arrival, her father was in one of his frenzies. Mechanically, she helped her mother strap him to the bed.

She had come back from one hell to another, and only thoughts of Emile sustained her 15 February 1952 was Léone's 23rd birthday. Would her lover remember? Last year he bought her a bicycle lamp – the only present of her adult life. She summoned up her courage, took the last of her savings, and boarded the coach back to Nantes. Humbly and apologetically she approached him at the garage and asked if they could meet on Sunday at the usual place. He showed no sign of remembering her birthday. But- to her intense joy – he agreed to meet at the rendezvous.

When he came, he brought no birthday present. Emile made love brusquely that Sunday and he did not stay the night as usual. It was on the following day that Léone went into Nantes and sought out one of the gunshops. There she bought a .22 automatic. The pistol had recently been declared a 'sporting weapon'. Léone, who could barely sign her name, did not need a licence.

She lived now only for their Sundays. Léone hung around in Nantes waiting for the next meeting, living from day to day in the dockside area by taking men into hotel bedrooms. When the grey haze of waiting hours was over she hastened to their rendezvous at Cholet. Emile was not there. She scoured the town and eventually found his motorbike parked outside a cinema. When the film was over she ran to meet him, but he brushed her off. He had flu, he said. He was going straight home. She must wait for the coming Lent carnival.

Fate, which had dogged Léone all her life, had reserved its completing irony for this meeting. It was at Cholet's Lent carnival that the couple had enjoyed their first night together two years earlier. It was at the Lent carnival too, with its hurdy-gurdy gaiety, that Léone Bouvier was to kill her lover.

Yet it started so well. Emile roared up on his motorbike at their rendezvous and she mounted pillion on the back just as in the old days. She kissed him as they rode into the town centre to mingle with the carnival crowds. They moved gaily among the stalls, the streamers and the balloons. Emile stopped by a shooting range to demonstrate his prowess. The weapon (fate again) was a .22 automatic. And above the staccato crackle of gunshot he told her he was leaving to work in North Africa. He was going, he said, for good.

'But what about me?' We were going to get married...'

'So what?'

'You don't want to marry me any more, then?'

'*C'est la vie.*' Emile shrugged and mumbled platitudes, telling her she would find someone better than him. Léone was incredulous. She asked again. Again he said no, he would never marry her.

Emile drove her back to her bicycle, locked up at their rendezvous. There she implored him, 'Emile, you aren't going off and leaving me like this?'

Emile said nothing, but returned to his motorcycle and climbed on, preparing to leave. Léone took the gun from her handbag and slipped it under her coat. She came up behind him. 'Emile,' she whispered, 'kiss me for the last time...'

He did not respond. She put her left arm around his neck and pulled him tenderly towards her. Gently, she kissed his cheek. And as she did so she withdrew the pistol and placed the barrel-end against his neck. Then she pulled the trigger.

There was only one shot.

Afterwards she mounted her bicycle and fled, pedalling blindly to the only place she knew that offered sanctuary. It was to Angers that she cycled, to her sister's convent.

She arrived there in distress, without explaining what had happened. Georgette gave her coffee and put her to bed – the poor, ruined child come like a ghost from her past.

The police came the following afternoon. Léone was arrested in the convent, but such are the procedures of French law that it was not until December 1953 that she was brought before the Assizes of Maine-et-Loire. French courts are traditionally flexible in the handling of a *crime passionnel*. Léone's misfortune was to face an unusually aggressive prosecutor and a hostile judge.

Judges play a more active role in the French courts than their English equivalents do. They may examine and cross-question a defendant at some length. And at Léone's trial in Angers, the judge showed himself entirely lacking in the subtlety associated with the French legal mind. What he had in abundance was the stubborn hypocrisy of the French provincial bourgeois.

He simply could not see that Léone's blighted childhood or her lover's callous rebuffs made one jot of difference to the case. Why did she not stay at her parents' hearth instead of wandering the dockside at Nantes? The answer should have been evident when Léone's father was brought to the witness box, sweating and shaking under the ordeal of a morning without a drink. The experts declared him an hereditary alcoholic. The mother, too, frankly admitted that they had all lived in mortal fear of his violence. But she explained that she'd done the best she could, adding the fateful reflection that her other daughter was a nun.

The judge pounced.

'You see!' he called, rounding on Léone, 'There was no need for you to go wrong. Why did you go wrong?' It is hard to exaggerate the part played by this circumstance. It seemed to nullify every mitigating factor of Léone's background. The writer Derrick Goodman has made the point eloquently: they did not come down hard on Léone because she had murdered her lover. It was because her sister was a nun.

The judge continued with his tirade, dwelling on the fact that Léone had killed Emile as she kissed him. This was a detail that seemed to him an incomprehensible outrage: *'atroce!'* he fumed, *'atroce!'*

Léone stood quietly in the dock, her head bowed low.

'Why did you kill him?' demanded the judge.

Tears were streaming down her cheeks as Léone raised her head.

'I loved him', she said simply.

The prosecution had called for the death penalty on the charge of premeditated murder. For reasons stated in the case of Pauline Dubuisson, there was no likelihood of Léone being executed. In fact, the defence had every right to expect a lenient judgement. What was Léone's crime if not a *crime passionnel?* Middle-class ladies had walked scot-free in cases of this nature.

The jury was out for only a quarter of an hour. And it would seem that they arrived at the same formula as in the case of Pauline Dubuisson. They avoided the charge of premeditated murder, for that carried an automatic death penalty, and found her guilty of murder – but without premeditation.

The foreman complacently suggested that the prisoner be given the maximum penalty of penal servitude for life – a minimum of 20 years. The judge readily agreed. And so, with the afflictions of a simple mind and a warm heart, a horrific childhood and a succession of rejections, Léone Bouvier fell victim to the full weight of French law.

The Real Mrs Mainwaring

The town of Colditz in Upper Saxony is remembered today for its castle, built high above the River Mulde, which housed some of the most determined escapers of World War Two. But long before its masonry knew the silent excavations of the Allied POWs, that brooding silhouette had looked down on a drama of a very different kind.

It was to Colditz that, in the summer of 1871, there came an English gentleman named Mainwaring with a beautiful companion that everyone took to be his young wife. Mainwaring booked in at a well known hotel, and engaged a suite of apartments for his honeymoon. He even received letters there, postmarked from Ferrybridge in Yorkshire. All, it appears, went on as merry as a marriage bell until one day an Englishwoman, travelling incognito, arrived at the hotel, taking two rooms on the same floor as the loving couple.

Her name was Mrs Mainwaring.

For a day or two, the real Mrs Mainwaring bided her time, apparently maturing her plan for revenge. Then, one night, she crept stealthily along the passage leading to her husband's bedchamber. Entering, pistol in hand, she saw her husband and his partner together among the sheets. Without a second thought she levelled the gun and fired. the ball passed through Mr Mainwaring's head – he died almost instantly.

This classic Victorian drama of love and venegeance had a fittingly tragic outcome. The real Mrs Mainwaring, her 'fell purpose' accomplished, was duly arrested and taken to prison. However, she was found dead in her cell that next morning. According to The *Illustrated Police News* which reported the story, she had managed to conceal poison about her person and must have swallowed it soon after her incarceration. The doctors were unanimous in their opinion that she had been dead for several hours.

A Life for a Life

Early in July 1955, north country publican Albert Pierrepoint received official notice that he would be needed in London on the 13th. A small, tidy man, Pierrepoint made the appropriate arrangements for a journey he had made many times before. On the afternoon of 12 July he arrived at the gates of Holloway Prison in North London. Admitted by the authorities, he was given a cup of tea and then taken to the door of a cell where, through the peep-hole, he could see a pale young woman reading a Bible.

The officials supplied the statistics he needed to know: Height – 5 ft 2 inches; Weight – 103 lbs. Albert Pierrepoint, official hangman, studied her file and proceeded to the execution chamber where, using a sandbag for dummy, he tested the spring-loaded mechanism of the trap.

At 09.00 the following morning, 28-year-old Ruth Ellis entered the chamber to become the last woman hanged in Britain. She faced the noose with the same extraordinary calm as she had exhibited throughout her trial and her ordeal of waiting. Ruth Ellis asked neither for sympathy nor for mercy. From the condemned cell she had written, 'I say a life for a life.'

The hanging was efficiently accomplished. The post mortem noted the fractures to spine, thyroid and cartilage, but reported the air passages clear. She had not been stran-gled like so many before her: 'No engorgement . . . No asphyxial changes . . . Cause of Death: Injuries to the cen-tral nervous system consequent upon judicial hanging.'

Yet neither the prisoner's calm, Pierrepoint's expertise, nor any amount of paperwork could mask the essential horror of what had transpired. 1955 was the year when Rock 'n 'Roll hit Britain; the first year of commercial television. Yet at Holloway Prison, an Old Testament form of tribal retribution had been enacted upon Ruth Ellis. For days beforehand, friends, relatives, lawyers and MPs had been pressing desperately for a reprieve. On the eve of the execution, the crowds had already started to assemble outside the prison gates, equipped with Thermos flasks and sleeping bags, so as to be near as the macabre drama was played out. Among them was a vociferous minority chanting for the abolition of a penalty which seemed more barbarous than murder itself. The hanging of Ruth Ellis did not only shock because the condemned woman was young and blonde and attractive. It exposed an iron inflexibility in the British legal system. Even in 1955, there was hardly another country in the civilised world where a crime of passion was punishable on the scaffold.

Born Ruth Hornby at Rhyl in 1926, the condemned woman had led a chequered life. At 15 she had escaped from a difficult home background to start work as a waitress. In due course she found employment at a munitions factory and was already dyeing her hair with the peroxide that was to distinguish her in all the press photographs. Ruth was no shy maiden. With a slender, somewhat predatory sensuality she found it easy to acquire dancing partners among servicemen at the wartime clubs she began to frequent in London. In 1944, she had a child by a Canadian soldier, and no sooner had her figure returned than she took up a job as nude model in a Camera Club. In the years of postwar austerity, West End vice lords were already spinning their webs of sleazy excitement. Ruth became a club hostess and call girl. In 1950 she married George Ellis, an alcoholic dentist who frequented her low-life locales. The couple had a daughter but separated soon afterwards, and Ruth returned to the circuit. It was while working as manageress at the Little Club, a seedy upstairs drinking room in Knightsbridge, that she met David Blakely, the man she was to murder.

Blakely came from a very different background. Born in 1929, the son of a well-to-do Sheffield doctor, he was given a public school education at Shrewsbury, and throughout his brief life he retained his boyish good looks. Blakely remained immature in temperament too. For all his suave charm and his well-bred accent, he never held down a steady job. Feckless, emotionally vulnerable and prone to sulks, Blakely maintained abiding enthusiasms only for alcohol, for women and – above all – for racing cars. When he drank he became obstreperous, provoking fights he was too cowardly to see through. With his women he was a braggart and a largely unsuccessful lover. And his experiences on the motor circuits were hardly any happier.

Blakely raced at Silverstone and other well-known tracks, including Le Mans in France. But though he consorted at clubs and meetings with stars like Mike Hawthorne and Stirling Moss, victory almost always eluded him. Nor did racing offer him a career. His obsession for cars, as for drink and women, was financed chiefly by private money, including a £7,000 legacy from his father.

Blakely first met Ruth Ellis in 1953. The young racing driver was drunk and insulting on that occasion, and Ruth referred to him afterwards as a 'pompous ass', telling a friend, 'I hope never to see that little shit again.' But she did – with consequences disastrous to both.

Blakely took to frequenting the Little Club, where Ruth succumbed to his charm and expensive manners. David was 'class', and before long they were sleeping together at her flat above the premises. Ruth, at the outset, was clearly the dominant partner, confident and self-possessed while he was weak and ineffectual. Moreover, as Blakely frittered away more and more of his resources, he came to depend on her to subsidise his drinking.

After having a child of Blakely's aborted in December 1953, Ruth tried to cool the relationship by cultivating a more dependable lover, company director Desmond Cussen. At about the same time she lost her job at the Little Club, partly because of the time and money she had expended on David.

Ruth first moved into Cussen's apartment, and later to a flat to Egerton Gardens. Cussen loaned her the rent and was a frequent visitor there. But Ruth could not entirely break with her younger lover. She continued to sleep with Blakely, who eventually moved in with her at Egerton Gardens. It was a period of savage quarrels and recriminations between Ruth and David. He was intensely jealous, drank heavily, and sometimes beat Ruth so badly that she had to use make-up to camouflage the livid bruises on her limbs. She had a second abortion by him, and under the strain of the tempestuous relationship consulted a doctor who prescribed tranquillisers for her depression. Blakely, meanwhile, had invested what little capital he possessed in building a racing car. Predictably, the vehicle broke down in practice before its racing debut.

What bonded Ruth to her young lover? Love? Social ambition, or his periodic promises of marriage? Blakely had become a liability to Ruth, yet during this period of frenzied passion, the see-saw of emotional need began to tilt. Blakely, meanwhile, had not lost his middle-class expectations, and to friends of his, a married couple called the Findlaters, he confided his despair and his own need to make a break with Ruth Ellis. Ruth had long suspected that David was having an affair with Mrs Findlater, and the more time he spent in the company of the married couple, the more her own jealousy quickened. Ruth could dish out violence as well as take it; once, it seems, she slashed Blakely in the back with a knife.

Things came to a head at Easter, 1995. On Good Friday,

8 April, Blakely confessed to the Findlaters that he was getting frightened of Ruth. They suggested he spend the weekend with them at their apartment in Tanza Road, Hampstead. Though he was due to meet Ruth at 19.30 that night, Blakely gratefully accepted.

For two hours, Ruth waited at Egerton Gardens for her lover to turn up. At 21.30 she phoned the Findlaters to find out if David was there. The au pair took the call and told her that neither Blakely nor the Findlaters were in the flat. An hour later, Ruth phoned again, and this time Anthony Findlater answered. Though he claimed to know nothing of her lover's whereabouts, Ruth did not believe him. Again and again that night she rang Tanza Road, and in the end Findlater simply hung up the receiver whenever her voice came on the line. At the trial it was learned that Blakely was indeed at Tanza Road – shaking with fear on the couch.

Frenzied with suspicion, Ruth had Desmond Cussen drive her round to Tanza Road. When she saw Blakely's green Vanguard parked outside the flat, she ran in fury to the front door and repeatedly rang the bell. No-one replied. Eventually, she vented her spleen on the Vanguard, thumping in its side windows which were held in place only by rubber strips. The glass did not break, but the noise brought Anthony Findlater to the door in his pyjamas.

There was a furious scene in the street where Ruth kept demanding that Blakely come down, and Findlater denied that he was there. Already, the married couple had prudently phoned for the police. An inspector turned up and tried to calm the situation; after warning Ruth against breaching the peace he drove away.

Findlater slammed the door, leaving Ruth still fulminating in the street. Nor did she leave at once, but kept prowling around the Vanguard until a second police visit forced her from the scene. The long-suffering Desmond

Cussen, who had waited and watched throughout the whole performance, drove her back to Egerton Gardens.

His role in the affair deserves a word of explanation. Cussen was infatuated with Ruth but, lacking David's youth and glamour, knew he must wait until the flame of her earlier love was extinguished. For that reason, it appears, he was prepared to acquiesce with Ruth in what became an ever more obsessive quest.

Ruth did not sleep that night. Early the next morning she took a taxi to Tanza Road and kept watch on the Findlaters' from a darkened doorway. At about 10.00 Findlater emerged, and beckoned Blakely out into the street. Having examined the damaged cars, the two men got in and drove off down the road.

Ruth's suspicions were confirmed – the Findlaters *were* shielding David from her. Armed with this certainty, she spent the next hours in attempts to track down her lover's movements. After lunch, she and Cussen took her ten-year-old son to the London Zoo, leaving him there with enough money for the afternoon. Then, with Cussen as chauffeur, she continued the hunt for her quarry.

Cussen drove her back to Hampstead where they located the now-repaired Vanguard outside the Magdala public house. After considerably more furtive reconnoitring, they returned to Ruth's flat, gave her son his supper and put him to bed. That night, Cussen again drove her to Tanza Road where the Findlaters were holding a small party. Listening from the street, Ruth could hear David's voice – and a woman giggling at his remarks. A new suspicion took root in Ruth's fevered mind. David was not pursuing an affair with Mrs Findlater – but with the couple's au pair! A trivial occurrence seemed to confirm this idea: at a certain point, the blinds went down in what Ruth took to be the girl's bedroom; and at the same time, she ceased to hear David's voice. The Findlaters, Ruth convinced herself, were using the au pair to prise her young lover away from her.

Cussen drove Ruth home at about 21.00, and she spent a second sleepless night, chain-smoking and nursing her mute fury. By the following evening, on Easter Sunday, she must have been practically unhinged. 'I was very upset', she acknowledged at her trial. 'I had a peculiar feeling I wanted to kill him.'

By her own account, Ruth Ellis made her way by taxi to Hampstead that evening. In her handbag she carried a heavy .38 Smith and Wesson revolver. Arriving at Tanza Road she saw no sign of the Vanguard, so she made her way on foot to the Magdala pub where she sighted David's car by the kerb. Peering through the windows of the hostelry, she could see David and a friend, Mayfair car salesman Clive Gunnell, drinking at the bar. In fact, the two men had only come to replenish stocks for an evening at Tanza Road. Having downed their drinks, they came out into the street carrying cigarettes and three quarts of light ale.

Neither noticed Ruth at first. With a quart of beer under his arm, David approached the Vanguard, fumbling in his pocket for the keys.

'David!' she called, but he did not seem to hear. Ruth approached, taking the revolver from her bag. 'David!' she called again, and this time he turned to see the blonde with the Smith and Wesson.

Immediately, he ran towards the back of the van. Two shots echoed in quick succession. Blakely was slammed against the side of the vehicle, then staggered towards his friend for cover.

'Clive!' he screamed.

'Get out of the way, Clive,' Ruth hissed in response. And as Blakely tried again to run for safety she fired a third shot that span him to the ground. Then, with every appearance of icy calm, Ruth Ellis came at her fallen lover and drilled two more bullets into his prone body. A sixth bullet ricocheted off the road to strike the thumb of a passing bank official's wife.

From the doorway of the pub, people were spilling out onto the street. An off-duty officer was among those present and he moved slowly towards her. 'Will you call the police?' Ruth asked softly as he took the gun. 'I *am* the police', he replied.

That, in bare outline, was the sequence of events that led Ruth Ellis to trial at the Old Bailey. In purely legal terms, it seemed a clear-cut case of wilful murder against which Ruth offered no substantial defence. She refused to ask for sympathy as a downtrodden mistress; in the dock she glossed over Blakely's beatings: 'He only used to hit me with his fists and hands, but I bruise very easily.' With all passion and anguish spent, Ruth Ellis *wanted* to die for the murder of her lover, and indulged in no tearful theatricals. To the disquiet of her lawyers, she even insisted on appearing in the dock with a full peroxide rinse. In the argot of the day she appeared the very archetype of a 'brassy tart'. Ruth's fate may have swung on that bottle of peroxide – with the chance injury to the bank official's wife's thumb.

In cross-examination, the prosecutor posed only one question.

'Mrs Ellis, when you fired that revolver at close range into the body of David Blakely, what did you intend to do?'

'It is obvious,' she replied with fateful simplicity, 'that when I shot him I intended to kill him.'

That, in effect, was that. The judge in summing up pointed out that jealousy was no defence under British law; the intention to kill was all-important. 'If, on the consideration of the whole evidence, you are satisfied that at the time she fired those shots she had the intention of killing or doing grievous bodily harm, then your duty is to find her guilty of wilful murder.'

191

The Hangman's Verdict

For hanging Ruth Ellis, Albert Pierrepoint collected a fee of fifteen guineas (plus travelling expenses). He left Holloway practically besieged by a storming mob and needed police protection to get through. Pierrepoint returned to his pub, the Rose and Crown at Hoole, near Preston, and the wife who had never asked questions. And there he came to a decision: he would give up his macabre profession.

His had been an hereditary vocation, his father and uncle both having been listed as qualified executioners on the Home Office files. When the press learned of his resignation, it was rumoured that something exceptionally grim must have transpired in the death chamber. It had not – Ruth Ellis was 'the bravest woman I ever hanged' and there was 'nothing untoward'. Pierrepoint resigned because the furore caused him to examine his own conscience. Did hanging really deter murder? He concluded that it did not: 'Capital punishment, in my view, achieved nothing except revenge.'

Ruth herself had admitted her intention. The twelve members of the jury were out for only 23 minutes, and found the prisoner guilty of murder. Donning his black cap, the judge intoned the terrible words: 'The sentence of the Court upon you is that you be taken hence to a lawful prison, and thence to a place of execution, and that you there be hanged by the neck until you be dead...'

It all seemed so clear-cut. Yet, even under British law, it was not inevitable that Ruth Ellis should have hanged. Much about the case was never fully explored at the trial. Ruth's mental state, for example, was not discussed at any length; the effect of her second abortion, and the fact that she was taking tranquillizers on medical advice. The drugs, combined with alcohol she had consumed on the fateful day, may well have produced a state of serious psychological disturbance. Even on the given evidence, Blakeley's violent provocations might have led the jury to

recommend mercy. In the case of Kittie Byron, such a recommendation had saved the prisoner from the gallows.

Then there was the question of the murder weapons.
Ruth Ellis stated that she had been given the Smith and
Wesson about three years ago by a man in a club whose
name I don't remember.' Nobody believed this version of
events even at the time. It was widely rumoured that
Desmond Cussen had supplied the murder weapon, and
also driven her to Hampstead on the fateful night.
Interviewed in 1977, Cussen firmly repudiated the sug-
gestions. The defence did not pursue the matter at the
trial, since a hint of conspiracy to murder would have
jeopardised the case for manslaughter, and the chance of a
reprieve. Yet if someone did put the gun in Ruth's hand
and drive her – befuddled with drink, tranquillisers and
lack of sleep – to the murder scene she would have been
less easily presented as a cold-hearted blonde avenger.

During the last frenzied efforts to win Ruth a reprieve,
this issue became electric. On the day before her execution, Ruth Ellis made a written statement to her solicitor
Victor Mishcon:

> I, Ruth Ellis, have been advised by Mr Victor
> Mishcon to tell the whole truth in regard to the
> circumstances leading up to the killing of
> David Blakely and it is only with the greatest
> reluctance that I have decided to tell how it
> was that I got the gun with which I shot
> Blakely. I did not do so before because I felt
> that I was needlessly getting someone into
> possible trouble.
>
> I had been drinking Pernod (I think that is
> how it is spelt) in Cussen's flat and Cussen
> had been drinking too. This was about 8.30
> p.m. We had been drinking for some time. I
> had been telling Cussen about Blakely's treat-

ment of me. I was in a terribly depressed state. All I remember is that Cussen gave me a loaded gun ... I was in such a dazed state that I cannot remember what was said. I rushed out as soon as he gave me the gun. He stayed in the flat.

I had never seen the gun before. The only gun I had ever seen there was a small air pistol used as a game with a target.

Before signing the document, Ruth added:

There's one more thing. You had better know the whole truth. I rushed back after a second or so and said 'Will you drive me to Hampstead?' He did so, and left me at the top of Tanza Road.

One view of this is that Ruth Ellis had no interest in saving her life at that stage, and was only persuaded to make her statement so that her ten-year-old son should know the truth. Desmond Cussen, however, in the 1977 interview, reiterated his claim to know nothing about the revolver, adding: 'She was a dreadful liar, you know.'

With only a few hours to spare, the statement was rushed by messenger to the Home Office. Scotland Yard was notified and Fleet Street buzzed with the news. Cussen, however, could not be found to comment on the statement and lacking a confession from him, the Home Secretary refused to consider the most urgent representations.

No reprieve was granted. Early in the morning of 13 July, Ruth Ellis wrote her last note to a friend from the condemned cell: 'The time is 7 o'clock a.m. – everyone (staff) is simply wonderful in Holloway. This is just to console my family with the thought that I did not change my way of thinking at the last moment. Or break my promise to David's mother.' That promise had been made in an earlier letter, in which Ruth had asked forgiveness and written, 'I shall die loving your son.'

And perhaps Ruth Ellis did die loving David Blakely. She spent her last hour in the death cell at prayer before a crucifix. Just before 09.00, the grim procession of officials entered and told her the time had come. They offered her a large measure of brandy which she gratefully accepted. then, having thanked the authorities for their kindness, she walked steadily to the execution chamber where Albert Pierrepoint was waiting.

Suspicion

When Pauline Grandjean, a young dressmaker, became engaged to a man named Drouant she confessed a secret to her fiancé. The name she used, she said, was not her real one. There were good reasons for adopting the alias, but she was not prepared to divulge them.

Drouant accepted the arrangement, but he harboured his own suspicions. And when, one day in June 1905, he called unexpectedly at the girl's flat, those suspicions appeared fully confirmed. In her apartment was a postcard which bore the words: 'I shall come and see you this morning. You have my love in spite of all that has happened, and we will try and forget the past.'

His pulse quickening with jealous rage, Drouant concealed himself in the flat and awaited the arrival of the postcard's author. An hour or two later Pauline returned. She was followed almost immediately by a man who, on seeing her, fell into her arms.

Drouant sprang from his hiding place, forced the loving couple apart and plunged a knife deep into the man's back. The victim fell to the floor, his life ebbing with the blood that gushed from the wound.

'Murderer!' screamed the girl. 'You have killed my brother!'

It was a tragic episode which might have come straight from one of the stage melodramas of the period. the girl's brother had just served two years in prison and the pair had changed their names to avoid the stigma of his criminal record. He had written the card on the day of his release, intending to visit his sister briefly before going to look for a job in Paris.

The victim was taken to hospital in his death throes. He refused to lay charges against his aggressor.

Murder by our Paris Correspondent

How intrepid journalists are in detailing crimes of passion – how fearless in exposing lust and violence. These qualities were turned in on the profession by the great Morton-Bower scandal of 1852. The drama unfolded in Paris, and its male leads were both foreign correspondents.

Representing the *Morning Advertiser* was Mr Elliot Bower, aged forty and a bit of a wag. His friends knew him as a capital fellow much given to practical jokes. Once, for example, Bower crept up behind a blameless old gentleman who was studying the menu at an outside café table. The prankster suddenly grabbed him by the neck collar and the seat of his trousers and ran him along the boulevard. My, how they roared!

Representing the *Daily News* was Mr Saville Morton, elegant young man-about-town. Wealthy and much travelled, Morton was well known in the literary circles of the day. He was an intimate of Thackeray among other eminent writers, and became a foreign correspondent more for amusement than anything else. He did not need the money.

Both were Cambridge men who had been undergraduates together. And since they shared broadly the same liberal views, they worked closely together in Paris: swapping political gossip and sharing their insights into the latest intrigue. Morton was a bachelor, but Bower had married a Fanny Vickery in 1842. As chance would have it, Morton had known his friend's wife in London before the marriage. All seemed to conspire to cement the bonds of friendship, and the trio became boon companions who went to theatres and dined out constantly together. Sadly, it was not very long before the trio became a triangle.

Bower came to detect a threatening intimacy developing between his wife and his bachelor friend. At one stage there was a bitter quarrel, and Morton stopped visiting the Bowers' home in the rue de Sèze. The dispute was patched up, but it left an aura of mistrust which perhaps never entirely evaporated.

Elliot Bower, the jealous husband, was by no means irreproachable as far as the opposite sex was concerned. It must be remembered that the Paris of the day had a diamanté sparkle all of its own. This was the golden age of the *cocotte* and courtesan, of champagne and of *soupers intimes*. For the idling Englishman, the whole city glittered with temptation. And who could blame Mr Bower if, once in a while, he succumbed?

Mrs Bower could. The couple quarrelled frequently over Elliot's philandering ways. Some episodes sprang only from his prankster temperament: once for example, he strolled up to a carriage in the Bois de Boulogne where a lady was seated in her carriage. Elliot thrust his hand through the window and squeezed her knee. As she gaped in astonishment, he made an elaborate bow and sped off in a waiting cab.

But there were more serious misdemeanours: candlelit

suppers with *demi-mondaines* from which he came back late to the rue de Sèze. And things came to a head when Mrs Bower discovered that Elliot had been having an affair with an Englishwoman. Her name was Isabella Laurie, and Fanny found a letter from her husband's paramour, in which Isabella complained of having been seduced by Elliot and then cruelly cast aside.

Enraged, Mrs Bower turned to Saville Morton for comfort. Precisely what form that comfort took remains an issue in dispute. Certainly Mrs Bower wanted revenge against her husband, and was more than a little fond of Morton. The bachelor himself suggested a divorce and declared that he would marry her if she broke up with her husband. Mrs Bower, however, demurred. It was not that she was unwilling, but the timing was awkward. The trouble was, she was expecting a baby.

It was in fact to be her fifth child. In due course, the baby was born with its mother still seething with rage. Two days after the event she had a message smuggled out via the concierge's wife: 'Go at once to Mr Morton, and tell him from me that the child is just like him.'

It all depends on how you interpret the case. Morton's reported reaction was, 'Goddam! Oh, what a nuisance.' This strongly implies that they had had an adulterous liaison which now threatened to be exposed. But if their love had never been consummated, it is possible to speculate that Morton thought the woman had become seriously unbalanced.

Whatever the truth, Morton kept a low profile *vis-à-vis* the Bowers for a fortnight after the birth. The issue was forced when Mrs Bower developed a fever and, tossing and turning in her delirium kept calling out Morton's name. The doctors called for Morton to see if his presence would calm her. It did – and he stayed for several days and nights. The patient would only take medicine from Morton, who was put up in an adjoining room.

While the fever raged within her, Mrs Bower repeatedly insisted that her husband be kept away from her. Only once did she call him to her room. That was on the evening of 1 October 1852, and took the opportunity to shriek imprecations against his infidelities. The tirade ended with the patient pointing to her sleeping child, and the words: 'Listen to me, you villain. That is not your child. Saville Morton, and not you, is its father. Oh, Queen of England, come to my help and rid me of this scoundrel!'

How was Queen Victoria to help? Bower thought that his wife had gone mad and remained dutifully at her bedside. But she persisted. She referred to a particular period when he was in London ... she had spent a night with Morton.

Bower tensed. Suddenly, he rushed from the room and confronted Morton with the charge. Morton failed to reply, promptly making for the stairs instead. Bower grabbed a carving knife and hurried after him, brandishing the blade. With one lunge he gashed the bachelor with a wound that severed Morton's carotid artery. The blood spilled everywhere.

Panic-stricken servants had witnessed the whole affair, and it was Bower who told them to send for a doctor. In the confused comings and goings which followed the assault, he in fact showed remarkable composure. Bower did not wait for the police or the medical assistance to arrive. Instead, he changed clothes, grabbed a passport and made for the Gare du Nord. A train took him to Boulogne; a packet-boat to England and safety.

News crossed frontiers in 1852 that policemen seldom did. The Morton-Bower affair soon had newspaper readers enthralled on both sides of the Channel. But though Morton died as a result of his wounds, Bower remained at liberty. He strolled the London streets in perfect freedom without the need for disguise or alias. The French police did contact Scotland Yard, but they made no request for the fugitive's arrest. And lacking this formal requirement, the London police were in no position to act. Incredibly, Elliot Bower even gave his own account of the Morton-Bower case for the *Morning Advertiser*. It was a more accurate piece than many which had been published about the sensation, a unique exclusive, really: Murder by Our Special Correspondent, as it were.

What of Mrs Bower? She had been committed to a lunatic asylum shortly after the fateful event. But she did not take long to recover (there was doubt as to whether she needed treatment at all). And before long she too had returned to London. She did not meet Bower there though; Fanny would have nothing to do with her husband, and expressed complete indifference as to his fate.

What that fate was to be remained problematic. Though the French made no move to extradite the fugitive, they did set the official legal machinery in action. After police investigations, a *juge d'instruction* (examining magistrate) determined that the crime was not murder but homicide. This heartened Bower. And knowing French lenience towards jealous husbands in a *crime personnel*, it also encouraged him to make a bold move. Of his own free will, Elliot Bower returned to France and surrendered himself to the authorities.

The Assize Court in Paris was packed on 28 December as the Englishman faced his accusers. Bower entered the dock dressed in sober black, and his general demeanour was widely admired by the women in the courtroom. Not, however, by the *Gazette des Tribunaux*, which noted that the accused was 'a man of between 35 and 40 years of age, blond, like most Englishmen, with luxuriant whiskers and an unfashionable moustache.'

The trial that followed in no way resembled the trials known to phlegmatic Anglo-Saxons. Take the supposedly neutral indictment, for example: this was one long torrent of abuse against the accused man, couched in terms of the most florid rhetoric. Describing, for example, Bower's philanderings it read: 'The villain flaunted his misconduct. And this in Paris! Oh, shame upon him!' Having luridly portrayed the assault on the unarmed Morton, it continued: 'What next? The murderer, blood on his hands and crime on his conscience, fled to England – to Perfidious Albion, where assassins are sheltered from outraged justice...'

All this before the prosecution began! Very little, it seemed, could be said for perfidious Englishman with their unfashionable moustaches. The prosecution was an essay in defamation of character, in which foul innuendo, rank calumny and steamy prose jostled to take pride of place. Nobody disputed the fact that Bower had killed his rival. The main thrust of the prosecution's case was that the crime had been premeditated: Morton had been somehow enticed to the apartment in a cunning plot matured for some time beforehand. An absurd thesis, it is true, but it carried some weight when delivered with all the glowering malevolence that a Latin prosecutor can muster. Even Bower's voluntary surrender was scorned: a Frechman would have done the honourable thing and given himself up on the spot. What did Bower do? He fled. Fled like an Englishman and now came brazenly back to cock a snook at the majesty of French law.

'I demand death for the murderer Bower!' roared the prosecutor at the end of his vehement declamation.

Even Bower, a cool enough customer, must have trembled inwardly as the dread words rang out. But help was at hand in the shape of a defence counsel equally armed with Gallic passion. He described the dastardly seduction of a previously chaste wife by a man thought to be a friend. He dwelled on the furtive liaison which developed, the passing of notes and so on. Bower's counsel had witnesses who confirmed that, on at least one occasion, Morton had spent a night with Mrs Bower when her husband was in London. And all the time the trusting and hard-working husband had been innocent of his betrayal!

The crime, declared the defence, was Morton's, not Bower's: 'What man among you, what husband and father worthy of the name would have acted otherwise? I tell you, gentlemen, the blow struck did him honour. The wife of his bosom had been seduced, her person possessed by another; and, as a result, adulterous offspring had been foisted upon him . . .'

The public in the court hissed and cheered at appropriate points. Thee was even one moment when, overcome by his own portrayal of the outraged husband's plight, the defence counsel actually broke down and wept piteously into a large handkerchief; the judge himself was so moved that the proceedings had to be halted for a while.

Then came the finale. The defence ended with a stirring appeal to those patriotic emotions which the prosecutor had tried to whip up.

> 'Remember that the accused has voluntarily surrendered to our courts, demanding justice at your hands. He has done well. French justice will not fail him. He will, by your verdict, go back to England and tell his countrymen there of the religious attention with which a French jury listens to the evidence, and that our French justice is everywhere the admiration of the world!'

Wild cheers! In no time at all, the jury declared for acquittal. The crowd roared its approval – strangers surged forward to wring Bower by the hand – the gendarmes even kissed him. It was as if the Englishman had been given the freedom of the city.

Bower did not, in fact, go back to England to celebrate French justice and French juries. On the contrary, Paris itself suited him very nicely. He lived there happily for the next 30 years, dying, aged 70, in 1884.

Wild Bill and his Women

In the old West, where female company was scarce, jealousy probably motivated more murders than cattle or bullion ever did. From bar-room brawls to main street showdowns the quarrels flared. Life was cheap, and many a legendary lawman owned notches on his gun not to zeal for the law – but to love of women.

Take Wild Bill Hickock, for example. The famed Union scout and Indian-fighter used to boast of a great Rock Creek shoot-out that began his crime-fighting career. The pistoleer claimed to have slain the ten-man McCanles gang single-handed: six bullets saw off Dave McCanles and five henchmen; he used a knife to cut down the other four villains. The West was well rid of the gang, said Hickock, for they were 'desperadoes, horse-thieves and murderers' to a man.

Wild Bill, of course, was one of the Wild West's great self-advertisers. Six foot two inches tall (wearing high-heeled shoes), with auburn curls that cascaded to his shoulders, the 'Prince of Pistoleers' made such an impressive figure that dude reporters from the East lapped up every word he said. In reality, James Butler Hickock was a drunk, a liar and a womanizer. As it happens, there was a McCanles episode – but it was not quite as Wild Bill told it.

In 1862, Hickock was working as a humble stable hand at the Rock Creek pony express station in Jefferson County, Nebraska. The manager there was a Mr Horace Wellman, and the stockkeeper a J.W. Brink. And in the offing, too, was a certain Sarah Shull (Kate Shell), something of a local belle.

Hickock stole the lady's affections from David C. McCanles, a landowner of the neighbourhood. And on 21

July 1862, the jealous McCanles rode out to the station threatening to 'clean up on the people' there. He was clearly intending a Wild-West style crime of passion, but had no cohort of desperadoes with him: just two neighbours and his 12-year-old son.

When the smoke cleared at Rock Creek that day, only the boy returned.

Years after the event, historical investigators succeeded in tracing the boy, Monroe McCanles. And he gave an account of the affair which reflected no credit on the legendary lawman. Monroe stated that when his father entered the station manager's house, Hickock shot him in the back with a rifle from a hidden position behind a curtain. Then Wild Bill turned the weapon on one of the neighbours, but only succeeded in wounding him; the man was beaten to death by Wellman who used a hoe. McCanles's second companion fled out into the scrub and was killed with a shotgun – Monroe could not say by whom.

So much for the solo slaying of ten desperadoes. Monroe's version of events was broadly confirmed in 1927, when investigators dug up court records from Nebraska. It appears that three men – Hickock, Wellman and Brink – were charged with the triple murder. The accused escaped punishment, however, on a plea of self-defence.

And did Wild Bill ride off into the sunset with the lovely Sarah Shull? Not a bit of it. He had a succession of paramours, and in 1865, his liaison with a certain Susanna Moore was to lead to the first Wild West showdown on record. A man named Dave Tutt took up with the lady and incurred the pistoleer's jealous wrath. A disputed card game provided Wild Bill with his pretext, and he challenged his rival to a gun duel in the public square at Springfield, Missouri.

The duel is an age-old means of settling a love-triangle

quarrel: a kind of ritualised crime of passion. This one differed only from earlier gun duels in that the weapons were holstered. Tutt drew first, and missed. Before he had time to fire again. Hickock had put a bullet through his heart.

Off With Her Head!

Kings of the past possessed weapons of revenge unavailable to humbler citizens. A queen who took lovers threatened the royal succession. Adultery was treason, and two of Henry VIII's wives went to the block for the offence. The cases of Anne Boleyn and Catherine Howard were very different, but you could call each execution a judicial crime of passion.

Anne Boleyn was not, in conventional terms, an especially attractive woman. A contemporary described her as having a 'middling stature, swarthy complexion, long neck, wide mouth, bosom not much raised.' In fact, the observer declared, the Wiltshire girl had little to recommend her except for the king's appetite, 'and her eyes, which are black and beautiful and take great effect.'

Perhaps those dark eyes first drew Henry to her. Certainly, he wrote her some passionate love letters which have survived as evidence of real infatuation. Henry had his first marriage to Catherine of Aragon annulled in order to marry the English Anne. And though the first queen's failure to bear a male heir was a key reason for the divorce, Henry's love for Anne clearly strengthened his resolve.

When the pope refused to accept the divorce it sparked the immense upheaval of the English Reformation. And as for Henry and Anne, secretly married in January 1533, their union was not a success. The king's ardour soon cooled after the marriage and his eye started roving again.

Anne bore him a daughter (the future Elizabeth I) instead of the son he desired. A second child miscarried and a third – a male heir – was dead at birth.

The stillborn child was delivered on 29 January 1536. And the unhappy event seems to have set the wheels of vengeance moving, for on 2 May, Anne Boleyn was sent to the Tower charged with adultery.

Four young courtiers were cited as her lovers: Sir Francis Weston, Henry Norris, William Brereton and Mark Smeaton. The most sensational charge, however, was that Anne had had carnal relations with her own brother, Lord Rochford; an accusation instigated by his spiteful wife. All except Smeaton protested their innocence, the latter confessing to guilt. All went to the block, Smeaton declaring on the scaffold that he 'deserved to die'.

Anne for her part persistently professed herself innocent. When she heard of Smeaton's last words she erupted with passion: 'Has he not cleared me of that public shame he has brought me to? Alas, I fear his soul suffers for it and that he is now punished for his false accusation.' She was tried and unanimously condemned by a court of 30 peers. The sentence carried with it an option for Henry – she could be either burnt alive or beheaded, according to the king's pleasure.

Henry, bountiful in her mercy, opted for beheading. He event had an especially sharp blade imported from the Continent for, as the queen observed with sad vanity: 'I have but a little neck.'

Anne went to the scaffold on 19 May, behaving with courage and dignity. It was said that she had never appeared more beautiful than on that fateful day. Still professing her innocence, she graciously declared that the king had done her many favours: first in making her a marchioness, second in making her queen, third in sending her to heaven.

It is easy to imagine her a tragic victim of circumstance.

Nevertheless, her own uncle presided over the court of peers which found her guilty. They saw evidence which was subsequently destroyed. And no-one, not even her own daughter Elizabeth, later tried to retrieve her reputation. Smeaton's confession, her friends' silence, the peers' unanimous judgement – all tend to suggest that she may well have been an unfaithful wife.

Still, callous statecraft clearly played its part in the affair. The king craved a male heir and did not mourn his second wife's passing. He was seen immediately after the execution wearing bright yellow garb with a feather in his cap. And the very next day he became betrothed to Jane Seymour, his third wife. She was to die not long after giving birth to the boy child he so desperately desired (the sickly Edward VI). The fourth wife, Anne of Cleves, lasted no time at all. Henry only married her to effect a German alliance, and found her so ugly on sight that he divorced her immediately. It was then that the ill-starred Catherine Howard came into his life.

Catherine was the orphaned daughter of a noble and gallant soldier, and was brought up in the household of her grandmother. Agnes, Duchess of Norfolk. The girl was pretty, young and vivacious and Henry, now 50, fell passionately in love with her. He called her his ' rose without a thorn,' and she seemed to come fresh with all the innocence of virginal maidenhood.

Unfortunately for all concerned, this was an illusion.

Catherine had committed many youthful indiscretions. And almost immediately after wedding in July 1540, these came to the attention of the king's councillors. A former maidservant in the Duchess of Norfolk's household had confided to her brother Catherine's misconduct. The brother in turn approached Archbishop Cranmer. The queen, it appeared, had not been a virgin when she married, and the maidservant's story was as picturesque as it was disquieting:

> 'Marry, there is one Francis Dereham who
> was servant also in my Lady Norfolk's house
> which hath been in bed with her in his doublet
> and hose between the sheets an hundred
> nights. And there hath been such puffing and
> blowing between them that once in the house
> a maid which lay in the house with her said to
> me she would lie no longer with her for she
> knew not what matrimony meant.'

Nor was it just Dereham who had dallied with the
English rose. A man named Mannock 'knew a privy mark
of her body.'

This was an awkward business. Cranmer himself had
arranged the marriage and his reputation was at stake. He
is said to have been 'marvellously perplexed' as to what
to do about the report and called two other high officials
of state who were equally troubled. Cranmer, they decided, really must inform the king, even if the story was just
malicious gossip. The Archbishop agreed, but dared not
face his sovereign in person. Instead he submitted a written report and waited for the storm to break.

Henry was outraged. He refused to believe it. He questioned Catherine about the allegations, and she was fierce
in her denials. And though Henry desperately wanted to
believe her, his obligations required that he secretly
assemble a group of notables to investigate the allegations. Dereham and Mannock, the maidservant and her
brother, were all tracked down and closely questioned.
And when the various reports came back, the picture
looked very dark for Catherine.

Henry Mannock, for example, turned out to be a musician who admitted that he 'commonly used to feel the
secrets and other parts of her body.' Francis Dereham
seemed once to have been betrothed to Catherine, and
confessed that he had known her carnally 'many times

both in his doublet and hose and in naked bed.' He also named three young ladies who had joined with them in the bedroom athletics. And he said that Thomas Culpepper, Catherine's own cousin, was another of her lovers.

Henry VIII – bold scourge of the pope and the monasteries – wept like a baby when he heard the news. For some time he was so overcome with emotion that words failed him entirely. He loved his English rose and still refused to credit the stories. But he was like a man trying to cross a muddy field in gumboots. With every step he took, the mire went on loading his feet.

As investigations proceeded, it became clear that practically the whole household of the Duchess of Norfolk had conspired to keep up a pretence of Catherine's chastity. Lady Jane Rochford (the spiteful wife of Anne Boleyn's executed brother) was reported to have encouraged Catherine's youthful frolics. She too was arrested and questioned – and was to go to the block in due course.

Bitterly galling all this must have been to the deceived monarch. But so far, the allegations all concerned Catherine's behaviour before the marriage. There was worse – much worse to come. Henry discovered that after the wedding, Catherine had appointed the lusty Dereham to a post in her royal household. He had been writing some of the Queen's letters for her – they had been alone together in her bedchamber without the presence of servants or other members of the household.

Adulteress! The spell of the king's disbelief was broken and he had Catherine formally arrested. When questioned, she persisted in her denials until confronted with the haul of confession from miscellaneous lovers and servants. Faced with their frank statements, she broke down and admitted her youthful unchastity to the Archbishop. She still maintained, however, that she had been faithful as a wife.

The queen's confession was enough to seal the fates of the leading men in the case. Culpepper, a man of noble birth, was beheaded. Dereham and Mannock, both lowlier paramours, were hanged and quartered. Assorted members of the Howard family and household were arrested on the charge of misprision of treason – that is to say, concealing their knowledge of an intention to deceive the king.

Poor, wretched Catherine was now charged with adultery. But still the anguished king and his distressed councillors were reluctant to act decisively. The Lord Chancellor, for example, asked the Lords for a delay in the trial proceedings. The queen, he said, must be given a chance to clear herself of the charge. The Lords willingly agreed to the proposal. But within a couple of days, the king's own Privy Councillors pressed for a speedy resolution. They did, however, add a clause which speaks volumes for Henry's miserable state of mind. The king, they declared, need not actually attend Parliament as it assessed the evidence; he need only sign the documents when judgement was passed. This unusual arrangement was suggested because the 'sorrowful story and wicked facts if repeated before him might renew his grief and endanger His Majesty's health.'

Henry agreed to the proposal, which must have been a great relief to the Lords. They would now be able to speak their minds freely without their impetuous sovereign glowering at them from behind his beard. As in the case of Anne Boleyn, the trial records were subsequently destroyed. But it appears that Catherine did confess to 'the great crime she had been guilty of against the most high God and a kind Prince and against the whole English nation.' She asked no mercy for herself, but only for the friends and relations who had been implicated with her.

Catherine Howard was beheaded on Tower Hill on 13 February 1542. We do not know how she faced her end.

But we do know that the king took no more frisky nymphs to the altar. The following year he married the patient and motherly Catherine Parr – his 6th wife – who subsequently managed to outlive him.

The Headless Wife Case

It had all the ingredients of a Gothic horror story. They included the decomposing body of the beautiful wife – kisses delivered by her husband to the corpse – the severed head saved in remembrance. The story should have been set in some dark and sinister castle. But it wasn't. The drama unfolded in tranquil West Wycombe; it was a crime for the 1980s.

Michael Telling, 34, was a member of the vastly rich Vestey family behind the Dewhurst butchers' chain. His second cousin was Lord Vestey, multi-millionaire and polo-playing friend of royalty. In terms of material advantage, Telling enjoyed immense privileges. Being a beneficiary of the Vestey Trust, he received £1,200 a month pocket money – all his bills and credit card accounts were paid on top of that.

He could afford all the expensive toys he desired: fast cars, motorcycles, guns and stereo equipment. The Vestey millions paid for holidays all around the world. But they could not pay for the one thing that Telling needed. Money never did buy love.

He had had a miserable childhood. His father was an aggressive alcoholic who chased his pregnant mother brandishing swords. The mother herself was to testify that she had rejected her son. At an early age, Michael was packed off to boarding school, where he was bullied mercilessly. When he reacted by stealing, starting fires and playing truant, he was beaten by the staff.

He became a problem child: emotionally disturbed and

barely controllable in his actions. Twice expelled, he eventually went to a special school for maladjusted children, as well as becoming an inmate at a mental hospital. At home he was kept away from the family and raised by nannies and governesses. When only nine years old he was drinking sherry and smoking heavily. He kept carving knives in his room and once threatened his mother with a blade.

It was from this wrecked childhood that he entered adult life. In 1978, Michael Telling married his first wife, 18-year-old Alison, whom he had first met in Australia. The couple had a son, but the relationship was not to last. Telling was a 'coward who was unable to face his responsibilities,' she was to say. In 1980 he went to America to buy his latest toy, a Harley-Davidson motorcycle. While trying out his new machine at Sausalito near San Francisco, he pulled up at some traffic lights and fell into a conversation with a Mr and Mrs Zumsteg. They suggested that he meet their daughter, Monika.

Within three days of the encounter, he was sleeping with Monika. And shortly after his return to England, he informed his wife that he had found another woman. In 1981, a divorce was arranged. Less than a month later, Michael Telling married Monika Zumsteg.

Much was said at the trial about his bride. Monika was headlined in one paper as a 'SEX MAD GOLD-DIGGER', and she certainly lived her life in the fast lane. Monika drove a Pontiac Firebird and drank Benedictine and orange for breakfast. She used cocaine, heroin and marijuana. In her handbag she carried a gun and a vibrator.

The couple lived at opulent Lambourn House, West Wycombe in Buckinghamshire. Luxury items included a whirlpool bath on the lawn where Monika would frolic with naked party guests. Her husband used to sit on the sidelines, drinking. She said he was only good for money. On frequent occasions, she publicly belittled his sexual efforts, boasting to him of her own lovers, male and female.

When the marriage came to its gruesome end, neighbours were to confirm the stories. Richard Richardson, for example, was an odd-job man and a friend of the Tellings. He said that Monika told him she had no intention of making a life with her husband and that 'all she wanted was his money.' Once, she told Richardson that, 'I could f... any man, any woman better than any man can. I am AC/DC. Man or woman – I go with anybody.' She seemed to take a vindictive pleasure out of humiliating her husband. Richardson had been present on one occasion when Monika had ordered Telling to make coffee, shouting, 'Get off your f...arse, you mother-f... Make the coffee!' Telling begged her not to talk like that and affectionately ran kisses up her arm. On another occasion, the couple had a play fight in the kitchen. Monika took the opportunity to knee Telling in the groin. 'He went white, but said nothing.'

'He worshipped the ground she walked on,' said Richardson, 'but she showed no affection. She said she would only stay with him for two years to get money out of him.' Telling had to visit his son secretly because Monika disapproved, saying that the boy was horrible and she hated him.

Telling's first wife, Alison, told much the same story. Once, Monika had visited her home, bringing a bottle of gin and a cockatoo. She smoked cannabis, drank Drambuie and took four or five pills. She complained to Alison that Michael was no good in bed, saying she did not want a divorce until she'd got some of his money. Monika said that she was prepared to get herself pregnant and go back to America with the baby to get the cash.

Telling himself was to refer to countless humiliations. Once, he had seen her frolicking half naked with another woman on the living-room floor. Yet on their honeymoon night at the Hyde Park Hotel in London, she refused to have sex with her husband. In fact, she banned sex entirely with Telling for the last seven months of her life.

Monika was doomed to become the Headless Wife. She never got a chance to defend herself against these allegations in court. But her father was to claim that the stories were outrageous: 'She was certainly not a saint, but she was nothing like she was painted. She was too flippant sometimes, like when she told a neighbour she was AC/DC. It's the kind of things she would say for a laugh. Monika was a woman of great intelligence, kind and full of sensitivity.'

Whatever the truth, the relationship seems to have been founded on a disastrously flawed combination of personalities. She certainly liked fast living – he certainly needed love. And successive episodes illustrate how the marriage was heading for calamity. in 1982, Monika took up an Alcoholics Anonymous programme. Telling, meanwhile, underwent treatment in a psychiatric hospital. He was to claim that Monika tried to run him down with a car and attacked him with a whip. But he also admitted that he sometimes retaliated, and had attacked her on four occasions during their 17-month marriage.

The terrible climax came on 29 March 1983. By Telling's account, she was delivering a tirade in the living room, shouting that he ought to be sent to a mental hospital. The taunts finally shattered his eggshell personality. 'She came charging towards me. I thought she was going to attack me so I picked up the rifle and shot her.'

The weapon in question was a Marlin 30-30 hunting gun, and he shot her three times. She was hit in the throat and the chest. 'I kissed her then and said I was sorry. But I knew she was dead.'

If the case had ended there it would have been sensational enough. What happened next turned it into an almost unbelievable horror story. Telling left the body for two days where it was before carrying it into a bedroom: 'I went to look at her every day and kissed her often.' He also talked to the corpse as it lay on a camp bed.

214

Eventually, he dragged the body to a summer house, a building half-converted into a sauna. And there it remained for five months.

Telling told his friends that Monika had left him to return to her native America. As 'protection' for himself, he installed an elaborate security system at his home, and even employed private detectives to find his wife.

During this period, as Monika's body lay decomposing at Lambourn House, Telling started to see a former friend called Mrs. Lynda Blackstock. She spent three or four nights at his home, and he tried to woo her in his bedroom. But he could not make love successfully. 'He told me all about Monika', she was to say. 'He told me she was an alcoholic, a drug addict and a lesbian. Michael said she had gone back home to the U.S. – and he was glad.' At the trial, she was asked:

'There was not a hint that Monika lay dead in the very building you were visiting?'

Mrs Blackstock: 'Definitely not.'

Another recent girl friend, divorcee Mrs Susan Bright, also went to bed with Telling after he had killed his wife. She slept with him several times and the couple went out for meals together. She said: 'He was very talkative, although he seemed very nervous ... I asked him if he had heard from Monika at all and he said he thought she was in America.'

In September 1983, Telling hired a van and drove to Devon with the body. On Telegraph Hill outside Exeter he cut off Monika's head with an axe. He dumped the headless body there but could not bear to part with the head itself. Instead, he brought it home and hid it in the locked boot of his Mini in the garage. It was kept there wrapped in plastic.

Two days later, a Devon man stumbled on the headless body. Though badly decomposed by now, it still wore a distinctive Moroccan T-shirt. And although it had been decapitated, a chunk of hair and a few teeth were found at the site.

'The gruesome discovery made the national news, and Mrs Richardson's interest was alerted. She knew that Monika had a similar T-shirt, and was nonplussed when Telling confessed to her that he had killed his wife: 'She is in the sauna – it's stinking.'

Although Mrs Richardson did not believe him, she did eventually inform the police. At this stage, Monika was just one among many missing young women who vaguely fitted the description pieced together from the remains. But dental tests on the few teeth found revealed that the victim had suffered from a disorder of the gums. Monika, had recently undergone an operation for a gum infection.

Devon detectives went to the West Wycombe house and found the dead woman's skull in the Mini. Exactly a week after the body was discovered, Michael Telling was arrested.

He confessed the killing to the police. Asked why he had shot her he replied, 'There were 101 reason. I can't really explain. She kept pushing me. I just snapped in the end. She was horrible in many ways.'

Horrible in many ways – the phrase might serve as an epitaph on the whole case. Asked why he had cut off her head, Telling replied, 'I did not want her identified because of my family. Even when she died I wanted her to be with me.'

The case was tried at Exeter Crown Court in June 1984. He pleaded not guilty to murder, but guilty to manslaughter by reason diminished responsibility.

The press, of course, had a field day. 'MISTRESSES TELL OF SEX IN THE HOUSE OF HORROR' – 'SEX SESSIONS AS BODY LAY NEARBY', blared the headlines. The public learned that Telling had taken Mrs Bright out to a Chinese meal in High Wycombe just 24 hours after he had chopped off his wife's head.

If the press dwelled on the bizarre, macabre details, the courtroom wrangling revolved around Telling's state of mind. No-one denied that the defendant had killed his wife; he himself furnished most of the details. The question in dispute was whether he was responsible for his actions.

The prosecution pressed for a verdict of murder. It dwelt on the 'amazing catalogue' of gruesome lengths to which Telling went to avoid detection. He had told a psychiatrist that the seed of the crime was planted four days before the event. On the evening before the killing, the time and method were, allegedly, decided. 'Despite his mental abnormality, this man determined to kill his wife. He could have prevented himself from doing so if he wished.'

Afterwards, to conceal the crime, he used his wife's Cashpoint card until the account was almost depleted, so giving the impression that she was still alive. He hired the private detectives. He made an 'elaborate pretence' of going on a camping trip when he travelled to Devon to dump the body. As for the head, the prosecution alleged, he did not take it home for remembrance – but to avoid identification of the corpse.

Set against all this apparent cunning was the testimony of psychiatrists, friends and relations. The defence stressed the defendant's maimed and disordered personality. Telling's grey-haired mother appeared in the witness box and described how as a boy he had witnessed violent arguments between herself and his alcoholic father. She hold how he would run naked into the road in front of traffic; how he twice attempted suicide. She acknowledged that her son was a boy deprived of affection: 'Many of Michael's problems stem from his very lonely and unhappy childhood.'

Telling wept in the dock as his mother gave evidence, and he delayed the hearing by 15 minutes after passing a note to his lawyers asking for an adjournment. The note was strangely worded and misspelt: 'You get Mum away from this awful trial, or I will get up and let the bloody prosecutor hear what I think off.'

He was visibly moved too when a former school companion entered the box 'out of a sense of guilt' after reading newspaper reports. The man, Bertram Lilley, described the vicious bullying that Telling had endured: before the boys would let him join in a game they made him roll in a patch of stinging nettles until he resembled 'one large blister'. Even then he could not play because he was too badly hurt.

Lilley's parents had lived in Africa at the time and he once spent a half-term at the Tellings. There was more love, he said, across the many miles to Africa 'than across the living room of that house.'

Telling was close to tears as the testimony was given. otherwise he remained an enigma: slightly balding, dressed in Saville Row pinstripes and paying rapt attention to the trial. A psychiatrist described how Monika's sexual taunts and her ban on lovemaking would have been humiliating and distressing even to a normal man. But Telling was not normal; he did not know how to cope. His responsibility was 'substantially impaired' at the time of the killing.

The judge in summing up reminded the court that psychiatry is not an exact science. Ultimately, the jurors were as fit as anyone else to assess whether Telling was responsible for his actions. Yet they seem to have agreed with the psychiatrist. For after 2½ hours deliberation, the jury found the defendant not guilty of murder but guilty of manslaughter on the grounds of diminished responsibility.

Gaoled for life, Michael Telling was to remain in custody until those responsible felt it 'safe and proper' to release him.

Edgar the Peaceful

'The reign of Edgar was somewhat uneventful,' muses the *Encylopaedia Britannica*. King of a united England (959-975), this Anglo Saxon monarch was noted mainly for his church reforms and known as 'Edgar the Peaceful' in consequence.

Yet his personal life did not lack excitements. Aged 17, the king sired a child by a nun at the convent of Wilton; she refused to marry him. Then Edgar took his first wife, and not long afterwards hearing glowing reports about a beautiful Lady Elfrida, daughter of Devonshire's Earl Ordgar. To find out if the stories were true he sent his servant Athelwold to look her over as a prospective second wife. Athelwold went and found that Elfrida was all that had been rumoured. He fell in love with her and, instead of reassuring his monarch, sent a dispatch that the girl was stupid and ugly and he married her himself.

Athelwood took his new bride to his estate in Hampshire, and dared not present her at court. The king wondered why she never made her appearance, and so did Elfrida herself. Then came fateful day when the king came to hunt in nearby forests. He send word that he would spend the night at Athelwold's estate.

The courtier was in a quandary. He could not refuse his sovereign, and so ordered his wife to dress 'in fowle garments, and some evail favoured attire' so that her beauty would be hidden. Elfrida, however, refused to comply and decked herself out in all her finery. When the king saw her he was smitten with her loveliness. He took her husband hunting with him in a wood, 'not showing that he meant any hurt, till a length he had got him within the thick of the wood, where he suddenly stroke him through with his dart.'

219

Having murdered the deceitful courtier, Edgar the Peaceful married Elfrida. She bore him two sons (one of whom was Ethelred the Unready) and the couple presided together over the remainder of his tranquil reign.

Bunkum With a Capital B

The most infamous doctors in the annals of crime were generally cunning poisoners. Dr Ruxton's case was different. It is true that he used his medical knowledge to a gruesome degree in trying to cover up his atrocity. But all the facts indicate that the murder itself was an impulse killing accomplished in a state of high emotion. No science or stealth contributed to the initial act – his was a crime of passion.

He was born in Bombay as Bukhtyar Rustamji Ratanji Hakin and qualified in his native country. Moving to England, he was made a Bachelor of Medicine in London. After further studies at Edinburgh he took up a practice in Lancaster in 1930. It was at about that time that he changed his name by deed poll to that of Dr Buck Ruxton.

With him to London came Isabella Van Ess, a married woman from Edinburgh, Her husband divorced her when she followed the doctor down. And although Isabella never married Dr Ruxton she lived with him as his wife. She also bore him three children, and was known to everyone simply Mrs Ruxton.

They lived with the children at No. 2 Dalton Square, Lancaster. The doctor was highly regarded in his profession and well liked by all of his patients. This was despite the fact that the doctor and his 'wife' had an intensely emotional relationship. The couple quarrelled incessantly and often came to blows. But they always made up afterwards. At the trial, patients were to remember how Mrs Ruxton would rush into her husband's surgery and urgently embrace him to achieve a reconciliation.

The rows, though, were more than mere tiffs. Ruxton commonly threatened his wife and once held a knife to her throat. On two separate occasions the police were called in, but Mrs Ruxton never pressed charges. On the whole, she seems to have given as good as she hot. 'We were the kind of people who could not live without each other', the doctor was to admit.

Once, Mrs Ruxton attempted suicide to try and escape from the bonds that tied them together. And in 1934 she fled to her sister in Edinburgh intending a final breach. Ruxton, however, followed her and persuaded her to come back to him and to their children.

The root of the problem appears to have been Ruxton's obsessive jealousy. Constantly he accused his wife of infidelity, complaining on one occasion that she behaved like a common prostitute. His morbid suspicious were entirely without foundation, but jealousy feeds on chance happening and trifling coincidence. Things came to a head in autumn 1935, when Ruxton persuaded himself that she was having an affair with a young town clerk named Robert Edmondson.

On 7 September, the Edmondson family drove up to Edinburgh. Their party included Robert, his sister and parents. And they agreed to take Mrs Ruxton up too for a visit to her native city.

Seething with suspicion, Ruxton abandoned his surgery and followed them in a hired car. He discovered that his wife was staying in the same hotel as the family, rather than with her sister as planned. It was for a perfectly innocent reason, but back in Lancaster, Ruxton was to rant for days at his wife about her supposed liaison.

On 14 September, the following weekend, Mrs Ruxton made another blameless excursion. Taking the doctor's Hillman, she drove to Blackpool as she did once every year to see the illuminations with her sisters. She left the resort at 23.30 that night, intending to go back the next day. But she never did return to Blackpool. In fact, having driven back to Dalton Square in the car, she never went anywhere again. Not in one piece, that is.

It is known that she reached home, because Ruxton was using the Hillman the next day and in the period that followed. It is known too that the doctor was in the house with his three children and the housemaid, Mary Rogerson. The children were all under five; Mary Rogerson was aged 20. But she could give no account of what transpired that night, for Mary Rogerson disappeared with Mrs Ruxton. The next time anyone but the doctor saw the two women they were barely identifiable; no more than dismembered chunks of bone, tissue and skin all wrapped up in bloodsoaked packages.

The story emerged at the trial. It has to be assumed that Ruxton was waiting in a mood of frenzied suspicion. There was yet another row which this time reached its climax in bloody murder. Ruxton killed his wife with a sharp-bladed instrument, and Mary Rogerson no doubt saw everything. She had to die too – and afterwards began the grisly business of destroying the evidence.

From what is known of Ruxton's character, anguish, remorse – and concern for his children – must have been coursing through his veins. But he set to work like a Trojan on the bodies of the two women amid the welter of blood everywhere. Probably he worked all night while the children slept, and still there was much to be done.

One of the family's three charladies, Mrs Oxley, was due to arrive at 07.00 on Sunday morning. At 06.30, as she was preparing to leave her home, Dr Ruxton appeared on her doorstep. It was the astonished Mr Oxley who opened the door, with his wife standing not far behind him. Both heard what Ruxton said quite clearly: 'Tell Mrs Oxley not to trouble to come down this morning. Mrs Ruxton and Mary have gone away on a holiday to Edinburgh and I am taking the children to Morecambe. But tell her to come tomorrow.'

At the trial, Ruxton was to deny that he had ever been to the Oxleys' house.

Returning home, Ruxton made the children's breakfast. He received the Sunday papers and milk, delivery women noting that he seemed to be shielding an injured hand. On a brief excursion in the Hillman he bought a full tank of petrol and two spare gallons besides.

Nursing his wounded hand, Ruxton was busy all Sunday. A woman patient turned up at Dalton Square with a child needing treatment. Rutxon postponed the appointment, saying that he was busy taking up carpets because decorators were due the next morning. At mid-day, he asked a neighbour to look after his children for the afternoon, saying that his wife had gone with Mary to Scotland and that he had cut his hand opening a tin of fruit at breakfast.

That afternoon he toiled undisturbed at the house until it was in a more or less presentable state. Then, at 16.30, he called on a friend and patient, Mrs Hampshire, to ask if she would help him get the house ready for the decorators. It was in a strange condition when she arrived. The carpet on stairs and landing had been taken up, and straw was scattered around. It even bristled out from under the two main bedroom doors – which were locked and remained so all evening.

In one room was a bloodstained suit; in the backyard were bloodstained carpets. Ruxton asked if she would be kind enough to clean the bath. It was filthy, with a grubby yellow stain extending high around the inside of the tub.

At the trial, Ruxton was to claim that the blood marks all derived from the severely gashed wound to his hand. But there was an awful lot of it about and, daunted by the size of the task, Mrs Hampshire asked if she could get her husband to help. Ruxton agreed, and the business of cleaning up went on until 21.30. As a reward for their labours, Ruxton offered the pair the stained suit and carpets, which they took with them when they left.

Presumably, the bodies were in the two locked bedrooms. No doubt the doctor was not idle that night. And he must have had nagging fears about the stained articles he had given the Hampshires, for first thing on Monday morning, he went round their house and ask for the suit back. He stood there, dishevelled and unshaven, explaining that he wanted to send it for cleaning himself. Ruxton then demanded that she take the name-tag from it, claiming that it would be improper for her husband to go around wearing a suit with another man's name in it. She duly cut it off. 'Burn it now', he demanded, and she tossed the tag onto her fire.

Afterwards, she looked at the suit and found the waistcoat so badly stained that she also put that on the flames. As for the carpets, she was to testify: 'The amount of blood on the third carpet was terrible. It was still damp where the blood was, and it had not been out in the rain. I laid the carpet in the backyard and threw about 20 or 30 buckets of water on it to try to wash the blood off, and the colour of the water that came off was like blood. I threw it on the line and left it to dry, and when it was washday I had another go at it with the yard brush and water, and still could not get the congealed blood off.'

In the week that followed, the doctor kept fires going night and day in his own backyard. He called in the decorators. And when the charladies complained of peculiar smells about the house he replied by spraying Eau de Cologne around.

To neighbours, Ruxton gave varied and inconsistent accounts about why Mrs Ruxton and Mary were away. To one he confided, sobbing and agitated, that the pair had gone to London, where his wife had eloped with another man. But Mary's parents, the Rogersons, were not easily convinced. Eventually, Ruxton told them that their daughter had been got pregnant and that this accounted for her going away. Mr Rogerson was undeterred. He threatened to ask the police to find his daughter.

At some stage (probably Thursday 19 September) Ruxton must have driven up to Scotland. For ten days later, exactly two weeks after the women vanished, the first grisly package was discovered.

A woman found it by a bridge near Moffat, off the Carlisle-Edinburgh road. She saw what seemed to be a human arm protruding from a wrapped bundle at the water's edge. Horrified, she called her brother who in turn summoned the police. The constable found four bundles: 'a blouse containing two upper arms and four pieces of flesh; and four pieces of flesh; a pillowslip enclosing two arm bones, two thigh bones, two lower leg bones, and nine pieces of flesh; part of a cotton sheet containing 17 pieces of flesh; and another piece of sheet containing the best portion of a human trunk and the lower portions of two legs.'

More parcels were to turn up in due course. The police determined that pieces from two separate bodies had been removed: some of the teeth, eyes and finger ends (presumably to prevent fingerprint identification). In fact, during the early investigation, the surgical removal of various organs made it impossible to discover the sex of the victims. The police began by announcing that they believed the bodies to be those of a man and a woman.

Reading this news in his daily paper seems to have given Ruxton some rare moments of good humour. In jovial mood, he told one of the charladies, 'So you see, Mrs Oxley, it is a man and a woman, it is not our two.' On another occasion: 'Thank goodness the other one in the Moffat case was a man and not a woman' – or people would be saying that he had murdered his wife and Mary.

But the police had already connected the Moffat bodies

with doctor's home town. One of the bundles had been wrapped in a copy of the *Sunday Graphic* dated 15 September (the murder morning). It happened to be special edition sold only in Morecambe and Lancaster.

On 9 October, the Rogersons reported their daughter a missing person. On that day too, Ruxton asked Mrs Hampshire what she had done about the suit: 'Do something about it', he insisted. 'Get it out of the way. Burn it!' On 14 October, the doctor was taken into custody and questioned at length. In the small hours of the next day he was charged with Mary's murder. Cautioned, he protested, 'Most emphatically not, of course not. The furthest thing from my mind. What motive and why? What are you talking?' Some days later he was also charged with the murder of his wife, and it was on this indictment that he was to stand trial at the Manchester Assizes.

Precisely identifying the two bodies remained problematic for the authorities. The affair was to become something of a textbook case in medico-criminal history. A team of pathologists and anatomists fitted together their grim jigsaw of remains, proving that the age and size of the missing women roughly matched those of Bodies I and II. But key features had been removed. For example, Mrs Ruxton had prominent teeth and these had been withdrawn. Miss Rogerson had a squint – the eyes had been taken from their sockets. Nevertheless, it did prove possible to identify Mary's body by fingerprints. And Mrs Ruxton was identified when a photograph superimposed on Head II matched exactly.

It was proved that the doctor had been delivered the local edition of the *Sunday Graphic* for 15 September. Moreover, the linen sheet in which one bundle was wrapped was the partner of a single sheet left on Mrs Ruxton's bed.

The doctor made a miserable impression in the witness box. He vehemently denied the testimony of his charladies and his neighbours, claiming for example that he never visited the Oxleys; that he never asked Mrs Hampshire to burn the suit. His own account of his movements was deeply implausible and his manner both pitiable and arrogant. Sometimes he sobbed and became hysterical; sometimes he waxed bombastic. Once, taxed with murdering his wife and disposing of the witness, he replied, 'That is absolute bunkum with a capital B'.

A fit verdict on his own hopeless attempts to clear himself. Ruxton was found guilty, and when an appeal failed he was hanged at Strangeways Prison. The date was 12 May 1936. Soon afterwards, his own terse confession was published, a note penned at the time of his arrest:

> I killed Mrs Ruxton in a fit of temper because I
> thought she had been with a man. I was Mad
> at the time. Mary Rogerson was present at the
> time. I had to kill her.

It had been one of those cases that haunt the public imagination, and in the streets and playgrounds the children chanted their own summary in rhyme:

> Red stains on the carpet, red stains on the knife,
> For Doctor Buck Ruxton had murdered his wife.
> The maidservant saw it and threatened to tell,
> So Doctor Buck Ruxton he killed her as well.

Love Lives of the Medici Family

The great Medici family, merchants and bankers of Florence, are remembered both for their political eminence and their lavish patronage of the arts. Their love lives, however, left a very great deal to be desired.

Take Cosimo I, Grand Duke of Tuscany (1519-74). He

cruelly poisoned his faithless wife Eleanor of Toledo after having her lover done to death. It is said that Cosimo later rejoiced in the brutal double murder, boasting openly that 'killing the bull first and the cow after made the sacrifice all the more pleasing.'

Cosimo himself enjoyed the favours of his own daughter, the beautiful and intelligent Isabella. The artist Vasari once witnessed their incest while painting a ceiling at the Palazzo Vecchio. There was a dark moment afterwards when Cosimo suddenly remembered that the painter might be at work, and climbed the scaffolding dagger in hand. But Vasari prudently pretended to be asleep and so escaped assassination.

Isabella was married to the Duke of Bracciano. However, she enjoyed an illicit liaison with Troilus Orsini, one of her husband's bodyguards. When her lover got her pregnant he fled to France, but was tracked down there by Bracciano's men and murdered. Isabella sought protection with her loving father Cosimo, who sheltered both her and her illegitimate child. Bracciano did not dare to take his revenge on his wife immediately. Not long after Cosimo's death, however, Bracciano lured Isabella to his estate at Cerreto. There, on 16 July 1576 he strangled her.

The Worm That Turned

The French have a useful expression to describe a certain sort of husband in a love-triangle quarrel. The term is *mari complaisant* (complaisant husband) and it refers to a man who is perfectly aware of his wife's adultery but meekly acquiesces in it. He is a stock figure of fun in French fiction and folklore, and recurs time and again in real-life cases.

One such was René de Villequier, an eminent nobleman in the court of Henri III. For some 15 years he tolerated the infidelities of his wife Françoise de la Marck. He knew all about the life she was leading, occasionally remonstrated with her, but also harnessed her appetites to serve his own political career.

Attending the court at Poitiers on the morning of 1 September 1577, de Villequier went into his wife's bedroom and after joining her between the sheets, joking and laughing with her, he gave her four to five thrusts with a dagger. He called one of his men to finish her off. Then having stabbed a maidservant for good measure, he had his wife's body placed in a litter which was paraded before the king and his nobles.

Having taken the corpse back to his house for burial, de Villequiet returned and put in an appearance at court. There he triumphed in his avenged honour. He declared that he would gladly have killed her lovers too, but since they formed a small army there might be difficulties.

Henri III records the scandals in his *Journal,* and censures both the killer and his victim. But of course, no action was taken against de Villequiet. They have always been funny like that, the French.

All in the Family

When West German building firm owner Hans Appel married Renate Poeschke, each brought to the household a child by a previous marriage. Then Renate bore Hans a daughter – and the family expanded further when in 1973. Renate's brother Juergen moved in.

Hans made a shattering discovery one night as he was putting the children to bed. One of the infants confided that mummy and uncle Juergen had spent an afternoon in bed together – with no clothes on.

Incest possesses a power to shock as perhaps no other sexual transgression. Hans was appalled, but when he confronted the guilty couple neither replied with a firm denial. Instead, brother and sister quit the household and moved into the Sachsenhausen home of 21-year-old Dieter Poeschke. He was Renate's other brother, a garage mechanic and a married man.

The construction boss was still in love with his wife despite what he now suspected. While giving her presents to try and win her back, he also took to carrying a revolver. But he remained on good terms with Dieter Poeschke. On 7 January 1974, Appel accepted a lift in his brother-in-law's Mercedes which was going from Wiesbaden to Frankfurt.

As the car travelled along the road, Hans Appel unburdened himself of his problems. It seemed incredible, he said, but he suspected that Renate was having an affair with Juergen. Did Dieter believe such a thing?

'Of course,' replied the driver, 'Juergen and I both sleep with Renate all the time.'

Double incest! Appel was to say that something inside him snapped at that point. Witnesses saw the car swerve onto a pavement. Dieter rolled out and as he staggered to his feet, Appel shot him twice with the pistol. Then the outraged husband got out of the Mercedes and disappeared down the street.

It did not take the police long to discover the killer's identity. But the bizarre circumstances of this particular crime of passion provided strong mitigating factors. Tried in July 1974, Appel was sentenced to 21 months imprisonment. In fact, he never served any time at all, for the sentence was set aside on appeal.

As for Renate, she would not return to her husband but went on living with her brother Juergen.

A Crime That Rocked a Kingdom

It was an odd, odd business. The scandal that rocked France in 1847 helped to bring down a dynasty. It involved one of the noblest families in the nation, and no *crime passionnel* in French history has provoked more discussion. There is no question about the identity of the murderer in the Praslin affair, nor of the horrific savagery of the crime. Thick dossiers of letters and statements still survive in the Paris National Archives, along with trunkloads of material evidence: a silken bell pull, bloodstained clothing, bronze candlesticks and a hunting knife among other items. But despite all that has survived and all that has been written, mystery lingers about the case, elusive as the aroma of expensive tobacco and the musk of Old French roses. Underneath, it was an odd, odd business.

The young Théobald de Praslin married Fanny Sébastiani on 19 October 1824. He was only nineteen, she was two years younger, and they were very much in love at the time. The families on both sides being of immense wealth, the wedding was a glittering occasion. The young marquis was heir to the great Praslin dukedom, and his bride was an honorary goddaughter of Napoleon. Big interests blessed the marriage, which began rich in promise as an idyll of domestic happiness.

She bore him children – nine of them is less than fifteen years – perhaps too many in the light of what was to come. For under the strain of successive pregnancies and births, the Marquise lost her radiant looks. Her dark, romantic features – inherited from Corsican blood – thickened and became swart. She grew corpulent, And her temperament, once agreeably capricious, soured into a volatile and domineering nature.

Her husband, in contrast, was a passive, introverted

231

man little given to displays of emotion. The more she nagged, ranted and threw tantrums the more he retreated into a shell of cold reserve. Fanny continued to love Théobald in her tempestuous fashion; but on his part, love turned slowly into detestation.

Before 1839, when their last child was born, the decline in their relationship had begun. Already he had taken to shunning her bedroom, and she was writing him letters of complaint. They were eloquent letters which sprang directly from the heart, but the themes were monotonously reiterated: she regretted her fits of temper, tried to patch up the latest quarrel, craved his pity for her uncontrollable emotions. 'I am no longer the mistress of my feeling', she wrote at one point. 'Something over which I have no control takes possession of me.'

The Marquis merely became more disdainful. And in 1840, things took a terrible turn for the worse when he required her to sign an extraordinary document. By the terms of this private agreement, Madame de Praslin was to give up her natural rights as a mother. The family's governess was to have sole charge of all that concerned the children: clothes, schooling, recreation and so on. Madame de Praslin was not even permitted to see them unless in the company of the governess.

It was, by any standards, an appalling document for a mother to sign, and historians have long puzzled over its implications. Madame de Praslin wrote privately about it, claiming that she had sacrificed all to try and regain her husband's affection. But there are hints that some specific incident or discovery lay behind her renunciation. Was it some violent outburst which had frightened the children and led her husband to think them unsafe in her presence? Or was it something darker than that?

A charge of somehow 'corrupting' the children seems to have been laid against Madame de Praslin. It is known that her own governess at one time had been a certain

Mademoiselle Mendelssohn, suspected of lesbian relations with her pupils. Did the Marquis suspect his wife of the same proclivities? Had she interfered with her own children?

It is just one of the affair's lingering mysteries. The contract, the shunned bedroom – all this was in private. In public, the couple continued to appear amid the plush and chandeliers of the Court, to receive guests and dispense their hospitality. In June 1841, Théobald's father died and he became the fifth Duc de Choiseul-Praslin, inheriting not only some nine million francs but the magnificent château of Vaux-le-Vicomte.

This superb building survives as one of the great splendours of French Baroque style. With its domes and towers, fountains and tree-lined avenues, it was to provide the grandest backdrop imaginable for the drama which was to unfold.

To Vaux, with the new Duke and Duchess, came a new governess only recently hired. The orphaned and illegitimate daughter of a Bonapartist soldier, she had dragged herself out of a miserable childhood to serve with a noble English family. Fair-haired, green-eyed and socially accomplished, she came to the Praslins with the best possible credentials. In due course, the whole of France was to become fascinated by the Mademoiselle: her name was Henriette Deluzy.

Partisans of the Duchess were to paint her as a scheming adventuress who brought shame to a noble household. Others saw her as a decent girl placed in an intolerable position. History's verdict must draw a little from each portrait. Henriette Deluzy did not create the unhappy marriage – it was in a disastrous state when she arrived. Nor (this seems quite clear) did she and the Duke ever become lovers in the carnal sense. But the pretty young governess was both intelligent and ambitious. Coming from her own insecure background, the splendours of Vaux, the Praslin millions, all the ranks and privileges which went with them – these lures combined with the manifest unhappiness of the Duke must surely have excited her thoughts. After all, even decent girls may dream a little . . .

Praslin told her at the outset about the contract he had made with his wife. Though it struck her as strange, it also gave her unique powers in the household. Mademoiselle Deluzy accepted the position and was soon supervising all that concerned the children. Two of the daughters, Berthe and Louise, came quickly to adore her. The young instructress was bright, vivacious and thoroughly sane – in marked contrast to their unbalanced, faintly terrifying mother.

It was not long before the Duke, too, came to seek refuge from the chill of his marriage in the governess's warm little circle. He loved his children and he loved to see them happy. Temperamentally indolent as well as reticent, the Duke spent more and more time in their company.

The Duchess, of course, was reduced to paroxysms of rage. Mademoiselle Deluzy quickly became 'that woman', and night after night in her lonely bedchamber the Duchess wrote long impassioned letters to her husband. The governess, she fumed, was 'bold, familiar, dominating, thoughtless, inquisitive, gossipy, insolent and greedy.' She had split the family, and set daughters against their mother. One accusation repeatedly made is of especial significance in the light of what was to come. The Duchess claimed that the scheming governess was deliberately *making it appear* as if she was her husband's mistress. The Duchess, however, never at any stage seems to have suspected that her rival was actually sharing his bed.

Everybody else, though, came to believe that she was. Within a year or so of Mlle Deluzy's arrival the rumours were beginning to spread. In a Paris society that drank gossip like fine wine, the scandal began to ferment. In the summer of 1844 the Duchess publicly threatened suicide, creating such an embarrassing scene that the Duke decided that a break was called for. He took three of his daughters, with their governess, off on a long Mediterranean holiday. The Duchess remained at Vaux. And for the first time in print, there appeared in a Paris gossip column, a snippet concerning the Praslin ménage. The Duke, it was said, had gone off for a vacation with his mistress.

This delicious little item did not go unnoticed. The story circulated not only around the Paris boulevards, but reached the courts of Europe as well. Mademoiselle Deluzy would have to leave the household now, all the well-informed tattlers said. But she did not. To do so would only give credence to the rumours, and the Duke determined to remain aloof from such malicious gossip.

Shamed beyond endurance, the humiliated Duchess took to eating all her meals in the solitude of her bedchamber. She refused any contact with the governess and penned ever more eloquently hysterical letters to her husband.

The whole miserable business dragged on. In 1846, an unaccountable reconciliation appeared to occur, when the Duchess suddenly started making herself agreeable to the governess. It can only be explained as a change of tactics, though, for Madame de Praslin still fulminated in her letters to her husband about the 'little pair of green eyes behind your shoulder.' In reality, the mortified mother was maturing a plan for revenge.

She struck in June 1847. In that month, the Duke was suddenly but formally informed by his father-in-law that if the governess did not leave the household for good, his wife would sue for divorce and claim sole custody of the children.

The threat had terrible implications. The Duke himself clearly believed (for whatever reason) that his children were unsafe with their mother. Not only would he lose them to her, but the furore of the divorce would seriously affect his daughters' marriage prospects. The scandal would be immense, and what right-minded noble family would take on girls from his adulterous ménage? He could not doubt that Madame de Praslin would win her case – the scandal-mongering press had seen to that.

Now the governess really did have to go. After fierce but hopeless argument with his father-in-law, the Duke regretfully informed Mlle Deluzy that she should quit the household, with a generous life pension and a good reference for future employment.

She took it badly. Whatever private fancies she may have entertained about her future at Vaux, she certainly loved her charges; for six years the Praslin girls had comprised the only family she had ever known. That night she wept uncontrollably and swallowed laudanum in quantities that nearly took her life. But the next day she recovered, and in time she capitulated. She signed the annuity agreement.

And so the whole affair might have ended, but for the dark passions which the episode had engendered. The girls, for example, were unspeakably distressed by their separation from their beloved Mademoiselle. The Duke, meanwhile, was reduced to cold fury, a refrigerated rage which chilled even the triumphant Duchess. In a private memoir she wrote: 'He will never forgive me for what I have done . . . Every day the abyss between us will grow deeper. The more he thinks about what he has done, the more he will hate me and the more he will wreak vengeance on me. The future appalls me. I tremble when I think of it . . .'

There was not much of a future left, as it transpired, for either the Duke or the Duchess.

The discharged governess sought lodgings in Paris. But wherever she was accepted she would immediately find herself thrown back out onto the street. A certain Abbé Gallard was going the rounds, warning the owners off.

Mlle Deluzy, said the cleric, was an immoral woman soon to be named in a divorce court. Also, he implied that she was pregnant. The Abbé Gallard was the Duchess's confessor.

Eventually, the embattled governess found a small room at the Pensionnat Lemaire, a school for young women in one of the seedier quarters of Paris. She was desperately unhappy and wrote pitiful letters to the Praslin girls imploring them not to forget her. They answered with equal *tendresse:* they had had terrible scenes with their mother, they wrote. Also: 'You are our real mother.'

On 26 July, Mlle Deluzy briefly met two of the Praslin children with their father in Paris. His face at that time seemed to have crumpled. And during the brief meeting he told the ex-governess something about the Duchess that quite appalled her.

We do not know what that something was.

It is another of the lingering mysteries. Among all the documents preserved in the National Archives, references to the dark secret seem to have been excised. From allusions that have survived it is known to have involved *'horrors'*, 'secret carryings-on' and the Duchess's 'corruption of her sons'. Horace, the ten-year-old boy, had 'confessed infamies' to his father.

Some have interpreted these elusive references in the most literal way, suggesting that the Duchess had seduced at least one of her young sons. A more probable solution is proposed by Stanley Loomis in his authoritative study of the case, *A Crime of Passion* (1967). We know that after the governess had gone, the Duchess continued to threaten the divorce unless Mlle Deluzy actually left the country. That was what lay behind the persecutions of the Abbé Gallard. And it is possible that the Duchess had persuaded one or more of the boys to speak out against his father and the governess. He might even lie, pretending, for example, to have witnessed the couple in bed. Pure speculation, of course. What we do know is that the cold, reserved and rather weak-spirited Duke now plotted the murder of his wife.

All the pent up rage inside him found expression in his plan of revenge. At the great Paris residence, the Hôtel Sébastiani, he began in the most comically inept way by removing the screws from his wife's bedposts. His idea was that the vast and weighty canopy above would collapse to crush or suffocate her. There is no doubt that he entertained his bizarre project, culled from the romantic fiction of the day. After the affair had reached its bloody climax, it was found that ceiling wax had been stuffed as camouflage into the holes where the screws had been.

Nor was this the Duke's sole preparation. At the Hôtel Sébastiani, he also used his trusty screwdriver to remove the bolt by which his wife could lock her door from his own connecting suite. If the canopy failed to kill the Duchess, he would then be guaranteed of access to finish the job. His plans made, the Duke gave orders that absolutely nobody should enter the Hôtel apartments until the next visit of his family to Paris.

That visit came on 17 August. While Madame de Praslin went straight to the Hôtel Sébastiani, the Duke and four of his children repaired first to the Pensionnat Lemaire for a tearful reunion with the discharged governess. During the brief call, the Duke promised that he would try and get letters of reference from the Duchess for Mademoiselle Deluzy.

Once back at the Hotel, father and children retired to their various quarters. The lights were out by 23.30; all looked set for a peaceful night. It was at about 04.30 that a succession of blood-curdling, barely human shrieks ripped the dawn air over Paris.

The Duke, having perhaps waited hours for the canopy to collapse, had resorted to a furtive assault. He crept stealthily into his wife's bedroom, carrying with him a pistol and hunting knife. Bruises found on the corpse the following morning indicate that he clamped one hand firmly over her mouth as with the other he tried to cut her throat. But he only half-succeeded. With blood spurting from a gashed artery, Madame de Praslin woke and grabbed the double-edged blade, cutting her hand in the process. A big, strong woman, she managed to break free, to scream and to tug at the bell rope. A horrific fight and chase ensued, the Duchess staggering like a wounded animal around the room, steadying herself against the walls with her bleeding hand, frantic to escape her maniacal husband. Chairs and tables were knocked over; the bell rope was torn from its mounting. Later that morning, the copious bloodprints all around enabled the police to map the whole struggle with fine precision. It was on the sofa before the fireplace that the fifth Duke of Choiseul-Praslin finally cornered his wife. There, using a weighty brass candlestick taken from the mantlepiece, he clubbed her to the ground.

From the moment that the first terrible yelp had filled the Hôtel, servants had been trying to break into the suite. But all the doors were locked. Eventually, it was the Duke himself who admitted the staff. 'What has happened?' he asked them, feigning ignorance. The Duchess died moments later, and though the Duke tried to brazen it out by claiming that an intruder must have been responsible, his guilt was quickly established. When the head of the Sûreté Nationale first examined the appalling scene he remarked: 'This is not the work of a professional. It is the work of a gentleman.'

The Duke had had time to try and destroy the evidence, but in no satisfactory way. Smoke was seen pouring from the fireplace in his own bedroom, where he had burned bits of bloodstained clothing as well as quantity of papers. The *robe de chambre* he was wearing was found to be damp with water applied to the red bloodmarks on the material. His hands were scratched and bitten, and the hunting knife was found concealed in his apartment.

Paris was in uproar. A crowd gathered immediately around the Hôtel, and called for the death of the murderer. For the indignant citizenry, the crime came to embody all the moral corruption with which the régime was tainted. The constitutional monarchy of Louis-Philippe was already reeling from a financial scandal in which two government ministers had been implicated. The next year the king was to be overthrown by revolution; and historians have identified the Praslin murder as being a key event which helped to trigger the insurrection.

In the public mind the issue was clear: the Duke had murdered his wife for love of an English-trained governess. In reality, there was no likelihood that this would happen. The Duke was brought to trial before a Court of Peers who fully recognised the need to appease the public. In fact, the peers' greatest worry was that the Duke might commit suicide before sentence could be passed. 'What a mess!' the king was heard to exclaim as he signed the order summoning the court to convene. For the government, Count Molé wrote to a colleague: 'Impress upon the Chancellor Pasquier (head of the court) that it will be a public misfortune if this monster escapes by a voluntary death the fate which the law has reserved for him.'

In the event, however, the Duke did deprive the court of the satisfaction of dispensing its justice. While under close guard, he managed to swallow a dose of arsenic. It took him six days to die of the poison – six days of atrocious agony. He remained tight-lipped to the end, answering only evasively the questions put to him, and refusing to confess his guilt.

All the weight of public interest now fell on Mademoiselle Deluzy. She was kept in confinement for three months after the murder and subjected to the most exhaustive questioning. Had she been the Duke's mistress? Had she encouraged the crime? Throughout her ordeal, the ex-governess remained adamant in her denials. In the end she was released a free woman, but with an official proclamation hanging over her. The document acknowledged that there was no evidence to connect her with the crime. It did, however, charge her with having had a 'culpable liaison' with the Duke.

A now notorious woman, Mademoiselle Deluzy left France in 1849 to make a new life in America. Wearied by her trials but unbroken in spirit, she there married a young Presbyterian minister named Henry Field. The couple became leading lights in New York's church community, and though her past was known it was not held against her. Mrs Field died in 1875 at the age of 63. The obituaries barely mentioned the Praslin affair, but fêted her for her generous hospitality, her good works and her shining intellect. Before she died she had even written about France for her husband's religious periodical, *The Evangelist*. In her articles Mrs Field expressed her conviction that, whatever political upheavals might rock the country of her birth, one quality would guarantee the survival and well-being of France.

That quality was the strength which the nation derived from its happy family life.

The Chalkpit Conspiracy

At dusk on 30 November 1946, a man walking the North Downs near Woldingham in Surrey saw what looked like a heap of old clothes lying in a secluded chalkpit. Curiosity prompted him to look closer; and he found that the clothes were inhabited. Lying rigid in the trench was the body of a young man, trussed by a rope around his neck. a dirty piece of green cloth was entangled in the noose; the dead man's face was purple. When the experts first examined the body, it looked very much like a case of suicide. Yet there was no tree from which he might have suspended himself. And, though his clothes were smeared with chalk and mud, his shoes were spotlessly clean. Maybe the body had been carried there for disposal.

In the victim's pocket was an old wartime identity card which declared him to be John McMain Mudie, 35. Recently demobbed, he was found to have been working as a barman at the Reigate Hill Hotel some 12 miles from the chalkpit. A handsome young man, well liked by all who knew him, Mudie was nobody's idea of a killer or a killer's victim. He was too plainly decent to be mixed up in murder.

Painstaking detective work led the police to uncover a conspiracy hatched in London. Three men in particular were implicated. One was Lawrence John Smith, a joiner; the second, John William Buckingham, who ran a care hire business. And the third was very much more august figure: he was Thomas John Ley, 66, colosally fat, and a former Minister of Justice in New Zealand. He had been a noted spokesman there for Prohibition, and was known as 'Lemonade Ley' in consequence.

Evidence against them included statements from two gardeners who had seen a man loitering suspiciously at the chalkpit on the day before Mudie disappeared. The man had driven away in a car whose registration plate bore the number 101. Smith had, it transpired, hired a Ford Eight, FGP 101, for three days over the murder period.

Then there was the rag found entangled in the noose. It had been torn from a French polisher's cloth found at 5 Beaufort Gardens, Kensington, where Thomas Ley lived. A pickaxe, moreover, was found at the chalkpit where it seemed to have been used in partially filling in the trench. This too was traced back to 5 Beaufort Gardens; it had served there for mixing concrete.

Significant evidence, all of it – but it needed something stronger to support it. That came on 14 December, when Buckingham turned King's Evidence.

The story that unfolded was one in which hot-blooded jealousy and cold calculation had conspired to produce a quite senseless killing. The ex-justice minister had, it appeared, long been involved in an affair with a widow from Perth named Mrs Maggie Brook. They had come to London in 1930 and pursued their liaison quite openly. At one time it had been a sexual relationship, but Ley had been impotent for a decade. His love had endured beyond his capacity, however. The couple saw each other as regularly as ever.

Mrs Brook, 66 emerged at the trial as a kindly and sweet-nature lady – no storybook scarlet woman. Ley, in contrast, was a blusterer and a bully consumed by quite irrational jealousy. He had accused his partner of having affairs with three separate young men at the Wimbledon house where she lodged. And one of these was the blameless Jack Mudie.

Mudie had not exchanged more than a dozen words with Mrs Brook; their contact extended to no more than chance greetings on the stairs or in the lobby. Perhaps the ex-justice minister had observed some such exchange. In all events, his suspicious were aroused.

Jealousy worked on Thomas Ley, spreading like infection until it inflamed his whole being. By late November in 1946, Ley was toxic with it.

He contacted Smith, the joiner, who had helped convert his Beaufort Gardens house into flats. Buckingham was introduced to him as a man who could 'keep his mouth shut' . Ley told the pair that he wanted to kidnap a black-mailer who was persecuting a lady of his acquaintance. The man should be brought back to his house, tied up and forced to sign a confession. Smith and Buckingham did not ask too many questions. Ley offered them money –

'more than a year's salary' for each of them.

The plot involved finding a way of getting Mudie peacefully into the house. Buckingham came up with the idea of using a woman. She should turn up at Mudie's bar with a chauffeur and limousine. Complimenting the proposed victim on his bar-tending skills, she would invite him back to her house to help out with a cocktail party of her own. One Lilian Bruce was hired for the role, with Buckingham's son to play chauffeur. Smith and Buckingham senior would follow in a second car, overtaking just before Beaufort Gardens, so that they could prepare a reception committee. Ley himself would be waiting there too – waiting for the delivery of his victim.

All went as planned on the evening of 28 November. Smith and Buckingham got into the house first through the front door. Mudie was ushered in by the back entrance. Mrs Bruce and her chauffeur then immediately disappeared, leaving the barman to his fate.

Nearly 55 years have passed since the Chalkpit Conspiracy was exposed. Yet even today, it is not known precisely what transpired at Beaufort Gardens. Buckingham claimed that once Mudie was tied up, his own role in the affair was over. Ley gave him £200 in one pound notes, and he left straight away with the payment. Smith, though, stayed some ten minutes longer . . . and it was Smith who, with Thomas Ley, was charged with murder at the Old Bailey.

Both denied the murder charge. Smith's statement roughly agreed with Buckingham's; he said that he too had left with Mudie trussed but fully conscious. But he gave no satisfactory reason for lingering that extra ten minutes. Moreoever, there were details which suggested that he knew very well that Mudie would not leave the house alive.

They had used the French polisher's rag to gag him. A rug had been thrown over the victim's head while he was being tied up. Mudie had cried out: 'you're stifling me.' And either Smith or Buckingham had retorted: 'you are breathing your last.'

The prosecutor taxed Smith on this point:

'He said, "you're stifling me"?'

'Yes.'

'And did you say the answer he got was, "you are breathing your last"?'

'That was only said in joking form.'

'Tremendously funny, do you think?'

'Well...'

'You appear to think it was extremely humorous.'

'No, not extremely humorous. No, it was done to frighten this man.'

Weighing much more heavily against Smith, though, was the fact that the car he hired had been seen at the chalkpit *before* Mudie disappeared. If he was at that time reconnoitring for a suitable grave, it can hardly have been for a living victim.

As for the precise mode of Mudie's death, the experts were in some disagreement. One inclined to the view that he had been subjected to a pretty heavy 'roughing-up'; another that all wounds were trivial apart from the rope-mark around the neck, which suggested that the victim had been suspended by the cord. Speculation along these lines might have been insignificant in themselves, but for the extraordinary testimony of a man named Robert Cruikshank.

He was brought forward by Ley's solicitors. And in a sensational development, he told the court that on the fatal night, he had been trying to burgle Ley's premises. He had found a man trussed up in a chair, and in panic had pulled at the rope. Had he accidentally killed the victim? Cruikshank, it transpired, had a police record, and his statements were widely disbelieved. Was he covering for Ley, hoping for a reward from him? It was doubtful that he was ever at the house.

As for Ley, he denied any knowledge of the conspiracy. He did not doubt that Mudie had been brought to his house, nor that he had been bound there and gagged with a rag which came from the premises. He simply brazened it out, offering no satisfactory alibi for the night of the murderer. He blustered and rambled, apparently relying on the lack of direct evidence connecting him personally with the crime. The ex-justice minister had, after all, plotted his vengeance from afar. The jury could take the word of a former minister of state, or of two paltry London working men.

There is always a problem in long-distance plotting, though – the problem of the pay-off. Both Smith and Buckingham testified that Ley had paid them on the night £200 in one-pound notes. Ley's bank records showed that he had made two withdrawals of £250 and £300 shortly beforehand. And the withdrawals were in one-pound notes. Ley stated that the sums were for 'curtain furnishings'. Why not pay by cheque! His suppliers wanted cash, said the defendant. But he had receipts? No, Ley admitted, he had no receipt for either transaction.

The trial lasted for four day, but the jury took less than an hour to consider its verdict. When they came back into court, they declared both Ley and Smith guilty. Ley formally complained that the judge's summing-up had been biased, but a subsequent appeal failed. Both men were sentenced to be hanged.

The whole case had begun with a head in a noose – but it did not end in that way. Statements made during the trial had revealed a crazed, obsessive element in Ley's jealousy. And while awaiting execution, the ex-justice minister was examined by a Medical Board of Enquiry. It found him to be insane; not just given to jealousy but paranoid in the medical sense. Only three days before he was due to be hanged, a reprieve was granted and Ley was committed instead to Broadmoor.

That decision appeared to leave Smith alone to endure the ultimate penalty for murder. But, in a startling and controversial decision, he was also granted a reprieve. There was no question of the joiner being criminally insane; he had murdered strictly for cash. The Home Secretary's decision can only be explained in very human terms of fair play. Ley was clearly the moving force behind the murder, and Smith was only his instrument. To let the mastermind live and hang his subordinate would have been too dark an irony. The quality of mercy (however illogically applied) offered the only way out of the dilemma.

Lawrence John Smith had his sentence commuted to life imprisonment. And as for Ley, he did not enjoy a long period of grace. Fate dealt him the blow which the Home Secretary had withheld: he died at Broadmoor on 24 July 1947, succumbing to a haemorrhage of the brain.

'Oh, God, I am Not Guilty!'

Writer George Orwell set the scene. It is a peaceful Sunday afternoon in pre-war England. You have enjoyed the roast and the steam pudding, washed down with a cup of mahogany-brown tea. The fire is lit, you put your feet up on the sofa and reach for the Sunday newspapers. 'In these blissful circumstances, what is it that you want to read about? Naturally, about murder.'

For preference, the drama should be one of stealth and unfold against a background of intense respectability. Orwell cites a handful of classics in his *Decline of the English Murder*. There was the affair of Dr Palmer, for example, a Victorian physician who secretly poisoned 14 people. There was Crippen of course. And there was also the case of Thompson and Bywaters.

The domestic setting in suburban Ilford was perfect.

Dark, driving passions lurked just beneath the surface. And Edith Thompson's sinister love letters seemed to prove that the crime was one of convenience, coolly arranged at a clandestine meeting beforehand.

And yet it wasn't like that. There were no carefully laid plans. And Edith Thompson's terrible cry rings as chill today as it did when the death sentence was passed upon her: 'I am not guilty; oh, God, I am not guilty!'

Percy and Edith Thompson had lived a largely uneventful life at their home in Ilford, Essex. He was a shipping clerk and she the book-keeper at a firm of wholesale milliners. Married in February 1915, both had their own careers, and the union produced no children. Still, all the neighbours agreed that they seemed a perfectly ordinary couple.

Young Frederick Bywaters came into their lives in the summer of 1921. He was one of a party of people who joined Percy and Edith for an August Bank Holiday on the Isle of Wight. There, he and Edith became mutually attracted, and after the holiday Bywaters lived for a while in the Thompsons' home as a lodger. But Percy grew suspicious: there was row, and Bywaters quit the household.

Bywaters was only 19 at the time, and worked as a ship's writer on the P&O line. Eight years younger than the married woman, he was nonetheless of a strong and domineering temperament. He suggested a divorce, which Percy refuse to grant, and the secret liaison continued for some time before the lovers managed to share a bed. Mostly, the affair was restricted to brief meetings in teashops and elsewhere. Because of his job on the *S.S. Morea*, Bywaters was only in England between voyages. And it was during the periods of separation that Edith wrote her fateful letters.

There was a mass of them. When the case came to trial, no fewer than 62 love letters were submitted by the prosecution. It was an extraordinary correspondence; passionate, sinister and utterly compelling.

Edith generally wrote to her lover as 'darling' (a diminutive of darlingest'). And in the missives to her distant paramour she described how she was trying to get rid of her husband by putting poison or ground glass in his food ('big pieces too – not too powdered'). She returned to the theme on several occasions, complaining that her poisoning attempts had aroused Percy's suspicions: 'he puts great stress on the fact of the tea tasting bitter "as if something had been put in it." he says . . . when he was young (he) nearly suffocated gas fumes. I wish we had not got electric light, it would be easy. I am going to try the glass again occasionally – when it is safe.'

Additionally, Edith sent her lover newspaper snippets concerning cases of death by poisoning. She hoped that the proposed crime would not affect their relationships: 'This thing that I am going to do for both of us will it ever – at all, make any difference between us, darling? Do you understand what I mean? Will you ever think any the less of me?'

And she encouraged Bywaters to feel jealous. One passage in particular was to take on special significance: 'Yes, darling, you are jealous of him – but I want you to be – he has the right by law to all that you have the right to by love – yes, darling, be jealous, so much so that you will do something desperate.'

All very damning on the surface. Yet the evidence suggests that Edith was playing mind-games: exciting herself with make-believe projects that many an unhappy wife may have entertained from time to time. Above all, she wanted to bond Bywaters to her. He was young, handsome and impetuous. By seeming willing to murder on his behalf, she hoped to secure his affections.

In September 1922, Bywaters returned from a voyage and the secret meetings resumed anew. On the afternoon of 3 October, the couple had a rendezvous in a London teashop. Afterwards, Edith went to the theatre with her husband. As they were walking home together from Ilford station along Belgrave Road, Bywaters sprang out from the shadows.

There was a brief quarrel. Bywaters pulled a knife and stabbed Thompson several times. A witness heard Edith scream: Oh, don't! Oh, don't!' The attacker fled back to the shadows as his victim fell, coughing blood, to the pavement.

Immediately, Edith ran for help, rushing until she met a group of people with the words: 'Oh, my God, will you help me, my husband is ill; he is bleeding.' A doctor was called for but arrived too late. Percy was dead, and Edith, now hysterical, sobbed: 'why did you not come sooner and save him?'

Although Edith did not name the assailant, Bywaters soon fell under suspicion, was tracked down and arrested. Some of the love letters were found in his ship's locker; others were at his mother's home. Of course, they horribly implicated his mistress, and the pair went to trial at the Old Bailey together. Frederick Edward Francis Bywaters was charged with murder, and Edith Jessie Thompson with incitement to the crime.

Thompson confessed to the killing, but claimed not to have intended murder. After he sprang from the darkness, the fatal quarrel allegedly ran as follows:

Bywaters: 'Why don't you get a divorce from your wife, you cad?'

Thompson: 'I've got her. I'll keep her, and I'll shoot you.'

Believing that Thompson was armed, Bywaters pulled a knife in fear of his life: 'I did not intend to kill him. I only meant to injure him. I gave him an opportunity of standing up to me as a man but he wouldn't.' Questioned about the love letters, he stated that it never entered his head that Edith had really tried to poison her husband: 'She had been reading books. She had a vivid way of declaring herself. She would read a book and imagine herself a character in the book.'

The prosecution alleged that the murder had been plotted in the teashop that afternoon. Bywaters repudiated the charge. But, given the mass of compromising material in the love letters, passion and premeditation seemed inextricably linked.

Edith's counsel had tried desperately to keep the damaging correspondence out of the courtroom as inadmissible evidence. The petition failed. The defence also failed in trying to persuade Edith herself to stay out of the witness box. She was not obliged to testify, and doing so only gave the prosecution a chance to cross-examine her about the letters. Edith, however, insisted on facing her accusers, and the damning passages were read out time and again in court.

And what of those sinister extracts? The selections read out in court were all passages chosen by the prosecution. In fact, only a very few refer directly to murder attempts. As in all love letters, the writer had obliquely mentioned all kinds of private secrets. The illicit lovers had considered many different ways out of their love tangle: divorce, elopement and even a suicide pact, for example. Murder was just one of the possibilities they toyed with, and many elusive references to a proposed 'drastic action' or similar were quite capable of a different interpretation.

Edith had penned thousands upon thousands of words, most of them just lover's 'gush'. It was only in the Edith version that the correspondence appeared purely murderous. Some of the most apparently sinister passages clearly refer, in their context, to something the defence counsel dared not explain. This was an abortion which Edith was trying to arrange ('I am still willing to dare all and risk all if you are'). The defence obviously felt that it could not afford to be explicit. Enough stigma was attached to adultery; to throw in abortion would make

Edith appear more infamous still.

The few direct references to murder attempts were Edith's calamitous fibs. She testified that she made them all up to try and bind Bywaters to her. If the prosecution was to be believed, Percy had been fed an almost daily diet of splintered glass and poison pellets. In fact, the pathologist stated that no trace of poison or of glass was found in Percy Thompson's body.

In effect, the evidence clearly indicates an impulse killing by Edith's lover. Bywaters had not specially armed himself for the encounter; the knife was one which he always kept in his coat pocket (seafarers, facing the hazards of foreign ports, commonly carry a blade). The witnesses' testimony agreed that the attack had dismayed and horrified Edith. She had cried: 'Oh, don't!', she had tried to summon help. 'Oh, God, why did he do it?' I didn't want him to do it,' she had sobbed when she first learned that Bywaters had been arrested.

Yet it was as the scheming older woman that she was depicted. Contemporaries have described how, in the witness box, she seemed to exude a heady sexuality which turned the jury against her. The judge was strongly hostile to both prisoners in his summing up, and referred to Edith's 'wicked affection' for her lover. The jury took some two hours to consider its verdict:

Clerk of the Court: Members of the jury, have you agreed upon your verdict?

Foreman of the Jury: We have

Clerk of the court: Do you find the prisoner, Frederick Edward Francis Bywaters, guilty or not guilty of the murder of Percy Thompson?

Foreman of the Jury; Guilty, sir.

Clerk of the Court: Do you find the prisoner, Edith Jessie Thompson, guilty or not guilty of the murder of Percy Thompson?

Foreman of the Jury: Guilty

Asked whether he had anything to say before sentence of death was passed, Bywaters answered: 'I say the verdict of the jury is wrong. Edith Thompson is not guilty. I am no murderer, I am not an assassin.' And when the dread penalty was announced, Edith cried out: *'I am not guilty; oh, God, I am not guilty!'*

An appeal failed. For Edith a petition signed by thousands was submitted to the Home Secretary, but no reprieve was granted. Edith's mother visited her in the condemned cell and asked: 'How could you write such letters?' The submissive mistress replied sadly: 'No one knows what kind of letters he was writing me.'

Bywaters himself protested Edith's innocence to the end. Calmly accepting his own fate he wrote: 'For her to be hanged as a criminal is too awful. She didn't commit the murder. I did. She never planned it. She never knew about it. She is innocent, absolutely innocent. I can't believe they will hang her.'

By they did. Thompson and Bywaters died within moments of each other on the morning of 9 January 1923. Frederick Bywaters faced his end bravely at Pentonville. At Holloway, Edith Thompson had to be carried to the scaffold; she was in a state of collapse as they fitted the noose around her.

The Deadly Apéritif

On Friday 24 August 1973, a registered parcel arrived at the home of Tranquillo Allevi. His wife Renata took it in, as her husband was out at the time. She placed it on his desk, and when he returned, Tranquillo opened it up to find a bottle of apéritif. It was made by a well-known firm of Italian liquor manufacturers, and the accompanying letter invited him to become their local representative in a new sales campaign.

Allevi was a prosperous dairy farmer who lived near San Remo on the north Italian coast. Such invitations were not uncommon, and the 50-year-old dairyman took the bottle to his office where he put it in the fridge. It was a welcome gift, whether he took up the office or not. Probably he forgot about it in his concern to get on with the day's business.

The bottle remained in the fridge that night and the whole of the following day. It was a Saturday – the day on which, by custom, he would take his wife to dine at the casino restaurant in San Remo. The evening passed pleasantly enough. Having driven Renata home after the meal, Allevi went on to his office to clear up some business. A salesman and another friend joined him there. The night was warm and the trio took off their jackets. Remembering the apéritif, Allevi went to the fridge and returned with the chilled appetizer.

He produced three glasses and poured out the drinks. Raising his glass in a toast, he tossed back its contents in one. The others only sipped – which was lucky for them. For, seconds later, Allevi crumpled to the floor. He was racked with spasms and gasping for breath.

Dismayed, his companions put down their glasses. One phoned the police who came quickly. The three men were rushed to hospital where the two friends were purged with emetics and recovered. Allevi, however, died.

Doctors were quick to diagnose death by poisoning. And in due course it was found that the apéritif contained enough strychnine to kill 500 men.

Who had tampered with the bottle? Enquiries at the manufacturers revealed that although they had sent out some samples with invitations, Allevi was not on their list. His letter followed their customary formula. But it had been typed on a plain sheet, not the company's headed notepaper. It was, moreover, unsigned.

Allevi had no special business rivals. He was generally

well enough liked. And suspicion fell initially on Renata, Allevi's grieving wife. She was some 12 years younger than her husband. Enquiries revealed that she had several male admirers outside her marriage: her husband's book-keeper; an Army officer; and a veterinary surgeon who had treated the dairy herds.

Renata, however, had been visibly distressed at the news of her husband's sudden death. She responded to questioning with every appearance of truthfulness. Far from trying to dissociate herself from the bottle, she her-self informed police that she had taken it into the house-hold. She also stated, unprompted, that it was her idea that the apéritif should be taken to the office and placed in the refrigerator to cool.

As investigations proceeded, the police checked up on the movements of her admirers on the fateful day when the parcel was posted. It had been sent from Milan, which seemed to let off two of the suspects. The bookkeeper could prove he had been in San Remo; the Army officer was on duty at the time. That left the veterinary surgeon, Dr Renzo Ferrari.

A suave professional man, Ferrari had been in Milan on the 23rd, renewing his veterinarian's licence. Moreoever, the police discovered that two days earlier he had bought six grammes of strychnine at a chemist's near his place of work. This was not in itself suspicious – the doctor often bought the substance there for treating sick cattle.

But there was stronger evidence against him. Checking up on typewriters he had access to, detectives discovered a machine at the town hall in Barengo. It appeared to match the typing on the poisonous invitation. Dr Ferrari was a local government officer. He used the town hall in his work.

Ferrari was charged with the murder, and the trial caused a sensation in Italy. This was no hot-blooded Latin-style *crime personnel*. The defence counsel fiercely challenged the forensic evidence, and there were problems surrounding the precise motive. Ferrari had only recently become engaged to the daughter of a wealthy family. Why should he jeopardise his future? Ferrari claimed that his relationship with Renata was purely sexual. He said he was happy to break off the liaison when he met his fiancée.

Renata, dressed in widow's black, told a different story in the box. She testified that it was she who broke off the affair. It happened, she said, when her husband found out that she had been deceiving him. Ferrari refused to accept the breach. She had weakened at first, but then came to a final decision: 'I will not return to you.'

'We'll see,' the veterinarian had replied.

The poison, according to the prosecution, had been inserted by syringe through the cork of the intact bottle. And the final, damning evidence was supplied by a representative of the drinks firm. He stated that although no bottle had been sent from the company to Mr Allevi, one had been dispatched – with an invitation – to Dr Renzo Ferrari.

On 15 May 1974, a panel of judges found the accused guilty of murder with premeditation. The sentence amounted to some 30 years, including consecutive sentences for the attempted murder of Allevi's two drinking companions.

It should be remembered that almost anyone – including Renata – might have sampled the deadly apéritif. This, if anything ever was, was a case of bottled rage.

Atrocities

The Mongol Hordes

'I have committed many acts of cruelty and had an incalculable number of men killed, never knowing whether what I did was right. But I am indifferent to what people think of me.' So said Genghis Khan in the thirteenth century.

In the career of Genghis Khan, one atrocity followed another. By the time he died in 1227, he had been responsible for the death of around 20 million peoples around one-tenth of the population of the known world. He began his atrocious career by murdering his brother after a dispute over a fish; he was just 12 at the time.

At the age of 33, he became undisputed leader of the Mongol hordes – the Genghis Khan, meaning 'universal ruler'. In 1211, he began his conquest of imperial China, burning and pillaging every town and village on the way. Three years later he controlled the Addle Kingdom – China north of the Yellow River – and forced those outside his rule to deliver him 500 young men and women, plus 3,000 head of livestock, as the price of peace. In 1217, he left his champion Muqali there as viceroy to mop up any further resistance and went home to the steppes. It was then he looked to the west and started a campaign that would take him to the gates of Europe.

The King of Gulja, to the west of Mongolia, paid homage to Genghis Khan. He was assassinated by Cuchulug, the Emperor of Qara-Khitai in what is now Kazahkstan, and his widow and son called on Genghis Khan for help. This he happily provided, sending his general, Jebe, who killed Guchulug and, within a year, had delivered the whole of the Qara-Khitai empire to the Khan. This brought Genghis Khan into direct contact with the world of Islam.

To the west of Qara-Khitai was Khwarezam, which covered what is now north-east Iran, Afghanistan, Turkmeniya, Uzbekistan and Tadzikistan. In 1212, following a coup d'état, Shah Mohammed had installed himself as ruler of the important trading city of Samarkand.

Khan had no desire to go to war against Khwarezam. As the nomads of the steppes did not weave, it was important for them to maintain good relations with Khwarezam, as they bought cloth from Samarkand. Genghis Khan sent a caravan to the Shah carrying exquisite jade, ivory and gold bars and felt made from perfectly white camel hair. The 300 caravanners were accompanied by a Mongolian noble who carried a message from the Khan. It read, 'I know your power and the vast extent of your empire. I have the greatest desire to live in peace with you. I shall regard you as my son. For your part, you must know that I have conquered the Middle Kingdom and subdued all the tribes of the north. You know that my country is a swarm of warriors, a mine of silver, and that I have no need to covet further domains. We have equal interest in encouraging trade between our subjects.'

The Shah was a little suspicious of this message; he accepted the Khan's gifts but sent his messenger back without a reply. Genghis Khan sent a second caravan, this time consisting of 500 camels, laden with the fur of beaver and sable. With it was Uquna, an official of the Mongolian court.

At the frontier town of Otrar, the local governor had 100 of the caravanners including Uqurta – butchered and their cargo confiscated. Genghis Khan had one more go at diplomacy, sending a new emissary, this time a Muslim. The Shah had him put to death and his entourage returned to the Khan with their heads shaven. As a final insult to the Khan, he confirmed the governor of Otrar in office.

There could be only one response. In the summer of 1219, Genghis Khan assembled between 150,000 and 200,000 horsemen, many of them battlehardened veterans of the conquest of China. Together with his horseman, his best generals, his four sons and one of his wives – Qulan, which means 'she-ass' Genghis Khan set off to make war.

Shah Mohammed's army easily outnumbered Genghis Khan's, but he did not know where the Mongols were going to attack so he deployed his men all along the border. This was an idiotic strategy – they were spread so thinly that wherever the Mongols attacked they were bound to win. If the Shah had thought about it for a moment, he would have known where Genghis Khan was going to attack: at Otrar, of course – the governor there had killed his emissary.

Otrar was a walled city, though this was no problem for the Mongols. During their campaign in China they had captured a great deal of siege machinery along with Chinese soldiers who could use them. The Chinese had also perfected gunpowder and knew how to make bombs and mortars; they had rockets and bombards – primitive cannon – which fired metal balls.

The Mongolians also had siege engines of their own, dating back 1000 years. They were massive crossbows mounted on trestles that fired huge arrows over 200 yards, and catapults that could fling huge boulders with great force. Under covering fire, sappers tunnelled under the walls. Towers with retractable ladders were trundled up to the walls, while the gates were pummelled by huge battering rams.

The governor knew what fate awaited him if the city fell. He fought shoulder to shoulder with his men, who held off the Mongols for a month. Then, when the city fell, the governor retreated to the citadel with his men and fought on. When they ran out of arrows, he took to hurling bricks at the assailants. However, eventually he was overcome and taken. Trussed up with leather thongs and taken before the Khan, who ordered that he suffer an exemplary punishment, molten silver was poured into his ears and eye sockets.

A second Mongolian column, under the command of the general jochi, lay siege to the citadel of Sighnaq and demanded unconditional surrender. When this was not forthcoming, he attacked. The citadel was taken after a week and Jochi had the throats and bodies of all the inhabitants of the town slashed open.

A third column, under Alaq-Noyan, attacked Banakat to the west of Tashkent. After three days, the Turkish mercenaries who were defending the city sued for peace. Once the Mongols entered the city, the inhabitants were enslaved. The city's craftsmen were assigned to combat units or sent back to Mongolia; the women were distributed among the clans; the rest of the citizens were taken as hostages, who could be used as a human screen in the next battle.

The next objective was Khojend. Its commander was Temur Malik, who had a reputation as a skilled tactician and a courageous leader. With 1,000 crack troops, he retreated to the citadel, a fortified castle that stood on the riverbank. It was so well fortified, it needed 20,000 Mongols and an army of 50,000 prisoners to take it.

The Mongols set their prisoners to work building a bridge of boats across the width of the river. Then they filled the boats with rocks and sunk them, damming the river. Temur Malik's men tried to harry them but they were hopelessly outnumbered. He knew that, once the river was dry and the foot of the walls exposed, the fort was done for, so he and his men jumped in boats of their own and escaped with enemy squadrons in hot pursuit. He made it back to the Shah's camp safe and sound.

The Mongols entered the city of Nur disguised as caravanners. Once they were inside the city walls, the authorities capitulated and paid a tribute of 1,500 dinars; yet that did not save the city – the people were driven out, the city looted and the booty sent back to Mongolia.

Next to fall was Bukhara, which was one of the finest

cities in the west. For Muslims, it was a place of worship and was famed for its carpet weaving. When the Mongols attacked, the Turkish garrison tried to break out. They were hunted down and slaughtered. The Mongol prisoners were sent to break the gates down and catapults shattered the defences. Genghis Khan entered the city personally while fighting was still going on in the citadel. When it was captured, the last of the defenders were put to death. The inhabitants were lined up and told to leave; any found hiding in the city were stabbed to death on the spot.

Genghis Khan himself rode into the great mosque, believing it to be the Shah's palace. As sacred Koranic books were thrown in the dirt, hundreds of devoted Muslims killed themselves rather than submit to the barbaric invaders. Men slaughtered their wives rather than let the Mongols take them – the Mongols made a practice of making men watch while they raped their womenfolk. Among those who died by their own hand was the imam.

'It was an appalling day,' says a Muslim historian. 'Nothing was heard but the sobbing of men, women and children, separated forever as the Mongol troops parcelled the population among themselves.'

To Genghis Khan were attributed the words, 'I tell you I am the scourge of Allah, and if you had not been great sinners Allah would not have brought down my wrath upon your heads.'

The city was then burnt to the ground. For dozens of years afterwards Bukhara lay uninhabited. Thousands of corpses there, too many to be buried, exuded diseases which drove away the living. Those who lived in the surrounding region moved away. The irrigation ditches collapsed; the fields turned to desert and the animals, left to their own devices, perished. All that was left were the ruins.

Genghis Khan then turned on Samarkand. Behind him trudged a swelling army of prisoners, forced to work as slave labourers to destroy their own country. Samarkand was a city steeped in history. It had been ancient when Alexander the Great had conquered it in 329 BC, now it was one of the foremost trading centres in the world. It sent melons as far as Baghdad, packed in lead boxes lined with snow to keep them fresh. It boasted goldsmiths, silversmiths, coppersmiths, tanners, saddle-makers, wood carvers, cabinetmakers and swordsmiths. Even paper was made in the city, using a technique imported from China. Chain mail, carved ewers, ceramics and beautifully inlaid woodwork produced in the city were traded in the ports of the Mediterranean.

Samarkand had recently been fortified. In the ramparts were four great gates, symbolising the city's dependence on trade. It had a huge garrison, manned largely by Turkish mercenaries, so few of the inhabitants thought that it would suffer the same fate as Bukhara.

Genghis Khan was impressed by the defences, too. When he arrived in the spring of 1220, he camped outside the city and waited for reinforcements. Meanwhile, he deployed a curtain of troops round the city. When two of his sons turned up with thousands of prisoners, they decided the best ploy was to impress the enemy with their numbers. They took the prisoners' clothes from them and dressed them as Mongols. Then, under close guard and Mongol banners, they marched them towards the city walls.

The city's garrison charged the attackers. The Mongols turned and fled, leaving the unarmed prisoners to absorb the assault, then turned and counterattacked, hacking though the Turkish mercenaries. After a severe thrashing the Turks deserted, leaving the city defenceless.

The town's leaders came out to talk to the Mongols. Genghis Khan promised that all those who left the city would be spared. Once they were gone, Samarkand was sacked; the die-hards who stayed on were butchered, and part of the city was set on fire. Genghis Khan considered the Turkish mercenary criminals. One Persian chronicler says 30,000 were massacred. Some 50,000 citizens bought their freedom with a ransom that totalled 200,000 dinars. Those too poor to pay the ransom were taken as slave labourers by the Mongol units. Craftsmen were sent to Mongolia. It was said that when those who had paid the ransom returned to Samarkand there were so few of them they could only repopulate a quarter of the city.

The capital of Khwarezam was not Samarkland but Urgench, 300 miles up the Amudar'ya River towards the Aral Sea. Again, it was defended by Turkish mercenaries. However, this time they were ready, having carefully stockpiled weapons, food and water, ready for a long siege.

Genghis Khan charged three of his sons to take Urgench. One of them, Jochi, was named ruler of Khwarezam, so it was in his interests not to destroy the city completely. With them were three of the Khan's most experience generals and 50,000 horsemen.

An emissary was sent demanding unconditional surrender. The offer was declined, so the Mongols laid siege to the city. There were no boulders in the area for the catapults, so prisoners were sent out to find mulberry trees and their trunks were sawn up to make ammunition. Meanwhile other prisoners, under fire from the city walls, began filling in the moat – it took 12 days. That done, sappers advanced under the cover of siege engines and started chipping away at the brickwork.

During these long preparations, two of the brothers fell out. One wanted everything done meticulously, while the other was more gung-ho. The dispute could have been disastrous. But Genghis Khan resolved the situation by putting the third brother in charge of the other two.

Soon after, the walls were breached. But, aware of what would happen to them if they were defeated, the defenders fought ferociously, house to house. Both sides used burning naphtha to set fire to houses where their foes took shelter, the consequence being high loss of life for the civilian inhabitants.

The Mongols were used to fighting huge sweeping battles; this sort of fighting therefore did not suit them and they paid a heavy price. Having taken one half of the city, they attacked the bridge over the Amudar'ya River that led to the other half, and were repulsed – this action alone cost them 3,000 men.

The Turkish mercenaries continued their stout defence from the ruins of the city, supported and supplied by the remaining inhabitants. After seven days, the Mongols lost their patience and torched the rest of the city. The Turks were forced to pull back but hundreds of civilians were burnt to death. Eventually, members of the city council indicated that they wanted to parley. One begged the Mongols to have mercy on the brave men who had defended the city, 'We have seen the might of your wrath; now show us the measure of your pity," he said.

Unfortunately, the Mongols were in no mood for this kind of talk and the fighting continued.

'Everyone fought,' wrote an Arab historian, 'men, women and children, and they went on fighting until the Mongols had taken the entire town, killed all the inhabitants, and pillaged everything there was to be found. Then they opened the dam and the waters of the river flooded the city and destroyed it completely... Those who escaped from the massacre were drowned or buried under the rubble. And then nothing remained but ruins and waves.'

Genghis Khan was not at all happy about the destruction of Shah Mohammed's capital. The siege of Urgench had lasted six months; Mongolian losses were much higher than he was used to. Even worse, his sons had seized all the booty from what little remained of the city, without reserving any for their father. He refused to see them for three days. When he did, he lost his temper. Advisors calmed him down, pleading that his sons were young and inexperienced. They would soon toughen up if he sent them against the caliph of Baghdad.

Meanwhile, the Khans generals pursued Shah Mohammed, whose troops deserted in droves. City after city fell to the Mongols until the whole of Khwarezam was in their hands. Shah Mohammed died of pleurisy on the shores of the Caspian in what is now Azerbaijan.

Genghis Khan took a summer break at the oasis of Nasaf, before going north to Termez. When the city refused to surrender, he lay siege to it for seven days. It fell and the usual massacre ensued. Everyone was disembowelled after one woman swallowed some pearls rather than hand them over.

Next he headed for the ancient city of Balkh, capital of the kingdom of Bactria in what is now northern Afghanistan. As a city, it had been known for 3,000 years. Alexander the Great had occupied it and married Princess Roxane there. But Genghis Khan was not interested in such niceties. When the city surrendered itself to him on the understanding that its citizens would go unmolested, he went back on his promise and put thousands to the sword. When he passed that way again in 1222, he massacred the survivors.

'Wherever there was a wall still standing, the Mongols tore it down,' said an Arab historian, 'and for a second time swept away an traces of civilisation from the region.'

A Chinese monk travelling through the region at the time did not record the destruction being that complete, but reported that the great city of Balkh was a ghost town with dogs barking in the street.

Genghis Khan spared some cities, but if there was the slightest sign of opposition, he was merciless. As well as massacring the inhabitants, he would destroy the irrigation system that had taken centuries to construct. Many cities ravaged by the Mongols were destroyed forever.

Nessa resisted. When it was taken, the inhabitants were ordered to tie themselves together outside the city walls while Mongol archers cut them down for target practice. Those only wounded were despatched by sabre. Some 70,000 in all were killed.

Occasionally, there were setbacks. When Genghis Khan's son-in-law, Toguchar, was besieging Neyshabur he was hit by a defender's arrow and mortally wounded. The Mongols lifted the siege, but laid waste all the surrounding villages in vengeance.

In February 1221, Genghis Khans fourth son, Tolui, and 70,000 horsemen arrived in Mery, now called Mary, in Turkmeniya. It was a rich city famed for its ceramics, but its fortifications were particularly impressive. Tolui and 500 horsemen spent all day inspecting them. Twice he assaulted the city and was driven back, but the governor then surrendered, having received assurances that no one would come to harm.

Tolui did not keep his word: he evacuated the city and picked out 400 craftsmen and some children to keep as slaves – the rest were put to the sword. This was a formidable task. The population had to be divided up among the army units. Each man, it was said, had to kill between 300 and 400 people. One source says that Tolui left 700,000 corpses there. Another said he stopped counting after 1,300,000.

Tolui then went to Neyshabur to avenge Toguchar. The city tried to surrender but Tolui would have none of it. It was bombarded by boulders and incendiary bombs filled with naphtha. In two days, the walls were demolished completely and the inhabitants marched out. The craftsmen were separated out and sent off to Mongolia, then the slaughter began. Toguchar's widow and her entourage gleefully joined in. Again, everyone was disembowelled in case they had swallowed precious gems. Severed heads were stacked in pyramids. There were three – one for men's heads, one for women's heads, and one for children's. Not even the cats and dogs were left alive. The city was then flattened until there was hardly a trace that it had ever been there.

In Herat, after a siege that lasted eight days, only the mercenaries were massacred. Later, the populace revolted, killing the Mongol governor and the Khan's resident minister. In revenge, the Mongols slaughtered the population, then withdrew and waited. When survivors emerged from the rubble and those who had taken refuge in nearby caves returned, the Mongols went back and killed them too. One source says there were 1.3 million dead, another 2.4 million injured. 'Not a man, not an ear of corn; no scrap of food, not item of clothing remained,' it was said.

Mongol contingents were also sent back to Merv and Balkh to slaughter anyone who had returned to the cities they had laid waste. Next on the list was Bamiyan, where huge Buddhas were carved in the rocks. It was the jewel of Khwarezam, a stop off on the Silk Route and an unparalleled centre of culture. The story goes that the city was betrayed by Princess Lala Qatun whose father was trying to marry her off against her will; she sent word to Genghis Khan, telling him how the city's water supply could be turned off.

However, during the siege, Genghis Khan's grandson was killed. The Khan was so angered by the loss of his grandson that he did not even stop to put his helmet on before he started slaughtering the enemy. The boy's father was away at the time; when he returned the Khan rebuked his son falsely for having disobeyed him and asked his son whether he was now ready to obey any order his father gave him. His son swore he was.

'Well,' said the Khan. 'Your son has been killed and I order you not to lament.'

Revenge was taken in the normal way: the entire population was massacred. Even Princess Lala Qatun was not

269

spared – she was stoned to death for her treachery.

After the death of Shah Mohammed, power passed to his son Prince Jalal a-Din. With an army of Turkish mercenaries and Kwarezamian conscripts numbering around 60,000, he held up in a fortress at Chazi, 100 miles south of Kabul. The Mongols attacked but, after losing 1000 men, were forced to withdraw.

The Khan's adopted brother was in charge of the assault. Short of men, he thought he would fool Prince Jalal into believing he had more men than he had. He mounted straw dummies on horseback and rode them up to his camp as if they were a relief army. The ruse did not work – the Prince attacked. For the first time on Muslim territory, the Mongols suffered a defeat. The Muslim soldiers were said to have surpassed even the Mongols in their savagery, driving nails into the ears of their prisoners.

When Genghis Khan heard of this, he leapt into the saddle. It was said that with fresh troops he rode continuously for two days to reach Ghazi. They did not even stop to eat or drink, but rather – in the Mongol way – cut a nick in the back of their horse's neck each time they felt peckish and nourished themselves with the blood.

By the time they reached Chazi, a dispute had broken out between the Turkish mercenaries and the local troops and Prince Jalal was forced to withdraw. The city's inhabitants were deported or killed and its defences destroyed.

The Prince planned to escape to the Punjab but was caught on his back to the river Indus. There he surrounded himself with a square of troops and made a stand. The Mongols steadily hacked away at his lines of defence. When he had only a handful of men left, the Prince made a break for it and jumped off a cliff on horseback into the river. Genghis Khan was full of admiration – first for how the Prince had saved his own life at the expense of those of his men's, and then for the leap. He was an example to all Mongols, the Khan said, and was allowed to escape. The men who had made the jump with the Prince were not accorded the same respect: Mongol archers rained arrows down on them in the water. Prince Jalal eventually found refuge with the Sultan of Delhi.

Genghis Khan only made a brief incursion into India, laying waste to a few villages around Lahore, but then turning back into Khwarezam to take a closer look at the land he had already conquered.

Meanwhile, following the death of Shah Mohammed, the Khan's general, Jebe, had moved on northwards into Georgia, defeating the Georgian cavalry who were supposed to be the mightiest in the region. Then he moved on into Russia.

At the Battle of Kalka, the Mongols were attacked by 80,000 knights under Prince Mstislav. The Mongols, numbering only 20,000, used their tried and tested tactic. After a short engagement, they withdrew, apparently in disorder. The Russians pursed them at high speed – this stretched out their army. Then, when they outnumbered the advanced guard, the Mongols turned and fought. When they rest of the army arrived, they would come upon a scene of appalling butchery, which usually put them off fighting. If not, the Mongols slaughtered them as well.

The Russian knights wore steel armour and had shields, axes, swords and lances, but they were heavy and slow compared to the Mongol horsemen, and were easy prey for the Mongolian archers. They were easily defeated and Prince Mstislav was captured. He was executed by being wrapped up in a carpet and suffocated; this was a sign that the Mongols held in him great respect – they would not shed his blood.

The rest of the Russian army were intimidated by Mstislav's defeat and withdrew. The Mongols went on to plunder the warehouses of Sudak in the Crimea; they looted the kingdom of the Bulgars, then turned for home, cutting a swathe through Kazahkstan.

Genghis Khan himself returned to Mongolia where he died on the shores of Lake Baikal in 1227. He left orders that, if anyone gazed on his coffin, the next coffin would be theirs.

In 1237, ten years after the death of Genghis Khan, the Mongolian 'Golden Horde' attacked Russia again, employing similarly barbarous tactics. In 1347, during the Siege of Caffa on the Crimea, they invented biological warfare, catapulting the corpses of plague victims over the walls to infect those within. The Mongols continued to plague the Russians for centuries. As a traditional Russian tale called The Story of the Destruction of Ryazan puts it: 'They devastated the churches of God and before the consecrated altars they spilt quantities of blood. And none was spared, all perished equally and drank the cup of death to the lees. No one remained to sob or weep for the dead – neither father nor mother for their children, nor children for their father and mother, neither brother for brother, nor cousin for cousin – for all without exception lay lifeless. And this happened in requital of our sins.'

Auto-da-Fé

In 1231, Pope Gregory IX set up the Inquisition to suppress widespread heresy. It went about its barbarous business mainly in northern Italy and southern France. However, when the Muslims were driven out of Spain the political authorities in Aragon and Castile were looking for a way to impose their authority on the rest of country and, in 1478, persuaded Pope Sixtus IV to authorise a separate Spanish Inquisition.

They set to work and the first *auto-da-fé* took place in Seville in 1481. Hundreds were burnt alive and the Spanish Inquisition was so savage that the Pope tried to ban it. But the civil authorities had found the Spanish Inquisition such a powerful political tool that they restored it and named their own Inquisitor-General. They chose the Dominican Tomás Torquemada who, in his 15-year career, was personally responsible for burning more than 2,000 people at the stake.

Tomás Torquemada was the nephew of the famous theologian Juan de Torquemada, who was made a cardinal for promoting the idea of papal infallibility. From an early age, Tomás was exceedingly pious. After a brilliant scholastic career, he joined the Dominicans. This was a disappointment to his father, a nobleman who wanted his only son to marry and continue the family line.

Torquemada withdrew to the Monastery of Santa Cruz in Segovia, where he lived an extremely austere life. He refused to eat meat and, unlike other Dominicans, he refused to wear linen under his coarse habit; if that was not chafing enough, he often resorted to wearing a hair shirt. And he always went barefoot.

As his reputation for piety spread, Torquemada was made confessor to Isabella, the sister of Henry IV. He got her to promise that if she were ever made queen, she would restore the Inquisition. She did become Queen and, good to her word, she re-introduced the Inquisition and made Torquemada its head.

In the Middle Ages many people joined the church for the wealth and power it brought them. Torquemada was not one of them. This made him all the more dangerous. What he wanted to do was force the austerity that he enjoyed on other people; he did not care how he did it. He also earned the title 'the Scourge of the Jews'. Though his own grandmother was Jewish, he persecuted Jews – even those who had converted to Christianity – as heretics. One did not even have to be Jewish – it was enough that someone said one was.

As soon as he was made Inquisitor-General, Torquemada

produced a new set of rules for the Inquisition – 28 articles. At each new place the Inquisition visited, an eloquent priest or one of the inquisitors would give a sermon. At the end of it, faithful Christians were to come forward and swear their allegiance to the Inquisition and promise to work for it. Anyone who had lost their faith or practised heresy – which included Jews and any remaining Muslims – was given 30 or 40 days to come to the Inquisition and confess. They would not be dealt with harshly – that is, they would not be burnt at the stake – provided their repentance was sincere and that they confessed, not only their own sins, but those of their neighbours.

There would, of course, be some punishment – those who had offended God's holy law could not expect to get off scot-free. They would have to perform penances and give up wearing jewellery and fine clothes; they were not to ride horses or bear arms, and they would be liable to forfeit some of their property to Queen Isabella and King Ferdinand to help in their Holy War against the Muslims in Granada.

Anyone guilty of heresy or apostasy who did not come forward during the period of grace, but came forward voluntarily later, would again be treated mercifully. They would simply have to surrender all their property and would be sentenced to life imprisonment – but no fire. This punishment could not be evaded – if you gave your property away beforehand, the Inquisition would seize it from whoever you had given it to.

The slaves of those condemned by the Inquisition would be freed giving them ample incentive to inform on their master. Children who had become heretics due to the teachings of their parents were treated especially kindly. Provided they told the Inquisition of their parents' heresies, they would be given light penances and be taught the true faith. The children of those condemned by the Inquisition would be sent to monasteries and convents; the girls were supposed to be given a small dowry so that they could marry, but this never happened.

Anyone arrested for heresy or apostasy could ask for reconciliation with the church, but they would have to prove that their confession was sincere. The only way to do that was to inform on friends. If it were judged that their confession was not sincere, they would be handed over to the civil authorities and be put to death.

If a suspect fled, his name would be posted on the doors of all the churches in the area. He would be given 30 days to present himself to the Inquisition, otherwise he would be judged guilty of heresy. Those who had successfully fled the country were burnt in effigy, which did not hurt nearly as much.

There was no hiding place from the Inquisition: if a count or a duke refused to let the Inquisition into his realm, he would be found guilty of aiding and abetting heresy. Even death was no escape – if someone was found guilty after they were dead, their body would be dug up and their corpse burnt at the stake; their estate would naturally be forfeit.

Officers of the Inquisition were not allowed to take gifts from suspects. If they did, they would have to forfeit twice the value of the gift and might suffer excommunication – which would put paid to a lucrative career in the church. Torquemada reserved the right to sack inquisitors for other misdemeanours – such as not being harsh enough.

Torquemada took a broad definition of heresy. Besides the crime of being Jewish, bigamy was also a heretical sin as marriage was a sacrament. Sodomy was punished by burning, but ordinary, unmarried fooling around was okay, provided that the participants did not say it was all right – that would be contradicting the word of God.

One reason this was not included was that the Spanish priesthood was notoriously debauched. It was not until the sixteenth century that a screen was put in confessionals separating the priest and the penitent. Before that time licentious priests would lure attractive young women into the confession boxes and give them a few extra sins to confess. Torquemada would have loved to sweep this sort of behaviour from the church with his Inquisition but, by that time, Innocent VIII was Pope. He was a proud family man. His children lived with him in the Vatican, so he was hardly in a position to condemn amorous activity in those beneath him.

One priest was brought before the Inquisition because he had been sent to a convent as confessor and promptly seduced five nuns. But, he told the inquisition, he had been told to go the convent and take care of the nuns . . . and, as a good and faithful servant, he had done exactly that. Another priest was caught sodomising a 14-year-old boy in his care. As a priest, he was confined to a monastery for a year. The boy was not so lucky; he was made to wear a mitre full of feathers and whipped so severely that he died.

When a man or woman was suspected of heresy, they would be called to the Holy Office. All that was required to condemn a person was the testimony of two witnesses. The names of the witnesses were kept secret in case reprisals were taken against them. Theoretically, the accused could be represented by an advocate; in practice, no one was foolhardy enough to stand up to the Inquisition.

There were no guards at the Holy Office and so theoretically the accused could simply walk out; but that would invite condemnation as a heretic. Once accused by the Inquisition, there was very little hope of getting off. Both church and state wanted a uniformly Catholic country and the exchequer was eager to get its hands on as much confiscated property as possible. The odds were, of course, stacked against the accused. If a case was not proved, the suspect would have to undergo torture to see if they could clear the matter up by confessing. If they confessed, the confession would have to be repeated within three days.

Arrests often took place at night. Alguazils or familiars of the Inquisition would knock and, if there were any resistance, they would force entrance. The victim would be told to dress and they would leave immediately. The alguazils liked to work silently, bringing a painful gag for anyone tempted to cry out and alert their neighbours. It was shaped like a pear and was forced into the mouth. Screws then enlarged it, forcing the jaw open. Silence and secrecy made the alguazils' terror tactics more effective: everyone felt vulnerable.

Inside the Holy Office, everything was designed to intimidate the suspect. The 'trial' was held in a darkened room. The inquisitors wore white habits with black hoods and sat at a table swathed in black velvet; it had a crucifix, a Bible and six candles on it.

The trial would take place in camera, the public not being permitted to observe. A secretary would read the charges from a pulpit; there followed a long pause. Torquemada instructed his inquisitors to spend time examining papers before they spoke to the suspect as a method of instilling fear.

The prisoner would then be asked for their name and address, as well as whether they knew why they had been arrested. If the prisoner said they did not know why – which was usually the case – the inquisitor was instructed to study the papers before him once more.

After a while the prisoner would be asked if they had any enemies and whether they attended confession regularly. What was their diocese? Who was their confessor? When did he last go to confession?

Torquemada instructed his inquisitors not to be moved by anything the prisoner might do or say. Any sobbing, weeping, begging or heart-rending tales should be ignored – heretics were a crafty lot. Had they not pretended to be good Catholics while practising their heresy in secret? The inquisitors were reminded that the condemnation of one man might be the salvation of thousands. After all, heretics not only practised heresy themselves – they often persuaded others to follow in their diabolical ways.

If the prisoner stubbornly refused to be intimidated into confessing, the inquisitor was instructed to soften his expression. The prisoner was told that they were an errant child and, like a father, the inquisitor was merely trying to make them recognise the error of their ways. The Church was ready to forgive them and welcome them back, but first they had to unburden their soul by confessing and show true penitence, which, of course, meant revealing the names of those who, shared in their sin. Many fell into this trap and willingly provided more fodder for the Inquisition.

If the prisoner still refused to confess, they would be taken back to prison to think about it. If the suspect remained firm, the inquisitor would tell them that, although they appeared to be innocent, their jailers were not convinced. They would have to stay in prison, but would be moved to more comfortable quarters and be allowed visitors. Visitors would be sent by the Inquisition to encourage the prisoner to be careless in their talk. Prisoners were told that, if they confessed, they would get off with a light penance. An officer of the Inquisition was concealed so that they could overhear any conversation. They searched for any words that could be construed as an admission of heresy. Sometimes the suspect would be made to share a cell with another prisoner who was actually an agent of the Inquisition. The agent would talk openly of their own feigned heresy in the hope of entrapping the prisoner.

If all this failed, the prisoner would be taken back before the Inquisition and cross-examined at lightning speed. It would be a long and wearisome interview. The inquisitor would try to force the suspect into contradicting themselves. For those quick-witted enough to avoid the inquisitor's snares there was but one reward – the torture chamber.

Torture was largely Torquemada's contribution to the Inquisition. It had been used against the Knights Templar in France in the fourteenth century, but successive popes had declared that it was unfair to force confessions out of men and women using torture that was so severe that if they did not confess they knew they would die. Torquemada had no such qualms.

He instructed that torture could be used in any case where heresy was 'half proven' – in other words, an accusation had been made but no confession had yet been extracted. Simply being brought before the Inquisition was enough. Being a good Christian, Torquemada said that no blood must be shed; however, he conceded that people did often die under torture. If this happened, the inquisitor must immediately seek absolution from a fellow priest. Torquemada gave all his priests the power to absolve one another of murder.

The inquisitors did not use the word torture – prisoners were simply put to The Question. There were five carefully thought-out stages to The Question. The first was the threat; the prisoner would already have heard about the cruel methods that the Inquisition employed, but the inquisitors felt it was their duty to remind the prisoner of the danger they faced in the hope that they would become weak with fear.

The second was the journey to the torture chamber. The victim would be taken ceremonially in a procession by candlelight. Also lighting the way would be braziers, which would take on their own terrifying significance. The torture chamber would be dark and dismal. The victims would be given a little time to glance around it and see the hideous devices that were employed; they would see them being used on other victims who had refused to confess;

and they would see the torturers, who wore black hoods with eyeholes cut in them.

In the third stage, the prisoner would be seized and stripped, leaving them naked and vulnerable. The fourth stage was to introduce the victim to the particular instrument that was to be used on them and strap them on to it. Only then, in the fifth and final stage, would the pain begin.

It was against the law to repeat The Question. Once a victim had been tortured and survived, they could not be tortured again. However, there was no law against continuing the torture. It could go on day after day, week after week, with any interval merely being a 'suspension'.

Although the rack was used by the Inquisition, most prisoners were subjected to the hoist or water torture and, frequently, both. The victim's hands were tied behind their back and the rope was passed over a pulley – this was used to hoist the victim from the floor. If they did not confess after an hour or so, weights would be attached to their feet. If this still did not do the trick, the victims were to be let down with a jerk.

Next, they would be tied to a sloping trestle so their feet would be higher than their head. The head would be held in place with a band of metal. The nostrils would be sealed with wooden pegs and the jaw opened with piece of iron. A piece of linen would be put over their mouth and water would be poured down their throat, carrying the linen with it. The victim would swallow automatically pulling the linen into the gullet. They would cough and wretch and reach a state of semi-suffocation. When they struggled the ropes would cut into them. More and more water would be brought – up to eight jars were used.

Sometimes the Spanish Chair was also employed. This was an iron chair with metal bands that held the victim so they could not move. Their bare feet would be put in stocks next to a brazier. Their feet were covered in fat and slowly allowed to roast, more fat being applied from time to time so that the flesh did not burn away too quickly. Sometimes the victim had to be taken to the *auto-da-fé* in the chair because their feet had been completely burnt away. Flogging was also used and fingers and toes were cut off, usually one a day.

One Jew who converted to Christianity was delivered to the Inquisition by a servant whom he had whipped for stealing. He refused to confess to heresy. He had a linen bag tied over his head so tightly he almost suffocated. When it was taken off, he was asked to confess: he refused. Next, his thumbs were bound so tightly that blood spurted up from under the nails. His limbs were attached to pulleys and the ropes jerked violently so that his joints were dislocated. Then he was struck on the shins so viciously that he fainted with pain. Finally, he was tied up so tightly that the ropes cut into his flesh. He was only released when he had lost so much blood that his torturers feared he might die. Not that they cared, but it was much better for all concerned that, if people were going to die, they did so at the *auto-da-fé*. Public burning was a far more effective way of instilling the fear of God in other people. This particular man did not suffer that terrible fate. He was forced to wear the *sanbenito* – the garment of shame – for two years, then was banished from Seville.

A Scotsman named William Lithow was arrested in Malaga, accused of being a spy. As a Protestant he was taken before the Inquisition as a heretic. When he refused to convert to Catholicism, weights were put on his legs. The torture left him unable to walk. He was held in a prison overrun with vermin; his beard, his eyebrows and his eyelids were so infested that he could barely open his eyes. Every eight days, the vermin were swept off him. He was given a pint of water every other day. His cell had no bed, blanket, pillow or window.

After 47 days, he was taken by carriage to the torture

chamber, where he was racked for five hours. His torturers were so clumsy that they took an inch of flesh off his heel. From then on, the carriage drew up outside his cell every morning at the same time, so that he would think he was being taken back to the rack. When he still refused to convert, he was kicked in the face by the inquisitor and sentenced to 11 different tortures. Finally, he was taken to Granada to be burnt.

Two slaves – a Turk and a black woman – were to look after him so that he would be well enough to be burnt. They were very kind to him and another servant, a Flemish boy, was so impressed by his courage that he got word to the English ambassador who rescued him.

The inquisitors were particularly fond of torturing attractive young women. In Cordova, one 15-year-old girl was stripped naked and scourged until she bore testimony against her mother.

In Toledo, a woman named Elvira del Campo was charged with not eating pork and putting out clean linen on a Saturday. Terrified of torture, she admitted that these were criminal acts, but denied any heretical intentions. The inquisitors were not satisfied. When they sent her to be tortured, she fell on her knees and begged them to tell her what they wanted her to say.

She was taken to the torture chamber where she was told to tell the truth, but she had nothing to say. She was stripped and asked again. Her suffering was detailed in the records of the Inquisition at Toledo.

'Señor,' she said. 'I have done all that is said of me and I bear false-witness against myself, for I do not want to see myself in such trouble. Please God, for I have done nothing.'

She was told not to bear false-witness against herself but to tell the truth. They began tying her arms.

'I have told the truth, what more do I have to tell?' she asked.

A cord was tied around her arms and was twisted until

she screamed.

'Tell me what you want as I don't know what to say,' she said.

She was told to tell them what she had done. She had not done that. That was why she was being tortured.

'Loose the ropes, Señor,' she said, 'and tell me what I have to say. I do not know what I have done. Lord have mercy on this sinner.'

Another turn was made.

'Loosen the ropes a little so that I may remember what I have to tell,' she begged. I don't know what I have done. I did not eat pork for it made me sick. I have done everything they say. Loosen the ropes and I will tell the truth.'

Another turn of the cord was ordered.

Loosen me and I will tell the truth,' she begged. 'I don't know what I have to tell. Loosen me for the sake of God. Tell me, what I have to say. I did it, I did it. It hurts, Señor. I did it – I have nothing to tell. Oh, my arms. Release me and I will tell you everything.'

She was asked again what she did and she responded, 'I don't know, I don't eat pork because I don't like it.'

Asked why did she not like it, she replied, 'Loosen me, loosen me. Take me out of here and I will tell you. I will tell why I don't like it.'

She was then asked what she had done that was contrary to the Catholic faith and she replied, 'Take me out of here and tell me what to say. It hurts. Oh, my arms, my arms.' She repeated this over and over again.

Asked again what she had done against the one true faith, she said, 'I don't remember. Tell me what I have to say. Oh, wretched me. I will tell you anything you want, Señor. You are breaking, my arms. Loosen me a little. I did everything I am accused of.'

She was then asked to tell them in detail what she had done. 'What do you want me to say? I did everything. Loosen me. I don't remember what I have to tell you. Don't you see that I am a weak woman? Oh! Oh! My arms are breaking.'

More turns were ordered and she cried. At this point, there were 16 turns in the cord. The pain was unendurable, but mercifully, when they tried to add another turn the rope broke.

She was put on the rack.

'Señores, why will you not tell me what I have to say?' she said as they strapped her on.

They told her to tell them what she had done wrong.

'I don't remember,' she said. 'Let me go. I did what the witnesses said.'

She was asked what the witnesses had stated.

'Señor, I – have told you, I do not remember,' she said. 'Señores, release me. I don't remember.'

Again, she was told to tell them.

'I don't know,' she said. 'Oh! Oh! You are tearing me to pieces. I have said I did it. Let me go.'

She was told to tell.

'Seflor, it does not help me to say that I did it, and I have admitted that what I have done has brought me to this suffering,' she said. 'Señor, you know the truth. Señor, for God's sake have mercy on me. Oh Señor, take these things from my arms. Señor, release me, they are killing me.'

The cords tying her to the rack were tightened.

'Remind me of what I have to say for I don't know,' she begged. 'I said I did not eat pork – I only know that I don't eat it because I don't like it.'

She repeated this many times. Again, she was ordered to say why she did not like it.

'For the reason that the witnesses said. I don't know how to tell you. Miserable am I that I don't know how to tell you,' she said. 'I said I did it. My God, how can I find the words to tell you?'

She said that she didn't do it, so how could she tell them. 'You won't listen to me,' she said. 'You want to kill me.

Release me and I will tell the truth.'

Again she was told to tell the truth and she said, 'I don't know how to say it. I have no memory. Lord, you are witness that if I knew how to say anything else I would say it. I have nothing more to say than that I did it and God knows it.'

She said this many times.

'Señor, Señor, nothing helps me. You, Lord, hear that I tell the truth and can say no more. They are tearing out my soul. Order them to loosen me.'

'I do not say that I did it. I said no more.' And then, 'Señor, I did it to observe the law.'

She was asked what law.

'The law that the witnesses say. I admit it all, Señor. I don't remember which law it was. Oh, wretched was the mother that bore me.'

Asked again what law she had meant, she said, 'If I knew what to say I would say it. Oh, Señor, I don't know what I have to say. Oh! Oh! You are killing me. If you would tell me what to say. Oh, Señor. Oh, my heart.'

She was asked whether she wished to tell the truth before they began the water torture. She said that she could not speak and that she was a sinner. The linen was then placed in her mouth.

'Take it away,' she screamed. 'I am strangling. I am sick.'

A jar of water was then poured down her throat. Afterwards she was told to tell the truth. She begged to be allowed to confess; she was dying. The inquisitor told her that the torture would continue until she told the truth. She had to tell it. Then she was repeatedly cross-questioned, but she said nothing. Seeing she was exhausted by the torture, the inquisitor ordered it to be suspended.

All this had been noted down by a secretary who attended the torture sessions. On this occasion, Elvira del Campo seems to have got off lightly. Only one jar of water was poured down her throat and, according the secretary's meticulous notes, she did not scream or cry very much. But her sufferings were by no means over.

She was left for four days. By this time her limbs had stiffened, making any renewed torture doubly painful. Then she was brought back to the torture chamber. This time when she was stripped, she broke down completely and begged to be allowed to cover her nakedness. It made no difference. Her interrogation and torture continued. This time her replies were even less coherent than before. Eventually, she confessed to judaism, repented and begged for mercy. The torture was suspended.

Legally, confessions extracted under torture were not valid. So, 24 hours later, she was taken back to the Holy Office, where her confession was read out. Under oath she had to swear that it was correct in every detail. If she did not, the suspended torture would be resumed. That done, she was reconciled to the Church at a public *auto-da-fé*.

There were other, worse, tortures. In the prison of the Inquisition at Toledo, a statue of the Virgin Mary covered with nails and blades was found. When a lever was pulled, the Virgin Mary's arms embraced the victim, whose naked flesh was pulled on to the spikes in a vicious mockery of the faith. Probably the most nauseating torture involved a number of mice that were placed on the victim's stomach. A large dish was put over them upside down, and a fire was lit on top of the bowl. As it grew hotter the mice would panic and try to get away from it. The only way out was for them to burrow through the victim's flesh.

The Holy Office were not allowed to take life, so when a suspect had admitted heresy they were handed over to the secular authorities as enemies of the state. The Inquisition, wanting its hands to be clean, said it 'abandoned' its victims in secular hands and beseeched the authorities to show mercy. However, the secular authorities did not dare to show mercy. If they did, they risked being hauled in front of the Inquisition and charged with heresy themselves.

Even the inquisitors admitted that mistakes were made. Thousands of good Catholics were falsely accused, tortured into making a confession and unjustly condemned to death at the *auto-da-fé*. But they were seen as privileged – they were being allowed to die for the faith. And for their glorious death, they would be admitted straight to paradise, so they had nothing to complain about.

The execution of heretics was no new thing. In the fourteenth century, Pope Innocent IV had issued a Bull, instructing the governments of all Catholic countries that it was their duty to arrest and execute all heretics – or suffer excommunication and face charges of heresy themselves. The Spanish chose to do this in a particularly barbarous way.

Sometimes the Church was merciful. Some people who had been found guilty of heresy and asked to be reconciled with the church were spared. As an act of penitence, they had to be whipped half-naked though the streets in a procession to the local cathedral six Fridays in succession. After that, they would never be able to hold any rank or office, or wear fine clothes or jewellery. One fifth of their money would also be forfeit to the Inquisition. Unreconciled heretics, those who had relapsed into heresy and those the Inquisition did not choose to favour, suffered public burning at the *auto-da-fé*.

Auto-da-fé is the Portuguese for 'Act of Faith'. In Spanish it is *auto-de-fé* but, for historic reasons, the Portuguese variant has been adopted into the English language. These ghastly rituals took place on Sundays or other holy days, because more people would be able to watch.

The evening before the auto the heretics were brought before the Inquisition and told whether they would live or die. Every person condemned would then be allotted two priests to wrestle for their souls. Although the condemned were bound to die, it was still possible to save their souls.

In that case, if they were reconciled with the church, they would be strangled before the flames reached them.

Everyone found guilty of heresy also had to wear a tall cap like a mitre called a coraza, and a sanbenito, a loose-fitting tunic made of yellow sackcloth that came down to the knees. It was a garment regularly worn by penitents. Those found guilty of lesser crimes than heresy would be sentenced to wear the sanbenito on Sundays, or for a specific period. Normally, they would have blood-red crosses sewn on them. But the sanbenitos worn by those facing the auto-daft were decorated with flames and devils prodding the fires with pitchforks. If the flames pointed downwards, the Inquisition had been merciful. The victim had repented of their heresy and would be strangled. If they pointed upwards, the victim was persisting in their heretical believes and would suffer the worst atrocity: they would be burnt to death. Burning was the favoured method as, technically, it did not spill blood.

The next morning at around six o'clock the victims were lined up outside the prison in their sanbenitos with a rope around their necks and their hands tied together. They marched off in a procession led by priests bearing green crosses – the symbol of the Inquisition – draped in black material. Next came the alguazils: as well as arresting suspects and visiting victims in jail, urging them to repent, they were charged with protecting the inquisitors who were not always popular figures in the community.

Following them was a priest carrying the Host. Over his head was a canopy of scarlet and gold carried by four men. When he approached, the men, women and children in the crowd had to fall to their knees. If they did not, they would be marked out as heretics.

Then came more alguazils, followed by lesser criminals, some of whom bore the marks of torture. The victims came next, each flanked by two Dominican friars in their white vestments and black hoods. In some cases, these men were still trying to save the soul of the victim. Following after were the bodies of those who had been found guilty of heresy after their death and had been dug up for punishment. After them were the effigies of those who had fled Spain rather than face the Inquisition, carried on green poles. The effigies wore the sanbenitos and corazas of the condemned.

Then came the inquisitors, flanked on one side by banners emblazoned with the arms of the pope, entwined with those of Ferdinand and Isabella. On the other side were the arms of the Inquisition. Behind came more alguazils and other minor officials. The entire procession was flanked by soldiers carrying halberds. Bringing up the rear was the crowd, who followed the procession to the cathedral square.

Once there, each victim was read a list of their crimes before a sermon was preached. Often there were several hundred of them and this process could take all day. The victims were made to sit on benches swathed in black crepe; the benches were set on a platform so the crowd could see those who had been condemned. Being good Catholics, the crowds shouted insults at the victims and humiliated them. It was not unusual to set fire to Jews' beards. This was called 'shaving the New Christians'. An the white, priests, and monks harried the victims, still working hard to get last-minute repentance.

The inquisitors sat on another platform, surrounded by their blackdraped green crosses. Incense burnt – a wise precaution, as there were usually a large number of freshly disinterred bodies around.

Mass was celebrated; then there was another sermon. Following that, the Grand Inquisitor stood up and led the crowd in the oath. The onlookers were required to fall to their knees and swear that they could defend the Holy Office against all its enemies. They would be faithful to it in life and in death; they would do whatever it asked of them; and they swore that they would pluck out their right eye or cut off their right hand if that was what it asked of them.

Ferdinand and Isabella refrained from saying 'this oath.' So did the Spanish monarchs that succeeded them – with the exception of Philip II who was a zealot. It was at this point that the Church washed its hands of the victims. It had done all it could for the sinners. Now they abandoned them to the secular authorities for the punishment for heresy to be carried out. The charges were read out again, this time by the secular authorities. The Grand Inquisitor then made a public plea for mercy, asking disingenuously that their blood would not be spilt.

The secular authorities were deaf to these pleas and took the victims to the quemadero – the place of burning. This was a field where the stakes had already been set up and the faggots piled high. Having been tied to the stakes, the victims were asked if they wanted absolution; the lucky ones were garrotted, then the faggots were lit. Monks chanted; people cheered; the inquisitors feigned shock at the wickedness of the world; and the smell of roasting flesh permeated the air.

After condemning so many people to death, Torquemada himself died peacefully in his bed in 1498. He was a happy man: he had lived to see the Muslims expelled from Granada and his own persecution had resulted in the expulsion of the Jews from Spain in 1492. At the time, many people called him the 'Saviour of Spain,' because he freed the country from the control of the Pope. Indeed, many of the Grand Inquisitors that followed him were worse than he was, but he had built the instrument through which they vented their sadism. In the end, the Spanish Inquisition weakened Spain and left it with a reputation for barbarism that it only threw off after the death of General Franco in 1975.

At its height, the Spanish Inquisition had 14 tribunals set

up in Spain, Mexico and Peru. The Spanish Inquisition established itself in Sicily in 1517, but efforts to set one up in Naples and Milan failed. In 1522, the emperor Charles V introduced it to the Netherlands in an effort to stamp out Protestantism.

Napoleon attempted to suppress the inquisition when he occupied Spain in 1808 and it was finally halted in 1834. The last *auto-da-fé* took place in Mexico in 1850. Estimates of how many people perished in the autos vary wildly, but the number probably runs into the hundreds of thousands.

The majority were women, some of them in their nineties. Children as young as 12 or 13 were frequently burnt when their parents were found to be heretics. In 1659, two ten-year-old girls were burnt in Toledo.

Two elderly nuns were burnt alive in Evora in 1673 with the name of Jesus on their lips. They had lived blameless lives in a convent for over 40 years. Garcia d'Alarcon was said to be the most beautiful woman in the country when she was burnt by the Inquisition in Granada 1593. Isabelle, the wife of Francisco Dalos of Ciudad Real, first appeared before the inquisition at the age of 22. She was arraigned five more times and spent 18 years of her life in the prisons of the Inquisition. Her last trial began in 1665, when she was 80, and lasted until 1670. She was tortured three times and eventually died. The Inquisition then sentenced her to a double punishment. Her body was burnt, along with an effigy. Having neglected to confess before she expired in the torture chamber, she died in a state of sin.

One of the most famous victims of the auto in the New World was Dofia Ana de Castro, a socialite in Lima. Her love affairs were legendary and it was said that she even shared her favours with the viceroy. It was possibly a rejected lover or a jealous rival who told the Inquisition she was secretly practising Judaism. She was burned in 1836.

In Sicily, a renegade Augustine Friar named Diego

Lamattina got his revenge. In 1657 he was charged with being, a heretical blasphemer, despiser of the sacraments and an insulter of sacred images. When he was in prison, he was visited by the Inquisitor General, whose brains he dashed out with his manacles.

Balthazar Lopez was an incorrigible joker. As court saddler in Castile, he had amassed a small fortune. After taking a trip abroad in 1645, he was arrested. Along with 56 others he faced the flame at the great auto held at Cuena in 1654. As they approached the quemadero, his confessor exhorted him to rejoice, as the gates of Paradise were soon to be opening freely for him.

'Freely,' scoffed Lopez. 'The confiscation of my property has cost me 200,000 ducats. Do you infer that I have been swindled?'

At the brasero – the brazier – he noticed that the executioner, Pedro de Alcald, was making a clumsy job of strangling two of his fellow victims. 'Pedro,' Lopez said, 'If you can't strangle me better than you are doing to those two poor souls, I'd rather be burned alive.'
The executioner then tried to bind his feet.

'For God's sake,' said Lopez, finding this the final indignity. 'If you bind me, I won't believe in your Jesus.'

He threw down the crucifix he was holding. The priest finally managed to persuade him to take it back and ask for forgiveness. Then the executioner started to strangle him and the priest asked if he was truly repentant.

'Father,' said the dying man, 'is this any time to joke?'

The Destruction of the Aztecs

The conventional view of the Aztecs is that they were the most bloodthirsty people who ever existed. While it is true that they practised human sacrifice and would sometimes dress themselves in the flayed skins of their victims, this is by no means the whole story. The Aztecs were the last of the four great civilisations the Ohnec, Teotihuacdn, Mayan and Aztlán – that had flourished in Mexico since the first millennium BC.

Their civilisation was destroyed by young Spanish noble-man Hernando Cortés in 1521. The Spanish considered the conquest of Mexico the last crusade. Battles against 'the infidel' were fresh in Spanish minds. Granada, the last great stronghold of the Moors, had only been recaptured by the Spanish in 1492. Muslims and Jews were expelled, and those who remained were forcibly converted.

Cortés conquered the Aztec empire with just 500 men, 16 horses and one canon. Almost as important was his mis-tress, a slave girl called Malinche, later baptised as Doña Marina. She spoke both Mayan and the Aztec language Natuatl, and acted crucially as his interpreter throughout the campaign.

The Aztecs had an inkling of their fate when between 1507 and 1510 strange ships were sighted off the coast of Mexico. Then came a series of ill omens – a comet appeared in the sky, lightning struck a temple and the sound of women weeping was heard at night. Although the Aztec ruler Motecuhzoma simply executed anyone who reported these portents of doom, it did no good.

A fatal flaw in the Aztecs' defence was their own legends. The Aztecs believed that the god Quetzalcoatl, the mythi-cal ruler of Toltecs, the Aztec's precursors, had been exiled and would return in the year I Reed, according to the

Aztec calendar. I Reed was 1519, when the Spaniards turned up, so Motecuhzoma assumed that the Spaniards were gods and that their ships were wooden temples.

He sent gold and magnificent costumes made out of feathers, in the hope that the gods would take the gifts and go. Instead, Cortés seized the messengers and put then in chains. He gave them a demonstration of his god-like powers by firing his canon, which made them faint. Cortés established himself at Veracruz and burnt his ships so that his men could not flee back to Cuba, then began his march on the Aztec capital, Tenochtitlán.

With armour, muskets, crossbows, swords and horses, the Spanish had overwhelming military superiority. War for the peoples of pre-Columbian Mexico was largely a ceremonial affair. They wore elaborate costumes and were armed only with a small sword made out of obsidian – volcanic glass.

Their object was to capture as many of the enemy as possible to use as human sacrifices later. If a leader was killed or a temple captured, the loser capitulated immediately and talks began over the amount of tribute that should be paid. Cortés did not play by these rules – he slaughtered as many as he could on the battlefield.

Motecuhzoma's only possible defence was guile. He tried to capture Cortés in an ambush at Cholula. But Cortés discovered the plan and massacred the citizens of Cholula. He destroyed the temple of Huitzilopochtli, the Aztec god of war, and set up an image of the Virgin Mary instead. It was a crucial psychological victory over the Aztec culture.

Cortés established an alliance with the people of Tlaxcala, who had only recently been conquered by Motecuhzoma. They rebelled and rallied to Cortés' cause.

Hearing what had happened at Cholula, other Aztec cities surrendered without a fight and Cortés marched on Tenochtitlán unopposed.

Motecuhzoma had no choice but to greet the Spanish graciously. He lodged Cortés in the palace of Axayacatl, Motecuhzoma's father, which was packed with gold ornaments. These were melted down; decorative stones and feathers they simply threw away. The gold was shipped back as bars directly to Charles V in Spain, bypassing Cortés' commander, the governor of Cuba, Diego Velázquez. Cortés also demanded that Motecuhzoma swear allegiance to Charles V of Spain. He would remain nominal ruler of the Aztecs while Cortés himself seized the reigns of power, with the aim of becoming viceroy.

To reassert his authority, Velázquez sent a force of over 1000 under Panfilo de Narváez to bring Cortés to heel. Leaving a small force under Pedro de Alvardo in Tenochtitldn, Cortés headed back to the coast where he defeated Narváez and used the troops to swell his own ranks.

Meanwhile, back in Tenochtitlán, the Aztecs were celebrating the festival of their war god Huitzilopochtli which, like all Aztec festivals, involved human sacrifice on an epic scale. Terrified by the extent of these bloodthirsty rituals, Alvardo's men turned on the Aztecs and slaughtered as many as 10,000 priests and worshippers. When Cortés returned to Tenochtitlán, he found the city in a state of open warfare. He tried to calm the situation by getting Motecuhzoma to talk to his people, but the Aztecs stoned Motecuhzoma to death as a traitor.

Cortés grabbed as much gold and treasure as his men could carry and tried to make a run for it. The Aztecs ambushed them and Cortés escaped with just 500 men. But in a monumental tactical error, the Aztecs did not pursue the Spanish and finish them off. This allowed Cortés to regroup. He turned back and laid siege to the city.

The Aztecs put up fierce resistance, but for months, they were starved and harried. Finally, they were defeated by an epidemic of smallpox brought by one of Namden soldiers. This killed Motecuhzoma's successor, his brother Cuitlahuac. Their cousin Cuahtemoc took over as emperor, but he was captured and tortured until he revealed fresh sources of gold. Later he was hanged on the pretext of treason against Charles V

Many of the priests and Aztec soldiers preferred to die rather than surrender to the Spanish. In order to quell any resistance, Cortés demolished Tenochtitlán, building by building, using the rubble to fill in the city's canals. Mexico City was built on the ruins. The surviving Aztecs were used as slave labour in the gold and silver mines. They were decimated by two further epidemics of smallpox. Forcible conversion to Christianity destroyed what remained of their culture and they lost themselves in drink.

What little we know of the Aztecs comes from Cortés and his men who were more interested in booty than scholarship, and the Franciscan friar Bernardino, de Sahageen who circulated questionnaires among survivors of the onslaught in an attempt to learn something of the culture they had destroyed. His work was inhibited by the Inquisition who investigated him for being too pro-Indian and confiscated his writings which, fortunately, resurfaced in the eighteenth century.

The Middle Passage

When Europeans began colonising the Americas in the fifteenth and sixteenth centuries, they found their great projects there hampered by the shortage of labour. The indigenous people were not prepared to work for wages and they did not make good slaves – it was too easy for them to escape and live among their own people.

In Africa, however, the slave trade was already well established. As in most places in the world, an informal system of slavery had been established from the earliest times – those who lost a war became the slaves of those who won – but slaving became a commercial enterprise. As early as AD 650, Arab slave traders began taking African slaves to Arabia and beyond. In 1444, the Portuguese started taking slaves from West Africa, so when the Americas opened up, it seemed the natural place to find cheap labour.

At first, European ships would sail to the West African coast with manufactured goods that they would exchange for the slaves, who had been brought to the beaches by the local chieftains or traders. The slaves would be transported to the West Indies where the slave markets were. From there, they were taken to the islands' sugar plantations or on to North or South America. The ships would then return to Europe with cargoes of sugar, rum, tobacco and coffee. As these slaving voyages had three legs, they were known as the triangular trade.

For the American ships, the triangular trade was somewhat different. They sailed out of Boston, Massachusetts and Newport, Rhode Island, and were called 'rum boats' as they carried rum to Africa – Africans had come to like rum more than French brandy. The cargo was exchanged for slaves who, again, were taken to the West Indies, where they were exchanged for molasses. This was taken back to New England, where it was made into rum.

The journey across the Atlantic was called the 'Middle Passage'. Over 11 million Africans made the trip. This compares with over 18 million Africans who were taken eastwards by Arab traders. Nearly half of those who went to the New World were carried by the Portuguese and were taken directly to Brazil.

By the eighteenth century, when the transatlantic slave trade was at its zenith, slave ships were practically floating coffins. At any one time, the ships of half-a-dozen nations were moored off the coast of West Africa waiting to pick up slaves. In some places, such as the Bonny River in Nigeria, there could be as many as ten ships waiting. It could take months for a large ship to fill her holds. Along the Cold Coast, where the competition was greatest, ships would have to make numerous stops, sometimes buying slaves one or two at a time. The Portuguese traded further south out of Angola where they had the market to themselves and the waiting times were less.

Once the ship was moored and its sails furled, the crew would make 'house'. This involved tying spars between the masts to make the framework of a roof. On it, they would lay rush mats. Underneath, the 'house' was divided into two rooms. In one, the captain entertained kings, tribal headmen and other slave traders; the other was a receiving area for the slaves.

These roofs were not very good at keeping the rain out and they were hot and stuffy, especially as braziers were lit on deck. The crewmen were eager to make their stay off the coast as short as possible as they were prey to all sorts of tropical diseases. As there were rarely enough sailors to control the slaves, they tried to purchase Africans from different nations, so they could not easily organise a mutiny. Some captains picked out a few slaves to guard over the others, armed with a whip.

The slaves were brought on board in dugout canoes, manned by Krumen fishermen from the Grain Coast who were expert at handling boats. The slaves were shackled in pairs with leg irons. Before they were purchased, they were given a rudimentary medical examination to make sure they were healthy. Special attention was paid to their teeth and any signs that they were ageing. Then their heads were shaved, their clothes taken away, and they were branded with a red-hot iron.

Once on board, the men were kept chained until the ship sailed, and sometimes for the entire voyage. Women and children were allowed to go free. On some ships sexual relations with the captives were forbidden. On most, the young women and girls were repeatedly raped by the sex-starved sailors.

The slaves were housed in the cargo hold. This was about five feet high, so it was impossible for most to stand upright. A worse method of cramming in even more of the human cargo was devised: a shelf six feet wide around the hold to hold a second tier of slaves. In larger ships, there were two shelves. These allowed slaves 20 inches of head-room. Slaves were packed in so tightly that they had to lie on their side rather than on their backs.

Some captains were, in the circumstances, kindly men. One, John Newton, went on to become a parish priest and composer of hymns; Hugh Crow boasted that he had black friends in the West Indies that had once been transported on his ship; but some were fiends, drunk with power. Captain McTaggart of the Alexander once had every one of his 50-man crew, except three, flogged. When one man jumped overboard to escape a flogging and was rescued from the sea, he was asked if he was not afraid of being eaten by sharks.

'I would prefer that to life on this ship,' he said.

Once out at sea, the slaves were brought up on deck every morning. Their shackles were attached to a chain running down the centre of the deck to stop them jumping overboard. A drummer, a piper or a man with a whip encouraged them to exercise. This was a mixed blessing. The heavy leg irons caused bruising and bleeding around the ankles; but few captains risked letting the slaves take them off.

The slaves were fed two meals a day of a coarse porridge made from maize of millet. Their diet was occasionally varied with beans, the kind fed to horses, and sometimes a little salted meat. When the slaves were out on deck, good captains had their quarters scrubbed out with vinegar, but many did not bother with this nicety. In rough weather, the slaves would not be let out – they would have to stay in the stuffy, dark, stinking hold day and night.

Ship's surgeon, Alexander Falconbridge, who wrote several books about his experiences, said that each man had less space than he would have in his coffin. It was impossible to move through the hold without walking on someone. Falconbridge would take his shoes off to avoid injuring anyone. Slaves would bite his feet if they came near their faces.

The slaves had to move about to try and reach the lavatories – which amounted to no more than two or three large buckets for 100 men. They would have to manoeuvre themselves there with the man they were chained to. Many suffered from acute dysentery and were not up to this struggle. Not surprisingly, the smell of the slave ships was so foul that other ships would sail to windward of them. One slave captain, Richard Drake, would carry a bag full of camphor in his teeth as a nosegay.

Tarpaulins were spread over the gratings and vents to keep rain and spray out – they also kept the foul smell in. When it was warm, the conditions were so stuffy that many fainted. Falconbridge compared the conditions to those in a slaughterhouse.

Africans were particularly vulnerable to smallpox and epidemics raged through the holds. Others died of no apparent cause. Some went mad and others managed to kill themselves. One man on the Brookes, a slaver sailing out of Liverpool, tried to cut his throat the first night they were at sea. The surgeon sewed it up, but the next night the man tore out the stitches with his fingernails. The surgeon patched him up a second time and tied the man's hands behind his back. Then he refused to eat; he was threatened and punished, but it did no good. Within two weeks, he was dead. This was unusual. Those who could not be flogged into eating usually had a special device jammed between their teeth which forced their jaw open so that food could be pushed into their mouth.

Some slaves believed that if they died on the voyage, their spirit would return to their homeland, making suicide an attractive prospect. If they got the chance, they would jump overboard, often with a look of joy on their faces. One captain threatened to have the bodies of drowned slaves fished out and decapitated. Then, he said, their spirit would have to go home headless.

More commonly, death came from what the slavers called 'fixed melancholy'. This had no apparent cause except for the extreme misery of the conditions. Sailors believed that by some supreme act of will the Africans could simply hold their breath until they were dead. This is impossible, but it was noted that, although Africans often recovered from the other diseases on board ship – even smallpox – no one ever recovered from the 'fixed melancholy'.

The conditions were not always as bad as Alexander Falconbridge described. Slaves were a valuable cargo and, usually, everything possible would be done to keep them alive. The mortality rate was, in fact, higher among the sailors. They were not valuable and were prey to tropical diseases and scurvy as they were longer at sea.

Hugh Crow made several voyages without losing a single slave or seaman, but this was rare. An epidemic could kill hundreds before they reached the Caribbean. Occasionally, every slave would be dead before the vessel arrived. Anti-slavery campaigner Thomas Clarkson recorded 20 voyages where, of a total cargo of 7,904 slaves, 2,053 died. This is just over a quarter. More usually around one in eight died. The dead were thrown overboard and the slave ships were invariably followed by schools of sharks.

Mortality depended on the length of the voyage as conditions deteriorated day by day. The trip from the Gambia to Barbados took a mere six weeks; the journey from

Angola to Cuba could take as long as three months, especially as ships often found themselves becalmed in the doldrums. In that case, ships ran low on food and water, worsening the conditions for slaves and crew alike.

There was the danger of shipwreck – slaves chained in pairs with heavy shackles were unlikely to survive. There were also pirates to contend with and privateers. Britain and France were regularly at war throughout the eighteenth century and the other's shipping and cargoes were considered fair game. In one case, a British ship's captain armed some of the slaves to repulse the French. He said that they fought with great spirit, but he sold them in Jamaica anyway.

On well-run slave ships, as they approached the West Indies, discipline was relaxed. Sometimes there was even a party with the African women dressed up in clothes that the sailors had given them, capering around. However, when they finally arrived in Kingston, Havana or Rio de Janeiro, they soon found there was no cause for celebration. The slaves had to undergo a humiliating physical inspection before being separated and sold at auction.

If there was a shortage of slaves at the time, there would be an unseemly scramble, with buyers swarming over the boats to try and secure the best of the cargo. Then the captains totted up their profits, scrubbed out the holds and filled them with produce, while the slaves were sent off to a life of servitude.

Occasionally, the slaves mutinied. In November 1749, the *Ann*, sailing out of Liverpool, moored off the coast of Guinea to pick up slaves. Six months later, she was still there. By this time, she had 60 slaves on board. Her crew of just 13 was ill and, in the middle of one night, the Africans turned on them. They seized the arms and ammunition and killed or wounded all the crewmen, except for two who hid. The Africans took over the ship and ran her aground, where she broke up, then jumped overboard and disappeared.

The *King David*, sailing out of Bristol, was also under-manned when she picked up a cargo of slaves from the Guinea coast in May 1750. Her captain was an easy-going man who did not keep the slaves in irons. One of the slaves had been a chief in his own country and spoke English well. The captain would sometimes invite him to his cabin for a chat. During these visits, the chief saw where the captain's weapons were stowed. Soon after the ship sailed, the chief and 15 of his men rushed the captain's cabin, seized the guns and took over the ship. The captain and five of the crew were killed; the rest shut themselves in the hold. The chief called for them to come out, saying they would not be killed. Those who surrendered were put in irons. However, the first mate refused to come out. A cabin boy was sent down to tell him that he would be cut to pieces if he did not give himself up. When the mate came out, he was clapped in irons like the rest of the crew. Then the Africans began throwing them overboard, but the chief stepped in to save the mate.

'If you throw him overboard, who will sail the ship?' he asked. He swore to kill any man who harmed the mate, who then sailed them to safety.

The most famous mutiny occurred on board the *Amistad*, which sailed out of Havana with a cargo of 53 slaves. Before being sold on in Honduras, the slaves were allowed on deck to 'refresh' them. A ship's cook, who was of mixed race, remarked that, when they arrived, they would be killed and their flesh salted and sold as meat. One of the slaves, whose named was Cinqué, led a revolt. He broke their chains and threw the captain overboard. The slaves' two owners were on board. Cinqué insisted that they sail back to Africa – eastwards, towards the morning sun. However, the slave-owners tricked him by sailing off course during the night. After two months, they grew short of food and water, and found themselves moored off

Long Island.

At first, the US authorities thought that the *Amistad* was a smuggler. The ship was seized and the Africans were jailed in New Haven. The Spanish ambassador in Washington demanded that both the ship and the cargo be returned to its owners. However, abolitionists in the US argued that the slaves should be freed. They persuaded the congressman and ex-President John Quincy Adams to represent the men. He took the case all the way to the Supreme Court and won. Cinqué and his companions were freed and returned to Sierra Leone.

However, it was not the slave mutinies that put an end to the transatlantic slave trade, but the atrocities committed by the slavers. One in particular caught the public imagination. On 6 September 1781, a British ship named the *Zong* left the Guinea coast bound for Jamaica. She carried a cargo of 440 slaves and a crew of 17. By the time she reached the Caribbean, the complement was down to 380 slaves and ten crewmen. Many were sick.

The *Zong* approached Jamaica on 27 November, but her captain, Luke Collingwood, steered away, saying that he mistook the island for another one. Two days later, he called the remains of his crew together and revealed his vicious plan. He proposed throwing overboard all the sick slaves. They were unlikely to recover he said, and they would fetch nothing at auction. His justification was that the ship was short of water and, by throwing some of the slaves overboard, he would be able to save the rest.

The real reason was an insurance swindle. Insurers would not pay out for a slave who died of natural causes, fearing that the slavers would simply let the slaves die. But the rule of the sea is that an insurer has to pay up for cargo thrown overboard if the reason for jettisoning it is to save the rest. Although, this rule was not written with a human cargo in mind, it still applied.

The mate, James Kelsal, objected. They were not short of

water, he said, and they were near land. There was no justification for throwing anyone overboard. However, after he had made his protest, Kelsal said no more. He was one of the men who threw 54 living people into the sea. Three days later, after it had rained and replenished their stocks of water, they threw 42 more overboard. A week later, when they neared land, an additional 26 were drowned. To prevent them swimming ashore, their arms were bound before they were thrown. Another ten jumped overboard of their own accord.

A few days later, the *Zong* anchored in the harbour in Kingston, Jamaica, where the rest of the slaves were sold. Collingwood duly put in a claim for the 122 men and women he and his men had drowned and the ten who had killed themselves. However, the insurers were suspicious. They investigated the claim and found out what had happened.

The insurers refused to pay up for the drowned slaves and were sued by the owners. The owners won the case by arguing that throwing 133 slaves overboard was no different, in law, than throwing 133 horses overboard. The insurers appealed, and in a landmark decision, Lord Mansfield reversed the decision on the grounds that human beings – even slaves – could not be treated simply as goods.

The case set the campaign for the abolition of the slave trade rolling. There were even calls to charge the *Zong*'s officers with murder, but Collingwood died and so nothing came of it.

Wounded Knee

The battle of Wounded Knee was the last battle of the Indian – that is, Native American – Wars. But it was not so much a battle as a massacre. The descendants of the Pilgrim Fathers and others wishing to live out their manifest destiny say that the US Cavalry went to Wounded Knee on 29 December 1890 to talk, not to fight. To them, the fact that 84 Sioux men and 62 Sioux women and children ended up dead was a tragedy; to the Indians it was an atrocity.

Wounded Knee was essentially the Cavalry's revenge for the Battle of the Little Big Horn, where General Custer and his entire command of 264 men had been wiped out by the Sioux. It had happened just a few days before 4 July 1876, the 100th anniversary of American Independence. That America's finest could be defeated by what the American people saw as a bunch of savages was a shock. Everyone clamoured for vengeance – the young nation's honour was at stake.

A few days later, Buffalo Bill shot down Chief Yellow Hand, taking 'the first scalp for Custer' and earning a considerable amount of fame into the bargain. Then General Miles began a winter campaign against the Indians. Rather than return to the reservation, the Sioux chief Sitting Bull fled to Canada. But Crazy Horse, who was low on supplies, led a procession of 800 braves into Fort Robinson, Nebraska, in an effort to save his people from starvation.

Crazy Horse had been one of the greatest Indian warriors and he found it difficult to adjust to life on the reservation. He did not trust the whites, who he thought were so evil that they would soon try to imprison the grass behind fences.

General Crook admired Crazy Horse and invited him to scout for him against his enemies the Nez Percé. It was a simply a strategy of divide and rule. Crazy Horse was keen: he sent word that he would fight until all the Nez Percé were dead. However, the message got distorted into an avowal to fight until all the whites were dead. The mix-up was straightened out, but afterwards the Cavalry found it impossible to trust him.

Crazy Horse's young wife died and he became increasingly restive. On the reservations, he found that jealous tribesmen spied on him and reported his every move to the authorities. He planned to leave but was first persuaded to attend a conference at Fort Robinson. Crazy Horse was on his guard – only the year before Sioux leaders had been murdered at Fort Keogh in Montana. When he arrived at the fort, Crazy Horse was informed that he would have to be locked in the guardhouse. He went for his weapons but even his own warriors tried to restrain him. In the resulting scuffle, a soldier stabbed him with a bayonet for 'resisting arrest'. He died that night.

In 1881, Sitting Bull returned to the United States and surrendered; but his warriors settled down to reservation life no better than Crazy Horse's followers. Then in 1888, the Ghost Dance came. A prophet named Wovoka who lived in the Nevada desert had had scarlet fever, which made him delirious. During a total eclipse of the sun he spoke with the Creator, who told him that the Indians had not come to the end of their trail. What they must do, the Creator said, was put aside the weapons of war and love one another. That way, they would have a special place in the afterlife. To herald the Judgement Day and the end of the world as they knew it, the Creator gave them the Ghost Dance, which had to be performed on five successive nights. The more often they did it, the sooner the Judgement Day would come.

By the time the Ghost Dance reached the Sioux, its prophecy had changed slightly. At Judgement Day, the suffering earth would die and with it, all the races of man. The whites, if they were reincarnated at all, would be reborn into a different world. But the Indians would be born back into the world of grasslands and buffalo, as it had been before the white man had come along. All the red people who had ever lived would be reborn in the flower of their youth, and heaven and earth would once again be in joyous harmony. When the Sioux danced the Ghost

Dance, they chanted, 'We will live again.'

Soon 6000 Sioux were doing the Ghost Dance. As it seemed the one sure way to get rid of the whites, they danced until they dropped. This worried the Indian agents who did not understand that the Ghost Dance was a religious revival. They thought it was a new war dance. The US military grew nervous: they banned the Ghost Dance and sent more troops to the reservations.

The agents received word that some of the medicine men were making Ghost shirts which they said no bullet could penetrate. Most frighteningly of all, it was said that Sitting Bull was going to the Pine Ridge reservation in South Dakota, where he too would perform the Ghost Dance.

Sitting Bull was now 56 years old and a proud man. The Indian Bureau had tried to break his spirit by withholding his rations. In response, Sitting Bull showed his contempt for the bureau by refusing to report to the agents. The US military feared his strength and not without good reason – the Indians attributed their victory at Little Bighorn to Sitting Bull's Sun Dance. During that dance he had cut 50 pieces of flesh off various parts of his body. In the trance induced by this self-torture, he saw US soldiers falling from the skies into his camp like grasshoppers.

The authorities need not have worried. Having travelled widely with the Buffalo Bill Wild West Show, Sitting Bull had seen just how numerous the whites were and he knew that military victory against them was impossible. He wanted to explore the Ghost Dance for religious rather than political reasons. However, other Indians believed that after Sitting Bull danced the Ghost Dance the Sioux would have an even greater victory than the Little Bighorn. This could not be allowed.

Indian police were sent to Sitting Bull's house to prevent him going to Pine Ridge. They found the house unguarded and its occupant asleep. Sitting Bull was willing to go with them peacefully, but soon his followers gathered, warning him not to go. Some called him a coward. His 17-year-old son begged him to resist: he should remember what had happened to Crazy Horse. Suddenly, he refused to go. Everyone went for their guns – when the shooting stopped, Sitting Bull and his son were among the dead.

The news spread like a prairie fire. Fearing they would be massacred on the reservation, Sitting Bull's men fled, intending hide in the Bad Lands of Dakota. On the way they ran into Big Foot, who was returning to the agency for supplies with a troop of 100 ill and ageing warriors. Big Foot himself had pneumonia and was so ill he could not ride a horse. While they were talking, a cavalry troop under Colonel Forsyth caught up with them. Big Foot raised a white flag for a parley, but Forsyth insisted on his unconditional surrender and escorted his prisoner to the post office near a small stream called Wounded Knee Creek.

Forsyth called for reinforcements and soon nearly 500 men of the Seventh Cavalry – many of whom had been with Major Reno's party who had narrowly escaped the massacre at Little Bighorn – were guarding 350 sick and hungry Indians: 120 men and 230 women and children. There was no hope of escape, as the cavalry stationed men with machine-guns on the heights above the camp.

On 29 December, the order came to disarm the Indians. At a little past eight in the morning, the men and grown boys were called to a council. They sat in a semi-circle to the south of Big Foot's tent. Forsyth made a speech that was translated into their language, Lakotah. He said that they were safe now; the soldiers were their friends; they would be bringing more food and no one would go hungry. However, there had been trouble recently and to prevent any fighting starting accidentally, he was asking for their guns.

For the Indians, a gun was a symbol of manhood. As hunters, they needed them to survive, and they had heard of Indians handing over their guns only to be shot once they were disarmed. Two men went to confer with Big Foot, who told them to hand over their old weapons, but to keep the good ones.

The Indians handed over just two old rifles, claiming that was all they had. The soldiers did not believe them. Earlier, when they had caught up with the fleeing Indians, they had plenty of guns. Big Foot, who was bleeding from the nose, was brought outside and ordered to tell his braves to co-operate. He insisted they had no guns.

'The soldiers at Cheyenne River took them all away from us and burned them,' he told Forsyth. This was not true and Forsyth knew it.

'You tell Big Foot that yesterday at the time of his surrender his Indians were well armed,' Forsyth commanded his interpreter.

Big Foot stuck to his story and Forsyth ordered a search of the entire camp. Officers were sent to scour the tents and were told to use the utmost tact. Enlisted men were to search the outside area. They were not well disciplined and started tipping the contents of the Indians' wagons on the ground. They ripped open packs and took axes, hatchets, butchers' knives, and women's quilting awls – anything that could conceivably be used as a weapon.

The Indians understandably were tense and the situation got worse when the officers began searching the women, several of whom were hiding rifles under their skirts. Although this encounter passed without incident, the young men grew restless.

Yellow Bird, the medicine man, began to pray that their Ghost shirts would protect them. Then he began to dance. Something bad was about to happen, he said. There were many soldiers and many bullets, but the bullets would not hurt those wearing the Ghost shirts. He threw a cloud of dust in the air, saying that was how ineffective the bluecoats' bullets would be as the dust drifted away in the breeze. Besides, he said, 'I have lived long enough' – a traditional Sioux war cry. Forsyth ordered him to sit down.

By 9.30, the Cavalry had found 38 rifles, but only a few of them were good Winchesters; the rest were old and useless. The day before, the Indians had been armed to the teeth with good rifles. If they were not in the tents and not under the women's skirts, Forsyth reasoned, then the men must have them concealed under their blankets.

At that moment, Forsyth spotted an Indian with a rifle under his blanket and ordered a sergeant to seize it. Through an interpreter, he told the Indians they must hand over their rifles if they did not want to undergo the indignity of being searched.

About 20 older men came forward and opened their blankets to show they were unarmed. However, Yellow Bird started chanting again and the younger men held back. Major Whitside roughly ordered them to step forward. Some reluctantly did so. They did have rifles under their blankets.

Seeing the rifles being taken away, a young deaf troublemaker called Black Coyote leapt to his feet. He pulled a Winchester from under his blanket and waved it in the air saying that he had given much money for his gun and was not going to give it up unless he got paid. While Yellow Bird chanted, another medicine man started singing a Ghost song and the other young men began to move away.

Tension grew. Forsyth tried to get one of the elders to calm the situation down. Black Coyote was trying to roll a cigarette; while he was distracted, two Cavalry sergeants tried to grab his gun. There was a scuffle; the gun pointed skywards and went off. At that precise moment, Yellow Bird threw another handful of dust in the air. The young braves took this as a sign, throwing off their blankets and levelling their guns; they were cut down by gunfire.

Big Foot caught a bullet in the head. Seeing her father fall, his daughter ran towards him. She was shot in the back and fell across him. Being badly deployed, as well as killing the Indians, the Cavalry hit each other in the cross-fire.

The machine-guns on the ridge opened up, pumping explosive shells into the Indians' writhing bodies at a rate of 50 bullets a minute. It was reckoned that half the casualties occurred within the first minute. Survivors threw themselves on soldiers using knives, clubs, fists and teeth; but within two or three minutes the situation was impossible and the remainder fled. Once they were dear of the troops, the slaughter began in earnest. Fleeing Indians were simply gunned down; the explosive bullets set the tents on fire; a party of men, women and children trying to escape down the road to the south were slaughtered.

The remaining Indians tried to shelter in a ravine, but were shelled and cut to pieces by shrapnel.

Back in the camp, a young trooper saw an Indian disappear into a tent. Before anyone could stop him, he charged in too. A shot rang out.

'My God,' he screamed. 'I'm killed.'

The rest of his troops raked the tent with gunfire, then set it alight. When the burning canvas fell away, it revealed Yellow Bird, still defiant.

Some Indians escaped the ravine, but were caught up with later. Dead bodies were found up to two miles away. Survivors reported that women and children were enticed from hiding places in rocks only to be abused and murdered.

Outraged by what had happened, the Indians in the ravine came out guns blazing. One Indian bullet struck artillery Lieutenant Hawthorne who was up on the ridge. The bullet hit his pocket watch, which saved his life, but the workings of the watch were scattered throughout his body and five operations were required to remove them all.

The Indians' last stand was futile; they were shot down

like dogs. When the guns eventually fell silent, any Indians remaining alive were told to come out they would not be harmed. When a wounded man staggered out, he was shot. Colonel Forsyth then stepped in and ordered no further shooting.

The injured were taken to a field hospital. There were 51 Indians, 37 soldiers and two civilians – an interpreter who had had his nose cut off and a priest wounded. The blue-coats had lost 25, largely as a result of 'friendly fire'. The Indians had lost 146 and the troopers proudly boasted that they had avenged Custer.

Massacre at Amritsar

After the annexation of Bengal, British conquests in the subcontinent continued rapidly. The Hindu Marathas were defeated in 1818 and when the Sikh kingdom in the Punjab fell in 1849 the whole of the subcontinent was under the control of the British East India Company. Following the Indian Mutiny in 1857-58, the British government in London took over.

In the 1890s, thousands of Sikhs moved to the west coast of Canada and the United States looking for better jobs and higher wages. They faced a hostile reaction from white workers and the Canadian immigration laws hurt their pride. Inspired by the Irish struggle for Home Rule, they began to seek some way of freeing India from British domination.

During World War I, India rallied to the British cause in the hope that their loyalty would win political concessions. Indian Muslims were in two minds about the war, though: they were loyal to Britain, yet Britain was not just fighting Germany, but also the Ottoman Empire. The Sultan of Turkey was Caliph – head of Muslims worldwide – and he called a jihad, or holy war, against the British in India.

India sent millions of pounds to help the British war effort and the Sikhs, with their fearsome military tradition, sent fighting men. Although they made up only seven per cent of the population of India, over half the troops who volunteered came from the Punjab. When they returned from the war, they were changed men. They were not prepared to go back to being second class citizens in their own country.

A worldwide flu epidemic struck; there was a drought, which bought on a famine; plague and cholera broke out in several parts of India. Exhausted by the war, the British had neither the money nor the organisation to respond to such disasters.

In 1918, the British parliament rushed through legislation ending direct rule and giving India a limited form of self-government. However, instead of letting the Indian people decide things for themselves, government was put into the hands of the Imperial Legislative Council. Those organising criminal conspiracies connected with the revolutionary movements in India were cracked down on. They could be arrested without a warrant, held without trial and, if tried, had no right of appeal. The Indian press was outraged, but despite protests from all quarters, the bill was enacted.

Mahatma Gandhi wrote to the viceroy informing him that he intended to start a campaign of civil disobedience. The government ignored him. The first protest day was to be 30 March 1919, but was later changed to 6 April. For 24 hours, no one would work; all shops, offices, factories and markets would be closed. People would fast, giving themselves over to discipline and self-purification, and attend public meetings.

In many places, people observed the first protest day on 30 March. In Delhi, the police tried to halt a procession, by opening fire. When a crowd gathered in front of the Town Hall, they opened fire again. Eight people were killed and many more wounded.

On 6 April, the whole of India was closed down. This time the police took no action and the day of protest remained peaceful.

The Punjab was ruled with an iron hand by Lieutenant-Governor Sir Michael O'Dwyer, who was fanatically opposed to political reform. He banned newspapers and excluded political leaders. During the war he had used pressgang techniques to recruit soldiers and he had little respect for the law. This caused enormous resentment. However, everything remained calm in the Punjab until the first week of April 1919.

On 29 March, a meeting was held at Jallianwala Bagh in Amritsar, which was the administrative centre of the Punjab. Home to the Golden Temple, Amritsar is a holy city and the centre of Sikhism. The Jallianwala Bagh was private property, held in common by a number of people. A walled rectangle about 250 yards long and 200 yards wide, it had once been a garden – and is again. But then it was open ground used for fairs and public meetings. The entrance was through a narrow lane which opened out onto a patch of raised ground that overlooked the rest of the Bagh.

Two local leaders spoke at the meeting. They said they had did not want to hurt the police as protesters did in Europe. To use violence, they said, was a moral degradation. Instead, they urged the crowd to follow Gandhi's dictum: 'Do not injure anyone but be ready to be injured.' The meeting went ahead without incident.

The following day, the whole of Amritsar was closed down and, in the afternoon, another meeting was held in the Jallianwala Bagh. It called for Hindu-Muslim unity, though once again the speakers urged the crowd to maintain the strategy of non-violence.

On 6 April, Amritsar was brought to a standstill for a second time. Muslims, Hindus and Sikhs all stayed away from work and 50,000 attended a protest meeting. The next day, Gandhi left Bombay for Delhi and Amritsar. He got as far as Palwal, where he was served with a written order banning him from Delhi and the Punjab; he was arrested and taken back to Bombay.

The Hindu festival of Ram Naumi was on 9 April. Muslims joined in as a gesture of solidarity. This worried the British, who had always used the Machiavellian tactic of 'divide and rule'. Observing the festivities, the Deputy Commissioner of Amritsar Miles Irving said, 'There will soon be a row here.'

The following day, he invited the local leaders who had. addressed the meetings at the Jallianwala Bagh to his bungalow, where they were arrested and thrown out of Amritsar. When news of the arrests spread through the city, a crowd marched on the Deputy Commissioner's house. They met numerous Europeans on the way, but harmed no one. The procession was stopped at a railway bridge that was guarded by the army. The protesters said that they only wanted to go to the Deputy Commissioner's house to lodge a protest. Despite the fact that they were unarmed, the soldiers opened fire and many people were killed and wounded.

The crowd returned to collect the bodies. This time they carried lathes or Indian quarterstaffs, but some lawyers tried to calm them. The Deputy Commissioner and the police gathered in force on the other side of the bridge. Some protesters threw stones at the police, who opened fire without warning.

The crowd scattered and rampaged through the city, some attacking the telegraph building. The telegraph master was dragged from his office and had to be rescued by the army. Rioters stormed the railway goods yard – the station superintendent was beaten up and barely escaped with his life. A guard was not so lucky and died on the spot. The manager and assistant manager of the National Bank were killed and the building was set on fire. The manager of the Alliance Bank was also killed; his bank and a local store were looted, and a lady missionary was knocked unconscious.

On 10 April, the Commissioner of the Lahore district, A.J.W. Kitchin arrived. He toured the city and reported back to the Lieutenant-Governor that the situation was beyond control. Miles Irving was told to hand control of the city over to the army. Brigadier-General Reginald Dyer, commander at Jullundur, took over; his first move was to arrest prominent Nationalists.

On 11 April, the people wanted a funeral procession to bury their dead. At first Dyer banned it, then let it proceed on the condition that it dispersed at 2 p.m. The procession went ahead, was peaceful and dispersed on time. Even so, Dyer cracked down all the harder on the city. The next day, he stationed armed men at strategic points throughout Amfitsar and cut off water and electricity supplies.

Baisakhi, the Indian new year was on 13 April. To Sikhs it was even more significant: it was the day that Gobind Singh Ji – the tenth and last guru of Sikhism found the Khalsa. This is the dominant order of Sikhism, with its familiar beards and turbans. It is the militant order, responsible for throwing off the tyranny of the Moguls. On 13 April, people from all over the Punjab flocked to Amritsar. Some 20,000 men, women and children assembled in the Jallianwala Bagh, but Dyer had issued a curfew and banned any procession.

'Any gathering of four men,' said the order, 'would be looked upon and treated as an unlawful assembly and dispersed by force of arms, if necessary.'

The proclamation was read out publicly, but not all parts of the city were covered and most people did not hear it.

At 4 p.m., General Dyer took a tour of the city to see if his order was being obeyed. He took with him an escort of 50 men – armed with rifles and kukris and two armoured cars. Half the men were Gurkhas; the other half came from the 54th Sikh Frontier Force and the 59th Rifle Frontier Force. At about 5 p.m., he arrived at the Jallianwala Bagh. Seeing the public meeting there, he deployed 25 of his men to the left and 25 to the right.

The meeting was peaceful. Some local leaders were sitting on the stage; one of them was reading a poem. The huge crowd listened attentively.

Some saw the soldiers and began to panic. 'Don't be afraid,' said the speaker. 'The army is not going to fire on innocent people.' But they were.

Without warning, Dyer gave the order to fire – he had been there just 30 seconds. The soldiers shot down the unarmed crowds, who were caught in a death trap. Dyer's men blocked the exit. Some people had the presence of mind to throw themselves flat on the ground. Others, in panic, ran this way and that and were cut down.

The Times correspondent Sir Valentine Chirol described the scene like this. 'One cannot possibly realise the frightfulness of it until one has actually looked upon the Jallianwala Bagh – a waste space frequently used for fairs and public meetings, about the size perhaps of Trafalgar Square, and closed in almost entirely by walls, above which rise the backs of native houses facing into the congested streets of the city. I entered by the narrow lane by which General Dyer entered with about 50 rifles. I stood on the same rising ground on which he stood when, without a word of warning, he opened fire at about 100 yards' range upon a dense crowd, collected mainly in the lower and more distant part of the enclosure around a platform from which speeches were being delivered. The crowd was estimated by him at 6,000, by others at 10,000 and more, practically unarmed, and all quite defenceless. The panic-stricken multitude broke-at once but for ten consecutive minutes he kept up a merciless fusillade on that seething mass of humanity, caught like rats in the trap.'

The crowd broke into two. Dyer would order his men to

fire on one group, then the other. Between fusillades, one could hear the low moaning of the wounded. In their effort to get away, the crowd converged, trampling each other; Dyer aimed fire at them. Men went down, others clambered over them. Some were hit again and again. In places the dead and wounded lay in heaps, so that those who were only wounded would find themselves buried beneath a dozen others.

Still the firing continued. Hundreds tried to scale the walls, at some placed just five feet high, at others seven feet or ten. They would run at them, trying to gain a hold on the smooth surface. Some almost reached the top when others, fighting to get away, pulled them down. The Jallianwala Bagh had turned from a peaceful meeting place into a screaming hell.

At the official enquiry Dyer admitted that, as far as he knew, they had committed no crime. He claimed that he feared that his force would be attacked, though he had no information that a single individual was armed. They were going to use lathes he said; but no one saw anyone carrying them. Sergeant Anderson, Dyer 's bodyguard, was certainly not afraid.

'I saw nothing to be afraid of,' he said. I had no fear that the crowd would come on us.'

The only reason Dyers men stopped firing after ten minutes was because they had run out of ammunition: 1,650 rounds had been fired. Dyer told the inquiry, 'It was unlikely that a man shooting into the crowd would miss.'

If the passage had been wider, he said, he would have taken the armoured cars in. The fire had not been indiscriminate, he maintained. From time to time, he checked his fire and directed it upon places where the crowd was thickest. He had made up his mind to punish the demonstrators for having assembled.

The fire was directed towards people who were running away and at those who were lying flat and posed no possible threat. 12 men trying to shelter behind a tree found themselves spotted by soldiers and cut down. There was a well in the Jallianwala Bagh and over 100 corpses were found down it. They had to be removed when the stink became unbearable.

At 5.15 p.m., Dyer ordered his men to shoulder their arms and march off. They left 381 corpses and another 16,000 wounded. 'The corpses were ten to 12 feet high in some places,' an eyewitness said.

That night the curfew was strictly enforced and 1000 wounded were left lying in the Jallianwala Bagh overnight. Asked why he had left the wounded to their own devices, Dyer said that he had done his duty and it was not his job to render aid. The wounded could go to hospital, he said. But they could not – he had imposed a curfew.

A number of women, many wives of the dead, defied the curfew and tended the wounded, but there were too few of them even to give water to all those who needed it. The next morning relatives removed the bodies, which were cremated five or six at a time. Other bodies lay out in the Jallianwala Bagh all the next day and were consumed by vultures and jackals.

Miles Irving was delighted. Once Dyer had fired on the mob, he said, 'the whole rebellion collapsed.'

Dyer had not finished his cruelty against the people. He declared Martial Law and instigated the infamous 'Crawling Order'. In the hours when Indians were allowed out of their houses, between six in the morning and eight at night, they had to crawl. This was enforced at bayonet point. People had not so much to crawl as to wriggle along on their bellies. Even the smallest offence was punished by flogging. Large numbers of people were arrested, tortured and humiliated, while special tribunals meted out summary justice.

The authorities cracked down right across the Punjab.

Professors were arrested; students were forced to walk up to 16 miles a day for a roll call and children as young as five were made to salute the Union Jack; a marriage party was flogged; Hindus and Muslims were left handcuffed together; Indian's cars were confiscated; property was destroyed; along with crawling orders there were skipping orders. Aeroplanes and Lewis guns were employed against unarmed civilians.

Winston Churchill condemned these actions. The crawling order, he said, 'violated every canon of civilisation'. But, Churchill said, 'one treacherous fact stands out: the slaughter of nearly 400 . . . That is an episode which appears to me to be without precedent or parallel in the modern history of the British Empire.'

The authorities had tried to cover it up. One woman who lost her husband in the Jallianwala Bagh reported that constables had come to her house four months later and offered her 25,000 rupees if she would forget all about it. More money would be forthcoming later. She declined the offer, saying she would prefer to remember.

Churchill's condemnation in the House of Commons ensured that the atrocity at Amritsar could not be covered up. Many moderate Indians began to hanker for self-government. The massacre had shaken their belief in British 'fair play'. Although it took another 26 years and another word war – in which Indian troops, yet again, played a major part – before India gained its independence, the massacre in the Jallianwala Bagh sounded the death knell of the Raj.

The Jallianwala Bagh is now a place of pilgrimage. In 1997, during an official visit to India, the Queen went to Jalhanwala Bagh and publicly apologised for what General Dyer had done there in her grandfather's name.

Guernica

Guernica is a small market town in the Basque country, 30 kilometres north-east of Bilbao in northern Spain. To the Basques it is a spiritual home. Their historic parliament building is there; and in its grounds there is an oak tree that is the symbol of Basque culture and independence. When the Spanish Civil War broke out in 1936, its 6,000 inhabitants stayed loyal to the Republican government, who promised the Basques self-government. By contrast, General Franco, whose Nationalist army invaded from Morocco, aimed to keep the whole of Spain under the direct control of Madrid.

Until the end of March 1937, the struggle for Spain centred on Madrid. The war seemed a long way away. Guernica was protected by three battalions of Basque troops and the inhabitants felt safe. However, fearing that Franco, their fascist brother, might lose, both Hitler and Mussolini secretly sent troops to help him. It was a way for the two dictators to give their men battle experience before the war that to them seemed inevitable. Along with 5000 ground troops, Hitler sent his Condor Legion. They were handpicked airmen who would spearhead his revolutionary new strategy of Blitzkrieg that allowed him to overrun most of Western Europe in a matter of months.

It was the Legion's commander in Spain who persuaded Franco to begin a new offensive in the north. The mountains that separated the Basque country from the rest of the country would have made conventional warfare a long and tedious process. Guns would have to be manoeuvred across the rugged terrain to soften up the opposition every time it took up a new defensive position. But under the Blitzkrieg strategy, the Condor Legion would act as aerial artillery, pounding the enemy before they had a chance to dig in. This would keep the front fluid and the Nationalists' motorised infantry could easily outrun the ill-equipped Republicans.

The Blitzkrieg was also used to terrorise the civilian population. Once the planes had dropped their deadly load, civilians knew that Nationalist troops would not be far behind. Franco's formidable troops from Morocco had a fearsome reputation. Stories spread of men being shot after surrender and women being forced to strip at gunpoint and submit themselves to rape.

As the Nationalists attacked, the population fled. Refugees jammed the roads, making it harder for the Republicans to withdraw and regroup. Refugees poured into Guernica, believing that there they would be safe. It was renowned worldwide as a historic centre of culture and democracy – surely the enemy would respect that.

By 25 April 1937, the Nationalists were just 20 miles from Guernica. But between them and the town was rugged terrain and thousands of Basque troops to provide protection for the inhabitants. Or so the Guernicans thought.

Monday 26 April was a market day. Although the livestock market had been suspended for the duration of the war, the street market was in full swing. At 4.30 p.m., the bells of Santa Maria Church began to toll. People were puzzled by this. By the time they realised that it was an air-raid warning, a single Heinkel 111 bomber was directly overhead. Some people ran for the cellars that had been designated as air-raid shelters. Others took refuge in the church of Santa Maria and, naively, in the railway station plaza.

The plane climbed high in the sky, then came screaming earthwards. This was only a practice run, giving the bombardier a chance to identify the target the Renteria Bridge across the River Mundaca. Again, the plane was climbing, and the anti-aircraft gunners, who had identified the plane as fascist, found that they could not elevate their guns high enough to see it off with ack-ack fire. By this time, the plane seemed to be retreating. The soldiers defending the town got to their feet and cheered. But now the aircraft turned and began the run again, this time dropping its bombs.

Even though the navigator on board the Heinkel was supposed to have been one of the most experienced bombardiers in the Condor Legion, the 3,000 pounds worth of bombs landed hundreds of yards from the Renteria Bridge, near the railway station plaza in the centre of town.

One 550-pound bomb sliced off the front of the Julián Hotel. The rubble engulfed a group of children playing in the street outside. Another bomb hit the back of the station, which collapsed. Others fell in the station plaza killing both the people waiting for the next Bilbao train and those who had sought refuge there, believing it to be a place of safety. No one knows how many people there were in the plaza, but it was probably 300-400.

One eyewitness saw a bomb hit a group of women and children. 'They were lifted high into the air, maybe 20 feet or so," he said, 'and they started breaking up. Legs, arms, heads, and bits and pieces flying everywhere.'

Some corpses had been decapitated; others were stripped of their clothing by the blast. Many, though dead, did not have a mark on them – the force of the blast had simply collapsed their lungs. The air was full of the screams of the wounded and bereaved. Survivors took no notice of the dismembered corpses and they tried to drag the injured free of the debris. Soldiers left their posts to help; people came out of the shelters – no one was expecting another attack.

However, the rest of the squadron – nine Heinkels with a fighter escort of six Messerchmitt 109s – were circling over the village of Garay, ten miles south of Guernica. At 4.40, they lined up and moved in.

Ten minutes later they began their descent along the River Mundaca. They came in lower this time, as the first attack had drawn negligible flak. They were so low that people on the ground could see the crewmen. Spotters also noticed that the planes were spread out in a wide formation. This meant they were not planning to attack one specific target. They aimed to destroy the whole town using the technique of 'carpet bombing' perfected by the Condor Legion during its attack on Oviedo the previous September.

The first three Heinkels came in at 2,000 feet. Travelling at 170 miles an hour, they made an elusive target. After spraying the skies with an ineffective burst of gunfire, one young machine-gunner dropped his weapon and started taking pictures of the raid. His photographs later formed a vital part of the propaganda war.

The first plane had dropped high explosives. The next three dropped incendiary bombs: a cluster hit a sweet factory, setting vats of boiling sugar on fire, along with the hair and overalls of the girls who worked there. Women came running out into the street, living balls of fire.

People still had no idea what had hit them. The factory manager walked calmly back in through the flames to rescue a fish he had bought for the meeting of his cookery club the following day. He simply could not believe that things would not continue as normal. Another eyewitness saw an old woman sitting outside her front door peeling potatoes with bombs dropping all around her. When she had finished, she got up and walked calmly indoors.

Two more waves of bombers came in, each plane dropping 3,000 pounds of explosives. One bomb hit a house where a girl was celebrating her 15th birthday with her widowed mother. The house collapsed, killing them; but by some freak circumstance, her birthday cake ended up sitting, unscathed, on top of the pile of rubble that had buried them.

The incendiaries exploded with a white flash, then flared, burning fiercely and scattering red and white fragments of Thermite. One landed in a bull pen in the market place, where two bullocks were sprayed with burning Thermite. Maddened with pain, they broke free and went charging through the burning stalls and burning people, before falling to their deaths in a bomb crater.

Fire tore through the canvas-roofed stalls. There was no way to stop it. The concrete roof of the fire station had collapsed, flattening the fire tender to a third of its original height. Firemen had to do what they could with buckets. A stable collapsed, so completely that it was three days before the body of the stable boy was recovered, mingled with the remains of two dray horses.

Mercifully, some of the bombs did not explode. The canisters were recovered and their German markings later displayed by the Basque government to show the world who had been responsible.

Sadly, that was not the end of the tragedy at Guernica. Next came ten Heinkels who peppered the town with more incendiaries. Junkers swept in at 200 feet, spraying the town with machine-gun fire and cutting down those who tried to escape. A mother who had left her house to tend to an injured girl was cut down. Seeing this, her three children rushed screaming from the house and were likewise cut down.

A group of 15 boys had taken shelter in a thick concrete pipe that carried flood water away from the town. They should have been safe, but four incendiaries fell at the mouth. The heat cracked the concrete and tons of earth collapsed on them. Their bodies were only found two weeks later after a flash flood washed them from their resting place.

The Heinkels flew back and forth, combing the streets for someone to kill. It was estimated that 50 people were hit in one strafing alone. Condor pilots swooped in on single figures fleeing down the street, shooting them and dropping grenades. The Heinkels lingered for half an hour before, low on ammunition and gas, they turned for home. They left at six, one and a half hours after the first attack.

Throughout the onslaught, the Renteria Bridge remained intact. People sheltering under it considered themselves very lucky indeed. Little did they know that worse was yet to come. At six, the main bomber force took off, 23 Junker 52s, carrying 100,000 pounds of high explosives between them, forming over Garay.

During this brief respite, the fire brigade started digging people out of collapsed buildings. They had just enough time to rescue one small girl. Lines of people with buckets tried to dowse the flames, while Guernica's Carmelite Convent was turned into a makeshift hospital. It was filled with dying people calling for absolution, but no priest to oblige.

Father Eusebio had heard that his church had been hit. He rah to see it and found it intact. Earlier in the day he had intended to take a photograph of it. His old plate camera was standing on its tripod outside. He ran to it, determined to make a record of the destruction of his town. As he reached it, he just had time to turn it skyward and see three Junkers through the viewfinder. He snapped the shutter, pulled out the plate and fled. Behind the Junkers, the sky was black with bombers. Moments later the church was hit by incendiaries and the camera consumed.

The first salvo of bombs hit a restaurant and a bank. People in the street and cows that had escaped from their pens were blown to pieces. Houses collapsed like packs of cards. Several bombs simultaneously made a direct hit on an air-raid shelter in Calle Santa Maria, hurling bodies out into the street. In other shelters, people were asphyxiated by the lack of air. In the shelter of a basement in a house in Calle Allende Salazar, all 20 occupants died, suffocated by smoke. Their unmarked bodies were discovered four days later. The Town Hall took three direct hits and three floors collapsed on the shelter beneath. One young woman crawled to safely. Over her shoulder she -saw a hand and thought. someone was trying to hold her back, only to discover that a severed arm had got caught in her belt. The moment she struggled free, the rest of the building collapsed, sealing the entrance to the shelter.

Father Eusebio led a mother and her five daughters to the Renterfa Bridge while buildings collapsed and people were blown to bits all around them. He told them that their only chance was to get out of town. He himself went back into town to warn the people in the church of Santa Maria. After seeing his own church destroyed, he realised that German airmen were no respecters of the Catholic faith, although now they were not even bothering to aim. The Junkers were high up and the town was obscured by dust, the bombardiers could not see their target, so dropped their loads indiscriminately. The pilots claimed it would have been dangerous to take them back to the airfield with them.

Baker Antonio Arazamagni saw a bomb hit his bakery. The building bulged outwards slightly, then collapsed on his prized Ford. He decided it was time to get out of Guernica.

There was only one legitimate target in the town – an arms factory. The owner was pro-Franco and believed that was why his factory was saved. In fact, the German pilots did not know about the factory or his sympathies. It was left unscathed because the line the bombers took across the town did not pass over it, and the fighters did not bother strafing it because the factory was built out of solid concrete. Nevertheless, the owner had the smile wiped off his face when a German bomb hit his mansion 100 yards away.

After the smoke from the first squadron's attack had cleared, the lead planes of the second squadron could see the Renteria Bridge and went in for the kill. They unloaded their high explosives and a shower of smaller incendiaries. Not one bomb hit the bridge – they simply rained down on the battered town once more. By this time, terror had given way to exhaustion among those who huddled in the shelters. Human beings, it seems, can become accustomed to anything even aerial bombing.

Father Eusebio was right about the Germans' attitude to the church. One 550-pound high-explosive bomb hit the local Augustine monastery, blowing it to smithereens. An incendiary dropped through the roof of the church of Santa Maria, landing in the chapel of Our Lady of Begonia and knocking Our Lady to the ground. Father Iturran was in the pulpit, leading the packed congregation in prayer, but Father Eusebio was on hand. He grabbed a vase and emptied its contents over the canister. The incendiary gave off clouds of smoke, but no flames.

'Bring more water,' yelled Father Eusebio.

People began to panic.

If our Lord could work a miracle by turning water into wine,' said Father Iturran, 'then perhaps he will allow us to use wine as water.'

The incendiary was snuffed out with communion wine and Iturran's calm words stemmed the panic.

Soon after 6.30 p.m., the last of the Junkers climbed away from the town. This last attack had killed a further 200 people, injuring 400 more. Three-quarters of the buildings in Guernica had been destroyed – or soon would be, by flames. The Renteria Bridge was still intact.

After the planes had gone, Father Eusebio counted out 60 seconds then instructed the congregation to get out. They streamed down the Calle San Juan, across the Renteria Bridge, up the Arteaga road to the safety of the caves in the rocky hillside. Over 500 found safety there.

Others were caught out on the roads. As civilians streamed out of the town, they were joined by deserting soldiers. They slowed their pace to those of the refugees, figuring that, from the air, it would be impossible to tell the difference between soldiers and civilians. It made no difference: a squadron of six Messerschmitts, strafed them anyway. They came in so low that those on the road stood no chance.

At 7 p.m., the Heinkel 51s, refuelled and re-armed, returned. After strafing those on the roads, they turned their attention back to the town. On the ground the anti-aircraft gunners were out of ammunition, but the Heinkels, made no attempt to attack them. Instead, they strafed the ruins, moving backwards and forwards, some-times in pairs, sometimes in a long line, sometimes in close formation as if they were trying out new tactics.

Eventually, at 7.30 p.m., they turned for home. The attack on Guernica was over. After a few minutes, a woman named Maria Ortuza emerged. She had been hiding under the corpse of a dead donkey, which had protected her from the strafing. She walked up to the Church of Santa Maria and looked out over the town, desperately searching for a sign of life 'to show I was not alone'.

She wandered the town for some time. Suddenly, she saw a horse rear up in flames. It had probably been dead for some time, but the heat of the fire made its muscles con-tract. As the flames consumed it, the animal fell back. Shortly afterwards she heard the voice of a man who was trapped under a pile of rubble. He had been lucky: moments before the building had collapsed on him, the street had cracked apart. He had fallen down a sewer, which protected him. With him was a young woman who had not been so fortunate. Her bones stuck out through her light cotton dress; she was dead and already her body had begun to smell.

In all, 1,654 were killed in the attack and 889 wounded. Many of the bodies lay face down, having been hit from behind while running away.

Miraculously, the houses of the rich on the western slopes of the town were largely intact. The rich supported Franco and it was rumoured that they had been spared intentionally. Townspeople scoured the buildings, looking for 'traitors' on whom to take revenge. But the rich had already fled. In fact, no orders had been given to spare them; they had been spared by chance because of the northeast-to-southwest bombing run across the town.

That night the Condor Legion celebrated in the brothels of Vitoria. Their leader, Lieutenant Colonel Wolfram von Richthofen, cousin of the World War I fighter ace, secretly reported to Berlin that the concentrated attack on Guernica was 'the greatest success'. On Thursday, 29 April 1936, the Nationalists reached Guernica. Spanish, Italian and Moroccan troops marched over the Renteria Bridge at about 8.30 a.m. They met some resistance – five Nationalist soldiers were killed and 28 wounded – but by 10.30 a.m., Franco's flag flew over the parliament building. The troops behaved well, even setting up a field kitchen to feed the survivors.

That night, Franco's headquarters issued a statement saying that Guernica had been burnt by retreating Republicans and that it was a he to 'attribute this atrocity to our noble and heroic air force'. The Spanish Church backed the story and the professor of theology in Rome said, 'The truth is there is not a single German in Spain.'

However, the photograph Father Eusebio took to Bilbao the following day and the unexploded incendiaries showed this to be a he.

Although the war dragged on for another two years, the Republican soldiers retreating from Guernica knew that their cause was lost. Their raggle-taggle army was not up to fighting such a ruthless enemy. Having taken Guernica, the Nationalists now had a new arms factory that, by fluke, had escaped the bombing.

When the painter Pablo Picasso heard about the bombing of Guernica, he was appalled. A communist, his sympathies lay with the Republicans. He was no stranger to the regions, having been brought up in nearby Galicia. He condemned the German attack in a huge painting entitled Guernica which became one of the great icons of pacifism. In 1940, when Germans marched into Paris, they came to his studio where the painting was leaning against the wall.

A German officer pointed at it and demanded, 'Did you do that?'

Picasso replied, 'No, you did.'

The Rape of Nanking

Since the 1870s, Japan had sought to expand into the mainland of Asia. Firstly, it took over Korea. Then, after a short war with Russia, it established a toehold in Manchuria. In World War I Japan sided with the Allies against the Germans and demanded that China cede its German concessions to the growing Japanese Empire. Being weak and without allies, China had no choice.

The Versailles Peace Conference rewarded Japan for backing the winners in World War I with more concessions in China. In 1931, the Japanese consolidated their hold on Manchuria and, when the Chinese objected, firebombed an entire district of Shanghai. The Chinese appealed to the League of Nations, which found in China's favour. Japan promptly withdrew from the league. China was further weakened by the fall of the last Emperor of the Manchu Dynasty, so Japan swallowed up Mongolia and parts of China's Hebei province.

Up until this time, the Japanese military had been constrained by a civilian government at home. But in 1936, the military seized power in Tokyo and signed a pact with Nazi Germany. Then in 1937, the Japanese commanders in Manchuria decided to 'solve the Chinese question once and for all' and launched a full-scale invasion.

In August 1937, Beijing fell; in November, Shanghai was taken. From there, the Japanese moved up the Yangzi towards Nanking, then the capital of the Chinese Republic. The Chinese government quickly withdrew to Wuhan while Generalissimo Chiang Kai-Shek considered the situation. Nanking, he quickly decided, was indefensible. He suggested declaring it an open city, so the Japanese would have no excuse for butchering its citizens. Although its loss would be a psychological blow to China, it would have no effect on the overall military situation. His chiefs of staff agreed.

There was one dissenting voice though. General Tang Shengzhi point out that Nanking contained the mausoleum of President Sun Yat-Sen, then considered the father of the nation. Tang said that if they did not sacrifice one or two big generals, how would they be able to account to the father of the nation in heaven? Honour had to be satisfied.

Chiang Kai-Shek was delighted: Tang got the job. Despite his noble sentiment Tang's defence of Nanking made no difference. The Japanese were making their way towards the city unopposed. Japanese pilots – who, in the Samurai tradition, carried a sword instead of a parachute – were indiscriminately bombing and machine-gunning unarmed civilians for the fun of it.

The Japanese, under General Matsui Iwane, army looted Suzhou on the way. An American missionary fleeing the fighting reported that he had to drive slowly to avoid running over the dead bodies that were strewn across the road. Matsui's forces were within sight of Nanking on 5 December. On 7 December, Chiang Kai-Shek flew out, after destroying all the petrol and ammunition that could not be saved.

'I intend to defend Nanking to the last man,' General Tang told an American observer. 'The Japanese will eventually capture the city, but they will pay a high price for it.'

This was mere hubris, the Americans concluded. The mechanised Japanese forces were unstoppable.

On 9 December, a Japanese plane dropped a letter from General Matsui. It was addressed to General Tang, demanding his surrender within 24 hours. Matsui pointed out that he would be hard on those who resisted, but would be 'kind and generous to non-combatants and to Chinese troops who entertained no enmity to Japan'. When he received no reply, the Japanese began shelling. It was a precision bombardment: the shells fell in a straight line that advanced 25 yards every half minute.

Soon the 100,000-strong garrison of Chinese troops was routed. The retreat was disorganised. Officers and men fled as they could. However, acting without orders, a small group of fanatically patriotic Chinese troops put machine-guns on the top of the city walls and strafed the men fleeing the city.

The gates to the city were then locked. Nevertheless, both soldiers and civilians still tried to escape. Access to the Xiaguan gate, which opened on to the river, was down a 70-foot long tunnel. Two military vehicles collided in it and burst into flames. Refugees fleeing the fire met those fleeing the city. Thousands were suffocated or trampled underfoot. Those who emerged were machine-gunned by the Japanese. Two Americans who went through the tunnel the next day reported having to drive over bodies 'two or three feet deep'. By the time the city fell on 13 December, 40,000 were dead.

Throughout the fighting, Japanese planes had been dropping pamphlets promising the citizens of Nanking the protection of the invading army and telling them that they would be allowed to live in peace under Japanese occupation. However, when General Matsui drove in triumph through the city gates, it became dear that these were empty promises. Although the General himself showed traditional restraint, behind him on a high-stepping white horse came Colonel Hashimoto. He was one of the new breed of arrogant super-patriots.

Even worse was the field commander of the occupying force, Lieutenant-General Prince Asaka Yasuhiko, who was married to the Emperor's aunt. As a royal, he brooked no opposition. It was he who gave the orders for the first massacres.

He was not alone in his lust for blood. The Japanese press carried news of two sub-leutenants who held a Samurai contest to see who would be the first to kill 100 Chinese using their swords. Both reached 100, but they could not decide who had got there first, so they continued to 150. One of them had to drop out when his sword was damaged by 'cutting a Chinese in half, helmet and all'; but the contest was only a friendly and the loser declared it to have been 'fun'.

Once inside the city, bloodthirsty victory celebrations began. The Chinese municipal authorities had fled and the Japanese organised no new ones. Law and order broke down. Japanese soldiers got down to the business of getting drunk, looting, raping woman and killing anyone who got in their way. Even though the Japanese troops could do pretty much what they liked, the generals were soon complaining that these 'celebrations' were taking place under the eyes of neutral observers. Some of these were Germans. One even handed over Nazi armbands and decorations to make the Japanese soldiers and officers stop committing atrocities – in his presence at least.

Nanking was the temporary home to 250,000 refugees from Shanghai. The refugees were terrified of the Japanese, but anyone who ran away was bayoneted or shot. Just 27 foreign missionaries, doctors and teachers had stayed on. They tried to organise what they hoped would be a 'safety zone', believing that the Japanese authorities would soon restore order. Instead, Nanking became what many of them described as 'a living hell'.

While the foreigners did as much as they could to protect the populace, the citizens of Nanking were robbed of their last possessions. They were lined up and shot, or used for bayonet practice. Even the homes of foreign dignitaries were looted and foreign flags torn down and insulted. When complaints were made to the Japanese Embassy, they were received politely, but nothing was done. A victorious army must have its spoils.

Some tried desperately to keep a record of the atrocities. On 18 December, for example, the following complaints were logged.

'One teahouse master's daughter, aged 17, was raped by seven Japanese soldiers and she died on the 18th. Last night three Japanese soldiers raped four girls between six and ten o'clock. In number 5 Moh Kan Road, one old man reported his daughter was brutally raped by several Japanese soldiers.

'There are about 540 refugees crowded in number 83 and 85 on Guangzhou Road. Since the 13th up to the 17th those houses have been searched and robbed many times a day by Japanese soldiers in groups of three or five. Today the soldiers are looting the places mentioned above continually. At present, women of younger ages are forced to go with the soldiers every night by sending motor trucks to take them. They are released the next morning. More than 30 women and girls have been raped. The women and children are crying the whole night through. Conditions inside the compound are worse than can be described.'

One girl scratched a Japanese soldier while he was raping her. He stuck a bayonet into her neck and severed the muscles on one side.

Two days afterwards a 17-year-old married girl, who was nine months pregnant, was raped by two Japanese soldiers at 7.30 in the evening. An hour and a half later her labour pains began; the baby was born at midnight.

'Mother is hysterical,' the report said, 'but the baby is doing wen.'

Some 140 refugees were dowsed with petrol and set on fire. Only one survived, and his eyes were burnt out.

On Christmas Day, the Japanese began the registration of refugees at the university. Disarmed Chinese soldiers were told that they could join labour details. Instead, the soldiers were grouped together and used for bayonet practice or simply machine-gunned. Meanwhile, the death toll of unarmed civilians climbed to 40,000. Some had been buried alive or roasted to death over fires. Yet even death did not end the horror: Japanese soldiers found it good sport to toss a grenade into a pile of dead bodies.

Still the complaints of rape poured in. A German observer estimated that there were 20,000 cases in all. On the university campus, girls as young as 11 and women as old as 53 were violated. Elsewhere it was reported that two women of 72 and 76 were raped repeatedly in broad daylight. When soldiers came to attack a 62-year-old woman, she complained that she was too old to be raped. One soldier responded by jamming a stick up her vagina instead. After a 60-year-old woman was gang-raped, one of the soldiers told her to 'clean his penis with her mouth'. Her grandson was stabbed twice for crying.

One doctor reported that a fourteen year old girl who had not yet reached puberty was raped so brutally that she needed surgical intervention; four soldiers gangraped a girl of ten; one man had both his legs broken with a rifle butt when he refused to supply a girl for a soldier; and when a young man of about 17 told a soldier that there was no girl in the house for him to rape, the youth was taken and sodomised.

These rapes were not just perpetrated by drunken soldiers on the rampage the officers indulged themselves freely too. One foreign resident reported that six women were forced to wash clothes for Japanese officers. That was their daytime occupation – at night they were repeatedly raped. The older women were raped between ten and twenty times, the younger women forty times a night.

A group of officers drove up to the university one night, held the nightwatchman up against the wall and raped three of the women. One was just 12. Another one was carried off by the officers.

Anyone who opposed the soldiers, including children, was bayoneted or shot. If a woman resisted, she risked being bayoneted. One woman had her five month-old baby next to her while she was being raped. When it cried, the soldier raping her smothered it to death.

The foreigners attempting to maintain the 'safety zone' eventually managed to get the Japanese to post sentries around the compound. But this did no good. The sentries went in and raped the women instead.

The rape of Nanking was only brought to a halt when venereal disease began to get out of hand – syphilitic men do not make good soldiers. One Chinese woman was admitted to hospital with virulent forms of syphilis, gonorrhoea and genital chancroids. She had been imprisoned by Japanese soldiers in their quarters, and they raped her seven to ten times a day for six weeks.

The Japanese authorities solved the problem by opening brothels, staffed by Chinese women who had been forced into prostitution. This was the beginning of the forced military prostitution that turned millions of enslaved Chinese, Koreans, Malays, Filipinos and captured Europeans into 'comfort women,' throughout World War II.

After the orgy was over, General Matsui held a service for the 300 Japanese who had died. He used it to berate his officers. Later he told an American correspondent that 'the Japanese army is probably the most undisciplined army in the world today'. He found this shameful. During the Russo-Japanese War of 1904, Japanese troops were renowned for their high standard of discipline and the scrupulous treatment of civilians and prisoners of war. But at that time, the officers had come from Samurai families with high codes of honour. The new officer corps was full of swaggering fascists like Colonel Hashimoto.

This new breed sought to justify their actions on the grounds that the Chinese had done the same to them. True, Chinese militiamen had mutinied against their Japanese officers at Tongxian on 29 July, two-thirds of the 380 Japanese in the city had been killed and all Japanese buildings burnt. Japanese soldiers had been tortured and Japanese women impaled on stakes. The Chinese also cut the ears or noses off the Japanese on battlefields to prevent their souls finding a resting place. But these atrocities were nothing compared to the wholesale barbarity that the Japanese inflicted on occupied China.

As regards the rape, Japanese apologists claim that it occurred because Matsui's front-line troops were middle-aged men who were more likely to get out of hand with women'. This is not true – when new recruits arrived in China, they were appalled at the atrocities, but the Japanese army took pains to habituate its men into practising the most barbaric torture on the Chinese as a matter of course. Mass executions were used as to terrorise the civilian population and mass rape was a way to humiliate the Chinese.

News of the rape of Nanking soon got out. The world was appalled. Prince Asaka Yasuhiko was recalled to Tokyo where the Emperor ordered that especially good treatment should be meted out to the inhabitants of Nanking. It was too late.

The Liquidation of the Warsaw Ghetto

The Nazis had proved that they were capable of mass murder at Babi Yar and numerous other places across occupied areas of the Soviet Union and the Baltic States. At least this suffering was mercifully brief. The torture of the people in the Warsaw Ghetto dragged on for four years and some 500,000 people were lost.

Between 1918 and 1939, the Jewish population of Warsaw became the largest concentration of Jews in Europe and the second largest in the world, after New York. When the Germans occupied the city on 7 September 1939, there were around 380,000 Jews in Warsaw, making up some 30 per cent of the population. The situation grew ugly immediately: many Poles were anti-Semitic and knew what their new German overlords expected of them. Jews soon found themselves subject to kicking and punching on the streets. They were thrown out of their homes and kidnapped for forced labour. Women were raped and people murdered by Polish rowdies as wen as by the Germans themselves.

As early as November 1939, the Germans made it clear to the Jews what was going to happen to them. Special 'educational' camps were going to be set up for them. Only one thing would be taught there: how to die.

In the meantime, all Jews had to wear armbands with the Star of David on them. This made it easier for the violent anti-Semite element of the Polish population to know whom to attack. Jews were also issued with identification papers marked prominently with the word 'Jude'. All Jewish assets of over 2,000 zloty per family were confiscated and, later, it became illegal for any Jew to earn more than 500 zloty a month – at a time when the price of bread rose to 40 zloty a pound. It became illegal for Jews to make bread, to buy from or sell to 'Aryans', to own gold or jewellery, to ride on trains or trolleycars or to leave the city without special permits. Jewish doctors were not allowed to treat 'Aryan' patients, nor were Jewish patients allowed to seek the help of 'Aryan' doctors.

Jews were regularly robbed, beaten and murdered on the streets, with no sanction against their assailants. They lived in constant fear of the only punishment for even the slightest infraction of the regulations – death. However, even carefully obeying the rules was no protection, as the regulations were constantly being tightened. Jews were persecuted, humiliated and subjected to ruthless acts of terror. All Jews bore responsibility for what any one Jew did. Hence, early in November 1939, all 53 of the male inhabitants of an apartment house at 9 Nalewski Street were summarily shot because one of the tenants had struck a policeman.

Actions such as these sent a wave of panic through the Jewish population. The constant degradation left them feeling dehumanised; they were systematically robbed of the self-confidence to fight back.

In January 1940, the Seuchensperrgebiet – or 'area threatened by typhus' was established, and was to be designated a Jewish area. The Germans decided that the world had to know that they were not the only ones who hated Jews. Over Easter 1940, a number of pogroms were arranged. In Warsaw, the German Air Corps paid Polish hoods four zloty a day to beat up and murder Jews. For the first three days, the hoodlums ran amok, unopposed; but on the fourth day, the Jews fought back. This resulted in running battles. The Jews published a mimeographed newspaper called The Bulletin to celebrate the event – the triumph was brief.

In November 1940, the Germans established the Warsaw Ghetto. Jews living outside the Seuchensperrgebiet were forced to move into it. Houses vacated by Jews were locked and their contents given to Polish merchants and peddlers. Poles living within the boundaries of the ghetto were ordered out, as the walls and barbed wire surrounding it grew higher day by day. By 15 November, it was sealed completely. Two weeks later, shops and small factories inside the ghetto were closed, meaning that Jews no longer had any way of making a living and were cut off from any contact with Jewish communities elsewhere.

The ghetto population was swelled by thousands of Jews being moved in from neighbouring towns. They were allowed to bring nothing with them. Many who knew no one in Warsaw died of malnutrition on the streets. The place became impossibly overcrowded. In spring 1941, the population peaked at 450,000 in just 307 hectares. Hunger and overcrowding brought with it disease and people, wrapped in filthy rags, their bodies impossibly swollen or covered with open wounds could be seen on the streets.

No newspapers were allowed in the ghetto, so the inmates knew nothing of the outside world. Only life inside the ghetto existed. For most, this meant somehow trying to get by on the meagre rations of soup and bread doled out by public kitchens. Some lived on potatoes recovered from garbage pits and begged pieces of bread; but those who still had a little money lost themselves in the chitchat of pavement caffis and the dance music of the nightclubs. This contrast between the poor and the rich, who grew fat on 'food smuggled in from "Aryan" sections', was exploited by the Germans, who used photographs from the ghetto in their propaganda.

Every day the situation deteriorated. Children and the elderly begged on the streets. Some 6-year-old boys crawled though the barbed wire to beg for food on the outside – this supported entire families. Often a single shot rang out, indicating the death of another under-aged foodsmuggler.

Starving shadows of boys became known as 'catchers'. They would snatch parcels from passers-by and devour their contents while they were running away. In their haste, they sometimes stuffed themselves with soap or uncooked peas, with disastrous results.

The Germans had organised the Jewish Community Council to try and give some semblance of order to this chaos. This comprised well-respected figures of the Jewish community, who had been forced to join on pain of death. The Germans also instituted a Jewish Police Force to maintain law and order, increasing the risks for the food smugglers and the catchers.

Deaths rose from 898 in January 1941 to 5,560 in January 1939. In all, 100,000 Jews died inside the ghetto, largely from starvation and disease. Some simply fell down in the street and stayed there. Those who died at home fared little better: they were stripped so that their clothes could be sold and their bodies left outside the house. Every morning, between 4 and 5 a.m., the Jewish Community Council sent round carts to pick up the bodies. They could be seen stacked high with naked corpses, heads and limbs bobbing up and down as the carts rumbled down the uneven streets.

Those who died were soon replaced by Jews who had been rounded up in other parts of Poland. The ghetto was so overcrowded that newcomers had to camp on the streets, or would have to go to the 'points'. These were the large unheated rooms of synagogues or disused factories. Hundreds of people would be living in each room with no washing facilities. Whole families were given enough room for one person to sleep in – usually a straw mattress on the ground. Some did not have the strength to rise. The Jewish Community Council provided only one slop of 'water soup' a day. The walls were filthy and mildewed.

Not surprisingly, typhus raged in the ghetto. The hospitals were full to bursting point: 150 people a day were being admitted to a single ward. The sick and dying were two or three to a bed, with others on the floor. Doctors could not keep up; those who were dying were urged to get on with it to make room for the next patient. The gravediggers could not dig fast enough. Even though hundreds of corpses were buried in every grave, hundreds more had to lie around, filling the area with a sweet, sickly odour. The epidemic grew out of all control, at one point as many as two per cent of the population dying every month.

Then came the news that, during November and December 1940, some 40,000 Jews of Lodz, another 40,000 from Pomerania and other areas that were going to be incorporated into Germany, along with several hundred gypsies, had been gassed in Chelmno. The victims had been told that they were being taken there to work. When they arrived in Chelmno, they were ordered to strip and given a towel and soap, having been told they were going to have a shower. It was a cruel hoax. As the Jews were transported in trucks towards mass graves in the woods near Chelmno, exhaust gas was pumped into the sealed vehicles. At the woods, Jewish gravediggers – under the watchful eyes of SS guards – unloaded the bodies and buried them, knowing they would be next.

Three people who had, miraculously, escaped brought the news to the Warsaw Ghetto. Most people did not believe them – the inhabitants of the ghetto were clinging to life so tenaciously that they could not comprehend how people could have died in such a fashion. Some of the youth groups, particularly the young communists, believed the stories, though. They noticed that German terror was increasing and decided they would not go meekly to their deaths like the people at Chelmno. They began to organise propaganda to alert the other inmates of the ghetto to the danger, and they smuggled the news abroad, along with a demand that retaliation be taken against the Germans. The communist delegate to the Polish government in exile in London broadcast the news to the world, but few people believed it.

When Germany attacked the Soviet Union in the summer of 1941, the Jews of the ghetto began to hear of mass shootings of Jews in Wilno, Slonim, Bialystok and Baranowicze. Tens of thousands of Jews were being slaughtered. Again, most of those inside the ghetto refused to believe it, or put it down to the antics of drunken soldiers rather than an organised policy of extermination.

At this point, the youth groups decided that they must organise resistance. They sent messages to the Polish Underground to ask for arms and in the meantime, they began training. Several thousand were involved in the resistance movement, though they were organised into cells of between five and seven. They established a cooperative barber's, a tailor's shop and a cobbler's as a front. Youth groups organised a choir, educational courses and put on plays to try to keep the cultural life of the ghetto going. They also produced one weekly and six monthly magazines in an effort to maintain morale.

On one occasion, the girl who was smuggling 40 mimeographed copies of The Bulletin was stopped by the Polish police. She pretended to be an ordinary smuggler and offered them a bribe of 500 zloty. This was an unusually high offer and therefore made them suspicious. They asked to see the 'merchandise' and from under the girl's skirt fell not food or stockings, but printed sheets. They were just about to take her to the Gestapo when a colleague, seeing she was in trouble, started a scuffle. The police ran off to stop it, leaving the girl to drop the 500 zloty and run for her life.

The Germans grew angry with the number of Jews managing to slip out of the ghetto to get a little bread or a few pennies. They established special courts to try any one caught on the 'Aryan side'. On 12 February 1941, 17 people, including three women and four children, were executed for leaving the ghetto. Cries were heard from the Jewish jail on Geisha Street from the 700 other prisoners waiting to be tried for the same offence.

Just in case the message had not got through, the German Commissar of the ghetto, Dr Auerswald, filled the ghetto with posters announcing the executions. The ghetto was so intimidated that no protest was made, but things still got worse. The Germans began shooting passers-by in the street for no reason. Between ten and 15 a day were slaughtered randomly. One particularly sadistic policeman claimed to have killed over 300 people in a month. More than half of them were children.

The Jewish Police were used to rounding up people for forced labour. The Germans maintained that the people being sent to labour camps were lucky. Although the conditions were harsh, it did give them the opportunity to survive the war. Forced labourers were even allowed to write to their families. However, when the letters arrived, they were full of stories of the mass killing of Jews. Again, the people remaining in the ghetto could not believe what they were being told. Even when they heard of the liquidation of the ghetto in Lublin, the people in Warsaw refused to believe it was going to happen to them.

People tried to convince one another that not even the Nazis would murder 300,000 people when there was a labour shortage – that the Germans were taking people from the Warsaw Ghetto for forced labour showed that they needed manpower.

They did not know about the change of policy in Berlin. Although the Germans had shot tens of thousands of people at Babi Yar and other places throughout the occupied areas of the Soviet Union. and the Baltic states, it was not a very efficient method of slaughter. On 20 January 1942, SS Obergruppenführer Reinhard Heydric, Adolf Eichmann and others met in the Berlin suburb of Grossen-

Wannseee, where they came up with what they called the 'final solution' to the 'Jewish question'. They planned to round up all Jews in occupied Europe and ship them to camps in the east where they would be systematically exterminated.

In the Warsaw Ghetto, the terror tactics continued. On the night of 17 April 1942, over 50 of the Jewish Community Council's workers were dragged from their beds by German officers and shot in the streets. The ghetto was shocked, hysterical, but the inhabitants concluded that this brutal action was aimed at the political leaders who urged resistance. On 19 April, a special edition of the resistance paper Der Weker was published, explaining that this was part of the German policy of systematic extermination of the Jews. It urged the people of the Warsaw Ghetto not to go to their deaths as 'meekly as those in Lublin or Chelmno had. However, the activists still had not managed to get any guns and their words fell on deaf ears.

Guns were promised, though. The Polish socialists said that a shipment of 100 pistols, a few dozen rifles and some grenades would arrive shortly. The communists in the ghetto organised more military training and tried to work out a plan of action in case the Germans stormed the ghetto.

Their task was not made any the easier by the fact that they were always losing members. Between 18 April and 22 July, the Germans entered the ghetto every night and killed ten or 15 people. None of the activists slept in their own beds. The whole ghetto was unsettled by the Germans' habit of shooting people from one group one night and another the next – smugglers, merchants, workers, and professional people.

Other random acts of violence terrorised the people into absolute subordination. A Polish policeman saw three children sitting one in front of another in front of the hospital and killed all three with a single shot. A German watched as a pregnant woman tripped and fell as she crossed the road. Instead of helping her up, he shot her. Every morning a man, shackled, was flung out of an Opel car on Orla Street and shot. It was a Jew who had been caught on the 'Aryan side'.

The Germans adopted a new tactic to stop smuggling. They would dress up as Jews with Star of David armbands and hide machine-guns in burlap bags. Thinking they were safe, smugglers would scale the ghetto walls, only to be gunned down.

In mid-May 1942, 110 people arrested for being on the 'Aryan side' were executed. The prisoners were led out of the central jail into special trucks to be gassed. Only one of the accused protested. A woman stopped on the steps of the trucks and shouted, 'I will die, but your death will be much worse.' Again, Dr Auerswald put up posters announcing the 'just punishment' of these 110 'criminals'.

In mid-July, the rumour circulated that the Deportation Board had arrived and that between 20,000 and 60,000 inmates of the ghetto were to be taken to build fortifications. Supposedly, the Germans planned to take all the ghettos' unemployed, leaving only those who had jobs. Those who had had enough money to sit in cafés all day quickly became clerks and mechanics. The women became seamstresses and the price of sewing machines went through the roof. Many paid what little they had to get work, but it did them no good.

On 20 July 1942, the doctors were rounded up, along with the managers of the Jewish Mutual Aid Committee and a number of the Jewish Community Council. They were locked up.

On 22 July, the Deportation Board arrived at the headquarters of the Jewish Community Council. They brought news – it was a small matter really: all unproductive Jews were going to be deported somewhere to the east.

Oberscharführer Hoefle dictated a proclamation that appeared under the Jewish Community Council's name on white posters the following morning. It said that all Jews, except those who worked for the Germans, the Jewish Community Council or the Jewish Mutual Aid Committee, would be deported. The Jewish police would be the agency responsible for organising this and they would report directly to the Deportation Board.

On the first day, 2,000 prisoners from the central jail, along with beggars and starving people picked up on the streets, were taken. From then on, the quota was to be 6,000 a day.

The following afternoon the activists met. Without guns, they decided, resistance was impossible. Their clear duty was to save as many people as they could. They thought they might be able to get help from their contacts inside the Jewish police, but it was too late. Germans and Ukrainians had moved in and surrounded a block on Muranowska Street. They took over 2,000, enough to fill the shortfall in the daily quota. Even those with papers saying they were working for the Germans were taken. From then on, the Germans said they would look after the 'technical details' of the deportations themselves.

In a meeting on the 23 July, the communists began urging resistance. But the majority feared that any actions might be provocative. If they handed over the required quota of Jews every day, the Germans might leave the rest of them alone, they argued. Still, the inhabitants of the ghetto did not believe that they were all going to be killed and those who thought that there might be some possibility of saving themselves willingly condemned others.

However, Adam Czerniaków, chairman of the Jewish Community Council, committed suicide. He knew that deportation meant that hundreds of thousands of Jews from the ghetto were heading for the gas chambers and he refused to take responsibility for it. Activists condemned him. He was a voice of considerable authority in the ghetto, they said; he should have made it his business to inform everyone, particularly the Jewish police, of the fate awaiting deportees. Instead, the communists rushed out an issue of their paper *On Guard*, warning people of the fate that awaited them and urging them to resist by any means at their disposal.

By the fifth day, the resistance knew for certain what was happening to those who were deported. A Polish contact had followed one of the transports to Sokolow. There he was told by a local railway worker that it had taken the branch line to Treblinka. Every day freight trains were taken down that branch, full of people from Warsaw: they came back empty. No consignment of food was ever sent down that line and civilians were forbidden to go anywhere near Treblinka railway station. The Pole also met two naked Jews who had somehow escaped. They told him about the mass extermination that was going on at a camp outside Treblinka.

Another edition of On Guard was prepared, explaining in full what deportees could expect; no one believed it. At the same time, the Germans began giving three kilograms of bread and one kilogram of marmalade to anyone who voluntarily registered for 'deportation'. It was a brilliant ruse. Ghetto inmates said, 'Why would they feed people they intend to murder?' Their hungry stomachs got the better of their reason. Thousands took the short walk down to the Umschlagplatz of their own volition. They waited in line in their hundreds; the transports had to be doubled to accommodate the demand: 12,000 people were deported daily, but still the trains could not accommodate them all.

Once all the volunteers had gone and the children's homes and refugee shelters had been emptied, the ghetto was emptied block by block. People with knapsacks would move from street to street, trying to guess which block was going to be cleared next.

The clearance was done by the Polish police, the Ukrainians and the Jewish police. The Polish police isolated the block; the Ukrainians surrounded the house; and the Jewish police would walk into the courtyards and summon the inhabitants.

'All Jews must come down. Only 30 kilograms of baggage is allowed,' they would say. 'Those remaining behind will be shot.'

People would come running, pulling on their clothes and carrying everything they could grab. They would assemble, trembling, in front of the houses. No talking was allowed. Then the Ukrainians would go in and search the apartments. According to regulations, the doors of the apartments had to be left open. If not, the Ukrainians would break them down with a boot or a rifle butt. There would be shots as anyone left inside was killed. Then they would move on to the next house.

The people in the street would be formed into columns. Any passer-by who had mistakenly walked down the wrong street would be taken too. The column would be marched off, with old people and children who had to be carried bringing up the rear. Outside the area cordoned off by the Polish police, relatives would desperately try to find their loved ones.

The column would be marched to the Umschlag or deportation point. The tall wall surrounding it had one narrow entrance, guarded by the Polish police. The deportees would hold out their identification papers and be told rechts – meaning life – or links – meaning death. Although argument was futile, people held out other papers, trying to prove how useful they would be to German industry. It made no difference. The gendarme's decision was quite arbitrary. Sometimes he ordered people to show him their hands and let all those with small hands live. Other days, he picked all the blondes to die. In the morning, short people might live; in the afternoon only the tall survived.

The Umschlagplatz was filled with more than enough people for four days' transports. They were left to camp out in the square or in the surrounding derelict buildings for four or five days before they were loaded into cattle trucks. Some people wore merely a housecoat or nightgown. Every inch of free space was filled. There were no toilet facilities – everything was covered in urine and excrement.

The people were given no food; on the second day, the hunger pains became unbearable. There was no water either; people's lips cracked. While waiting, children sickened and people became smaller and greyer. By now, they had no doubt as to what their fate would be.

The Germans were clever enough to tantalise those they had condemned to die with a glimmer of hope. They set up a children's hospital and an emergency aid station. The staff were clad in white coats and given working certificates. The personnel were changed twice a day, so it appeared that, if you had a white coat, you could walk in and out. White coats were soon fetching fabulous prices in the ghetto. Some nurses took strange children in their arms and walked out with them. If they were sick, older people could be sent to hospital or direct to the cemetery. Healthy people were also sometimes smuggled out in ambulances. But the Germans got wise and checked the condition of the sick. Those found fit had their legs broken without an anaesthetic.

It was possible to get the Jewish police to smuggle one out, if they were bribed enough. But those who escaped usually appeared in the Umschlagplatz two, or possibly three, times before they ran out of money and had to board the train like everybody else.

Some people, who did escape from the Umschlagplatz, survived. Others who were brave enough to come to the Umschlagplatz to try and help get someone else out were swept onto the trains themselves.

The transports left every morning and evening, so twice a day the crowd was rounded up and forced into the cattle trucks. To survive this, you had to be as far from the trucks as possible. The Ukrainians would encircle the square and force the people towards the train; thousands of people would be crushed together. Resist and the Ukrainians shot you. They could not miss at that range and with thousands of people huddled together, they would probably kill another one or two besides.

People would squeeze into the doorway of the hospital or take to the upper floors of the surrounding buildings; but the Ukrainians would run about, chasing them out like wild beasts. Some hid in the attics; three girls who hid up there for five days were eventually smuggled out by nurses.

The Ukrainians did not have to exert themselves too much, though. No matter how many escaped, there were always enough to pack the cattle trucks. Indeed, the people had to be beaten with rifle butts before the doors could be closed. Those who escaped that shipment would simply wait in the Umschlagplatz. They would either go on the next shipment or the one after that... or starve.

The resistance groups were losing a lot of their men. Still, they started to fight back. They set a few fires and beat up the commander of the Jewish police. They also tried to place their people with German firms in a vain effort to save them.

By the middle of August 1942, there were only 120,000 left in the ghetto 300,000 had been taken to Treblinka to be gassed. There came a short pause in the deportations, while the Germans started liquidating what remained of the Jewish settlements in nearby towns.

Then the deportations from the ghetto started again. This time they were hard to avoid as cleared areas had been sealed off and the ghetto was now much smaller. The people left had become more skilled at hiding, so the Germans gave every Jewish policeman a quota. They each had to prove seven 'heads' a day, whereas before the Jewish police had sometimes been helpful, they were now inflexible. They would grab women with babies in their arms, snatch stray children or tear the white coat off a 'doctor'. If they did not come up with their quota, they would be on the train to Treblinka themselves.

On 6 September 1942, the remaining inhabitants of the ghetto were ordered to move into the area bounded by just four streets. There the final registration would take place. The people remained in the small rectangular block for two days. Yet, even now the Germans did not leave them completely without hope. Some would go to German firms; along with members of the Jewish Community Council, they were issued with numbered slips that guaranteed them – for the moment – life. Instead of offering any last-minute resistance, everyone without a slip thought of only one thing – how to get one.

Finally, those with slips were marched away to the firms where they would be billeted. The rest were taken to the Umschlagplatz. The last to be taken there were the families of the Jewish police.

There was no escape from the Umschlagplatz now. Sick adults and children moved from the hospitals were left lying in empty halls. They relieved themselves where they lay as there was no-one to help. Nurses sought out their parents and gave them an overdose of morphine. One doctor poured cyanide into the mouths of sick children, saving them the horrors of a train ride to Treblinka. In two days, 60,000 people were deported to certain death. On 12 September 1942, the liquidation of the Polish ghetto was over.

Those left alive were some 33,400 Jews working in German factories and 3,000 employees of the Jewish Community Council. However, there were more hidden in cellars, attics and in any other corner the Ukrainians had not bothered to look. Building work began: new walls were put up to divide the ghetto into three. Jewish workers from nearby factories were billeted there. They were forbidden to communicate with one another and were forced to work at least 12 hours a day without a break. The food was minimal and soon there was another outbreak of typhus.

The garbage carriers and gravediggers became rich, smuggling out what valuables remained to sell on the 'Aryan side' under piles of garbage or in coffins. What was left of the resistance groups in the ghetto joined forces in the Jewish Fighting Organisation or, in Polish, ZOB. They organised themselves this time according to the sector they were billeted to, rather than along political lines. They heard that Polish resistance groups were now forming in the forests and they even managed to get some pistols from Polish communists. These they used to attack senior figures in the Jewish police.

ZOB also attacked Jewish foremen who had been harsh with the slave labourers under their care. During one attack, three ZOB men were arrested, but others disarmed the German guards and freed them.

In mid-November several hundred more Jews were deported, ostensibly to the concentration camp at Lublin. During the train journey, a ZOB man broke the bars on the carriage window, pushed six women out and jumped out himself. Before, such an escape had been impossible – the escapees were held back by others, fearful of the vengeance the Germans might wreak. Now everyone knew the deportation meant death and it was better to die honourably.

In December 1942, ZOB received ten pistols from the Polish Home Army, which had recently formed. They planned to take revenge on the Jewish police, but on 18 January they found the ghetto surrounded again as the

Germans started a second liquidation. This time, however, they were not unopposed. ZOB put up barricades and, for the first time in the ghetto, offered armed resistance. There was a full-scale battle on the streets and many ZOB men were killed. Realising that they were not ready to take on the Germans in this way – they did not have the weapons for it – they resorted to guerrilla tactics. Four guerrilla actions were organised, one of which attacked the SS. Again, it cost ZOB lives.

One ZOB battle group was caught unarmed by the Germans. They were taken to the Umschlagplatz, where their leader addressed them. When they were ordered to get on to the train, not a single man moved. Van Oeppen, the chief of Treblinka, shot all 60 himself, on the spot. Tragic though this was, it was an inspiration to others.

Both Polish and Jewish public opinion were altered by these ghetto battles. The halo of omnipotence had been ripped from the heads of the Germans and they were frustrated by these actions. At last, people realised that it was possible to oppose the Germans' will and might.

Although the resistance was puny, rumours began to circulate outside the ghetto that there were hundreds of dead Germans inside. Word spread throughout Warsaw that ZOB was invincible. The Polish Underground was so impressed that they sent 50 pistols and 50 hand grenades. ZOB organised itself into a tight military outfit with sentries and guard posts manned 24 hours a day – they did not intend to get caught napping by the Germans again.

Once more, the German propaganda machine got to work. Two of the Warsaw factories were to be moved to Jewish 'reservations where productive Jews devotedly working for the Germans would be able to live through the war in peace'. In February 1943, 12 Jewish foremen arrived from the concentration camp in Lublin and tried to persuade the Jews of the Warsaw Ghetto to volunteer. The working conditions in Lublin were 'excellent', they said.

That night ZOB surrounded the Lublin men's quarters and forced them out of the ghetto.

ZOB began putting its own proclamations on the ghetto walls. When the Germans tried to counter this, ZOB seized their posters from the printing shop and destroyed them: ZOB was now in control of the ghetto. Again, plans were announced, saying that German factories were being evacuated to 'Jewish reservations'. At one joinery shop, only 25 out of the 1,000 Jewish workers volunteered to go. ZOB burned down the joinery shop, causing one million zlotys-worth of damage. The Germans issued a statement saying the fire had been started by a parachutist, but no one in the ghetto had any doubt about who was really behind it.

The next factory, a brush maker's, was to be moved in March. Out of its 3,500 Jewish workers, not one registered to go. When the machinery was being moved, ZOB planted incendiary bombs with delayed action fuses so the machines burnt up on their way.

ZOB now had the backing of the whole ghetto, which supplied them with food. Money was donated to buy arms and ammunition, and they taxed those who would not pay voluntarily. Even the Jewish Community Council was taxed. The money was then smuggled over to the 'Aryan side' where weapons and explosives were bought. These were then smuggled back into the ghetto like other contraband – Polish policemen were bribed to look the other way as heavy packages were hurled over the wall. Inside the ghetto, the Jewish police had no say any more.

Petrol was smuggled in to make Molotov cocktails and explosives were used to manufacture hand grenades. Soon every member of ZOB was armed with a pistol with ten to 15 rounds of ammunition, four or five hand grenades, and four or five Molotov cocktails. Each area had two or three rifles and there was one machine-gun for the entire ghetto.

ZOB now decided to rid the ghetto of all those who had collaborated with the Germans. Death sentences were pro-

357

nounced on all Jewish Gestapo agents; those who were not killed, fled. Later, when four Gestapo agents entered the ghetto, three were killed and the fourth badly wounded.

Realising that those remaining in the ghetto were not going to go to their deaths voluntarily, the Germans began arresting people for minor offences. However, when ZOB heard that the people caught were going to be deported, they raided the jailhouse and freed them.

The Germans then tried arresting people en masse, loading them onto trucks and taking them direct to the Umschlagplatz; ZOB stopped the trucks and freed them. Finally, the Germans got so frustrated that they decided to forcibly liquidate the remainder of the ghetto, no matter what the cost.

At 2 a.m. on 19 April 1943, ZOB observation posts reported that the Germans were coming. German and Polish policemen surrounded the ghetto at 30-yard intervals. Within fifteen minutes, ZOB had manned its defensive positions. The inhabitants of the ghetto were warned and fled to pre-arranged shelters and hiding places in cellars and attics.

At 4 a.m., German soldiers arrived in threes and fours, hoping not to arouse the suspicion of the population. Once in the middle of the ghetto, they formed in companies and platoons. At 7 a.m., motorised detachments, including a number of tanks and armoured vehicles, entered the ghetto. Field guns were set up around the walls. SS men came marching in, their goose-stepping boots ringing down the silent streets of the ghetto – the mastery of their situation seemed complete.

However, they had chosen to form at exactly the wrong place – the intersection of Mila and Zamenhofa Streets. ZOB had been waiting for just such an opportunity, and they were manning all four corners of the intersection. They rained gunfire and hand-grenades down on the SS men. Even the machine-gun opened up on them, sparingly – ammunition had to be conserved. The SS tried to retreat, but found themselves cut off. Those still alive tried to find shelter in doorways, but were fired on from all sides. A tank was called up to cover the retreat; it was hit with a Molotov cocktail and burned out. Not one German left the area alive.

Another group of Germans tried to enter the ghetto, but they were pinned down. After dozens were killed and wounded, they were forced to withdraw.

In Muranoski Square, the partisans were cornered. But they fought so ferociously that they repulsed the attack, capturing two German machine guns and burning out a second tank. By 2 p.m., there was not a single German left alive in the ghetto. It was ZOB's first complete victory.

For the next 24 hours the ghetto was bombed and shelled. Then at 2 p.m. on 20 April, the SS turned up again in close formation. As they waited for the gate into the ghetto to be opened, a partisan set off a remote-controlled mine – 100 SS men were killed. The rest withdrew under showers of gunfire.

Two hours later, the Germans attacked again, this time in a loose formation. Although 30 Germans entered the ghetto, only a handful re-emerged; the Germans were forced to withdraw. They tried to attack again in several points around the ghetto but met with ferocious opposition – every house round the perimeter of the ghetto was now a fortress.

At this point the Germans changed tactics. They sent emissaries – three officers with machine-guns lowered and white rosettes in their buttonholes – who suggested a 15-minute truce to remove their dead and wounded. They also offered all the inhabitants of the ghetto safe passage to labour camps in the Jewish reservations. They would even be allowed to take their belongings with them. The response from ZOB was gunfire.

In one area, the Germans were taking such heavy casualties that, by dusk, they resorted to setting the buildings on fire. ZOB partisans were forced to withdraw, but their retreat was blocked by a wall. A gap in it was the only way to the central ghetto, but it was guarded on three sides by German and Polish police, and Ukrainians. Half the group managed to slip through in the darkness before the Germans found a searchlight and trained it on the wall. One well-aimed shot put the light out and the rest of the partisans escaped.

The ordinary inhabitants of the ghetto were not so lucky. Thousands perished in the flames; others ran out into the courtyards where they were seized by the Germans or killed on the spot. Hundreds committed suicide by jumping from the fourth or fifth storeys of apartment houses – some mothers jumped with their children to save them from the flames. The only consolation was that these scenes of horror were witnessed by thousands of Poles who lived in the surrounding area.

The Germans thought that such horrendous loss of life would subdue the ghetto. They announced a deadline for the inhabitants to report to collection points for deportation: no one turned up. The partisans now began to take the battle to the enemy. They tried to disrupt troop movements into the central ghetto; from balconies, windows and rooftops, they showered SS trucks with bombs. One such vehicle saw all but five of the 60 SS men it was carrying killed. ZOB even succeeded in blowing up a military vehicle outside the wall of the ghetto.

When the deadline had passed, the Germans tried to enter the ghetto again, with force. The partisans had planted mines, but the electricity supply had been cut off, so they could not detonate them. As a result, they began fighting house by house. Again, the Germans were forced to resort to arson. ZOB guided the inhabitants of the ghetto to underground shelters, where thousands sheltered for over a week.

When the burning was over, not a single building was left and the water supply was cut off. Still ZOB fought on – the Germans did not dare to enter the ghetto during the day. Ferocious fighting took place at night and there were heavy losses on both sides. Food and water were scarce, as was ammunition. ZOB knew that there were 20 rifles and more ammunition waiting for them on the 'Aryan side', but there was no way they could get them.

The Germans began looking for the shelters using police dogs and sensitive sound-detecting equipment. When they found them, battle raged. Although ultimately they could not resist the might of the Germans, ZOB fulfilled its aim the Germans did not evacuate a single living person.

On 8 March, Germans and Ukrainians surrounded ZOB's headquarters. After two hours of ferocious fighting, they hurled in gas bomb. Seeing the position was hopeless, the partisans committed suicide rather than be taken by the Germans alive. Some shot their families, then themselves – 80 per cent of the partisans perished there.

The remnants banded together. Ten days earlier, two partisans had been sent out of the ghetto to contact their liaison men to arrange the withdrawal of the battle groups from the ghetto when it fell. Now the liaison men turned up. Those who remained were taken down into the sewers to make their way out. The Germans had anticipated this, so the sewers were full of obstacles and entanglements that were booby-trapped and would explode at a single touch. In some places the sewers were only 28 inches high and it was difficult for the escaping partisans to keep their mouths above the level of the sewage. Every so often, the Germans would pump gas into the drains. At one place, where the sewer was not big enough for them to stand, they had to wait for 48 hours. Partisans kept losing consciousness. For some, the lack of water was too much to bear. Driven mad by thirst they drank the foul sewer water.

On 10 May, a manhole cover was lifted in broad daylight. A number of Jewish partisans emerged and escaped in a truck. Others were left in the sewer. Those who got out were taken out to the woods where they fought with the Polish Home Army. Most died eventually. Those who survived took part in the Warsaw Uprising of 1944.

As the Soviet army approached the city in July 1944, the Polish Underground staged an uprising against the Germans. They were members of the Home Army who were run by the Polish Government in exile in London. However, they knew that in east Poland, which had already been liberated by the Red Army, the procommunist Polish Committee of National Liberation was in charge. Hoping to gain control of Warsaw before the Red Army took it, the Home Army followed the suggestion of the Soviets and revolted.

The Home Army's Warsaw Corps numbered about 50,000 men. Against weakened German opposition, they had taken over most of the city by I August. However, the Germans counter-attacked, forcing the Polish Home Army into defensive positions which they bombed and shelled for the following 63 days. The Red Army occupied the suburb of Praga, across the Vistula River from the city and stopped there while the Germans bombed the city flat. The Soviets also prevented the British and Americans from supplying the rebels.

Out of food and ammunition, the beleaguered Poles had to surrender on I October. The remnants of the Home Army and the remaining Jews were taken prisoner and deported, and the rest of the city was destroyed. Only then did the Red Army move on.

This was an entirely cynical ploy by the Soviets: allowing the Germans to destroy the Home Army eliminated the main body of the military organisation that supported the Polish government in exile in London. So when the Soviets overran the whole of Poland there was little effective resistance to the communist-led puppet government they installed.

For the Jewish resistance fighters who had survived the Warsaw consolation was that these scenes of horror were witnessed by thousands of Poles who lived in the surrounding area.

The Germans thought that such horrendous loss of life would subdue the ghetto. They announced a deadline for the inhabitants to report to collection points for deportation: no one turned up. The partisans now began to take the battle to the enemy. They tried to disrupt troop movements into the central ghetto; from balconies, windows and rooftops, they showered SS trucks with bombs. One such vehicle saw all but five of the 60 SS men it was carrying killed. ZOB even succeeded in blowing up a military vehicle outside the wall of the ghetto.

When the deadline had passed, the Germans tried to enter the ghetto again, with force. The partisans had planted mines, but the electricity supply had been cut off, so they could not detonate them. As a result, they began fighting house by house. Again, the Germans were forced to resort to arson. ZOB guided the inhabitants of the ghetto to underground shelters, where thousands sheltered for over a week.

When the burning was over, not a single building was left and the water supply was cut off. Still ZOB fought on – the Germans did not dare to enter the ghetto during the day. Ferocious fighting took place at night and there were heavy losses on both sides. Food and water were scarce, as was ammunition. ZOB knew that there were 20 rifles and more ammunition waiting for them on the 'Aryan side', but there was no way they could get them.

The Germans began looking for the shelters using police dogs and sensitive sound-detecting equipment. When they found them, battle raged. Although ultimately they could not resist the might of the Germans, ZOB fulfilled its aim the Germans did not evacuate a single living person.

On 8 March, Germans and Ukrainians surrounded ZOB's headquarters. After two hours of ferocious fighting, they hurled in gas bomb. Seeing the position was hopeless, the partisans committed suicide rather than be taken by the Germans alive. Some shot their families, then themselves – 80 per cent of the partisans perished there.

The remnants banded together. Ten days earlier, two partisans had been sent out of the ghetto to contact their liaison men to arrange the withdrawal of the battle groups from the ghetto when it fell. Now the liaison men turned up. Those who remained were taken down into the sewers to make their way out. The Germans had anticipated this, so the sewers were full of obstacles and entanglements that were booby-trapped and would explode at a single touch. In some places the sewers were only 28 inches high and it was difficult for the escaping partisans to keep their mouths above the level of the sewage. Every so often, the Germans would pump gas into the drains. At one place, where the sewer was not big enough for them to stand, they had to wait for 48 hours. Partisans kept losing consciousness. For some, the lack of water was too much to bear. Driven mad by thirst they drank the foul sewer water.

On 10 May, a manhole cover was lifted in broad daylight. A number of Jewish partisans emerged and escaped in a truck. Others were left in the sewer. Those who got out were taken out to the woods where they fought with the Polish Home Army. Most died eventually. Those who survived took part in the Warsaw Uprising of 1944.

As the Soviet army approached the city in July 1944, the Polish Underground staged an uprising against the Germans. They were members of the Home Army who were run by the Polish Government in exile in London. However, they knew that in east Poland, which had already been liberated by the Red Army, the procommunist Polish Committee of National Liberation was in charge. Hoping to gain control of Warsaw before the Red Army took it, the Home Army followed the suggestion of the Soviets and revolted.

The Home Army's Warsaw Corps numbered about 50,000 men. Against weakened German opposition, they had taken over most of the city by I August. However, the Germans counter-attacked, forcing the Polish Home Army into defensive positions which they bombed and shelled for the following 63 days. The Red Army occupied the suburb of Praga, across the Vistula River from the city and stopped there while the Germans bombed the city flat. The Soviets also prevented the British and Americans from supplying the rebels.

Out of food and ammunition, the beleaguered Poles had to surrender on I October. The remnants of the Home Army and the remaining Jews were taken prisoner and deported, and the rest of the city was destroyed. Only then did the Red Army move on.

This was an entirely cynical ploy by the Soviets: allowing the Germans to destroy the Home Army eliminated the main body of the military organisation that supported the Polish government in exile in London. So when the Soviets overran the whole of Poland there was little effective resistance to the communist-led puppet government they installed.

For the Jewish resistance fighters who had survived the Warsaw ghetto, this was the ultimate betrayal – many of them had been communists. On May Day 1943, a week before the ghetto was finally liquidated, they had held a communist-inspired celebration. There were speeches and the sound of the Internationale had rung out across the smouldering ruins of the ghetto. Of the 500,000 Jews that had passed through the Warsaw ghetto, only a handful had survived.

Babi Yar

There is a ravine outside Kiev, capital of the Ukraine, called Babi Yar. In 1941, the Nazis butchered 200,000 Jews there. If anyone had ever had any doubt as to Hitler's intentions towards the Jewish people, it was dispelled by the atrocity at Babi Yar.

When the Germans marched into Kiev on 19 September 1941, many Ukrainians rejoiced. It was the end of Soviet – Russian – rule. Since the Soviets took over in 1919, the Ukraine had been decimated by collectivisation, purges and famine. Even the Jews welcomed the Germans. The Soviet newspapers had carried not a word about Nazi atrocities. Right up until Hitler's sudden attack in June 1941, the Soviet press had heaped praise on Stalin's ally Hitler. Nothing was said of the treatment of Jews in Germany and Poland. Some Jews even praised Hitler for being an able statesman. The older people recalled that, when the Germans had been in the Ukraine in World War I, they had behaved very well much better than the Russians. They had not been anti-Semitic then. The Germans were civilised Europeans with a respect for order. Most of all they were renowned for their consistency. Soon the Ukrainian Jews would discover, tragically, how wrong they were.

When the Germans entered the city, they headed straight for the Kreshchatik. This was the main street in Kiev where the party officials and secret policemen lived and worked. Naturally, these officials had already departed. The Germans set up their headquarters there, taking over the Continental Hotel and converting the Doctors' Club into a dub for German officers. Germans filled the boulevard cafés. Two enterprising Jewish barbers set up shop and did a roaring trade, cutting German officers' hair.

The first ominous note was sounded when the Germans took over the radio station – all Jews working there were ordered out. On 24 September, the new boss of the radio station was just telling those remaining that he wanted the world to hear 'the voice of free Kiev' when there was a massive explosion: the German headquarters had blown up. Explosions continued for the next five days, setting alight the centre of Kiev. Nobody knows how many Germans were killed. Neither the Nazis nor the Soviets would say. Long after the war, the Soviets denied blowing up the Kreshchatik, blaming it on the Germans; however, it is clear now that the Soviet authorities mined the whole area before leaving. A few soldiers had been left behind to detonate the bombs, but word quickly spread that the Jews were to blame.

On the morning of 28 September, a notice went up. It said in Russian, Ukrainian and German, 'All Yids living in the city of Kiev and its vicinity are to report by eight o'clock on the morning of Monday, 29 September 1941, at the corner of Melnikovsky and Dokhturov Streets (near the cemetery). They are to take with them documents, money, valuables, as well as warm clothes, underwear etc.

'Any Yid not carrying out this instruction and who is found elsewhere will be shot.

'Any civilian entering flats evacuated by Yids and stealing property will be shot.'

Ukrainians assumed that the Jews were being deported to Palestine, possibly as a reprisal for the Kreshchatik. Most Jews thought so too and did what they were told. The following morning the streets near the cemetery were full of women and children, the sick and the elderly; all able-bodied young men had already been conscripted into the Red Army. These were poor people too anyone with enough money to leave Kiev was long gone. Some had even managed to bribe their way out of the city after it had been occupied.

Many Ukrainians had no great love for the Jews: some hurled insults at them; others called for them to be confined in a ghetto. Some Jews already feared that they were going to their deaths. One woman had poisoned herself and her children; a young girl had thrown herself from an upper storey window. Her body lay in the street covered by a sheet – nobody bothered to remove it.

The crowd was moved off, a rumour having circulated that they were heading for the railway station. People carried suitcases; some seemed to have the entire contents of their houses strapped to their backs. Others had clubbed together to hire a lorry to carry their possessions.

The Russians and Ukrainians were not universally hostile to the Jews. Some had come to see old friends off while others helped them with their bags. German soldiers looked on, keeping an eye out for pretty Jewish girls.

The dense crowd edged along until they got to the Jewish cemetery. The entrance was guarded by German soldiers and Ukrainian policemen who told the crowd that anyone who entered would not be allowed back – with the exception of cabbies who could drop their fare and go back for another one. Jews were separated from non-Jews, husbands from wives.

Still, most people assumed that they were being taken to a train – there was a war on and they were being evacuated to somewhere safer. The Jews were going first, they reasoned, because they we're more closely related ethnically to the Germans than the Russians or Ukrainians.

Once inside the cemetery everyone was told to drop what they were carrying – foodstuffs on the right, baggage on the left; they would have to sort things out when they got to their destination. By now they could hear the occasional burst of machine-gun fire nearby, but could not admit to themselves that they were going to be shot. For one thing, there was such an enormous mass of people. Such things did not happen, they told themselves.

By the time they realised what was happening, it was too late. They found themselves walking through a narrow corridor lined by soldiers and dogs. The soldiers stood shoulder to shoulder, had their sleeves rolled up and were armed with clubs and sticks. As the crowd passed through, the soldiers beat them savagely, aiming for the ribs, the stomach and the groin, drawing blood. Those who fell to the ground were set upon by the dogs and trampled by those coming from behind.

Young women were propositioned by German soldiers who said that they could save them if they slept with them. Ukrainian policemen then ordered everyone to strip; those who hesitated had their clothes ripped off them. They were still being kicked and hit with knuckledusters and clubs by Germans who seemed to be in a sadistic frenzy. This was being done to keep the huge mass of people disorientated.

Bleeding, naked people formed lines at a gap that had been dug in the steep wall of sand. Some Ukrainians who had got mixed up with the Jews stood to one side there, but an officer ordered that they be shot anyway. He was afraid that if word got out of what was happening, no Jews would turn up the next day.

The lines of naked people were marched through into the ravine, and lined up on a narrow ledge in the quarry. It had been cut especially for the executions and was so narrow that victims automatically leant back against the sandstone. Below them was a sea of bodies covered in blood. On the other side, the machine-gun crews had built a fire, where they brewed coffee. When the ledge was full, they left the fire and returned to their guns. Then they loosed off a burst along the line. As each person was hit, they fell into the sea of bodies below. Around 34,000 people were killed that day.

One woman escaped, though. Her name was Dina Mironovna Pronichev. She was an actress and mother of two. Her husband was Russian; she did not look Jewish, spoke Ukrainian and could have passed as one. When she read the notice, she decided not to go. However, she would see her parents to the train, then return home to look after the children. When she realised what was happening, her parents told her she should save herself. She approached one of the Ukrainian policemen and showed him her union card, which did not mention her ethnic group. He set her to one side with the Ukrainians who had got mixed in with the Jews.

'We'll shoot the Jews first, then let you out,' he said.

But when a German officer turned up, he ordered that she should be shot anyway, They were the last batch that day.

When she stood on the ledge, she heard the bullets coming towards her. Before they reached her, she jumped. It was a long drop, but she landed softly on the bodies below and was splattered with blood. Beneath her, she could feel people moving. The Germans climbed down and walked over the corpses, shooting anyone still alive. One SS man caught his foot on Dina. He shone a torch in her face, then picked her up and punched her, but she hung limp and lifeless. He kicked her in the chest and trod on her hand so the bones cracked. Then he walked away.

Earth was piled on top of the bodies. Sand went in Dina's mouth and she realised that she would rather be shot than buried alive. She held her breath to stop herself coughing and wriggled free. It had been a long day for the Ukrainian policemen and they only covered the corpses with a light sprinkling of sand. In the dark, she crawled to the edge of the pit.

She dug handholds in the sandy sides and hauled herself out. Hearing a whisper, she nearly jumped back into the pit. It was a young boy who had somehow escaped too. Together, they crawled off into the night.

They made little progress. When it grew fight they hid in some bushes on the edge of another ravine. From there,

they watched the Germans sorting out people's belongings. An old woman and her six-year-old grandson came
by; the Germans shot them. Six or seven Germans led two
young women out on to a ledge on the other side of the
ravine and gang raped them. When they had finished,
they bayoneted them, leaving their bodies there naked
with their legs spread. All the time, in the background, was
the sound of shooting.

Dina fell into a trance and saw her mother, father and sister in long white robes. She was awoken by the boy who
said plaintively, 'Don't die, lady, don't leave me.'

When it grew dark again, they crawled on. Towards
dawn, the boy crawled ahead as a lookout. She heard him
shout, 'Don't move, lady, there are Germans here.'

Then she heard them shoot him. Luckily, they had not
understood what he had said and they did not come looking for her. She was so distraught that she temporarily lost
her mind, digging a small hole, then filling it up with sand,
as if she was burying the boy who had saved her.

The next day she took refuge in a rubbish tip, covering
herself with rags and boxes. Occasionally, she heard
Germans passing by. Across the road, she saw tomatoes
growing in a garden, so when it was dark, she crawled
over and ate them. Still she dragged herself on. At around
dawn she saw a barn behind a cottage and slipped inside.
Hearing a dog barking, a woman came out of the cottage
and sent her son to fetch the Germans. They took Dina to
a guardhouse where soldiers were drinking coffee. She
went to sit on a chair, but they shouted at her and made
her sit on the floor.

When the soldiers went, they left one behind on duty. He
was sympathetic and let Dina sit on the chair. Later he
gave her a rag and indicated that she should clean the window. He told her to look out of the window and pick out
the way she had to run. But before she could escape, an
officer turned up with two 15-year-old girls. They were

sobbing, kissing his boots and telling him he could do anything he liked with them – including have sex with them –
if he did not shoot them. The officer took them and Dina
back to the place where the victims had been stripped.
Around 40 old men and women were sitting among the
clothes; one was lying paralysed. They were guarded by a
single sentry.

'Don't look at me,' he shouted at Dina. 'I can't do anything for you. I have children too.'

A girl in a soldier's tunic and greatcoat approached, putting the coat around Dina, who was shivering in the cold.
She was a 19-year-old Russian nurse who had been left
behind in the Soviet retreat.

A lorry arrived and they climbed aboard. It took them to
a garage that was being used as a temporary prison. When
they arrived, an old woman got off and squatted down to
relieve herself. In response, a German soldier shot her in
the head. The garage was already full of people rounded
up on the streets, waiting to be shot, so the lorry pulled off
again, seemingly heading for the Brest-Litovsk highway. It
was going full tilt when Dina threw herself off. Either the
guards did not see her, or did not care, because the lorry
did not stop.

A group of people gathered around her. She explained
that she had meant to go to the market, but had missed her
stop and jumped off. They did not believe her, but took her
into a nearby farmhouse anyway. Half an hour later she
found refuge with her brother's wife, who was Polish.

Over the next two years, the slaughter continued.
Between 100,000 and 200,000 Jews, communist officials
and Russian prisoners of war were killed at Babi Yar.
When the Germans retreated in August 1943, they had
bodies exhumed by slave labour and burnt in huge pyres
in an attempt to conceal what they had done. Dina survived the war and was the only eyewitness to what had
happened at Babi Yar on 29 September 1941.

The Bombing of Dresden

After the Allies had successfully overcome the last serious German offensive in World War II, the Battle of the Bulge in the winter of 1944-45, the British and US to the west and the Soviets to the east were involved in a free-for-all, with each side seeing how much German territory it could seize.

However, Britain, the US and the Soviet Union were still ostensibly allies. So on the night of 13 February 1945, a matter of months before the end of the war in Europe, the Anglo-American air force made a show of helping the invading Red Army. They ordered some 1300 bombers to firebomb the medieval city of Dresden that stood in the path of the Russian invaders, reasoning that Dresden was a major communications centre. In reality, it had no strategic significance at all apart from a railway marshalling yard that was not targeted. There were no factories there either. However, the city was completely destroyed and as many 135,000 people were killed - almost twice as many as were killed by the atomic bomb dropped on Hiroshima. It was the biggest single raid of the war in Europe.

The people of Dresden could not be considered combatants. Most able-bodied men were away at the front. The women, children and the elderly left behind had been joined by refugees, again the young, the old and the female, from Silesia and Wargau. The peacetime population of 600,000 had swollen to one million. Before the bombing started one could hardly move in the station. Children were dying of hunger and cold; old people collapsed and died from the stress. Ironically, the only significant body of men in the city was Allied prisoners of war who had been drafted in as forced labour to help feed the population.

The idea of bombing Dresden was first floated at the conference at Yalta in early February 1945. The three great war leaders, Churchill, Roosevelt and Stalin, met in the Crimean resort to discuss how to finish off Hitler. In return for the Anglo-American bombing of targets in the path of the Red Army, Stalin promised to declare war on the Japanese once the war in Europe was won.

Although the Germans had come up with the idea of carpet bombing during the Spanish Civil War, it had been perfected by Air Marshal Sir Arthur 'Bomber' Harris, who had taken command of the RAF's Bomber Command in 1942. He believed that the war could be won by turning every German city into a pile of rubble. His reasoning was that, if one destroyed all of the enemy's industry and killed its workforce, the frontline troops would have no weapons to fight with. They could then be easily overcome by Allied troops equipped with weapons made in the United States, Canada and the far-flung regions of Siberia, which were beyond the range of German planes. Churchill was uneasy about the morality of such a wholesale onslaught on civilians but, in 1942, there was no other strategy.

The operation that had been decided on had to be undertaken immediately, in February. The return trip to Dresden was a nine-hour flight from England, much of it across hostile territory. Even though the nights were still long, some of the journey across Germany would inevitably take place during daylight and the hope was that the bad weather usually experienced at that time of year would keep German fighters on the ground.

Bomber Command would attack on the night of the 13th in two waves separated by three hours. The Americans, whose Flying Fortresses were better suited to daytime missions, would attack on the morning of the 14th. The RAP's first wave would consist of 245 four-engined Lancaster bombers with nine Mosquitoes to mark the target. The Lancasters would take ten to 15 minutes to pass over the target. The second wave would be 529 Lancasters, which would take 20-30 minutes to pass over the target. Each Lancaster would carry 1,447.7 tons of high explosive and 1,181.6 tons of incendiaries, along with 2,154 gallons of fuel for the long flight. The bombing would be concentrated by using a broad formation with planes at different heights.

That night, numerous other planes would be in the air to confuse the German defences and make dummy attacks on other targets. The following two days, 527 B-17 Flying Fortresses carrying 953.3 tons of high explosives and 294.3 tons of incendiaries would again attack the target. They would be escorted by hundreds of fighters who, when not defending the bombers, would fly low and strafe trains and trucks.

The plan was to bum the centre out of the city. The lead plane would mark the sports ground in the centre of Dresden with red target indicators. Then the rest of the formation would move in.

It was known that there were light air defences around the railway yards. One interesting piece of intelligence came from Colditz Castle, which was used to hold British officers who had made a habit of escaping from other prison camps. One of the inmates had asked a guard whether there were any barrage balloons over Dresden. He was told there were none. Otherwise, little was known about the city and the aircrew were not supplied with maps, so it is plain that the bombers were not aiming to take out specific military targets – their target was the city itself.

During the briefing, the aircrew was told that Dresden was one of the few centres of communication between Berlin and the Russian Front. The men were informed that the city was full of men and material on their way to the Russian Front, which was not true. Many trains were due, filled with refugees fleeing the air raids on Berlin. The bombing of Dresden was designed to cause maximum havoc and intended to break the morale of those left defending Berlin. It would give Berliners the idea that there was nowhere safe to run to. Even so, some of the aircrew questioned their orders. They could not see the justification for firebombing a city like Dresden. It was not a military target; rather it was a famous centre of art. Some asked why they could not concentrate on industrial targets like Cologne or the Ruhr. However, their commanders intimated that the order had come from Churchill himself. Many got the impression that the raid was being staged to impress the Russians with the power of Bomber Command. Although this left them uneasy, in modem war terrible things do happen to civilians. And British cities had taken their share of punishment.

The fliers were ordered that if they were hit they should fly as far as possible westwards before ditching their planes. They should not try and fly eastwards to safety behind Russians lines; tension between the Allies was already showing and downed British and American airmen had already been maltreated by the Soviets.

The Lancasters began taking off at 6 p.m. on the evening of 13 February The outward journey would take five hours, as the planes would zigzag to avoid flak and keep the Germans guessing about their destination. They had been told to expect harassment from enemy fighters. With such a long journey across enemy territory, almost to the point of no return, many of the airmen expected to be killed.

The Mosquitos left later and took a more direct route. Their flight time was two and a half hours. They were expected over the target at 10 p.m. It would then take them ten to 15 minutes to locate and illuminate the aiming points.

The attackers were lucky with the weather. Cloud cover

was total over the continent, which meant they had little trouble with night-fighters. However, the weather forecasters in England had predicted that the skies over Dresden would clear at about 10 p.m. and stay clear for only a short while: timing was of the essence.

The Mosquitos found the target using radio beams but, due to the curvature of the earth, they had to be high to detect them; even then, they were faint. When they picked them up, they found that they were 15 miles south of Dresden, so turned back towards the city.

Using radar they located the sports stadium and dropped a green flare on it. The cloud over Dresden was solid, almost down to the ground, meaning that any sort of precision bombing would be out of the question.

Suddenly it cleared below 3,000 feet. The Mosquitos went down and marked targets with red flares, going so low that they could see cars and people on the ground. The main marker had missed the sports ground by about 300 feet, but was, effectively spot on. When dropping bombs from the height the Lancasters were operating at, anywhere within a couple of miles was considered a direct hit.

The Lancasters could see the flares through the clouds, though they could not see the city itself. The Mosquitos dived again, planting more flares so that there could be no mistaking the target. Then the order was given for the Lancasters to start their bombing run.

Over the target there was no fighter cover. A petrol shortage kept the Luftwaffe on the ground. There was some light flak from a battery of 20 millimetre guns manned by schoolboys, but there were no serious defences, so the master bomber ordered the Lancasters to come in low. The heavy guns had been taken away to the Russian front. Dresden was, essentially, undefended.

The people were unprepared. Dresden had only suffered two small daylight raids. When the green flare was dropped over the sports stadium, illuminating the city with an eerie glow, some people went outside to see what was happening. When the sirens began, many people assumed that the raid was not on Dresden but on some other city in the area.

The ten o'clock train had been stopped in the station when someone accidentally pulled the communication cord. Police directed people to the air-raid shelter under the station. Some stubbornly stayed on the train; others, who had been in air raids in other German cities, knew that it was better to be anywhere else other than a railway station during an air raid. They were right: 3000 dead were found in the shelter and another 300 were found on the train – all of them burnt to death.

As the Lancasters began unloading their bombs, people took shelter wherever they could. The famous Dresden choir was singing when the Lancasters came. Bombs fell among the choirboys, killing them. The blasts of the four- or sometimes eight-ton bombs had a terrible effect. Later, numerous pregnant women were found with their bellies open and their mutilated babies literally blown out of them.

The focus of the attack was not the sports stadium, or the station, but the old town to the east with its timber-framed houses. However, bombs were falling miles from there. Some of the RAF's incendiaries had poor ballistic qualities and, once dropped, spread out over an extensive area.

The houses in Dresden's old town were butted up against each other to save space. Inevitably, once one caught fire the whole street would burn. The houses were built with a cellar underneath for storage, in which most people took cover. Although these cellars afforded some protection against blast, they were no help against incendiaries. Once they hit, people had to come out of the cellar and try to smother the incendiary bombs with sand or water before they burst into flames. This was a hazardous business. By 1945, some incendiaries were fitted with a small explosive booby trap to kill, maim, or at least discourage anyone from smothering them.

After the first couple of casualties, people gave up trying to extinguish the incendiaries and fled, leaving the houses to burn. Soon the old town was a raging inferno: dust and smoke made it impossible to see; survivors covered with wet blankets tried to find their way out, while they continued to be blasted from above. A boys' school that had been turned into a military hospital – with a red cross on the roof – was hit; 300 wounded men were killed when the building collapsed.

Soon the fire had taken such a hold that the fire brigade could do nothing to halt the conflagration. The air above the target became superheated, making it difficult for, the oncoming stream of bombers to identify any target other than the enormous fires. The markers were obscured by smoke and the violent winds caused by the updraft made it difficult to manoeuvre the Lancasters as they came in. As a result, the remaining aircraft simply dumped the rest of their bombs on the blazing city and turned for home. The final wave of high explosives blasted the fires horizontally a considerable distance.

Despite the horrific speed of the attack, Dresden had suffered no worse than hundreds of other town and cities across Germany – up to this point. No one on the ground realised that at the same moment the first flares were dropping, a second wave of planes – twice as big as the first – was taking off in England.

In all, the second wave of 529 Lancasters carried 650,000 tons of explosives in their dark bellies. Each plane also carried one 4,000-pound thinwalled blast bomb.

Again, the planes took a zigzag path across Germany. They needed no markers – the burning centre of Dresden was a beacon they could home in on from 50 miles away. When the master bomber got there, the city was lit up; he could not see the aiming point. There was no opposition so he flew in low. Being able to see people on the ground brought home to him the horror of what he was about to do.

When the sirens sounded again, the people of Dresden could not believe it. They could not believe that the British intended to raze their beautiful city the way they had the industrial cities to the west. Again, people took refuge in the cellars. When they emerged, they found the fire had turned into a firestorm. Those stuck in the cellars suffocated; many who braved the streets were burnt alive. As they tried to shed their burning clothing, people passed out from oxygen deficiency. Every last molecule of oxygen was being consumed by the burning buildings. People crawled on the ground to gasp what air they could; those who fainted in the streets were quickly charred.

Those who survived looked frantically for friends and loved ones. They searched among the dead, who littered the ground: some were black like charcoal and shrunk to half their size; others lay peacefully unmarked, as if sleeping, their lungs burst by the blast. Women and children sat on the trams as if they had nodded off, or lay around naked, their clothes blasted off them. Soldiers were only identifiable by their belt buckles. Some corpses lay in groups as if clawing at each other; arms, legs and heads poked out of the rubble. Static water tanks were full to the brim with corpses.

Temperatures at the centre of the fire reached 3,000 degrees – 1,200 degrees is the maximum sandstone can withstand so numerous buildings, collapsed. Other structures were blown down by the winds the fire drew. Some people were literally blown off their feet and sucked into the flames.

Even at 20,000 feet, the crews in the Lancasters could see a rosy glow in the sky above them. The light was as bright inside the planes as if the aircrew had walked on stage as the heavy aircraft heaved and buckled in the enormous columns of heated air.

The people on the ground began to believe that Churchill had ordered the firebombing of Dresden personally, and cursed the airmen for blindly following his orders. Some believed that the aircrew listened into German radio to hear which shelters people were being instructed to go to. The large bombs, they believed, were then used to pound the shelters, and when people ran out on to the streets smaller bombs were dropped to kill them. The truth was that there was so much smoke and the air was so turbulent that it was impossible for the aircrew to tell where the bombs were going.

A rumour spread that an English spy with a torch was guiding the planes in. The British SS men stationed nearby were blamed. They had betrayed England by backing Germany, and now the Germans were losing the war they were betraying Germany to the RAF; to escape the wrath of the populace they deserted.

No one knew how many dead there were. Figures circulated: 250,000, 300,000, 400,000. There was no possibility of fighting the fires – even when it had been attempted it had been counterproductive. People sheltering in the cellars were drowned.

The famous Zwinger museum went up in flames. Even though its art treasures were to be moved before the Soviets arrived, they sat in a lorry outside, where they were burnt.

When the castle caught on fire, people were trapped in the cellars. Young men, trying unsuccessfully to break though the walls with axes, perished in the flames. Others who escaped the cellars found that the castle's roof hand melted, raining down molten copper on them.

Incendiaries lodged in the dome of the Sarrasani Circus building. The horses and 16 boys and girls who were acrobat riders were killed by a blast bomb. Although the circus people managed to get some of the animals out, the tigers suffocated in their cages. Despite the burning building collapsing on Wally the hippopotamus, he survived because he was half submerged in a tank of water.

The hippopotami at the zoo were not so lucky – when their house collapsed, they were pinned underwater and drowned. Two dwarf hippos took refuge in a bomb crater. A keeper threw hay down to them; but later on they were blown to bits by a time bomb. A gibbon was destroyed after losing its hands; chimps suffocated; some apes escaped and were seen in the forest later. The yaks were burnt and died from their wounds. A mother bear was blinded, but her cubs survived to be suckled by another bitch. The polar bear cubs were not so lucky, though. Their badly burnt mother, who had saved them, had to be put down. They could have been reared by bottle, but there was no milk in the ruins of Dresden and they died of hunger soon after.

Some bison and red buffalo escaped and menaced the people fleeing the city. The vultures escaped too but despite the rich pickings offered by the ruined city, returned to the zoo promptly at feeding time.

As the firestorm raged, it could be seen up to 50 miles away from the ground. Allied prisoners of war who saw the devastation were appalled. Even German soldiers who had suffered the horrors of the Eastern Front said they had never seen anything like it.

The retreating Lancasters could see the firestorm they had left behind for 100 miles. For most, this had been the first raid they had been on where there had been no opposition – no night fighters, no flak to speak of. They felt like murderers: the people they had bombed had been defenceless. For many, the bombing of Dresden seemed like a cowardly act. They felt sorry for the people who had been blasted on the ground four miles beneath them.

One night fighter, a JU 88, did eventually tail the Allied planes, but it quickly turned away, realising that with the light of Dresden behind him he made a perfect target for the Lancaster's tail gunners.

On the ground, the sirens could not sound their all clear – the air-raid warning system had been destroyed. Buildings that had been spared by the bombing caught on fire as the flames spread and a column of people, some in night clothes, some with the hair burnt off their heads, began to make their way out of the city.

The following day, at their brief, some of the American airmen expressed misgivings about attacking Dresden. The city, they knew, was full of refugees fleeing the Russians. Nevertheless, following orders was now routine to them; some of the fighter escort even strafed the trails of people fleeing the burning city.

On the morning of the 14th, there was cloud cover over the city. The American bombers did not even see their target. They simply dropped their bombs where they were told. But survivors said that low-flying aircraft attacked the civilians who were huddling down by the River Elbe. While the zookeepers tried to erect a special tent to protect the giraffe from the freezing weather, an American fighter flew low, killing a number of the animals the keepers had saved the night before. He also killed some of the animal keepers of the Sarrasani Circus.

The writer Kurt Vonnegut was with a working party of 100 American POWs who took shelter with their guards in the huge underground meat safes of the Dresden slaughterhouse. Ironically, they survived, but emerged the following morning to be bombarded by American Mustangs. They took cover in the rubble and watched as the Mustangs went on to shoot German civilians.

On the ground, people were desperately trying to tend the wounded or search for relatives when the bombs started falling again. There were no warning sirens this time. The raid lasted for ten minutes. A total of 487.7 tons of high explosives and 294.3 tons of incendiaries were dropped – small beer compared to the raid the night before. It did little more than disturb the rubble. However, many of the bombs had delayed-action fuses, which made trying to rescue people trapped in cellars a dangerous business.

That night the RAF sent Lancasters to bomb Chemnitz, which was crammed with refugees who had fled Dresden. Dresden was targeted again that night, maybe by the RAF mistaking it for Chemnitz, or maybe by the Russians.

As the Lancasters were returning home in the morning, 211 Flying Fortresses carrying 456.6 tons of high explosives and no incendiaries were taking off to give the ruins of Dresden another pounding. That day it rained, turning the city into a sea of mud, wreckage and half-exposed corpses. Even so, the city burnt for four days. As it was overcast, the Americans simply dumped their loads on the city without any pretence of strategic bombing. The devices must have just churned the rubble once more. Neither German records nor later aerial reconnaissance showed they had any effect whatsoever but this didn't prevent low-flying fighters from continuing to strafe the ruins for another eight days.

As a communications centre Dresden had three distinctive features. One was the railway bridge over the Elbe. It was left intact; indeed, it had never been a designated target. The second was the railway yard and its rolling stock. It too survived, being outside the RAF's target area. The third was the Autobahn bridge outside the city to the west. It was never attacked. Though the city was destroyed and over 100,000 people killed, as a communication centre Dresden was virtually unimpaired.

As the Air Raid Patrolmen, Red Cross and Fire Brigade had been decimated by the air raid, detachments of SS Pioneers worked alongside slave labourers doing rescue work. It was an impossible task. Corpses lay in the streets for days, those that could be collected were buried in mass graves. The centre of the city was cordoned off and the army went in with flame-throwers to cremate the bodies on huge grids. Piles of body parts were heaped together, dowsed with petrol and burnt. No one realised that beneath the rubble there were still people alive, trapped in the cellars. Later, when they opened the cellars, everyone was dead.

At first, they tried lifting out the corpses. 'Thus began the first corpse mine in Dresden,' said Vonnegut, who had helped dig it. But later the stench became too overpowering. The cellars became awash with a green liquid that dripped from the corpses. The SS Pioneers came in with flame-throwers and cremated the bodies where they sat.

For weeks, men carried remains in wooden boxes, cardboard boxes, anything they could find, to the crematorium. But no matter what they did, they could not cope with the scale of the problem. Soon the weather warmed, the unburied corpses became a writhing sea of maggots and the city a cloud of flies.

Survivors found what shelter they could. Wounds were covered with paper as the city had run out of bandages. As well as the cold weather, people were menaced by wild animals that had escaped from the zoo. An ostrich was found 50 miles away, dead in the snow, the remains of a fox in its mouth.

Although many people cursed the British after the bombing of Dresden, many of the survivors also cursed Hitler. After all, it was he who had brought this holocaust on them. Some critics earned themselves a bullet in the back of the head for their pains.

Although the German papers described the British as 'terror-fliers', 'air-gangsters' and 'child-murderers' after the raid on Dresden, British prisoners of war did not find this attitude reflected in their guards, even among those who had lost relatives or entire families in Dresden. The war was nearly over and the guards would far rather be captured by the British or Americans than by the Russians.

Some of the people took out their frustration on the

American POWs who were helping to clear the rubble, though. They were cursed and spat on. There were rumours that Americans had been shot for looting; there was one such case, but he was not a POW. He was a 45-year-old schoolteacher and former recruiter for the Free America Corps, who was then an infantryman in the SS. He had found a battered teapot in the rubble, and was court-martialled for looting and executed by a firing squad. At the time, his son was on the other side, serving in the US Marine Corps.

A massive 15 square kilometres of Dresden were destroyed completely. After the war, the authorities considered bulldozing the remains of the city and rebuilding the place from scratched. Instead, the castle and the Zwinger museum were restored, while the rest of the city was rebuilt in an undistinguished eastern European style. One of the loveliest cities of Europe had been lost forever.

My Lai

By 1968, the Vietnam war had been under way for three years and the Americans already knew they were losing. The war was the last act in a liberation struggle that had begun when Vietnamese leader Ho Chi Minh gate-crashed the Versailles Peace Conference in 1918, after the end of the World War I. He asked when the French, the colonial power occupying Indo-China, were going to leave his country. He was thrown out.

As part of the liberation struggle, Ho Chi Minh and his fellow Vietnamese nationalists became communists. They began an armed struggle against the French in the 1930s, then took up arms against the Japanese when they invaded during World War II. After the Japanese were defeated, the Viet Minh resumed the fight against the French, which they won in 1954. At a peace conference in Geneva, the country was temporarily divided in two for administrative purposes, with Ho Chin Minh's communists holding the North – the country would be reunited after a general election. That election never came.

As the Cold War grew colder, America saw Vietnam as a place in which they could stop the spread of communism. They were wrong; the Vietnamese had an entrenched military culture. They had been fighting the Chinese for centuries and knew the Americans did not have the stomach for a long war.

As guarantors of the Geneva Peace Agreement, America needed an excuse to go to war. In 1965, they pretended that one of their warships had been attacked by two North Vietnamese gunboats in the Gulf of Tonkin. Congress approved the money for the war and American troops went in. The alleged attack was a fabrication.

By 1968 the Americans knew they were out of their depth. Not only were they fighting a disciplined army from the North, but they also faced a guerrilla army, called the Viet Cong, in the South. Given that a Viet Cong guerrilla looked just like any other Vietnamese person, they were as hard for the Americans to find as a drop of water in a bucket of tears.

Worse was to come. The Americans realised that, as the Viet Cong could simply attack at will and run away, they could control their rate of casualties. Analysts in the Pentagon worked out that the Vietnamese were keeping the losses just below their birth rate. That meant that they could, essentially, fight forever.

Back home in the US, the American public saw the Vietnam as a small and backward place. They believed their massive military superiority should be able to crush any enemy on the planet. But even massive air strikes did no good. The Viet Cong simply crawled out of their shelters and began fighting again.

US ground troops were not highly motivated; many of

them did not even know where Vietnam was, nor did they care. Poorly trained US conscripts were rotated home after a year. All most of them wanted was to get through that year in one piece, but these half-hearted soldiers were put up against a ruthless and dedicated enemy who were fighting for their country.

The Americans were consumed with paranoia. No one could be trusted: prostitutes who sleep with GIs left bombs under soldiers' beds after making love to them; toddlers were booby-trapped – if an unwary American picked up the child, both soldier and child would be blown to smithereens. It is little wonder that Americans came to see every Vietnamese person – even women and children – as their enemy. It seemed quite legitimate to kill children, as they would one day grow up to be Viet Cong. The random massacre of Vietnamese civilians became commonplace, but one atrocity in 1968 shocked the world. It helped weaken support for the war in the US and, although American involvement continued for another six years, eventually lost it for them.

On the morning of 16 March 1968, three companies of the American troops were sent on a search and destroy operation in the My Son area near Quang Ngai. Their job was to seek out the enemy and kill them.

The soldiers were from the 11th Infantry Brigade, American Division. Company C's target was the Viet Cong's 48th battalion which intelligence believed was operating out of a hamlet marked on American maps as My Lai 4. Helicopters set troops down nearby. There was no resistance at the landing zone. The company commander Captain Ernest L. Medina sent the 1st and 2nd Platoons into the village. Seeing Americans coming, some villagers ran away and were gunned down. There was no resistance – the 2nd Platoon swept through the northern part of the village, hurling grenades into the huts and killing anyone who came out. They raped and murdered village girls, rounded up civilians and shot them. After half an hour, Medina order the 2nd Platoon on to the hamlet of Binh Tay, where they gang raped several more girls before rounding up some 20 women and children and killing them.

Appalling though these actions were, the name most closely associated with the massacre was that of Lieutenant William L. Calley, who commanded the 1st Platoon which swept through the south of the village, shooting anyone who tried to escape, bayoneting others, raping women, shooting livestock and destroying crops and houses. Survivors were rounded up and herded into a drainage ditch. Lieutenant Calley opened fire on the hapless villagers and ordered his men to join in. They emptied clip after clip into the tangled heap of human flesh until all the bodies lay motionless. When they stopped firing, miraculously, a two-year-old child crawled out of the carnage, crying. He tried to climb out of the ditch and run away. Calley grabbed him, pushed him back and shot him.

Half an hour later, the 3rd Platoon moved in to mop up. They shot wounded villagers to 'put them out of their misery', burnt houses, killed the remaining livestock, shot anyone trying to escape and rounded up a group of women and children and sprayed them with bullets.

No one is sure how many died. Estimates put the death toll at anywhere between 172 and 347 people. They were unarmed old men, women or children only three of them were known members of the Viet Cong. Captain Medina reported a body count of 90 Viet Cong, no civilians; the divisional press officer announced 128 enemy dead. The war that had begun with a lie continued with lies, until no one in the Pentagon or in the US government knew what was going on. There was just one American casualty, and the wound had been self-inflicted. The press officer said 13 Viet Cong suspects had been captured and three weapons taken. That just three weapons were being shared among

141 enemy soldiers should have alerted someone that something was wrong, but it was just another day in Vietnam.

The reason that, on this occasion, the truth was unravelled was that two pressmen – combat photographer Ronald Haeberle and army reporter Jay Roberts – had been assigned to Calley's platoon. They had witnessed the appalling carnage. One woman had been hit by such ferocious, continuous fire that bone flew off chip by chip; another woman was shot and her baby opened up with an assault rifle; a baby was slashed with a bayonet. One GI, who had just finished raping a girl, put his rifle into her vagina and pulled the trigger; an old man was thrown down a well and tossed a grenade – he had to choose to drown or blow himself up; and a child escaping from the carnage was brought down with a single shot.

There was another appalled witness. Warrant Officer Hugh C. Thompson, the pilot of a small observation helicopter circling the village, had begun dropping smoke flares to mark the position of wounded civilians so they could be medi-vaced out. He was horrified to see American foot soldiers following the smoke and shooting the casualties.

Gradually, the news leaked out. The men of Company C were not shy about boasting of their great victory at My Lai. Meanwhile, the Viet Cong distributed pamphlets denouncing it as an atrocity. The US Army halfheartedly investigated the rumours of a massacre that had eventually spread up the chain of command, but decided there was no basis for an official enquiry.

However, another soldier, named Ronald Ridenhour, who had ambitions to be a journalist heard about the massacre and took an interest. He made it his business to meet the men from Company C, especially Michael Bernhardt, who had refused to participate in the killing. The other members of Company C were beginning to get uneasy

about what they had done, too. They were about to be
rotated back to the US and realised that the rest of the
world did not operate in the same moral vacuum as
Vietnam. They knew that there was nothing they could do
without inviting murder charges, but they were happy to
unburden themselves to Ridenhour.

Ridenhour compiled what they told him, but realised
that if he took his evidence to the army they would stage a
summary investigation, which would result in another
whitewash. When he returned to the US he could not forget what he had been told, so he drew up a letter outlining
his evidence and dispatched 30 copies to prominent politicians.

One of the recipients was Congressman Morris Udall of
Arizona. He pressed the Pentagon to interview Ridenhour.
Six months later, and nearly 18 months after the atrocity~
Lieutenant Calley was charged with murder.

This posed a problem for the US military. What they
needed was a scapegoat who could be branded a madman
or psychopath – that way they could assure the world that
the My Lai massacre was a one-off. But Calley was just a
regular guy. He had been working as an insurance apprais-
er in San Francisco, when he had been called up in his
native Miami. He started to drive home, but ran out of
money just outside Albuquerque, so he enlisted right
there.

Calley was sent to Fort Bliss, Texas, for basic training and
went on to clerical school at Fort Lewis, Washington. By
this time, the US Army had a severe shortage of officers.
After introduction of the draft, the army did not have
enough West Point graduates to command the rapidly
swelling ranks. As the war grew unpopular the numbers
joining the Reserve Officer Training Corps at universities
and colleges declined rapidly. Consequently, poorly educated men such as Calley were picked for officer training.

After a so-called 'Shake 'n' Bake' course at the Officer
Candidate School at Fort Benning, Georgia, Calley gradu-

ated without even being able to read a map properly. Undoubtedly, the course did not dwell on such complexities as the ethics of war. Before graduating, Calley was asked to deliver a speech on 'Vietnam Our Host'. At his trial, he recalled saying that American troops should not insult or assault Vietnamese women – the rest he was foggy on.

Nothing could have prepared Calley for the moral morass that was Vietnam, and certainly not his sketchy training. He found himself unable to control his own men and incapable of resisting the mounting pressure from his superiors for a 'body count'. As the war in Vietnam had no clear military objectives, the body count had become all-important.

The problem was that Calley and his men could not find any Viet Cong. In his own book on the My Lai massacre Calley described how, when he went with a prostitute who showed communist leanings, he wondered whether he should have shot her. She was the only 'enemy' he had come close to. Out in the paddy field, he could find no one. His inept attempts at ambush were noisy enough to alert the enemy miles away, and the enemy were out there all right; although invisible, they kept taking potshots at Calley and his men.

Patrolling near My Son in the My Lai area in February 1969, Calley's radioman was shot. For three days the company tried to penetrate My Son but were driven back. Two men were killed by booby traps; another was hit by sniper fire. The patrol then blundered into a nest of booby traps, but when they extricated themselves unscathed, two more men were cut down by snipers.

On their next assignment, they were heading for the rendezvous point when an explosion tore through the early morning stillness and a man screamed. There followed another explosion and another scream. Each explosion was followed by another – they had stumbled into a minefield and, as men rushed forward to aid their wounded comrades, they detonated more mines. Severed limbs flew through the air, medics crawled from body to body and the explosions continued. The episode lasted for almost two hours, leaving 32 men killed or wounded.

On 4 March, the company was mortared and most of the men's personal possessions were destroyed. Ten days later, two days before the assault on My Lai, four men – including the last of the company's experienced NCOs – were blown to bits by a booby trap. In 32 days, Company C – whose field strength was 90 to 100 – suffered 42 casualties, and they had hardly glimpsed the enemy.

Calley had seen atrocities committed by the Viet Cong too. One night, the VC had captured one of his men and they heard him screaming all night. He was seven kilometres away. Calley thought the Viet Cong had a PA system and amplifiers. They didn't: they had skinned the GI alive, leaving only the skin on his face. They then bathed his raw flesh with salty water; his penis was torn off. Calley's company recovered the body the next morning.

Calley had also seen a village elder broken in spirit when the VC delivered an earthenware jar containing what looked like stewed tomatoes to his door one morning. There were fragments of bone in it, and hair and lumps of floating flesh. It was what remained of his son.

He had seen GIs shooting down civilians for fun or target practice. He had heard of helicopter gunships hired out for human turkey shoots and bored GIs going 'squirrel hunting' in civilian areas. He had seen US soldiers casually fire on each other for no reason at all, and he had heard of fragmentation grenades being tossed into officers' quarters when their men did not want to go out on patrol.

'I look at communism the same way a southern looks at a Negro,' he said in an interview. 'As for me, killing those men in My Lai didn't haunt me. I didn't – I couldn't kill for the pleasure of it. We weren't in My Lai to kill human beings, really. We were there to kill ideology that is carried by – I don't know – pawns, blobs, pieces of flesh. And I wasn't in My Lai to destroy intelligent men. I was there to destroy an intangible idea.'

He even wished, humanely, that he could shoot the philosophy part out of people's heads. Besides, he reasoned, it wasn't even really him doing it.

'Personally, I didn't kill any Vietnamese that day, I mean personally. I represented the United States of America. My country.'

Calley believed that he should put his duty to his country above his own conscience. He was not even worried about killing the aged, the women and the children. He had heard of mamasans, throwing grenades, children laying mines, girls carrying AK-47s. Besides, when the children grew up they would be VC, like their fathers and mothers. Where were all the men? My Lai was full of women, and children whose fathers must be VC.

As far as Calley was concerned, was what he had done any worse than dropping 500-pound bombs on them or frying them with napalm? The atomic bomb had killed women and children in Hiroshima, hadn't it? And what were these damn Yankees getting so worked about? He had done nothing worse than General Sherman had done in his march to the sea during the American Civil War. The wisdom of the time was, he noted, that 'The only way to end the war in Vietnam was to put all the dinks [South Vietnamese] in boats and take them out to sea, kill all the North Vietnamese... then sink the boats.'

Like many American servicemen, Calley eventually stopped believing in the war. He came round to thinking that to argue that communism had to be stopped in Vietnam, before it spread to Thailand, Indonesia, Australia and finally the US – the then fashionable 'Domino Theory' which was the nearest thing the US had to a strategic aim – was like a man coming around to your house to murder his wife because he did not want blood on his carpets, then murdering your wife for good measure.

He knew that it was the Viet Cong who were winning the hearts and minds of the Vietnamese people, not the Americans. After My Lai, Calley became a welfare officer who bought pigs for peasant farmers, arranged sewing lessons for prostitutes and took sick children to hospital. But he began to realise that even his best efforts were wasted. The Vietnamese people did not want his help. They did not care about democracy or totalitarianism, capitalism or communism. They just wanted to be left alone.

When Calley was eventually called to Washington, he thought he was going to be given a medal. He was shocked when he was arrested and charged.

Calley's trial split the US. Those for the war protested that he was only doing his duty. Those against the war said that Calley was a scapegoat. Massacres like that at My Lai were happening every day and it was President Johnson, Defence Secretary Robert McNamara and the army commander General Westmoreland who should be in the dock: but 80 per cent of those polled were against his conviction.

In all, 16 were charged with the massacre at My Lai. Calley went on trial at Fort Benning with six other defendants, including his commanding officer, Captain Ernest Medina. The jury went out on 16 March 1971, the third anniversary of the massacre at My Lai. They deliberated for two weeks. In the end, they found Lieutenant WiWam L. Calley guilty of murdering at least 22 civilians. He was sentenced to life imprisonment with hard labour. On review, this was reduced to 20, then ten years. He was finally paroled on 19 November 1974,, after serving three and a half years under house arrest less than two months for each murder he was found guilty of and less than four days for each of the civilians killed at My Lai.

Charges of premeditated murder and ordering an unlawful act – homicide – against Captain Medina were reduced to involuntary manslaughter for failing to exercise proper control over his men. Not convinced that Captain Medina actually knew what his men were doing in My Lai-4, the jury acquitted him.

Charges – including one of the Nuremberg charges of violating the laws and customs of war – were brought against 12 other officers and men. Only five of the accused were tried; none was found guilty.

A dozen officers – including Calley's divisional commander, Major General Samuel W. Koster – were charged with participation in the coverup. None was convicted.

Calley himself believed that he was no worse than most, and better than many, of the officers and men who served in Vietnam. 'I was like a boy scout,' he said, 'and I went by The Boy Scout Handbook.'

He believed that he did his duty to God and country, that he was trustworthy, loyal, helpful, friendly, courteous, kind, obedient, cheerful, thrifty, brave, clean and reverent. Yet there were 347 civilians killed in the atrocity at My Lai: 100 were slaughtered in a ditch, one of them a two-year-old child.

The Gassing of the Kurds

The Kurdish people are the largest ethnic group in the world to have no homeland. They occupy eastern Turkey, northern Iraq and western Iran, and have been fighting for their independence for centuries. But they have no more bloodthirsty opponents than Saddam Hussein, so when the Iran-Iraq War broke out in 1980, the Kurds thought they could use it to their advantage.

By 1988, the Kurds had a guerrilla army of some 60,000 men and controlled some 4,000 square miles of territory. This was causing Saddam some headaches, as suppressing the Kurds diverted men from the battlefront. As early as

1983, Saddam had begun using chemical weapons – mustard gas, nerve gas and cyanide – against the Iranians. Then, in April 1987, he began to use them against the Kurds.

The first place to be hit was Balisan, a large village of around 250 households with a population of some 1,750 people. It had a primary school, a secondary school and four mosques.

It was drizzling in the late afternoon of 16 April, when the people of Balisan returned home from the fields. They were preparing dinner when they heard the drone of approaching aircraft. Some stayed in their houses; others dashed to makeshift air-raid shelters. Dozens of planes hove into view, wheeling overheard and dropping bombs on Balisan and Seikh Wasan, a smaller settlement of about 150 households a little way to the north-east.

As the bombs hit, there was a muffled explosion. Until then, no government had ever used chemical weapons against its civilian population. Video footage the Iraqis shot shows towering columns and broad drifting clouds of white, grey and pinkish smoke. A cool breeze was blowing in off the mountains; it carried the gas into the village. Survivors have different memories of what the gas smelt like. Some said it seemed pleasant, reminding them of roses, apples and garlic; others say it was pungent, like insecticide.

One elderly woman from Balisan reported that everything went dark – the gas was like a fog. Everyone became blind; some vomited; faces turned black. Men experienced painful swellings under their arms, women under their breasts. Later, a yellow discharge oozed from their eyes – survivors lost their sight for up to a month.

In Sheikh Wasan, survivors watched a woman blindly staggering around with her baby, not realising that it was dead. Villagers close to the impact died immediately. Others ran into the mountains and died there. A second attack followed an hour later.

The following morning Iraqi troops entered Balisan, looted the villagers' deserted homes and razed them to the ground. Army engineers dynamited Sheikh Wasan and bulldozed it.

The survivors had already fled. The inhabitants of the nearby town of Beiro, sent tractor-drawn carts to evacuate people to Raniya. At a resettlement camp there, they buried 50 or 60 people. A local doctor dressed wounds and administered eye drops, though these did little to help restore vision.

The next day the Iraqi security police turned up, ordering everyone out of the hospital and into vans waiting outside. These would take the survivors to the city of Erbil for medical attention – but they were told they would be treated only if they told the doctors at Erbil they had been attacked by Iranian planes. Of some 200 people taken, four died on the way.

By the time they had reached Erbil, the victims' eyes had dried out and were glued shut. Doctors applied eye drops, washed burns and gave everyone an injection of atropine, a powerful antidote for nerve gas. The origin of their injuries was not discussed. The doctors and nurses were afraid: the hospital knew of the reputation of the security police all to well. Their morgue held the bodies from the local branch headquarters. Some showed signs of having been beaten to death; other seemed to have been executed by firing squad, The bodies had been stripped of their wrist-watches, identification papers and personal property.

The morgue staff were ordered, on threat of death, not to contact the dead people's families or reveal their names. They were forbidden to touch the bodies and merely had to supply a death certificate. Sometimes the morgue was full to overflowing and the staff had to borrow a bulldozer to dig a mass grave. The morgue staff were forbidden to wash the bodies or prepare them for burial facing Mecca as Muslim tradition demands.

'Dogs have no relation to Islam,' said one security police officer.

The security police turned up at the hospital and ordered the doctor, at gun point, to remove the dressings from the survivors' wounds. They were going to be transferred to the military hospital, the chief policemen said. Later, when the doctor called the military hospital to see that his patients were all right, he was told that they had not arrived there.

Instead, they had been taken to the local security police headquarters, which over the next three days provided the morgue with 64 more bodies. The morgue staff who went to pick them up saw the gas-attack survivors there; they were in a pitiable state. The men were later taken off in a sealed bus and, presumably, executed. The women and children were driven three hours out of the city at night and abandoned in a deserted area – many children died of exposure. It is estimated that around 400 people from Balisan and Sheikh Wasan died as a result of the gas attack.

Kamal, a Kurdish guerrilla, heard of the attack on Balisan and Sheikh Wasam and rushed home to his family, who lived in the nearby village of Upper Bileh. He found they had taken refuge in some caves in the mountains, but it was bitterly cold and he persuaded them to return home. At 6 a.m. on 27 May 1987, his wife woke him to warn him that the village was under attack.

'We knew it was chemicals,' said Kamal, 'because the sound of the explosions was not loud. There were many bombs. I told my family that it wasn't a chemical attack. I did not want to scare them, but they knew what it was. So we began burning the branches we had stored for animal feed, and they made a very strong fire. We also soaked cloths and headscarves at the spring. My aged father was there. The attack was so intense that we were unable to leave the village. That was why we lit the fires. There was a separate spring for the women and I told everyone, men and women, to jump into the water. The attack lasted until 10 a.m. I sent my brother to get medical help. By sunset, the situation was getting worse. Several people had gone blind.'

After sunset, they crossed the stream and moved into a rocky area outside the village. They had all been affected by the chemicals and their situation was going from bad to worse.

'We had trouble seeing, and we were short of breath. We had nosebleeds and fainting spells. We sent someone to the surrounding villages to fetch water. I offered to pay them whatever they asked for, but the villagers were afraid to come, thinking that the chemicals were contagious. But the people from the village of Kandour were brave. They came to bring us milk.'

By that time that Kamal's brother had reached the local guerrilla headquarters to get help, but on the way back they lost their sight and collapsed. People from other villages collected them on mules and brought them back to the survivors from Upper Bileh; they had with them eyedrops and medicine. A doctor arrived and the guerrillas sent money to buy horses to take the injured Kurds to Iran. By this time the women, particularly, were in a terrible condition, and had to be spoon-fed, while the small children were hardly breathing.

'We went to Malakan,' said Kamal, 'where it was colder. We thought the fresh air there would help. Then we reached the Sewaka area. There were people there who raised animals and they took pity on us. They wept a lot and gave us food. Next morning we left for Warta. We had to cover our faces because the bright light hurt our eyes. It was like needles were being stuck into them.'

Eventually, the survivors escaped to Iran where they were given medical treatment.

After the Balisan valley chemical attacks, Iraqi troops

bulldozed at least 703 Kurdish villages. Over the next months there were a further 67 chemical attacks. The worst came on 16 March 1988, in Halabja, a bustling Kurdish town with a population of 40-60,000 or more. The town was full of refugees and Iraqi troops had already bull-dozed two entire quarters of in May 1987. It lay on the very edge of the war zone. All the villages between Halabja and the Iranian border had been razed and their inhabitants had come to live in camps around the town.

On 13 March, the town came under three days of Iranian shelling. The Iraqi forces pulled back, leaving the town open on 15 March. The Baghdad regime could have rein-forced the garrison, but it had other fish to fry. Iranian and Iraqi Kurds took over.

Reprisals began on the following morning. At first, the town was subject to conventional artillery and air strikes. Next came incendiaries – phosphorus and napalm. The planes flew so low that those on the ground could see their Iraqi markings. At around 2 p.m., a single bomber turned up. It dropped bombs that spread a yellow and white cloud through the town, which contained a mixture of mustard gas and cyanide.

Around 3 p.m., people in the makeshift air-raid shelters noticed an unusual smell. They compared it to sweet apples, perfume, cucumbers or, according to one witness, 'snake poison'. There was immediate panic. People tried to pack cracks around the entrances to the shelters with damp towels, while others pressed wet cloths to their faces or made fires.

When darkness fell, people came out of the shelters. There were no streetlights – power had been knocked out by artillery fire. In the dusk, those emerging from the shel-ters saw horrific scenes. There were dead bodies – human and animal – everywhere. They were huddled in door-ways and slumped over the steering wheels of cars. Survivors stumbled around laughing hysterically, before collapsing. The only ones left alive on the streets of Halabja were Iranian troops in gas masks and full chemical suits.

Some victims made it out of the town. Their eyes felt like they were being jabbed by needles and their urine was streaked with blood. They headed for the Iranian border. Freezing rain had turned the path to mud. Many victims were barefoot; children who died along the way were abandoned. Thousands of refugees huddled in the ruins of villages on the Iraqi side of the border, while Iranian doctors came and gave shots of atropine, before ferrying them across the border.

At least 5,000 people died as a result of the gas attack on Halabja. When Iraqi forces retook the town, they dynamited what was left of it, along with the neighbouring town of Sayed Sadeq, and left the bodies of the people killed there to rot in the street.

Tiananmen Square

Tiananmen Square in Beijing is one of the biggest squares in the world. It was frequently used for mass rallies during the long reign of Mao Tsetung. After his death China began changing: in the 1980s, under the leadership of the ageing revolutionary Deng Xiaoping, it was slowly being opened up to free market economics. However, some young men in the administration wanted the pace of change to quicken.

One of these was Hu Yabbang. As Secretary-General of the party, he was the first in the communist leadership to wear Western-style suits. He even suggested that the Chinese give up chopsticks and eat with a knife and fork. This was seen as a leap too far for the Mao-suited old guard and, in 1987, he was sacked. Hu was no democrat, but he was seen as young and honest while many of the old guard were known to-be corrupt; and slowly, Hu came to be seen as a symbol of liberalisation and democracy.

When he died on 15 April 1989, he suddenly became a martyr. Under the pretext of mounting for Hu, students took to the streets several times, demonstrating in Tiananmen Square and bringing the traffic in the centre of the city to a standstill. These demonstrations were witnessed by the large corps of foreign journalists who were in town to report the forthcoming visit of Mikhail Gorbachev, another idol of China's growing democracy movement.

The great mausoleum of Mao Tsetung flanks Tiananmen Square, as does the Great Hall of the People. In the middle is the Monument to the People's Heroes. It was there in 1976 that people had risked their lives to mourn for Zhou Enlai and call for the arrest of the Gang of Four. The resulting coup may have put Deng Xiaoping in power, but the Monument seemed the appropriate place for the students of Beijing to mourn for Hu Yhobang and make their call for democracy.

On 26 April, an editorial in the Communist party newspaper, the People's Daily, warned that a 'handful of people' were planning a 'conspiracy and a disturbance'. In the communist world, these are serious charges. Incensed, the students demanded the paper withdraw the accusations. On 27 April, they occupied Tiananmen Square and demanded a dialogue with the government. Having brought sleeping bags and blankets with them, they stayed the night. When they awoke the next morning, the students were surprised that the authorities had not tried to evict them, and they gained confidence. That day the speeches were about democracy and freedom. One of their leaders, Chai Ling, claimed passionately that democracy was their 'natural right'.

Posters went out to other universities and colleges, and 100,000 people flocked to the square. The debate raged about how long they should stay. One problem was that, on 30 April, Gorbachev was scheduled to lay a wreath on the Monument to the People's Heroes. Some wanted to withdraw partially to allow Gorbachev's visit to go ahead as planned. Chai Ling wanted to remain in occupation for the entire four days of his visit. This was not meant as an insult to Gorbachev, who was seen as a hero – he had brought an openness to the Soviet Union that the students wanted in China – however, such a demonstration would damage two unpopular figures in the regime, the President Yang Shangkun and the Prime Minister Li Peng, both of whom were educated in the Soviet Union. Better still, it would upstage Deng Xiaoping. Gorbachev's visit marked an end of the Sino-Soviet split. This was to have been Deng's last great coup. After it, at the age of 85, he planned to retire in favour of Hu Yacibang's successor as party secretary Zhao, Ziyang. Deng, they knew, would be angry at any demonstration.

Deng was a fearsome adversary and not to be underestimated. Although he ran the country, he had no constitutional or party position. The only official title he held was chairman of the Central Military Commission. He was in charge of the army and the students knew that he would have no qualms about causing bloodshed.

A faction of the students under Wuer Kaixi withdrew from the Monument, but the majority, under Chai Ling, stayed. Zhao Ziyang, who was embroiled in a leadership struggle with Li Peng at the time, turned up in the square and saw that no ceremonial wreath-laying could take place there. Effectively, Tiananmen Square was no longer under the control of the government. Furthermore, some of the students had started a hunger strike.

In many ways, Deng Xiaoping was a liberal. He even introduced limited free speech into China – though, in 1979, he ordered the clearing of Democracy Wall where people had been allowed to post anything they wrote when someone put up a poster critical of the Communist

Party. However, he had been a victim of the Red Guards in Mao's Cultural Revolution. He had been ousted and his son had been crippled when the Red Guards had thrown him out of an upstairs window. He was therefore deeply suspicious of young people with political ideas.

The Beijing government could have cleared the students out of the square before Gorbachev turned up, even though the world's press was there. That they didn't was due to the fact that the representatives of the Asian Development Bank were also in town at the time – China wanted a loan and the last thing the government needed was a bloody riot on its hands.

When Gorbachev arrived, he was greeted at the official reception at the Great Hall of the People. Normally, the route from the airport would have taken the motorcade across Tiananmen Square. Instead, it had to be directed down grubby backstreets.

In the square, demonstrators had banners proclaiming 'We are Fasting for the Liberty of this Nation' and T-shirts that proclaimed they would rather die than live without democracy. Portable radios were turned into the BBC Chinese Language Service, which was an offence. Although the secret policemen moved through the crowds taking photographs and jotting down names, they arrested no one.

The students made it clear that they were not demonstrating against Gorbachev or challenging the government. They made only limited political demands, largely to do with cleaning up corruption. All they wanted, they said, was to have a dialogue with the government. However, cleaning up corruption was not a simple matter. The leadership was steeped in it – the new free market economics encouraged foreign investment and no one was checking the books.

The ordinary people of Beijing supported the students, bringing food and water. Doctors set up a field hospital in the square to look after those suffering from heat exhaustion and the hunger-strikers, whose numbers had swelled from 400 to 3,140. Student marshals now controlled the square and checked people's passes. The police withdrew.

Gorbachev visited the square and wished the demonstrators luck. By this time the demonstration had grown so big that he was hardly noticed. The students gained some comfort from the fact that, at the televised banquet laid on for Gorbachev, Deng Xiaoping looked old and frail. It was rumoured that he was on heavy medication. However, Zhao Ziyang, whose liberal views were supported by the students, made a great show of backing Deng.

On 10 May, 10,000 cyclists took a 25-mile ride around the city, ending up outside the offices of the People's Daily, where they demanded the editorial of 26 April be withdrawn. This did not happen, but workers from the People's Daily turned up to lend their support in Tiananmen Square.

By mid-May, ordinary people outnumbered students. About 600 hunger strikers had ended up in hospital. The police appeared to support the demonstration and on a daily basis, criticism of Deng Xiaoping was growing. On 18 May, the rumour spread through the square that Deng would resign at 7 p.m. There was an outbreak of spontaneous clapping and singing. Even government officials seemed to believe this was true.

However, Deng did not resign. With Gorbachev gone, he began making plans to bring in the army. Li Peng backed him, Zhao Ziyang did not, but both of them made a televised appearance at Beijing hospital to show sympathy with the hunger striking students who had ended up there. The reception was hostile. The students lectured them, one telling them that they should make the government popular 'like in the United States'. Another said they should punish nepotism – it was well known that Deng's crippled son was milking the system.

Li Peng had a meeting with student leader Wuer Kaixi in the Great Hall of the People, which turned into a shouting match. In a country where deference is shown towards the aged, there was no precedence for this. Li Peng stormed out. Wuer Kaixi went back into the square and argued that the hunger strike should stop. Chai Ling opposed him and it continued.

That night, Deng Xiaoping called a meeting of the central standing committee of the politburo. They discussed declaring martial law. Zhao Ziyang found himself in a minority of one. Nevertheless, he and Li Peng went to Tiananmen Square and begged the hunger strikers to end their fast. The next day, martial law was declared and Zhao was arrested.

On 19 May, the army began to move into the city. With Zhao gone, it was clear that Deng Xiaoping was still very much in charge. The students grew wary and decided to give up their hunger strike, but they would not leave the square.

Li Peng and Yang Shangkun went on TV, promising action against the demonstrators. 'We've restrained ourselves for over a month now,' said Li. 'But a government which serves the people must take strong measures to deal with social unrest.'

Yang sought to draw a distinction between the mass of students, whom everyone supported, and a small bunch of troublemakers who egged them on. 'I would like to make it clear that by sending in the troops we are not intending to deal with students,' he said.

Those in Tiananmen Square heard the speeches on loud-speakers. They saw this as a declaration of war and more students and workers rallied to their cause. When the troops tried to drive into the centre of the city, the people of Beijing blocked their way. Their lorries were marooned in a sea of chanting people, many of them middle-aged. Nevertheless, it was quite good-natured – some people even brought food for the beleaguered soldiers. The people meant no harm to the troops; they just did not want them to attack their sons and daughters who were in the square. It was rumoured that one army commander had even refused to issue ammunition to his troops because his daughter was one of the protesters.

The following morning, the inhabitants of Tiananmen Square could not believe that they were still there. They had been expecting the army to come that night and drive them out. But things were indeed hotting up. At 9 a.m., a martial law order was issued prohibiting demonstrations and placing reporting restrictions on foreign journalists. Helicopters buzzed over the square, dropping leaflets supporting Li Peng. The students tore them up. That evening, they started building barricades.

The next day a troop train arrived in the central station. The students, however, had had advanced warning, and headed to the station to besiege the train. All the troops could do was sit there sullenly until the train pulled out again.

A newsreader named Xue Fei, who stumbled over his words when reading the martial law decree, was sacked when a banner saying 'Long Live Xue Fei' appeared in Tiananmen Square. The government ordered banners proclaiming the martial law orders to be displayed down Beijing's central avenue. Mysteriously, the letters peeled off after a couple of days. Even the sub-editors at the People's Daily joined in, running prominent headlines criticising the use of martial law and urging old men to retire from politics or stories that reported these things in other countries.

Despite these guerrilla actions, Deng knew all he had to do was wait. Although most people in the cities backed the students, 800,000 of China's population of a billion lived in the countryside. They supported Deng because his land reforms had transformed their lot.

By June, the students were drifting back to their studies. The square's makeshift latrines were overflowing and stinking, and the students' marshals had become officious – occupying Tiananmen Square was not exciting or fun any more. Though there were still speeches and slogans demanding democracy, troops now ringed the square.

Deng left Beijing and called his army commanders to a meeting at Wuhan. They offered him their support. The troops, who had been kept isolated from the news, were told to study the speeches of Li Peng and the People's Daily editorial of 26 April. Former supporters of Zhao Ziyang issued statements condemning the 'handful of people' who were controlling the students.

The government then worked on black propaganda. Three agent provocateurs went into the square and threw ink over a portrait of Mao Tsetung. The students handed them over to the police, but the damage was done. A lone soldier drove a truckload of guns and ammunition into the square and ran off; again, the students handed it over to the police, even helping to unload the truck. This was filmed by a Chinese camera crew and when the footage was shown on TV an entirely different construction was put on the event.

Then the weather turned against the demonstrators – a storm came and people left the square to take cover from the rain. Only a couple of dozen students braved it out. The protest in Tiananmen Square was now in trouble - half-a-dozen troops in sou'westers could have taken the square that night.

However, on 29 May, a small group of students from the Central Institute of Fine Art turned up, erecting a 30-foot high fibreglass and plaster-of-Paris model of a woman, like the Statue of Liberty holding a torch. Chai Ling dubbed her the Goddess of Democracy and people came flooding back. She stood directly opposite Maos portrait with her torch practically in his face: this was a deliberate insult to the government.

On the night of 2 June, the army moved in again. This time they had chosen their route carefully, and did not come in lorries but on foot, at the double. This tactic back-fired; before they even reached the square, they were exhausted. Already confused and disheartened, they were easily disarmed. Their equipment was piled in the middle of the street; they sat on the ground, the officers lowering their eyes, while students shouted slogans at them. Eventually the students and the officers reached a deal and the soldiers returned to their barracks.

The following night, the army returned with tanks and armoured personnel carriers. Government loudspeakers boomed out a chilling message. 'Go home and save your lives,' it said. 'You will fail. You are not behaving in the correct Chinese manner. This is not the West. It is China. You should behave like good Chinese. Go home and save your lives. Go home and save your lives.' No one moved.

People began shouting that the army was coming. Students began shoring up the barricades; young men were suddenly brandishing knives, clubs, bricks, coshes, spears; some even had Molotov cocktails. People were afraid, sure that they were going to die. Nevertheless, the speeches and the singing continued.

An APC came hurtling into the square, running people over and ripping their legs off with its metal tracks. It was pummelled with Molotov cocktails and sped away. A second APC arrived, killing more people. It rammed into a concrete barricade and got stuck. Petrol was poured over it and it was set alight. When three soldiers at the back emerged, their guns were grabbed from them. Two of them were beaten to death by the mob, the other one was saved by some students in a bus; the two men in the front seat were burned to death.

The students sang the Internationale. Some were crying and knew that they had just suffered their first defeat. So

410

far the demonstration had been successful because it had been non violent. They now realised that the two APCs had been sent in to the square in the hope that one or both of them would get caught. Once some soldiers had been killed, the blood of their comrades would be up. Now there would be a massacre.

Troops began pouring in through the Gate of Heavenly Peace. They charged across the north end of the square, clearing it. Tanks rolled over the tents some students had taken refuge in. Those close by heard their screams. At least 200 died that way.

At 4 a.m., the lights went out in the square to prevent foreign TV crews filming what was going on. A pop singer named Hou Dejian, who had joined the demonstrators, negotiated a peaceful withdrawal for the students; by 4.40 a.m., they were starting to leave. Then all the lights suddenly came back on. A line of well-armed troops was approaching the students. The police began hitting the students with clubs studded with nails and cattle prods. Scores of bleeding youths retreated up the stairs of the monument. They held hands and sang the Internationale again, while completely surrounded by soldiers. The police rushed at them repeatedly until the crowd collapsed. The soldiers then shot over the heads of the students, and into the crowd itself. They also shot at the journalists watching from the Beijing Hotel and the secret police were sent to arrest them. Workers and ordinary citizens took up sticks and charged the soldiers. They were shot down.

The students tried to escape, but the only hole in the line of troops was quickly filled with tanks. They managed to force a way through between the tanks and some escaped.

Outside the square, the crowd remained defiant, shouting at the troops who answered with gunfire. It is estimated that between 1,500 and 3,000 lost their lives in Tiananmen Square. Their bodies were burnt and the

411

Goddess of Democracy was smashed by the tanks. Next day, the leadership came to the square in a helicopter to see the ruins of the lady. Around the city, the shooting continued.

The student leaders were dispersed. Many of them escaped, via Hong Kong, to the United States. Those who remained were arrested. These days, the Chinese democracy movement exists only on the Internet. Unfortunately, not many people in China have personal computers – especially not the aged leadership.

Serial Killers

The Boston Strangler

The man who came to personify the modern serial killer was the Boston Strangler, who terrorised the USA's Boston area for two years. No one was ever charged with the Boston Strangler killings, but a mad did confess to them: his name was Albert DeSalvo.

DeSalvo was the son of a vicious drunk. When he was 11 he watched his father knock out his mother's teeth before bending back her fingers until they snapped – this was just another ordinary day in the DeSalvo household. When they were children, DeSalvo's father sold him and his two sisters to a farmer in Maine for just $9. DeSalvo escaped, and after he had found his way home his father taught him how to shoplift by taking him to a shop and showing him what to steal. His father would also bring prostitutes back to the family apartment and make the children watch while he had sex with the women.

Perhaps unsurprisingly, the young DeSalvo soon developed a lively interest in sex. He made numerous conquests among the neighbourhood girls, as well as earning a healthy living from the local gay community, members of which would pay him for his services. DeSalvo continued his sexual adventuring in the army until he met Irmgaard, the daughter of a respectable, Catholic family, in Frankurt-am-Main, Germany. After marrying Irmgaard, DeSalvo returned to the USA with his wife, where he was dishonourably discharged from the army for sexually molesting a nine-year-old girl; he only escaped criminal charges because the girl's mother wanted to protect her daughter from publicity.

DeSalvo next became a professional thief, making his living by breaking and entering. At home he appeared to be the perfect family man, although his prodigious sexual appetite was more than his wife could cope with: his demands for sex five or six times a day annoyed, and finally repelled, Irmgaard. DeSalvo then began to hand around the campus area of Boston on the lookout for apartments shared by young, female students. He would knock on the door with a clipboard and introduce himself as the representative of a modelling agency before asking whether he could take the measurements of the women who lived here. He was a charming man and sometimes succeeded in seducing them (occasionally they would seduce him). On other occasions he would just take their measurements – either when they were clothed or, as he preferred, naked – and promise that a female representative would call later. He never assaulted any of the women, who sometimes complained that no one had made the promised, follow-up visit. The police called him 'Measuring Man'.

At around that time DeSalvo was arrested for housebreaking and was consequently jailed for two years. Prison soured him, and when he was released he began breaking into houses throughout New England, tying up women and raping them. Known as the 'Green Man' because he wore a green shirt and trousers, the police throughout Connecticut and Massachusetts guessed that his assaults numbered in the hundreds. DeSalvo himself later claimed more than a thousand, bragging that he had tied up and raped six women in one morning.

In 1962 DeSalvo began to concentrate his activities on Boston, also adding murder to his repertoire. His first victim was the 55-year-old Anna Slesters, whose body, which had been left in an obscene pose, was found in her apartment. DeSalvo had strangled her and had then tied the cord that he had used to kill her in a bow around her neck. This became his trademark. Two weeks later he murdered the 55-year-old Mary Mullen, whom DeSalvo subsequent-

416

ly said had reminded him of his grandmother. Then he raped and strangled an 85-year-old nurse, Helen Blake. For her part, Nina Nichols fought back, scratching some flesh from his arms before he strangled her. On 19 August the 75-year-old Ida Irga was raped and strangled and on the following day DeSalvo murdered the 67-year-old Jane Sullivan.

The Boston police force soon realised that a maniac was at work and began questioning all known sexual deviants. DeSalvo, however, had a police record for house breaking alone – the details of his sexual deviancy appeared only in his army file.

DeSalvo took a long autumn break from his murderous activities, but by the time of his wedding anniversary – 5 December 1962 – his brain was so overheated by violent sexual images that he felt that it was going to explode. Seeing an attractive girl go into a apartment block, he followed her and knocked on the door of her apartment, pretending to be a maintenance man who had been sent by the landlord to check the pipes. She did not let him in, so he tried the same ploy at the next apartment, whose door was opened by a tall, attractive 25-year-old African-American woman called Sophie Clark. This time DeSalvo reverted to his 'Measuring Man' routine and remarked upon her curvaceous figure. When she turned her back he pounced on her, and after he had subdued her he stripped, raped and finally strangled her. As with his other victims, before leaving he propped up her naked body, spread her legs and tied the cord that he had used to strangle her in a bow under her chin.

Three days later DeSalvo made a return call on one of the women, a 23-year-old secretary, whom he had previously visited as the 'Measuring Man'. After Patricia Bissette had invited him in for a coffee she turned her back, whereupon he grabbed her around the throat, raped her and then strangled her with her own stockings.

DeSalvo's next victim, however, fought back so violently – biting, scratching and screaming – that the Boston Strangler fled and she escaped with her life, but she was so distraught that the description that she gave of her attacker was practically worthless.

The failed murder seems to have marked something of a turning point in DeSalvo's career of crime, because from then on his attacks became even more violent. On 9 March 1963, for example, he entered the apartment of the 69-year-old Mary Brown on the pretext of fixing the stove. He had brought a piece of lead pipe with him, which he used to beat in her head. When she was dead he raped her and then stabbed her breasts with a fork, which he left sticking from her flesh. Although he maintained his *modus operandi* by strangling her, this time the victim was already dead when he did so.

Two months later DeSalvo took a day off work and drove to Cambridge, Massachusetts. Spotting a pretty girl, a 23-year-old student named Beverley Samans, on University Road, he followed her back to her apartment. Once inside, he tied her to her bedposts, stripped, blindfolded, gagged and then repeatedly raped her before strangling her with her own stockings. But this was no longer enough for him and before he left the apartment he pulled a penknife from his pocket and started to stab her naked body. Once he had started he could not stop, and when her body was discovered it was found to bear 22 savage wounds. After his frenzy had subsided DeSalvo calmly wiped his fingerprints from the knife, dropped it into the sink and went home.

On 8 September 1963 the Boston Strangler struck again. This time it was a straight for ward case of rape and strangulation, the 58-year-old Evelyn Corbin being strangled with her own nylons, which he left tied in his signature now, but around her ankle, in a departure from his usual style.

By this time the people of Boston and the surrounding area were in a state of panic. The Strangler seemed to come and go at will. The police had no useful description of the killer and no clues – they seemed powerless. In desperation they brought in a Dutch psychic, Peter Hurkos, who had had some success in other cases, but he failed to identify the Boston Strangler.

While the USA – and particularly John F Kennedy's home state of Massachusetts – was in mourning following the assassination of the president, the Boston Strangler struck again, raping and strangling Joan Gaff, a 23-year-old dress designer, in her own apart ment before tying her black leotard in a bow around her neck. DeSalvo later said that he did not know why he had killed her; 'I wasn't even excited', he commented. After he had left her apartment, he revealed, he had gone home, played with his children and watched the report of Joan's murder on television. Then, he said, he had sat down and had his dinner, without thinking of her again.

On 4 January 1964 the Boston Strangler killed for the last time. His victim was the 19-year-old Mary Sullivan. He gained access to her apartment, tied her up at knife point and raped her before strangling her with his bare hands. Her body was left sitting up in bed, with her head lolling against her right shoulder. Her eyes were closed and a viscous liquid dripped from her mouth down her right breast. Her breasts and sexual organs were exposed and a broom handle protruded from her vagina. More semen stains were found on her blanket and a New Year's greeting card that the killer had found in the apartment was placed between her toes.

Later that year a woman reported having been sexually assaulted by a man who had used the Measuring Man routine, but otherwise the Boston Strangler's activities stopped. This was because DeSalvo had again been arrested for housebreaking. In jail his behaviour became increasingly disturbed and he was transferred to a mental hospital in Bridgewater, where he was diagnosed as being schizophrenic.

Although DeSalvo was in custody, the police still had no idea that they were holding the Boston Strangler. But in the Bridgewater hospital another inmate – who had killed a petrol-station attendant and was himself a suspect in the Boston Strangler case – listened to DeSalvo's deranged ramblings and began to put two and two together. He then persuaded his lawyer to speak to DeSalvo. In his taped interviews with the lawyer DeSalvo discussed facts about the murders that the police had not revealed. He spoke of the positions in which he had left the bodies, the ligature that he had used to strangle each victim, as well as the other wounds that he had inflicted. He also admitted to two murders that had not yet been attributed to the Boston Strangler.

Despite his admission DeSalvo was a mental patient who was plainly unfit to stand trial and whose confession was legally worthless. He was therefore not prosecuted for the rapes and murders to which he had admitted. There was no doubt, however, that he was indeed the Boston Strangler, even if he could only be charged with robbery and other sexual offences unconnected to the Strangler's activities. He was sentenced to life imprisonment and transferred to Walpole State Prison. On 26 November 1973 the 36-year-old DeSalvo was found dead in his cell, stabbed through the heart.

The Campus Killer

Like Albert DeSalvo, Ted Bundy also had the power to charm women, many of whom paid for their susceptiblity with their lives. For three years during the 1970s Bundy preyed on young female students on college campuses across the USA, killing at least 19 young women and maybe as many as 40.

Bundy was well educated, ran his own business, had been a noted high-school athlete and worked for both the Republican Party and the Washington State Crime Commission. He even became a counsellor at a Seattle-rape-crisis after having been screened for 'balance and maturity'. He had one significant problem, however: his sexual impulses were so strong that he could not control them. He later said that after his first attacks he had had to wrestle with his conscience, but had subsequently begun to desensitise himself to his crimes. He claimed not to have caused his victims unnecessary suffering, but said that he had had to kill them after he had raped them in order to prevent them from identifying him. He admitted deliberately terrorising his victim – or rather victims – in only one case: when he kidnapped two girls at the same time, intending to rape each in front of the other before killing them both.

From an early age Bundy had been a compulsive masturbator, and after glimpsing a girl undressing through a window he had become a Peeping Tom. He later became obsessed by sadistic pornography. His long-time girlfriend, Meg Anders, described how he like to tie her up with her own stockings before having anal sex with her, but said that she had put a stop to this sex game when he almost strangled her. For years they maintained a normal sexual relationship while Bundy indulged his perverse cravings elsewhere. And what he craved was total control over an anonymous victim, whom he often strangled during sex. Indeed, his attitude to sex was ambivalent: although his victims were always attractive young women, he liked to defile their bodies by stuffing twigs and dirt into their vaginas or sodomising them with aerosol cans or other foreign objects. When they were dis-

covered, some of the bodies of his victims, although partly decomposed, were found to be wearing newly applied
make-up and to have freshly washed hair – he had kept
them for the purposes of necrophilia.

Bundy began his murderous career in his home town of
Seattle. His first victim was Sharon Clarke, into whose
apartment he broke while she was asleep before hitting
her around the head with a metal rod. Although she survived – albeit with a shattered skull – she could not identify her attacker; nor was there any indication of the motivation for the attack.

Soon afterwards, young women began disappearing
from the nearby campus of the University of Washington.
Six went missing within seven months. The clue to what
may have happened to them came from the Lake
Sammanish resort in Washington State, when a number of
women reported having been approached by a young
man calling himself Ted. He had had his arm in a sling
and had asked them to help him to lift his sailing boat off
the roof of his car. Once in the car park, however, they had
found that there was no boat, whereupon Ted had then
said that they would have to go to his house to get it.
Although most of the women had declined his invitation
to accompany him, it seemed that Janice Ott had agreed to
go. And a few hours later Denise Naslund went missing
from the same area; she had been seen with a good-looking, dark-haired young man. The remains of Janice Ott,
Denise Naslund and another unidentified young women
were later found on waste ground. Their bodies had been
dismembered and eaten by animals. Witnesses at the
University of Washington subsequently said that they had
seen a man wearing a sling, and more bodies were also
found on wasteland.

The police had two suspects: Gary Taylor and Warren
Forrest. Taylor, a former convict, had been arrested by the
Seattle police for abducting women under false pretexts.

For his part, Forrest , a park attendant, had picked up a young woman who had agreed to pose for him. He had taken her to a secluded part of the park, where ha had stripped her naked and tied her up. He had then taped up her mouth and had fired darts at her breasts before raping and strangling her and leaving her for dead. His victim had survived, however, and had identified her attacker. the problem for the police was that although both men were in custody the attacks continued.

By now Bundy's girlfriend was growing suspicious of him and called the police anonymously to give them his name. But her tip-off was just one among the thousands of leads that the police had to follow up and it was overlooked.

Nevertheless, things were becoming a bit too hot for Bundy in his home state, so on 30 August 1974 he quit his job in Seattle and moved to Salt Lake City, where he enrolled at the University of Utah's law school. On 2 October he abducted Nancy Wolcox after she had left an all-night party. On 18 October he raped and strangled the 18-year-old Melissa Smith, the daughter of the local police chief; her body was found near Salt Lake City. He abducted the 17-year-old Laura Aimee from a Hallowe'en party in Orem; her naked body was discovered at the bottom of a canyon. He tried to pick up a pretty young French teacher outside her high school, but she refused to go with him. The 17-year-old Debbie Kent did, however, disappearing on 8 November from a school playground in which the key to a pair of handcuffs was found later.

A week later he approached the 18-year-old Carol DaRonch in Salt Lake City. Bundy said he was a policeman and asked her for the licence number of her car, explaining that someone had been trying to break into it. He then invited her to accompany him to the police station in order to identify the suspect and she obligingly got into his car. Once they were in a quiet street he handcuffed her and put a gun to her head when she began to scream. Despite being handcuffed, Carol managed to get out of the car, whereupon Bundy chased after her with a crowbar, which he swung at her head. Carol was just able to deflect it when at that moment a car drove down the street. Seizing her chance, she threw herself in front of it, forcing it to stop; after she had jumped in the car drove away.

Carol gave a good description of her attacker to the Utah police, but shortly thereafter Bundy moved to Colorado. In January 1975 Dr Raymond Gadowsky reported that his fiancée, Carolyn Compbell, was missing from her hotel room in Snowmass Village, a ski resort. A month later her naked body was found in the snow; she had been raped and her skull smashed in. Julie Cunningham disappeared from nearby Vail, and the remains of Susan Rancourt and Brenda Bell were found on Taylor Mountain. The body of Melanie Cooley was discovered just ten miles (16 kilometres) from her home. Unlike the other victims she was still clothed (although her jeans had been undone), but the police were nevertheless convinced that the motive for her murder was a sexual one. The Colorado attacks continued: Nancy Baird vanished from a petrol station, while Shelly Roberston's naked body was found down a mine shaft.

One day a highway patrolman was cruising through Granger, Utah, which had recently been plagued by a series of burglaries. He noticed Bundy's VW driving slowly, without its lights on, and indicated that he should pull over. Instead of complying, however, Bundy sped off, causing the patrolman to give chase. On catching up with him the patrolman asked him what he had in the car, to which Bundy replied 'Just some junk'. The junk turned out to be a ski mask, handcuffs, some nylon stockings and a crowbar. Bundy was detained for having committed a traffic offence and was later released. On the following day he was arrested at his apartment in Salt Lake City and charged with possessing tools with which to commit burglary, but he was again released on bail.

The police had impounded Bundy's car, however, in which they discovered maps and brochures of resorts in Colorado, some of which coincided with the places from which the girls had disappeared. Forensic experts found a hair in the VW that matched that of Melissa Smith. A witness recognised Bundy from Snowmass Village. Furthermore, Carol DaRonch picked him out of a line-up.

Bundy was charged with kidnapping and was subsequently tried, found guilty and sentenced to a period in jail of from one to fifteen years. Then he was extradited to Colorado to stand trial for the murder of Carolyn Campbell. In court Bundy came across as an intelligent and personable young man – the sort who could have had any girl whom he wanted – and it seemed unlikely to many that he could have been responsible for the terrible sex attacks.

In Aspen, Colorado, Bundy was given permission to conduct his own defence, even being allowed to use the law library. It was there that he managed to give his guard the slip, jump from a window and escape. He was recaptured eight days later. Bundy continued to protest his innocence and was able to spin out the pre-trial hearings by using skilful, legal, stalling tactics. In the meantime he had lost weight. One day, while standing on a stack of legal books in his cell, he managed to cut a hole under the light fitting with a hacksaw blade. He then squeezed through the 1-foot-square (30-centimetre-square) hole, stole a police car and got clean away.

Bundy made a murderous tour of the USA before settling in Talahassee, Florida, a few blocks from the sorority houses of Florida State University. On the evening of 15 January 1977 Nita Neary saw a man lurking in front of her own sorority house. She was about to phone the police when a fellow student, Karen Chandler, staggered from her room, blood streaming from her head, screaming that she had just been attacked and her jaw broken. The 21-year-old Margaret Bowman had been sexually assaulted and strangled with her own tights. The 20-year-old Lisa Levy had also been sexually assaulted: Bundy had bitten off one of her nipples and had sunk his teeth into her buttocks before beating her around the head. She died on the way to hospital. Cheryl Thomas had been viciously attacked in another building, too, but survived. The police could elicit only a sketchy description of the attacker from his victims.

On 8 February, in Lake City, Florida, Bundy abducted the 12-year-old Kimberly Leach, sexually assaulted and strangled her, mutilated her sexual organs and dumped her body in a pig shed.

Bundy was now short of money, so he stole some credit cards, along with a car, and did a moonlight flit from his apartment, on which he owed rent. But the stolen car was a giveaway and he was stopped by a highway patrolman, whereupon Bundy attacked him and tried to escape. The patrolman caught up with him, however, and clubbed him unconscious. At the police station Bundy admitted that he was wanted in Colorado. For their part the Florida police had begun to link him to the Tallahassee attack. When they tried to take an impression of his teeth he went berserk and it took six men to hold his jaw open. The impression was subsequently found to match the teeth marks on the buttocks of the murdered student, Lisa Levy, as well as those on the body of Kimberley Leach.

Bundy was charged with the murder of the child. At his trial he again conducted his own defence, cannily using points of the law with which to prolong the court case and charming the jury with his personality. The evidence against him was too strong, however, and Bundy was found guilty of murder and sentenced to death. All the while protesting his innocence, he managed to postpone his execution for another ten years. Eventually, when all the legal avenues had been exhausted, he broke down and confessed to nearly 40 murders. 'I deserve to die', he said.

At 7am on 24 January 1989 Bundy went to the electric chair. He is said to have died with a smile on his face. On death row Bundy had made a detailed confession, thereby aiding a number of academics who were studying serial killers. He had also received sacks full of mail from young women whose letters dwelt on various cruel and painful ways in which to make love – it seems that even on death row he had not lost his charm.

Jerry Brudos

On 10 May 1969 a fisherman angling from a bridge across the Log Tom river in Oregon, in the USA, saw what he took to be a large package floating in the water. On looking closer, however, he realised that it was the bloated body of a young woman, which had been weighed down by a car's gearbox. The body was identified as being that of the 22-year-old Linda Salee, who had vanished two weeks earlier. The corpse had been in the water for too long to determine whether Linda had been raped, but it was noted that curious burn marks surrounded puncture wounds a few inches below her armpits.

Police frogmen searching the area then found another body, which had been anchored in the water by means of a cylinder head. It belonged to the 19-year-old Karen Sprinkler, who had disappeared on 27 March; it was estimated that her corpse had been in the water for six weeks. The dead woman was fully clothed and was wearing a black bra had been padded out with screwed-up paper. Both Karen and Linda had been strangled.

The skeleton of the 16-year-old Stephanie Vilcko was

later washed up in a creek along the same river. She had disappeared from her home in Portland, Oregon, the year before. The Oregon state police also had two other missing girls on their books: the 19-year-old encyclopaedia seller Linda Slawson, who had gone missing during a sales trip in the Portland area; and the 23-year-old Jan Whitney, whose broken-down car had been discovered on a highway near Lebanon, Oregon.

Linda Salee and Karen Sprinkler's bodies had both been tied up with electrical flex and the police therefore thought that the murderer might be an electrician. But the corpses had been weighed down with car parts, too, so it was equally possible that he might be a mechanic. As Oregon was full of electricians and car mechanics, these speculations did not take them further forward.

Karen Sprinkler had been a student who lived on the Corvallis campus of Oregon State University. Several of the other girls there now reported that they had received phone calls from a man who claimed to be a psychic, as well as a veteran of the Vietnam War. He had used a variety of names and had always ended the conversations by asking the girls for a date; when they had refused he seemed offended. However, one of the more daring girls had indeed met him for a date. He had been fat and freckled, she said, and she had thought that there was something odd about him. During their conversation he had told her that she should be sad. When she asked why he replied 'Think of those two girls whose bodies were found in the river'. When she declined his invitation to go for a drive with him he said that she was right to be circumspect, asking 'How do you know I wouldn't take you to the river and strangle you?'

A week later the man phoned the girl again, whereupon she called the police, who seized him when he arrived at the college to pick her up. His name was Jerry Brudos and he was a 30-year-old electrician who lived in

Salem, which lies between Corvallis and Portland. The police did not have any evidence on which to hold Brudos, so they had to release him, but while investigating his background they soon discovered that he had a history of violence towards women and had spent time in a state mental hospital because of his sexual deviancy.

Brudos' deviant behaviour had begun when he was five and had taken home a pair of women's patent-leather shoes that he found in a rubbish dump. He was trying them on when his mother discovered him. She was furious and told him to throw the shoes away, but he nevertheless kept them and wore them secretly. When his mother learned of this she burnt them and beat him. At school he became obsessed with women's high-heeled shoes and even stole a pair of his teacher's. When he was caught and made to confess he was asked why he had done it, but he responded that he did not know and ran from the room.

At 16 he lured his neighbour's daughter to his bedroom. While Brudos was out of the room a masked man burst in brandishing a knife and forced the girl to strip, after which he took pictures of her nude. When the masked man left Brudos reappeared. The masked man had locked him in the barn, he said.

At 17 he had taken another girl for a drive when he stopped on a deserted road, dragged her from the car and forced her to undress. She was saved by a passer-by who had heard her screams. This time the police were called and Brudos lamely protested to them that this girl had been attacked by a weirdo. When the police searched his bedroom, however, they found a box of women's shoes and underwear. Brudos was sent to Oregon State Mental Hospital for treatment and was discharged after nine months.

His condition did not improve and he began attacking young women and stealing their shoes. Members of his family were afraid that he was well on his way to becoming a rapist, but then, to their great relief, he fell in love with a 17-year-old girl called Darcie and married her. They had their first child eight months later. Married life seemed to calm Brudos. His wife even indulged his obsession with photographing her in the nude, but later became concerned about the increasingly disturbing poses that he wanted her to adopt. Then, when his wife was in hospital having their second child, Brudos saw a young woman in the street who was wearing attractive shoes. He followed her home and choked her until she was unconscious before raping her.

As well as being an electrician, Brudos was also a mechanic who ran a one-man car-repair business from the garage of his home. He had furthermore been working in Lebanon, Oregon, close to the place where Jan Whitney's car had been discovered. The police found lengths of rope in Brudos' home, too, one of which was tied in the same kind of knot that the killer had used when trussing up the corpses.

Although the police were convinced that they had identified the right man they still did not have enough evidence with which to make an arrest. Then they discovered that they had a potential eyewitness to Brudos' criminal activities: a 15-year-old schoolgirl had been attacked by a fat, freckled man with a gun in Portland just two days before Linda Salee had disappeared. She had screamed, but the man had grabbed her around the neck, whereupon she had bitten his thumb and he had beaten her unconscious. When a car had fortuitously approached he had run off.

The girl identified Brudos from his mug shot and the police were on their way to arrest him when they saw his station wagon driving towards Portland. When it was stopped by highway patrolmen Brudos' wife was found to be driving; Brudos himself was hiding under a blanket in the back of the car. When he was made to change into prison overalls at the police station it was revealed that he was wearing women's underwear.

Brudos withstood questioning for five days. After that he began to talk about his interest in women's shoes and admitted tailing a pretty girl before breaking in to her home in order to steal her shoes. Next he shared his obsession with women's underwear; his favourite fetish, he said, was a large, long-waisted, black bra that he had stolen from a washing line. It was the type of bra that had been found on the body of Karen Sprinkler.

Then Brudos confessed everything, including the murder of the two missing women whose bodies had not been found. In January 1968, he revealed, Linda Slawson had come to his house selling encyclopaedias and wearing high-heeled shoes that he had found irresistible. Brudos had told her that his wife had visitors and asked her if she would mind discussing the encyclopaedias in his workshop. Having agreed, she was sitting on a stool running through her sales patter when he knocked her unconscious with a lump of wood. Then he strangled her. His mother and children were upstairs in the house at the time, so he gave them money and told them to go to a local hamburger joint. When they had gone he rushed back to the workshop and undressed the corpse, discovering to his delight that Linda was wearing attractive underwear. Making use of a box full of women's underwear that he had stolen from clothes lines he began to dress and undress the corpse as if it were a doll. That night he also chopped off Linda's foot, which he kept in the freezer and used to try on women's shoes. He dumped the rest of her body in the river, using a cylinder head with which to weigh it down.

Ten months later he was driving home from his job in Lebanon when he noticed that a car had broken down on the motorway. Brudos stopped and explained to the driver, Jan Whitney, that although he was a car mechanic they would have to drive to Salem to get his tool box. On arriving at his house together, he then ran inside alone, ostensibly to get his tools. Instead, however, he went in to check that his wife was not at home. Having ascertained that Darcie was not in he slipped silently into the back seat of the car, threw a leather strap around Jan's neck and strangled her. He then sodomised her corpse before beginning his game of dressing and undressing the body. This time he took photographs, breaking off from time to time in order to violate the body. Brudos then decided to prolong his pleasure by leaving Jan's body hanging from a hook in the locked garage. In that way he could come and play with it whenever he felt the need. He later cut off one of her breasts to make into a paperweight.

Two days after the murder his perverted secret was almost discovered when a car crashed through his garage wall. Although a policeman looked into the garage he did not spot Jan's body hanging there, shrouded as it was by dust and gloom. That night Brudos weighed down the corpse with scrap iron and dumped it in the river.

Four months later, while Brudos was driving past a department store, he spotted a young woman wearing a miniskirt and high-heeled shoes. He parked the car and chased after her, but she vanished into the crowd. On his way back to his car he saw Karen Sprinkler in the car park, pulled a gun and forced her to get into his station wagon. Brudos' family was away, so he knew that he was in no danger of being disturbed. Karen begged for her life, saying that she would do anything he wanted if he did not kill her. He asked if she was a virgin, to which she replied that she was and also told him that she was having her period. It made no difference, for he made her lie on the garage floor and raped her. Next he forced her to pose in high-heeled shoes and sexy underwear while he took pictures of her. After that he tied her hands behind her back, put a rope around her neck and threw the end of it over a beam, pulling it slowly until she suffocated. 'She kicked a little and died', Brudos said. He then violated Karen's corpse, cut off her breasts and dumped her body in the river.

Linda Salee was buying her boyfriend's birthday present when Brudos flashed a fake police badge at her and told her that he was arresting her for shoplifting. He then drove her to his garage. When they arrived Brudos' wife came out the house on to the porch, so Brudos ordered Linda to stand still in the darkness. At that moment a single scream could have saved her life, but instead Linda meekly did as she was told. After Darcie had gone back inside Brudos took Linda into the garage and tied her up before going to have his dinner. When he returned he found that she had freed herself. Although there was a telephone in the garage she had not called the police – 'She was just waiting for me, I guess', Brudos told his interrogators with a smile. Linda then tried to fight back, but the petite 22-year-old was easily subdued by Brudos, who put a leather strap around her neck. 'Why are you doing this to me?' she gasped. Pulling the rope tight, he raped her as she died. Brudos then strung up her corpse and jabbed two syringes into her sides, through which he ran an electric current intended to make her dance, but only succeeding in burning her flesh. On the following day he raped her corpse again. He considered cutting off her breasts, but did not like her pink nipples, preferring brown ones; he nevertheless made a mould of her breasts before throwing her body into the river.

On searching Brudos' garage the police found his lingerie collection, along with photographs of his victims either posing in the underwear or hanging from the ceiling. Brudos had incriminated himself in one shot by capturing on film his own reflection in the mirror. A female breast, hardened with epoxy, was also found on the mantelpiece in the living room.

After pleading guilty to four counts of murder, Brudos was sentenced to life imprisonment. Utilising his gift for all things electrical, he set up a computer system in jail, being permitted to order shoe and underwear catalogues from the outside world in return.

The police could not believe that Darcie Brudos was unaware of her husband's murderous activities. She was charged with abetting the murder of Karen Sprinkler, but was subsequently found not guilty.

A year after Brudos was sent to jail the body of Jan Whitney surfaced. It was so badly decomposed that it could only be identified by means of dental records. Linda Slawson's body was never found.

Carl Panzram

During the early years of the twentieth century the German-American Carl Panzram went on a life-long campaign of murder and mayhem. He claimed to have killed 21 people, to have committed thousands of burglaries, robberies and arson attacks and to have sodomised more than 1,000 men.

Born in 1891 to a family of immigrant Prussian farmers in Warren, Minnesota, Panzram became a criminal as a young boy. His father had deserted his family soon after Panzram's birth and his mother could not control him. When he was just eight years old he was brought before a juvenile court for being drunk and disorderly. Then, after burgling the house of a well-to-do neighbour, he was sent to reform school, where the discipline was rigid, if not sadistic. Panzram burned the place down.

Released in 1906, he began his war against the world in earnest, starting in the west, where he committed a string of robberies and assaults. While travelling the country he was raped by four hoboes, which instilled a new mode of revenge in him: 'Whenever I met a hobo who wasn't too rusty looking,' he later wrote in his autobiography, 'I would make him raise his hands and drop his pants. I wasn't very particular either. I rode them old and young, tall and short, white and black'. Having ended up in Montana State Reformatory, he quickly escaped from jail, robbing and burning down several churches over the next couple of months. Then he joined the army, only to be court-martialled on 20 April 1907 for insubordination and pilfering US-government property. Three years spent at Fort Leavenworth, where he crushed rocks under the blistering Kansas sun, honed his meanness to the sharpness of a razor's edge.

After his release in 1910 Panzram headed for Mexico, where he joined up with the rebel leader Pascaul Orozco, who fought alongside Pancho Villa and Emiliano Zapata during the Mexican Revolution. He later returned to the USA, leaving a trail of murder, robbery, assault and rape in his wake as he moved north through California and the Pacific Northwest region.

Arrested in Chinook, Montana, for burglary, he was sentenced to a year in prison, but escaped after eight months. A year later Panzram was arrested again, this time while using the alias Jeff Rhoades; he was given a two-year jail sentence. Paroled in 1914, he immediately resumed his life of crime. In Astoria, Oregon, he was once more arrested for burglary and was offered a minimal sentence if he revealed the whereabouts of the goods that he had stolen. Although he kept his side of the bargain he was sentenced to seven years' imprisonment. Outraged at this injustice, Panzram escaped from his cell and wrecked the jail. After the guards had beaten him up he was sent to Salem's correctional facility, the toughest prison in the state. Almost as soon as he arrived there he flung the contents of a chamber pot into a guard's face, for which he was beaten unconscious and chained to the floor of a darkened cell for 30 days. This punishment did not break his spirit, however, and he spent his time in the hole screaming words of defiance.

The facility's warden was shot dead during an escape attempt, and although the new warden was even tougher Panzram still managed to burn down the prison's workshop, as well as a flax mill. He also went berserk with an axe and incited a prison revolt, for which he was given another seven years in jail. By now, however, the atmosphere in the prison was so tense that the guards would not venture into the yard, so the warden was dismissed. The next warden was an idealist who believed that Panzram might respond to kindness. When Panzram was next caught trying to escape the warden told him that he was the 'meanest and most cowardly degenerate' that the prison authorities had ever seen. Panzram agreed with this description, but to his astonishment instead of punishing him the warden let him leave the jail on condition that he returned that evening. Although Panzram walked through the prison gates with no intention of going back he did, in fact, return that evening. The liberal regime was maintained and Panzram continued to respond to it, that is until he got drunk with a pretty nurse one night and absconded, only to be recaptured after a gunfight. He was returned to a punishment cell, where he was fed a diet of bread and water, also being beaten and sprayed with a fire hose. Finally, the ever resourceful Panzram constructed his own tools and hacked his way out of the prison in May 1918.

He headed east, stealing $1,200 from a hotel in Maryland and then boarding a merchant ship bound for South America. He jumped ship in Peru, where he worked in a copper mine. In Chile, he became a foreman for an oil company, later, for no apparent reason, setting fire to an oil rig. Back in the USA he stole $7,000 from a jewellery shop and $40,000 in jewels and liberty bonds from the New Haven home of the former US president, William Howard Taft. With the money he bought a yacht, and after hiring sailors to help him to refit it he raped and shot them before dropping their bodies in the sea. He killed ten in all.

Panzram served a six-month jail sentence in Bridgeport for petty theft before being arrested again for inciting a riot during a labour dispute. Jumping bail, he headed for western Africa, where he continued his murder spree. On one occasion he was approached by a 12-year-old boy who was begging for money. 'He was looking for something. He found it, too', wrote Panzram later. 'First I committed sodomy on him and then I killed him.' He smashed in the boy's head with a rock: 'His brains were coming out of his ears when I left him and he will never be deader', Panzram enthused. Panzram once decided to go crocodile-hunting and hired six black porters and ended up feeding them to the crocodiles.

Back in the USA Panzram raped and killed three more boys. In June 1923, while he was working as night watchman for the New Haven Yacht Club, he stole a boat, killing a man who clambered aboard and tossing the body into New York's Kingston Bay. He was eventually caught attempting to rob an office in Larchmont, New York, and was sentenced to five years in Sing Sing. The guards there were unable to handle him, however, and he was sent to Clinton Prison in Dannemora, which was considered to be the end of the line for hard cases such as him. There he received savage beatings and also smashed his leg after falling from a high gallery. He spent his days plotting his revenge against the whole human race, amongst other things planning to blow up a railway tunnel when there was a train in it; to poison an entire city by putting arsenic in its water supply; and to start a war between Britain and the USA by blowing up a British battleship in US waters.

When he tried to escape from Clinton Prison he was tortured by having his hands tied behind his back and then being suspended by a rope from a beam. He could endure this for 12 hours on end, all the while screaming and cursing his mother for having brought him into the world. Despite his horrendous treatment at the hands of the guards, one of them, Henry Lesser, sympathised with Panzram and persuaded him to write his autobiography. Panzram did so, making no excuses for himself in it, saying that he had broken every law of God and humanity and furthermore commenting that if there had been more laws in existence he would have broken those, too.

Released yet again in 1928, Panzram hit the Washington-Baltimore area like a one-man crime wave, committing eleven robberies and one murder. He was soon arrested. At his trial he addressed the jury, saying 'While you were trying me here, I was trying all of you. I have found you guilty. So I hate the whole human race'. The judge sentenced him to 25 years in jail. 'Visit me', Panzram retorted.

At Fort Leavenworth Panzram told his guards 'I'll kill the first man that bothers me'. True to his word, he murdered the mild-mannered, civilian prison laundry supervisor Robert G Warnke with an iron bar. After a hasty trial Panzram was sentenced to death by hanging. Meanwhile, Lesser had been hawking Panzram's autobiography around the literary establishment, which included the legendary newspaperman H L Menken. People were impressed by it, but when Panzram heard that they were thinking of starting a movement to work for his reprieve he protested, saying 'I would not reform if the front gate was opened right now and I was given a million dollars when I stepped out. I have no desire to do good or become good'.

The Society for the Abolition of Capital Punishment also stepped in to try to save his neck, but he told it to forget it. Hanging would be a 'real pleasure and a big relief' for him, he said. 'The only thanks you or your kind will ever get from me for your efforts is that I wish you all had one neck and I had my hands on it. I believe that the only way to reform people is to kill them. My motto is : "Rob'em all, rape'em all and kill'em all."' He even turned on Lesser in the end, writing in his last letter, 'What gets me is how in the heck any man of your intelligence and ability, knowing as much about me as you do, can still be friendly towards a thing like me when I even despise and detest my own self'.

The end could not come soon enough for Carl Panzram. He was standing on the gallows on 11 September 1930 when the hangman, a son of Indiana, asked him if he had any last words. Panzram replied 'Yes, hurry it up, you Hosier bastard. I could hang a dozen men while you're fooling around'.

Harvey Glatmen

The Los Angeles Times journalist Robert Dull had separated from his pretty, young, blonde wife, Judy, because he objected to her modelling in the nude for other men, but the bust-up had not been acrimonious. She had invited him to her flat on 1 August 1957 to talk about a divorce, but when he arrived she was not at home. Her flatmate, Lynn Lykles, said that she had left several hours earlier with a photographer called Johnny Glynn. Over the next two hours two other photographers called, saying that the 19-year-old Judy had failed to turn up for a session. No one answered the phone number that Glynn had left, so Dull called Judy's family and friends. After ascertaining that none of them had seen her he called the police.

Lynn gave the Los Angeles Police Department (LAPD)

439

a description of Glynn: he was short, with jug-handle-like ears, she said, and looked rather scruffy and dishevelled. He had visited the flat two days earlier, when another of her flatmates, Betty, had showed him Judy's portfolio, which had captivated him. He had phoned that morning, she continued, saying that he had a rush assignment and asking Judy to act as his model. Judy had been reluctant to do so, however, as she had a busy schedule ahead of her; Betty's description of him had made her rather suspicious, too. But when Glynn had said that his studio was being used for another assignment and that they would therefore have to shoot the pictures in her flat she had agreed. When he had turned up at the flat he had brought no photographic gear with him because, he explained, a friend had lent him his studio. He had agreed to the fee that Judy asked and the two of them had then left. That was the last time that anyone saw Judy alive.

Descriptions of both Judy and the mysterious photographer were circulated, but there was little else that the LAPD could do. However, Judy's disappearance did make the newspapers and for weeks Police Sergeant David Ostroff was kept busy following up potential leads. Ostroff also studied the file on a beautiful young actress named Jean Spangler, who had vanished eight years earlier.

Five months after Judy's disappearance, a rancher and his dog discovered a skull lying in the desert near the Interstate 60 motorway, over 100 mile (161 kilometres) east of Los Angeles. When the police arrived they unearthed a half-buried skeleton clad in women's underwear and the remains of a brown dress like the one that Judy was wearing when she was last seen. Tufts of hair attached to the skull showed that the dead woman had been a blonde; furthermore, the skeleton measured 5 feet 4 inches (1.6 metres), the same height as Judy.

Eight months after Judy Dull went missing another woman in the Los Angeles area disappeared. A divorcee and mother of two, the 24-year-old Shirley Ann Bridgeford had gone on a blind date with a short, dishevelled man with prominent ears called George Williams. Police Sergeant Ostroff soon came to believe that Johnny Glynn and George Williams were the same man. Three months later Ruth Rita Mercado, 24-year-old stripper and nude model who used the stage name Angela, also vanished. Although Ostroff added her file to his dossier he was still no nearer to catching the culprit. Then, however, the police got lucky.

On the evening of Monday, 27 October 1958, Officer Thomas F Mulligan, of the California Highway Patrol, turned into a dark street in the dusty town of Tustin, 35 miles (56 kilometres) south of Los Angeles. The light thrown by his motorcycle headlamp revealed a couple struggling, so he stopped and called out to them. Seeing that the woman was holding a gun and that her clothes were in a state of considerable disarray, Officer Mulligan pulled out his own pistol and ordered them to stop, whereupon they put up their hands. The woman, who identified herself as Lorraine Vigil, claimed that the man had tried to rape and kill her. The man did not deny her allegations.

Lorraine was a secretary who was determined to break into modelling, she later explained. A friend, who ran a modelling agency, had called her that evening and had asked her if she wanted to undertake a photographic assignment. Although her friend knew the photographer, who was called Frank Johnson, she had warned Lorraine to be a little wary of him. Lorraine had accepted the job and the photographer had later picked her up from her flat on Wiltshire Boulevard. Heading downtown, he had driven past the modelling studio on Sunset Strip that the agency had said would be the venue for the session. When Lorraine had mentioned this he had said that he was taking her to his studio in Anaheim, but then he had driven through Anaheim as well.

He had stopped on the dark road in Tustin and had pulled out a gun. Having ordered her to keep quiet, he had then produced a length of rope. Seeing this, Lorraine had said that she did not want to be tied up and would do anything that he wanted. At that moment a car had driven by and Lorraine had made a lunge for the door handle, whereupon the gun had gone off, the bullet grazing her thigh. In the resultant split second of confusion she had thrown herself at her assailant, causing the car door to fly open. They had fallen out of the car on to the road. He had then dropped the gun, which she grabbed. She was in the process of trying to shoot the fake photographer who had attacked her when Officer Mulligan arrived.

At Santa Ana police station the photographer who called himself Frank Johnson revealed that he was, in fact, Harvey Murray Glatman, aged 30. It was furthermore discovered that Glatman lived no more that a few streets from Ruth Rita Mercado's San Pico Boulevard flat. When they visited the address that he had given the police found a run-down, white-shingle bungalow. Inside, the walls were covered with nude pin-ups, some of which featured bound and gagged young women. Among Glatman's meagre possessions were found a number of lengths of rope.

Glatman agreed to take a lie-detector test; when the name Angela – Ruth Rita Mercado's professional name – was mentioned the stylus leapt, and within minutes Glatman had confessed to killing Ruth. Then he said 'I killed a couple of other girls, too'. It turned out that he had quite a story to relate.

Harvey Glatman was born in Denver, Colorado, in 1928. He was a mummy's boy who did not get on well with other children. When he was 12 his parents noticed red welts encircling his neck and after persistent questioning forced him to admit that tightening a rope around his neck gave him sexual satisfaction. The family doctor told his worried parents that he would grow out of it. At school Glatman was unattractive to girls and would instead gain their attention by grabbing their purses. This was not a very effective method of courtship, however, and at 17 he therefore took more direct action by pointing a toy gun at a girl and ordering her to undress. After she had screamed and run away Glatman was arrested, fleeing to New York on being released on bail.

In New York Glatman turned his perverted urges into a way of life, robbing women at gunpoint and later graduating to burglary, for which he spent five years in Sing Sing. He seemed to respond to psychiatric help in prison and became a model prisoner. On his release he went back to Colorado and began working as a television repairman – a job that allowed him to enter other people's homes quite legitimately (he would sometimes sneak into their bedrooms). His mother then lent him the money with which to set up a television-repair business in Los Angeles.

Glatman confessed everything to the police. Judy Dull, he said, had been the girl of his dreams. After he had picked her up he had driven her to his makeshift studio, where he had asked her to take off her dress and put on a pleated skirt and cardigan instead. He had then produced a length of rope and had tied her up. The shots that he was taking, he had explained to her, were for the cover of a true-life crime magazine, which was why she had had to be bound and gagged.

He had taken some pictures of her, but the sight of the helpless Judy had been too much for him; bound as she was, she could not resist as he had slowly undressed her. After that he had put a gun to her head and had told her that he would kill her if she cried out for help; she had nodded, whereupon he had untied her gag. Glatman had next made her pose on the sofa for more explicit bondage photographs and had then raped her twice. When he had finished he told her that he would take her to a remote spot in the desert, where he would release her.

He had let Judy put on her brown dress and had then driven her into the Nevada Desert. After spreading a blanket on the ground in a lonely spot he had again made her pose for erotic photographs, some with a noose around her neck. When Glatman had grown tired of taking pictures he had tied the loose end of the noose around her ankles and had pulled it until she was dead. Glatman had apologised to Judy's corpse before burying it in a shallow grave and had kept her shoes as a keepsake. Although he had originally intended to get a thrill from photographing and raping a beautiful woman – naked, bound and gagged – Glatman found that the killing had given him the greatest satisfaction of all and was determined to do it again.

Glatman had then registered in the name of George William with a dating agency and the agency had fixed him up with a date with Shirley Ann Bridgeford. When he had picked up Shirley he could see by her reaction that she found him a disappointment, but she had nevertheless gone with him.

Glatman had driven her south, out of Los Angeles towards San Diego. He had stopped in the Anza Desert and had tried to put his arm around her, to which she had responded that she did not feel that this was appropriate behaviour on a first date. He had then suggested that they went for a meal and she had seemed relieved. He had driven with one hand on the steering wheel while trying to fondle her with the other. She had again tried to fend him off and he and soon grown angry. He had stopped the car and had pulled out his automatic pistol, ordering her to get into the back of the car and undress. She had refused, so he had torn off her clothes and then raped her.

That had not been the end of Shirley's hideous blind

date, however. Next he had driven her into the desert, where, after unpacking his photographic gear, he had made her pose on the same blanket on which he had killed Judy Dull. After having forced her to lie on her front he had tied a rope around her neck and garrotted her. He had taken her red knickers as a memento and had left her body where it lay, covered with brushwood because the ground was too hard to dig a grave in.

Five months later Glatman had spotted an advertisement in the newspaper offering the services of a nude model called Angela. He had called her before visiting her on the evening of 23 July 1958. She had taken one look at him, however, and had refused to let him in, but because he had liked her appearance he had pulled out his gun and had forced his way into her flat.

He had ordered Angela to undress at gunpoint and had then tied her up and raped her. After that he had announced that they were going for a little picnic, whereupon he had driven her to a deserted spot about 30 miles (48 kilometres) from where he had murdered Shirley Ann Bridgeford. Much as he had enjoyed killing Shirley and Judy, he had later thought that those murders had been over too quickly and had decided that in this instance he would take his time. The two of them had accordingly spent the day together, eating, sleeping and drinking. Glatman had also occasionally forced Angela (or Ruth Rita Mercado, as she was known when she was not at work) to pose for him. He had furthermore repeatedly raped her. Ruth had been very compliant, he said, clearly having decided that her only chance of surviving was to try to please him. After 24 hours spent toying with his victim, however, Glatman had garrotted her in the same manner in which he had dispatched his previous two victims.

After making his detailed confession Glatman helped the police to find the remains of Ruth Rita Mercado and Shirley Ann Bridgeford. Although his lawyers suggested that he plead guilty but insane, Glatman pleaded guilty without caveat, thus opting for a quick execution rather than a life spent in mental institution. He died in the gas chamber on 18 September 1959.

The Moors Murderers

Ian Brady and Myra Hindley still rank as perhaps the world's most infamous killers. Their bizarre and deviant sexual relationship drove them to torture and murder defenceless children for pleasure in a case of serial killing that appalled the world. The idea that Hindley may one day be released from prison elicits howls of protest from the public. Nobody – least of all himself – however, has ever contemplated freeing Brady.

When Hindley met Brady he was already deeply warped: a 21-year-old stock clerk at Millwards (a chemical company in Manchester), his mind was full of sadistic fantasies. He had a collection of Nazi memorabilia and listened to recordings of Nazi rallies, while in his lunch hour he read Adolf Hitler's autobiography *Mein Kampf* ('My Struggle') and studied German grammar. He believed in the Nazi cause and regretted that he had not been part of its terrible excesses.

For her part, Hindley was known as a loner. Her first boyfriend had died when she was 15; she had not been able sleep for days afterwards and had turned to the Roman Catholic Church for consolation. At school it was noted that she was tough, aggressive and rather masculine, and that she enjoyed contact sports and judo, none of which suited her to the genteel life of 1950's Britain. At the age of 19 she became a typist at Millwards, where she met Brady. He impressed her immediately: she considered most of the men whom she knew to be immature, but Brady dressed well and rode a motorbike. 'Ian wore a black shirt today and looked smashing... I love him', she confided to her diary.

For nearly a year Brady took no notice of her, however: 'The pig. He didn't even look at me today', she wrote more than once. Finally, in December 1961, he asked her out. 'Eureka!' her diary says. 'Today we have our first date. We are going to the cinema.' (The film that they saw was Judgement at Nuremberg, which was about the trial of Germany's leading Nazis following World War II.) Hindley rapidly surrendered her virginity to Brady, later writing 'I hope Ian and I love each other all our lives and get married and are happy ever after'. Yet their relationship would not be as innocent as her hopeful words suggest, for Hindley soon became Brady's sex slave. He introduced her to sexual perversion and urged her to read his books on Nazi atrocities. They took pornographic photographs of each other and kept them in a scrapbook; some showed weals across Hindley's buttocks that had been left by a whip.

Hindley subsequently gave up babysitting and going to church. Within six months she and Brady were living together at her grandmother's house; because her grandmother was a frail woman who spent most of her time in bed they had the run of the place. Brady persuaded Hindley to bleach her brown hair a Teutonic blonde and dressed her in leather skirts and high-heeled boots. He often called her Myra Hess – or 'Hessie' – after a sadistic, Nazi, concentration-camp guard.

Life with Brady made Hindley hard and cruel. She did anything that Brady asked of her and did not balk at procuring children for him to abuse, torture and kill. Their first victim was the 16-year-old Pauline Reade, who disappeared on 12 July 1963 on her way to a dance. They persuaded Pauline to go for a walk on the nearby Saddleworth Moor, where they killed and buried her. Four months later Hindley hired a car and abducted the 12-

year-old John Kilbride; when she returned the car it was covered with mud from the moors. Brady and Hindley laughed when they read about the massive police hunt that was undertaken to find the missing boy.

In May 1964 Hindley bought a car of her own, a white Mini van. During the following month the 12-year-old Keith Bennett went missing; like the other victims, Hindley and Brady had buried him on Saddleworth Moor. At Brady's behest Hindley then joined a local gun club and bought pistol for them both, which they practised firing on the moors. While they were there they visited the graves of their victims, photographing each other kneeling on them.

On 27 December 1964 they abducted the ten-year-old Lesley Ann Downey. This time they were determined to derive the utmost perverted pleasure from their defenceless victim. They accordingly forced her to pose nude for pornographic photographs and then tortured her, recording her screams, before strangling her and burying her with the others on Saddleworth Moor.

Brady now wanted to extend his sphere of evil influence, aiming to recruit Myra's 16-year-old brother-in-law, David Smith, to their perverted circle. Brady showed Smith his gun and talked to him about robbing a bank. He also lent him books about the Marquis de Sade (from whose name the word 'sadism' is derived) and persuaded him to write down quotations dictated by Brady. 'Murder is a hobby and a supreme pleasure' or 'People are like maggots, small, blind, worthless fish-bait', Smith obediently wrote in an exercise book under Brady's guidance.

Brady believed that he could lure anyone into his world of brutality and murder and bragged to Smith about the murders that he had committed. They were drinking at the time and Smith thought that Brady was joking, so Brady decided to prove his capacity for murder and simultaneously ensnare Smith by making him party to a killing.

On 6 October 1965 Brady and Hindley picked up Edward Evans, a 17-year-old homosexual, in a Manchester pub. They then called Smith and asked him to come to their house at midnight. When he arrived he heard a cry coming from the sitting room. 'Help him, Dave', said Hindley, and Smith rushed into the room to find a youth in a chair with Brady sitting astride him. Brady held an axe in his hands which he brought down on to the boy's head, hitting him at least 14 times. 'It's the messiest', Brady said with some satisfaction. 'Usually it takes only one blow'. Brady then handed the axe to the dumbstruck Smith. (This was an attempt to incriminate Smith by putting his fingerprints on the murder weapon.)

Although Smith was terrified by what he had seen he helped to clean up the blood while Brady and Hindley wrapped the boy's body in a plastic sheet; the couple made jokes about the murder as they carried the corpse downstairs. After that Hindley made a pot of tea and they all sat down. 'You should have seen the look on his face', said Hindley, who was flushed with excitement; she then started reminiscing about the murders that she and Brady had previously committed. Although Smith could not believe what was happening he realised that he would be their next victim if he showed any signs of disgust or outrage. After a decent interval he made his excuses and left; when he got back to his flat he was violently ill.

Smith told his wife what had happened, who urged him to go to the police. At dawn, armed with a knife and screwdriver, the couple went out to a phone box and reported the murder. A police car picked them up and took them to the police station, where Smith told his lurid tale to incredulous policemen. When the police visited Hindley's house at 8.40am to check out Smith's story, however, they found Edward Evans' body in the back bedroom.

Brady admitted killing Evans during an argument and then tried to implicate Smith in the murder. Hindley merely said 'My story is the same as Ian's...Whatever he did, I did'. The only emotion that she showed was when she was told that her dog had died: 'You fucking murderer', she screamed at the police.

The police found a detailed plan that Brady had drawn up for the removal from the house of all clues to Evans' murder. Curiously, one of the items listed was Hindley's prayer book; when the police examined it they discovered a left-luggage ticket from Manchester Station. The police reclaimed two suitcases containing books on sexual perversion, as well as coshes and photographs of a naked and gagged Lesley Ann Downey. The tape that had recorded her screams – which was later played to the stunned courtroom at Chester Assizes – was also discovered. Other photographs showed Hindley posing beside graves on Saddleworth Moor, and it was these that subsequently helped the police to locate the bodies of Lesley Ann Downey and John Kilbride.

At Brady and Hindley's trial the truly horrific nature of the murders was revealed. The pathologist disclosed that Edward Evans' fly had been undone and that dog hairs had been found around his anus; John Kilbride's body was discovered with his trousers and underpants around his knees. Hindley, it seemed, had been turned on by watching Brady perform homosexual acts on his victims. Later Brady let it slip that both he and Hindley had been naked when they had photographed Lesley Ann Downey in the nude, but otherwise the pair refused to talk about their crimes.

They were sentenced to life imprisonment. Brady did not bother to appeal against the sentence; Hindley did, but her appeal was rejected. They were refused permission to see each other in jail, although they were allowed to exchange letters.

Brady showed no contrition in prison and refused to allow his spirit to be broken, regarding himself as a martyr to his own perverted cause. He gradually became insane. Hindley, however, broke down and petitioned to be released. When her appeal was refused a warder (who was Hindley's lesbian lover) organised an abortive escape attempt, for which Hindley was sentenced to an additional year in jail.

She took an Open University degree and gave additional information about the whereabouts of her victims' graves to the police in a bid for mercy. Brady, however, countered her every move by revealing more of her involvement in the crimes, considering any attempt on her part to go free as an act of disloyalty to him. 'The weight of our crimes justifies permanent imprisonment', Brady told the Parole Board in 1982. 'I will not wish to be free in 1985 or 2005.'

Hindley still hoped for parole, but public opinion was resolutely against it: after all, the families of their victims were still suffering.

Henry Lee Lucas

Henry Lee Lucas holds the record for being the USA's most prolific serial killer. He confessed to over 360 murders, of which 157 were investigated by the authorities and proved to have been committed by him – as for the rest, they took his word for it.

Lucas' mother, a half Native American Chippawa, was drunk for most of the time on the corn liquor that she bought with the proceeds of prostitution. Known to be 'as mean as a rattlesnake', she sent the seven children from her first marriage to a foster home. Lucas' natural father worked on the railways and lost both of his legs in an accident; Lucas himself was brought up by one of his mother's lovers, Andrew Lucas. His mother beat her children constantly and after one beating he was unconscious for three days and suffered brain damage; another such incident resulted in a glass eye. Lucas was also made to grow his hair long and to wear a dress.

Lucas was introduced to sex at the age of ten by the educationally challenged Bernard Dowdy, another of his mother's lovers. Dowdy would slit the throat of a calf and have sex with the carcass, encouraging the boy to do the same. Lucas enjoyed the experience and from childhood onwards associated sex with death. Throughout his childhood he continued to have sex with animals, sometimes skinning them alive for his sexual pleasure. At 14 he turned his perverted attention to women, beating a 17-year-old girl unconscious at a bus stop and raping her; when she came to and started to scream he choked the life out of her.

Convicted of burglary, he was sent to a reformatory when he was 15. Two years of hard labour on a prison farm did nothing to reform him, however, and on his release started housebreaking again and was sent back to jail. He escaped from prison, whereupon he met and fell in love with a young woman called Stella. They stayed together for four years and she agreed to marry him. Then his mother turned up demanding that her son take care of her and after a violent row Lucas killed her. This time he was sentenced to 40 years' imprisonment.

By 1970 the authorities considered Lucas to be a reformed character and released him. He killed a woman within hours of getting out of jail. In 1971 he was arrested for attempting to rape two teenage girls at gunpoint; the only excuse that he gave at his trial was that he craved women all the time. Released again in 1975, he then married Betty Crawford, but the marriage broke up when Betty discovered that he was having sex with her nine-year-old daughter, as well as trying to force himself on her seven-year-old child. Lucas then moved in with his sister, only to be thrown out when he started to have sex with her daughter, too.

In 1978 he met another sex-murder freak in a soup kitchen in Jacksonville, Florida. Ottis Toole was a sadist with homosexual tendencies who often dressed as a woman and picked up men in bars – he had even started to take a course of female hormones in furtherance of his ambition to have a sex change. Toole was also a pyromaniac who had an orgasm at the sight of a burning building.

Lucas and Toole became lovers and together embarked upon a series of violent robberies which frequently involved murder – often for the sheer pleasure of it. In Toole's confession he admitted that at around that time they had seen a teenage couple walking along a road because their car had run out of petrol. Toole had shot the boy while Lucas had forced the girl into the back of the car. After he had finished with her he had shot her six times and they had then dumped her body by the side of the road. (This was one of the cases that the police would later confirm.) Another incident had occurred outside Oklahoma City, when they had picked up a young woman called Tina Williams whose car had broken down. Lucas had shot her twice and had then had sex with her corpse.

Later in 1978 Lucas and Toole were in Maryland when a man asked them if they would help him to transport stolen cars. This was much too tame a sport for such hardened criminals, they explained, so he enquired whether they would be interested in becoming professional killers instead. They answered that they would, to which the man replied that the one condition was that they joined a Satanic cult.

Lucas and Toole subsequently claimed to have been inducted into the Hand of Death sect in Florida by a man named Don Meteric. As part of the initiation ceremony

Lucas had had to kill a man. He had lured his victim to a beach and had given him a bottle of whisky; when the man had thrown back his head to take a swig of it Lucas had cut his throat. As part of the cult's activities Lucas and Toole kidnapped young prostitutes, who were forced to perform in pornographic videos which often turned out to be 'snuff movies' in which the prostitutes were killed. The pair also abducted children, taking them across the border into Mexico where they were sold or used as sacrifices in Satanic ceremonies.

At around that time Toole introduced Lucas to his 11-year-old niece, Becky Powell, who was slightly educationally challenged. Becky was then living in Toole's mother's house in Florida, where they were also staying. Toole – who had been seduced by his older sister, Druscilla, before he became a homosexual – enjoyed watching the men whom he picked up make love to Becky or her older sister, Sarah. After Druscilla committed suicide, however, Becky and her brother, Frank, were put into care. Lucas then 'rescued' them and by January 1982 they were all on the run together, living off the money that they stole from small grocery shops. Becky called Lucas 'Daddy', but one night, when he was tickling her innocently at bedtime, they began to kiss; Lucas then undressed her before stripping off himself. Becky may have been only 12 at the time, he said, but she looked 18.

During his time with Becky, Lucas continued his murderous rampage in conjunction with Toole. Lucas later outlined a typical two weeks in Georgia. In that short space of time they had kidnapped and murdered a 16-year-old girl before raping her dead body, as well as abducting, raping and mutilating a blonde woman. Another woman had been taken from a car park and stabbed to death in front of her children. During the course of one robbery the shop's owner had been shot; another man had died in a second robbery; in a third the owner of the shop had been stabbed; and in a fourth a woman had been tied up before being stabbed to death. Toole had also tried to force his sexual attentions upon a young man, whom he had shot after being spurned. Becky and Frank had often taken part in the robberies, also witnessing several of the murders.

Lucas and Toole eventually parted company, Toole taking Frank back to Florida while Lucas and Becky were given work with a couple named Smart who ran an antique shop in California. After five months the Smarts sent Lucas and Becky to Texas to look after Mrs Smart's 80-year-old mother, Kate Rich. A few weeks later Mrs Smart's sister visited her mother, only to find the house filthy. Lucas, it transpired, had been taking Mrs Rich's money in order to buy beer and cigarettes. On finding him drunk, in bed with Becky, the pair was fired.

They were trying to hitch a lift out of town when they were picked up by the Reverend Reuben Moore, who ran a religious community nearby called the House of Prayer. Lucas and the 15-year-old Becky quickly became converts and joined the community, living in a converted chicken barn. Becky then seems to have had a genuine change of heart and to have become homesick. She wanted to go back to Florida, she told Lucas, who reluctantly consented, whereupon the two set off to hitchhike to her home state. They settled down with their blankets in a field at nightfall. It was a warm, June night. A row then broke out about Becky's decision to return home and she struck Lucas in the face. He retaliated by knifing her through the heart, after which he had sex with her corpse, cut up her body and scattered the dismembered pieces in the woods. Becky was, Lucas later claimed, the only woman whom he had ever loved.

Lucas returned to the House of Prayer, where he, too, then seems to have had some sort of change of heart. One Sunday he dropped in at Mrs Rich's house to give her a lift to church. During the journey she asked him where Becky was, whereupon Lucas pulled out a knife and stabbed her; she died instantaneously and raped her corpse before stuffing it into a drainage pipe that ran underneath the road. He subsequently returned, placing her body in a dustbin bag and then burning it in the stove at the House of Prayer.

Sheriff Bill F 'Hound Dog' Conway, of Montague County, Texas, had begun to have his suspicions about Lucas when he reappeared without Becky. Now it seemed that he was linked to the disappearance of another woman, Mrs Rich, and Lucas was accordingly hauled into the sheriff's office for questioning. Lucas was both a chain smoker and a caffeine addict, so Conway deprived him of cigarettes and coffee, but still Lucas refused to break, saying that he knew nothing about the disappearance of Kate Rich and that Becky had run off with a lorry driver who had promised to take her back to Florida. Conway finally had to release him.

Soon afterwards Lucas told Reverend Moore that he was going to look for Becky. While heading for Missouri he saw a young woman standing beside her car at a petrol station; holding a knife against her ribs he forced her into her car. They then drove south, towards Texas. When she dozed off Lucas pulled off the road, intending to rape her. She awoke suddenly to find a knife at her neck, whereupon Lucas stabbed her in the throat, pushed her out of the car on to the ground and cut her clothes off her body. After he had raped her corpse he dragged it into a copse and took the money from her handbag. He abandoned her car in Fredericksburg, Texas, and then returned to the House of Prayer.

While he had been away Reverend Moore had told Sheriff Conway that Lucas had given Becky a gun for safe-keeping. Because Lucas was a convicted felon who had therefore forfeited his right to bear arms under US law this was enough to justify his arrest. After taking him into custody Conway again deprived him of coffee and cigarettes and this time Lucas began to crack; he was later found hanging in his cell with his wrists slashed.

After having been patched up in the prison hospital Lucas was put in a special observation cell in the women's wing. On the next night he cracked completely, starting to yell in the early hours of the morning. When his jailer arrived Lucas claimed that the light in his cell was talking to him. The prison officer, Joe Don Weaver, who knew that Lucas had already smashed the bulb in his cell, told him to get some sleep. Later on during the night Lucas called the jailer again and confessed that he had done some pretty bad things. Weaver advised him to get down on his knees and prey, but instead Lucas asked for a pencil and paper.

Lucas spent the next half an hour writing a note to Sheriff Conway, which read 'I have tried to get help for so long and no one will believe me. I have killed for the past ten years and no one will believe me. I cannot go on doing this. I have killed the only girl I ever loved'. Lucas then pushed his confession through the peephole in the door of his cell. After reading it Weaver called Sheriff Conway, who plied Lucas with coffee and cigarettes upon his arrival and asked about the murders. Lucas said that he had seen a light in his cell that had told him to confess his sins and then told the sheriff that he had killed Kate Rich. Sheriff Conway and Phil Ryan, a Texas Ranger, later asked Lucas what had happened to Becky Powell. Tears flowed from his one good eye as Lucas told of how he had stabbed, raped and dismembered her. The story left the two hardened law officers feeling sick and wretched. 'Is that all?' asked Ryan wearily, half hoping that it was. 'Not by a long way', replied Lucas. 'I reckon I killed more than a hundred.'

On the next day the Montague County police began to investigate Lucas' story. Near the drainage pipe in which

Lucas had temporarily hidden Mrs Rich's body they discovered some of her underclothes, as well as her broken glasses. At the House of Prayer they found burnt fragments of human flesh, along with charred bones. Lucas himself took them to the field in which he had killed Becky. There they found her suitcase, which was full of women's clothing and make-up. Her skull and other parts of her body were discovered in an advanced stage of decomposition in nearby woodland.

Lucas began to confess to other murders, too – often in breath-taking detail. These were also investigated and confirmed. A week after he had began to confess Lucas appeared in court, where he was charged with the murders of Kate Rich and Becky Powell. When he was asked whether he understood the seriousness of the charges against him Lucas replied he did, then admitting to about a hundred other murders. The shocked judge could scarcely credit this behaviour and asked Lucas whether he had ever had a psychiatric examination. Lucas replied that he had, but commented 'They didn't want to do anything about it ... I know it ain't normal for a person to go out and kill girls just to have sex'.

Lucas' sensational testimony made the headlines in every newspaper in the country. Police departments in each US state and county began to check their records, while Lucas' confession was also run through the computer at the newly formed national Center for the Analysis of Violent Crime.

Toole, it was discovered, was already in prison: he had been sentenced to 15 years' imprisonment for arson and was currently incarcerated in Springfield, where he had been regaling a cell mate with the gruesome tale of how he had raped, murdered, beheaded, barbecued and eaten a child named Adam Walsh. The police were now forced to take the lurid stories seriously. Indeed, both Toole and Lucas now began to admit their crimes freely. They confessed to a series of robberies of convenience stores, for example, saying that at one they had tied up a young girl who had had wriggled free, so Lucas had shot her in the head and Toole had had sex with her dead body.

Lucas was next taken on a 1,000-mile- (1,609-kilometre) long tour of his murder sites. In Duval County, Florida, he confessed to eight unsolved murders. The victims had been women ranging in age from 17 to 80; some had been beaten, some strangled, some stabbed and others shot (Lucas claimed that the Hand of Death had said that he should vary his coup de grâce.) Near Austin, Texas, Lucas pointed to a building and asked whether it had once been a liquor store; on being told that it had, Lucas confessed to having murdered its former owners during a robbery in 1979. Lucas then led the police to a field in the same county in which he had murdered and mutilated a girl called Sandra Dubbs – he even pointed out where her car had been found.

It transpired that Lucas and Toole had cruised the Interstate 35 motorway murdering tramps, hitchhikers, men who were also robbed of their money and old woman who had been abducted from their homes. Over a period of five years they had killed more than 20 people up and down that highway alone. One of their victims was a young woman whose corpse was later found naked, except for a pair of orange socks, near Austin. She had been hitchhiking along Interstate 35 when Lucas had picked her up; according to Lucas she had refused to have sex with him, so he had strangled her and taken what he wanted. Although she was never identified it was for her murder that Lucas was sentenced to death.

Despite his subsequent withdrawal of his confession to the murder of Becky Powell and his plea of not guilty, Lucas was found guilty of the crime and sentenced to life imprisonment, in addition receiving four further life sentences, two sentences of 75 years each and one of 67 years, all for murder.

During his confession Lucas had told the police that Toole had poured petrol over a 65-year-old man before setting him alight; the pair had then hidden so that they could watch the fire engines arrive. The police identified the man as being George Sonenberg, who had died four days later. Until then they had assumed that the fire was an accident, but Toole freely admitted to the killing and furthermore claimed to have started hundreds of other fires. It was this particularly horrific murder, however, that Toole was also sentenced to death.

Both Lucas and Toole enjoyed their brief period of notoriety and relished revealing the ghoulish details of their shocking crimes. Further information about the Hand of Death was not forthcoming, however.

Dennis Nilsen

Dennis Nilsen was Britain's most prolific serial killer. Sadly, of all of his 15 victims only one – a Canadian tourist – was missed; the rest were homosexual drifters who were looking for money, love or just a place to stay for the night.

Nilsen was born in Fraserburgh, a small town on the bleak, north-eastern coast of Scotland, on 23 November 1945. His father was a Norwegian soldier who had escaped to Scotland following the German invasion of his country in 1940 and had married Betty Whyte, a local girl, in 1942. The marriage did not work out, however, and Betty continued to live with her parents before the couple divorced a few years later.

Dennis grew up living with his mother, elder brother and younger sister, but the strongest influence on his young life was that of his stern and pious grandparents. Their faith was so strict that they banned alcohol from the house and regarded the radio and cinema as instruments of the devil. Nilsen's grandmother would furthermore not cook on Sunday – the Lord's day – and their dinner therefore had to be prepared on Saturday.

The young Nilsen was sullen and intensely withdrawn. The only person who could penetrate his private world was his grandfather, Andrew Whyte, Nilsen's hero. A fisherman, he would regale the little boy with tales of the sea and of those of his ancestors who had been lost beneath its churning waves. When Whyte died of a heart attack at sea in 1951 he was brought home and laid out on the dining-room table. Dennis, aged six, was invited to view his grandfather's body and thus got his first sight of a corpse. From that moment on the images of death and love were fused in his mind.

He left school at 15 and joined the army. After basic training he was transferred to the catering corps, where he was taught how to sharpen knives and to dissect a carcass. During his time in the army Nilsen had only one close friend, whom he persuaded to pose for photographs sprawled on the ground, as if he had been killed in battle. On one night in Aden the drunk Nilsen fell asleep in the back of a taxi. He woke to find himself naked and locked in the boot of the car. When the taxi driver appeared Nilsen played dead, but as the Arab manhandled him out of the boot Nilsen grabbed a jack and beat him around the head with it. Nilsen never knew whether he had killed the man, but after he began having nightmares about being raped, tortured and mutilated.

After spending 11 years in the army Nilsen left to join the police force. Part of his training included a visit to a mortuary; the partially dissected corpses that he saw there fascinated him. Although he did well in the police force his private life was gradually disintegrating. Death became an obsession with him, and he liked to masturbate while pretending to be a corpse, lying naked in front of a mirror with blue paint smeared on his lips and his skin whitened with talcum powder. His incipient homosexuality also began to bother him. After 11 months in the police force he caught two men committing an act of gross indecency in a parked car; because he could not bring himself to arrest them he decided to resign.

He then went to work interviewing unemployed applicants for benefit at the Jobcentre in London's Charing Cross Road, becoming the branch secretary of the civil-service union and developing increasingly radical political views. His work was nevertheless good enough to earn him promotion to the position of executive officer at the Jobcentre in Kentish Town, north London.

Despite his professional progress Nilsen was lonely and yearned for a lasting relationship. He had been aware of his attraction towards other men since his teens, but had somehow managed to repress it while in the army and police force. In 1975 he met a young man called David Gallichen outside a pub, with whom he later moved into a flat at 195 Melrose Avenue, in the Cricklewood district of London, along with a cat and a dog called Bleep. Gallichen, or 'Twinkle', as Nilsen called him, stayed at home and decorated the flat while Nilsen went to work. They made home movies together and spent a lot of time drinking and talking. The relationship did not last, however, and when Gallichen moved out Nilsen was again plunged into a life of loneliness.

On New Year's Eve in 1978 Nilsen met a teenage Irish boy in a pub and invited him back to Melrose Avenue. They had been too drunk to have sex and when Nilsen woke in the morning the boy was lying fast asleep beside him. He was afraid that when the boy woke up he would leave, and Nilsen wanted him to stay.

Their clothes were thrown together in a heap on the floor. Nilsen lent over and grabbed his tie, wrapping it around the boy's neck and pulling it tight. The boy immediately awoke and began to struggle. They rolled on to the floor while Nilsen kept on pulling the tie. Although the boy's body went limp about a minute later, he was still breathing. After going into the kitchen and filling a bucket with water Nilsen took the bucket to the bedroom and held the boy's head under water until he drowned. Now he had to stay with Nilsen. He carried the dead boy into the bathroom and gave him a bath. He then dried the corpse lovingly, before dressing it in clean socks and underpants. For a while he lay in bed holding the dead boy; after that he put him on the floor and went to sleep.

On the following day he decided to hide the body under the floorboards, but rigor mortis had stiffened its joints, making it hard to handle. He therefore left the body as it was while he went to work. After the corpse had loosened up Nilsen undressed it and washed it again, this time masturbating beside it. He found that he could not stop playing with, and admiring, the boy's body. All the time that Nilsen was playing with the corpse he expected to be arrested at any moment, but no one came: it seemed that the dead boy had not been missed by anyone. After a week of living happily with the corpse Nilsen hid it under the floorboards; seven months later he cut it up and burnt it in the garden.

Nilsen's first experience of murder had frightened him. He was determined that it would not happen again and decided to give up drinking. But because he was lonely and liked to go to pubs to meet people he soon slipped off the wagon. Nearly a year later, on 3 December 1979, Nilsen met Kenneth Ockenden, a Canadian tourist, in a pub in Soho. Nilsen took the afternoon off work to join Ockenden on a sightseeing tour of London, after which Ockenden agreed to go back to Nilsen's flat for something to eat. After a visit to the off-licence they sat in front of the television eating ham, eggs and chips and drinking beer, whisky and rum. As the evening wore on disturbing feeling to began to grow inside Nilsen. He liked Ockenden, but realised that he would soon be leaving to go back to Canada. A feeling of desolation swept over him – it was the same feeling that he had had when he killed the Irish boy.

Late that night they were both very drunk. Ockenden was listening to music through earphones when Nilsen wrapped the flex of the earphones around Ockenden's neck and dragged him struggling across the floor. When he was dead Nilsen took off the earphones and put them over his own ears. He then poured himself another drink and listened to records. He stripped the corpse in the early hours of the morning and carried it over his shoulder into the bathroom. When the body was clean and dry he placed it on the bed and went to sleep next to it.

Later that morning he put the body into a cupboard and went to work. In the evening he took out the corpse and dressed it in clean socks, underpants and a vest. He then took some photographs of it before arranging it next to him on the bed. For the next two weeks Nilsen would watch television in the evening while Ockenden's body was propped up in an armchair next to him. Last thing at night he would undress it, wrap it in some curtains and place in under the floorboards.

Because Ockenden had gone missing from a hotel his disappearance made the news for a few days. Nilsen was again convinced that he was about to be arrested at any moment – after all, people in the pub, on the bus and in the off-licence had seen them together. But when there were still no knock on the door Nilsen felt that he could pursue his macabre hobby unfettered. He began deliberately to seek out his victims, going to pubs where lonely, young homosexuals hung out, where he would buy them drinks, offer advice and invite them back to his flat for something to eat. Many accepted.

One of those who did was Martin Duffey, who, following a disturbed childhood, had run away from home and had ended up sleeping in railway stations in London. He went home with Nilsen and crawled into bed after drinking two cans of beer. When he was asleep Nilsen strangled him and then dragged his unconscious body into the kitchen, filling up the sink and holding his head under water for four minutes. After that Nilsen went through his now standard procedure of stripping and bathing the corpse before taking it to bed. He talked to it, complementing it on its physique, kissing it and masturbating over it. Nilsen kept the corpse in a cupboard for a few days; when it started to swell he put it under the floorboards.

The 27-year-old Billy Sutherland, on the other hand, died because he was a nuisance: Nilsen hadn't fancied him, but after meeting him on a pub crawl Sutherland had followed him home. Nilsen later said that he vaguely remembered strangling him – there was certainly a dead body in the flat on the following the morning.

Nilsen would go out to work as if all was perfectly normal, but when he got home in the evening he would retrieve his latest corpse from its hiding place an play with it. To him it was a thrill to own such a beautiful body and he would engage the corpse in a passionate embrace and talk to it. When he was finished he would stuff it under the floorboards again.

Some of his murders were terrifyingly casual. Nilsen came across one of his victims, the 24-year-old Malcom Barlow, for example, after he had collapsed on the pavement on Melrose Avenue. Barlow was an epileptic and said that the pills that he was taking made his legs give way, so Nilsen carried him home and called an ambulance. When he was released from hospital the next day Barlow returned to Nilsen's flat. Nilsen prepared a meal and Barlow began drinking, even though Nilsen warned him not to mix alcohol with the new pills that he had been prescribed. When Barlow indeed collapsed Nilsen could not be bothered to call the ambulance again and therefore strangled him, after that carrying on drinking until it was bedtime. By now the space under the floorboards was full of corpse, so the following morning Nilsen stuffed Barlow's body into the cupboard under the sink.

As the place was full up Nilsen decided that it was time to move. There were six corpses under the floorboards; several others had been dissected and stored in suitcases. He decided that he had better dispose of the bodies first and after a stiff drink pulled up the floorboards and began cutting up the corpses. He hid the internal organs in the garden, where birds and rats dealt with them. The other body parts were wrapped in a carpet and thrown onto a bonfire; a tyre was placed on top to disguise the smell.

Nilsen then moved to an attic flat at 23 Cranley Gardens, in the London district of Muswell Hill, in a deliberate attempt to put a halt to his murderous career – he could not kill people, he reasoned, if he had no floorboards under which to hide their corpses and no garden in which to burn them. Indeed, although he had several casual encounters at his new flat, when he picked up men at night he let them go in the morning, unmolested. He was elated because he believed that he had finally broken the cycle of killing.

When, however, John Howlett – or 'Guardsman John', as Nilsen called him – came back to Cranley Gardens Nilsen could not help himself and strangled Howlett with a strap before drowning him. A few days later he strangled Graham Allen while he was eating an omelette. The death of his final victim, Stephen Sinclair, a drifter and a drug addict, upset Nilsen. When they met Nilsen felt sorry for him and bought him a hamburger. Having gone back with Nilsen to Cranley Gardens, Sinclair slumped in a chair in a stupor and it was then Nilsen decided to relieve him of the pain of his miserable existence. He first got a piece of string from the kitchen, but finding that it was not long enough he instead used his one remaining tie to choke the life out of his unconscious victim.

Killing at Cranley Gardens presented Nilsen with a problem: how to get rid of the bodies of his victims. With no floorboards or garden he was forced to dispose of the corpses but dissecting them, boiling the flesh from the bones, dicing up the remains and flushing them down the toilet. Unfortunately, the drains in Muswell Hill were not built to handle bodies and those at 23 Cranley Gardens had been blocked for five days when, on 8 February 1983, the drain-clearance company Dyno-rod sent Michael Cattran to investigate.

Cattran quickly determined that the problem was not inside the house, but on the outside. Locating the manhole that led to the sewers at the side of the house, he removed the cover and climbed in. At the bottom of the access shaft he saw a glutinous, grey sludge, which smelled awful. As he was examining it more sludge came out of the pipe that led from the house. He called his manager and told him that he thought that the substance that he had found had originally been human flesh.

On the following morning Cattran and his boss returned to the man-hole, only to find that the sludge had vanished. No amount of rainfall could have flushed it away, which meant that someone must have gone down there and removed it. Cattran put his hand inside the pipe that connected the sewer to the house and pulled up some meat and four small bones. One of the tenants living in the house told them that they had heard footsteps on the stairs during the night and that they suspected that the man who lived in the attic flat had been down to the man-hole. They then called the police.

Detective Chief Inspector Peter Jay took the flesh and bones that Cattran had recovered to Charing Cross Hospital, where a pathologist confirmed that the flesh was indeed human. The tenant of the attic flat was still at work when Jay visited Cranley Gardens, but when Nilsen returned at 5.40pm Jay met him at the front door and introduced himself, saying that he had come about the drains. Nilsen remarked that it was odd that the police should be interested in drains, prompting Jay to explain that the drains contained human remains. 'Good grief! How awful', exclaimed Nilsen. Jay told him to stop messing about and asked 'Where's the rest of the body?' After a short pause Nilsen replied 'In two plastic bags in the wardrobe next door. I'll show you'. He then pointed out the wardrobe to Jay, the smell that emanated from it confirming what he was saying. 'I'll tell you everything'. Nilsen said. 'I want to get it off my chest, not here, but at the police station.'

The police could scarcely believe their ears when Nilsen admitted killing 15 or 16 men. In the wardrobe in Nilsen's flat, however, they found two large, black, dustbin bags, one of which held a shopping bag containing the left side of a chest and an arm. A third held a torso which had no arms, legs or head, while a fourth was full of human offal. The unbearable stench indicated that the bags had been closed for some time. In the second dustbin were two heads – one whose flesh had been boiled away, the other largely intact – and a torso, whose arms were still attached to it although the hands were missing. One of the heads belonged to Stephen Sinclair (Nilsen had severed it four days earlier and had started to simmer it in a pot on the kitchen stove). The police found Sinclair's pelvis and legs under a drawer in the bathroom. There was another torso in a tea chest in Nilsen's bedroom, along with a skull and more bones. The police also examined the garden at 195 Melrose Avenue, where they identified human ash and enough fragments of bone to determine that at least eight people, and probably more, had been cremated there.

Nilsen was eventually charged with six counts of murder and three of attempted murder. His solicitor had one simple question for Nilsen: 'Why?' 'I'm hoping you will tell me that', Nilsen replied.

Nilsen had intended to plead guilty, in order to spare the jury and the victims' families the details of his horrendous crimes, but his solicitor instead persuaded him to claim diminished responsibility. He was sentenced to life imprisonment, with the recommendation that he serve at least 25 years.

Jeffrey Dahmer

Like Dennis Nilsen, the Milwaukee mass murderer Jeffrey Dahmer kept the corpses of his victims lying around his home. He went one step further than Nilsen, however,: in an effort to possess them more completely he began eating their flesh, reasoning that they would thus become a part of him and therefore stay with him forever.

Dahmer began his murderous career at the age of 18, at a time when his parents were going through an acrimonious divorce. Dahmer was alone in the house, feeling very neglected. He therefore went out to look for company and picked up a hitchhiker, a 19-year-old youth named Stephen Hicks who had spent the day at a rock concert. They got on well and Dahmer took Hicks back to his parents' house, where they had a few beers and talked about their lives. When Hicks said that he had to go Dahmer begged him to stay, but Hicks was insistent, so Dahmer made him stay by picking up a heavy dumbell, clubbing him around the head with it and then strangling him.

Dahmer dragged Hick's body into the crawl space under the house and dismembered it with a hunting knife (he had had plenty of practice because his childhood hobby had been dissecting animals). Even though he had wrapped Hicks' body parts in plastic bags the stench of rotting flesh soon permeated the house, so that night Dahmer buried them in a nearby wood. Becoming afraid that local children would find the grave, he then dug up them up again, stripped off the flesh and pulverised the bones with a sledgehammer before scattering the remains around his garden and the neighbouring property. It would be ten years before Dahmer would kill again.

After that Dahmer moved to Milwaukee to live with his grandmother. A loner, he hung out in gay bars. If another customer chatted him up he would slip drugs into their drink and they would often fall into a coma. Dahmer made no attempt to rape them – he was simply experimenting – but when the owner of the Club Bar ended up in hospital Dahmer was barred from it. In 1986 Dahmer was sentenced to a year's probation for exposing himself and masturbating publicly in front of two twelve-year-old boys. He claimed that he had been urinating and promised the judge that it wouldn't happen again.

Six days after the end of his probation period he picked up the 24-year-old Stephen Tuomi in a gay club and went to the Ambassador Hotel with him to have sex. When Dahmer awoke he found Tuomi lying dead; there was blood surrounding his mouth and bruising around his neck. Dahmer had been drunk the night before and realised that he must have strangled Tuomi; now he was alone with a corpse in a hotel room and at any moment a porter would be checking to see whether the room had been vacated. In a controlled state of panic he rushed out and bought a large suitcase, into which he stuffed Tuomi's body before taking it back by taxi to his grandmother's house, the taxi driver even helping him to drag the heavy case inside. Dahmer then cut up the corpse and put the pieces into plastic bags, which he left outside for the refuse collectors. (He performed this task so well that he left no traces at all: when police investigating the disappearance of Tuomi called at the house there was no sign of the body. Dahmer had got away with his second murder.)

Companionship, sex and death were now inextricably linked in Dahmer's mind. Four months later he picked up a young, male prostitute and went back with him to his grandmother's house to have sex in the basement. Dahmer then gave the boy a drink laced with a powerful sedative and when the young man was unconscious he strangled him. He then dismembered the corpse, stripped off the flesh, crushed the bones to powder and scattered the remains. Two months later Dahmer met an impoverished, 22-year-old homosexual and offered him money to perform in a video. Having agreed, the man had oral sex with Dahmer in his grandmother's basement. When it was over Dahmer offered him a drink, drugged and strangled him and finally disposed of the corpse.

Dahmer's grandmother began to complain about the terrible smell that persisted even after the rubbish had been collected; she also found a patch of blood in the garage. By way of explanation Dahmer said that he had been skinning animals there, an excuse that she accepted, although she made it clear that she wanted him to move out. Dahmer consequently found himself a small flat in a run-down, predominantly black, area. On his first night there he lured Keison Sinthasomphone, a 13-year-old Laotian boy, to the flat and drugged him. The boy managed to escape, however, and Dahmer was arrested. Charged with sexual assault and enticing a minor for immoral purposes, he spent a week in jail before being released on bail.

Dahmer could not control his compulsion to kill and while out on bail picked up Anthony Sears, a handsome, 26-year-old bisexual. Fearing that the police were watching his flat, he took Sears to his grandmother's basement instead. After they had sex Dahmer drugged Sears and dismembered his body, disposing of his corpse in the rubbish, but keeping his skull as souvenir.

In court the district attorney pushed for a sentence of five years' imprisonment for Dahmer's assault on Sinthasomphone. For his part, Dahmer's attorney argued that the attack was a one-off offence, continuing that his client was a homosexual and a heavy drinker who needed psychiatric help, not punishment. Dahmer was sentenced to five years on probation, as well as a year on a correctional programme. It did not help, however, for Dahmer was now set in his murderous ways.

After picking up a young stranger in a club he offered him money to pose for nude photographs. Back in Dahmer's flat the youth accepted a drink, which Dahmer had drugged. When he lapsed into unconsciousness Dahmer strangled and stripped him before performing oral sex on the corpse. He then dismembered the body, again keeping the skull, which he painted grey. He picked up another notorious homosexual, known as the 'Sheikh', and did the same to him, except that he engaged in oral sex before drugging and strangling him.

His next victim, a 15-year-old boy who accepted Dahmer's offer of $200 for posing in the nude, was luckier. Although the boy undressed, Dahmer had neglected to drug him before attacking him with a rubber mallet; Dahmer then tried to strangle him, but the boy fought back. Eventually Dahmer calmed down, and after the boy had promised not to inform the police he let him go, calling him a taxi. When he went to hospital for treatment the next day, however, the boy broke his promise and told the police what had happened. But because he begged them not to let his foster parents find out that he was a homosexual they dropped the matter.

The next time that Dahmer picked up a victim, a few weeks later, he craved more than his usual formula of sex, murder and dismemberment, having decided to keep the skeleton and to bleach it with acid. Although he dissolved most of his victim's flesh in acid he left the biceps intact and stored them in the fridge. When his neighbours began to complain about the smell of putrifying flesh that was coming from Dahmer's flat he apologized, saying that his fridge was broken and that he was waiting to have it fixed.

Dahmer's next victim, the 23-year-old David Thomas, was not gay. Although he had a girlfriend and a three-year-old daughter he nevertheless accepted Dahmer's offer to come back to his flat for money. After drugging him Dahmer realised that he did not fancy his latest pick-up, but killed him anyway, fearing that Thomas might otherwise cause trouble when he woke up. This time he took more pleasure in the dismemberment process, photographing it step by step.

The 19-year-old Curtis Straughter, an aspiring model, was engaged in oral sex with Dahmer when the sleeping potion took effect. Dahmer strangled him and again photographed his dismemberment; his skull was also kept as a trophy. The 19-year-old Errol Lindsey's murder proceeded along exactly the same lines, Dahmer offering him money to pose for nude photographs before drugging, strangling and dismembering him. The grisly process was once again recorded photographically and his skull was added to Dahmer's collection. The 31-year-old deaf-mute Tony Hughes also accepted $50 to pose in the nude and was duly murdered, but by this time Dahmer had become so blasé about the whole procedure that he kept Hughes' body in his bedroom for several days before cutting it up.

Dahmer's next victim was Keison Sinthasomphone's older brother, the 14-year-old Konerak. As in Keison's case, things went badly wrong for Dahmer, who, after drugging, stripping and raping the boy, went out to buy some beer instead of strangling him. On his way back to the flat Dahmer saw a naked and bleeding Konerak talking to two girls on the street. When Dahmer tried to grab him the girls hung on to Konerak; one of them had called the police and two patrol cars soon arrived.

The police wanted to know what the trouble was about and Dahmer claimed that he and Konerak had had a lover's tiff. He managed to convince them that the 14-year-old Konerak was really 19, and after taking them to his flat showed them Polaroids of Konerak in his under-wear which seemed to back up his story that they were lovers. The police, however, did not realise that the pho-tographs had been taken earlier that day, while Konerak was drugged. Throughout all of this Konerak sat passive-ly on the sofa thinking that his ordeal was over. In fact, it had only just begun: the police accepted Dahmer's story and left, whereupon Dahmer immediately strangled and then dismembered the boy. (The three policemen in ques-tion were later dismissed.)

On one occasion Dahmer was returning home after attending Gay Pride Day in Chicago when he picked up another would-be model, Matt Turner. Turner was also strangled and dismembered at Dahmer's flat. On meeting Dahmer in a gay club the 23-year-old Jermiah Weinberger asked his former roommate whether he should go with him, to which the roommate replied 'Sure, he looks okay'. Dahmer seems to have liked Weinberger, for they spent the whole of the next day together having sex. Then, when Weinberger looked at the clock and said that it was time that he went, Dahmer asked him to stay for just one more drink. His head ended up next to Turner's in the freezer.

When Dahmer lost his job he knew that one thing alone would make him feel better. He accordingly picked up 24-year-old man called Oliver Lacy and took him back to his flat, where he strangled him and sodomised his corpse. Four days later the 25-year-old Joseph Bradeholt – who was married, with two children – accepted Dahmer's offer of money for nude photographs and willingly engaged in oral sex with him. His dismembered torso was left to soak in a dustbin filled with acid.

By the time that Dahmer had killed 17 men – all in much the same way – he was becoming so casual about murder that it was perhaps inevitable that he would be caught. On 22 June 1991 Dahmer met Tracy Edwards, a young man who had just arrived for Mississippi. He was with a number of friends, so Dahmer invited them all to his flat for a party. He and Tracy would go ahead in a taxi to buy beer, he said, instructing the others to follow later. Edwards went along with this plan, but did not realise that Dahmer was giving his friends the wrong address.

When he got there Edwards found that he did not like Dahmer's flat: it smelled funny and there was also a fish tank in which Dahmer kept some Siamese fighting fish. As Dahmer told lurid tales about the fish fighting each other to the death Edwards glanced nervously at the clock as he sipped his cold beer. After he had finished the beer Dahmer gave Edwards a drugged drink of rum and coke. When Edwards became drowsy Dahmer put his arms around him and whispered that they would go to bed. Within an instant Edwards was wide awake and telling Dahmer that it was all a mistake and that he had to be going. Before he knew it, however, his hands had been handcuffed and Dahmer was poking a butcher's knife at his chest while ordering him to undress. Realising the seriousness of the situation, Edwards knew that he had to humour the man, to make him relax, and slowly unbuttoned his shirt.

Dahmer then suggested that they go into the bedroom, and escorted Edwards there at knife point. The room was decorated with Polaroid photographs of naked young men; there were also pictures of dismembered bodies and chunks of meat. The smell in the room was sickening; the putrid aroma seemed to be coming from a plastic dustbin under the window. Edwards thought that he could guess the rest.

Dahmer wanted to watch a video with his captive

friend, so they sat on the bed and watched The Exorcist. The gruesome film made Dahmer relax, while Edwards was frantically thinking of ways in which to escape. If Edwards did not comply with his requests, Dahmer then threatened, he would rip out his heart and eat it. Next he told Edwards to strip so that he could photograph him in the nude. As Dahmer reached for the camera Edwards seized his opportunity and punched Dahmer in the side of the head. When Dahmer crumpled up Edwards kicked him in the stomach and ran for the door. Dahmer managed to catch up with him and offered to unlock the handcuffs, but Edwards ignored him, wrenching open the door and running for his life.

Halfway down 25the Street Edwards spotted a police car and ran over to it, yelling for help. Once inside the car he explained to the policemen that a maniac had tried to kill him and directed them to Dahmer's flat. The door was answered by a well-groomed man who seemed calm and composed; the police began to have doubts about the story that Edwards had told them – that is, until they noticed the strange smell.

A contrite-looking Dahmer admitted that he had threatened Edwards, explaining that he had just lost his job and had been drinking. But when the police asked for the key to the handcuffs he refused to hand it over and became violent, whereupon the policemen pushed him into the flat and forced him to lie face down on the floor while they read him his rights. Then they began to look around the flat, one of them opening the fridge door. 'Oh my God,' he exclaimed, 'there's a goddamn head in here.' Dahmer began to scream like an animal and the police rushed outside to get some shackles with which to restrain him. After that they began their search of the flat in earnest.

They ascertained that the fridge contained meat – including a human heart – in plastic bags. There were three human heads in the freezer. A filing cabinet contained grotesque photographs, three human skulls and a collection of bones. Two more skull were found in a pot on the stove. Another pot contained male genitals and severed hands, while the remains of three male torsos were found in the dustbin in the bedroom.

At the police station Dahmer seemed almost relieved that his murderous spree was over. He made a detailed confession and admitted that he had now reached the stage at which he was cooking and eating his victims' bodies.

Dahmer's cannibalism and necrophilia were the cornerstones of his plea of insanity, but the district attorney pointed out to the jury that if Dahmer were found insane and sent to a mental hospital his case would be reviewed in two years' time, further explaining that if he was then found to be sane he could be released. The jury found Jeffrey Dahmer guilty of 15 murders, for which he received 15 life sentences.

The Candy Man

The Texan town of Houston's Candy Man, the killer Dean Corll, did not realise that he was homosexual until he was drafted into the army at the age of 25. After being discharged 11 months later he went back to work in his mother's sweet factory. Although he was late in recognising the true nature of his sexuality he quickly learnt how to exploit his personal situation and began giving sweets to local boys, also being in a position to hire any boys that he fancied. Furthermore, his mother covered up for him; when one boy complained about Corll's sexual advances she sacked him. For their part, the other teenagers on the workforce made sure that they were never left alone with Corll.

At around that time Corll met a 12-year-old boy called David Brooks, who had a deeply insecure background. Brooks liked Corll, considering him to be good and generous (Corll paid him $5 a time for oral sex.) By the time that Brooks was 15 he was using Corll's flat as his second home. Corll lived in the run-down Heights area of Houston, in which children were always short of money and often high on drugs, making things easy for a predatory homosexual like Corll. Even after the sweet factory closed down Corll continued to be known as the kind man who gave sweets to children; the boys also knew that he gave away money in return for oral sex.

Corll seems to have committed his first murder during this period, for it is thought that he picked up and took home Jeffrey Konen, a 21-year-old student at the University of Texas who disappeared while hitchhiking. Konen's body was discovered three years later on High Island Beach (which later became one of Corll's favourite body-dumping grounds.) It was so badly decomposed that forensic experts were unable to determine the cause of death. It was certainly murder, however, because the body was found bound hand and foot.

In 1970 Brooks visited Corll's flat, where he found two dead, naked boys strapped to a board. Corll, who was also naked, explained that he had killed the boys during sex and offered Brooks a car if he kept quiet. From then on Brooks, who was soon seen driving around in a green corvette, acted as Corll's accomplice, helping to lure boys to Corll's flat, where Corll would rape and kill them while Brooks looked on. Brooks found the whole business highly lucrative, for Corll seemed to have an insatiable desire for young boys and penetrated them anally before strangling them. 'He killed them because he wanted to have sex and they didn't want to', Brooks later explained.

Corll developed a taste for double murders. In December 1970, for example, he picked up the 14-year-old

478

James Glass and the 15-year-old Danny Yates when they were on their way back from church. Glass already knew and liked Corll and had visited his flat before. On this occasion, however, he and his friend ended up being tied to the board before being raped and strangled. Six weeks later the same fate befell the 17-year-old Donald Waldrop and his 13-year-old brother, Jerry.

Then, on 29 May 1971, the 13-year-old David Hilligiest and his friend, the 16-year-old George Winkie, vanished while on their way to the swimming pool. They had been seen together getting into Corll's white van. Although their disappearance was reported the police showed no interest in following up these cases and – like the others who had disappeared before them – listed the two missing boys as runaways. This was not good enough for David Hilligiest's parents, however, who had posters printed offering a $1,000 reward for information about their son's whereabouts. One of the boys who distributed the poster was Wayne Henley, a lifelong friend of David Hilligiest.

Later that summer the Hilligiests' younger son, the 11-year-old Greg, revealed that he had once played an exciting game of poker with David, Wayne Henley and David Brooks, who had once worked at the neighbourhood's sweet factory. David Hilligiest had gone missing once before, his parents then recalled. On that occasion they had found his bike outside the sweet factory and had discovered David inside with the manager, Dean Corll, a nice man who had given him sweets. They still did not put two and two together, however.

It later transpired that sometime before David Hilligiest went missing David Brooks had taken Wayne Henley to meet Corll, guessing that he could be a potential victim. Corll, however, had quickly realised that Henley was a popular boy, and also that he would do anything for money. He soon began paying Henley $200 a time to deliver his friends to him. Henley would sit in the car while Corll cruised the district offering young boys a lift. With one teenager in the car already they felt that it was safe to get in, but would then be driven to Corll's flat to be raped and killed.

Henley soon took over from Brooks as Corll's major source of supply. He subsequently admitted to being present at the murders of at least nine boys and furthermore confessed to killing one himself. Henley had shot the boy in the head, he said, but his victim had not died immediately. When he had looked up at Henley and had said 'Wayne, why did you shoot me?', Henley had pointed the gun at him and had shot him again. Henley had also played an active role in the murder of the 18-year-old Scott Mark, who, unlike the younger boys, was no pushover. Mark had grabbed a knife and had tried to stab Corll, but Corll had disarmed him. Henley had then seized Corll's pistol and had aimed it at Mark while Corll strangled him.

Between them Henley and Brooks regularly supplied Corll with victims aged between nine and twenty. Corll continued to rape and kill the boys singly, as well as in pairs; he sometimes also castrated his victims. The local people were becoming increasingly concerned about their missing children, but still the police did nothing. Indeed, Corll's killing spree only came to an end when Henley made a near-fatal mistake and brought Corll a girl instead of a boy.

Henley had comforted the 14-year-old Rhonda Williams after her boyfriend, the 18-year-old Frank Aguirre, had gone missing (he was another of Corll's victims). She soon considered herself to be Henley's girlfriend and the two decided to run away together. This suited Corll, who was becoming tired of murder and was planning to go straight.

Corll now had a regular boyfriend, Guy, whom he had picked up in a public lavatory before taking him back to his flat, where they had become lovers. When Guy had expressed interest in a locked room in the flat, Corll had vowed that he would never take Guy into it and nothing more was said. Corll also had a girlfriend called Betty Hawkins, whom he had been dating on and off for five years; she had two children, who called Corll 'Daddy'. Corll promised Betty that he would finish with Guy and they then planned to move to Colorado together.

Henley and Rhonda had planned to run away together on 17 August 1973, but Rhonda could not wait and left home nine days early, on 8 August, to join Henley. Henley had invited a friend named Tim Kerley to a paint-sniffing party that was being held at Corll's flat on that night and had no choice but to take Rhonda along. When they arrived Corll was furious: 'You weren't supposed to bring a girl', he yelled.

Corll eventually calmed down and they soon began to get high by sniffing acrylic paint that had been sprayed into a paper bag. Within an hour they had all passed out. When Henley awoke he found that he had been hand-cuffed and bound; the other two youngsters had been tied up as well, and Kerley was naked. Corll was now furious again: 'I'm going to kill you', he told Henley, 'but first I'm going to have my fun'. He then dragged Henley into the kitchen, holding a .22 pistol against his stomach. This was the moment that Henley had long feared would happen: he had always believed that Corll would kill him one day, in order to get his hands on Henley's 14-year-old brother, Ronnie.

Having procured victims for Corll for two years Henley understood him well and knew how to sweet-talk him. He therefore said that he would be willing to partic-ipate in the rape and murder of the other two: Henley would rape Rhonda while Corll had Kerley. Corll agreed to this suggestion and released Henley. They then carried their bound victims into the bedroom, where Corll turned up the radio in order to drown the sound of any screams. Next he gave Henley a knife and ordered him to cut away Rhonda's clothing. After that Corll set about raping Kerley, but when Kerley began to struggle Rhonda grew distressed. 'Why don't you let me take her out of here?' Henley asked Corll. 'She doesn't want to see that.' But Corll ignored him, so Henley grabbed Corll's pistol and told him that they were going. 'Go on Wayne, kill me, why don't you?' taunted Corll, whereupon Henley pulled the trigger and hit Corll in the head with a bullet, causing him to stagger forward a few paces. When Henley fired again Corll fell through the bedroom door and Henley then emptied the clip full of bullets into his back.

After he had untied the other two they called the police. When they arrived Henley admitted to killing Corll and the others vouched for him – after all, he had done it to save them, they believed. A chance remark of Henley's alerted the police to the true story, however: he had told Kerley that if he hadn't been his friend he would have got $1,500 for him. The police then found a 17-inch-(43-centimetre) long dildo in Corll's flat, along with other tools of the sadist's trade. Inside his white Ford van they also discovered rings, hooks and lengths of rope.

When questioned about all of this Henley confessed that he had taken money from Corll in return for procuring boys for him, furthermore admitting that he and Corll had also killed boys. There were a lot of them buried in a boat shed that Corll had hired three years earlier, Henley volunteered, later helpfully taking the police to it. Inside they found some possessions belonging to the missing boys, as well as bags of lime. They then started digging up the floor and soon the naked bodies of 17 boys were revealed. They had been bound and gagged; their genitals had sometimes been buried separately; and there were also body parts that did not belong to any of the 17 victims. Henley then told the police that more bodies were buried around lake Sam Rayburn, as well as to the south, at High Island Beach. Twenty-three bodies were found in all; although Henley said that two more bodies were buried on the beach they were never located.

Brooks was surrendered to the police by his father. When Henley saw him he told him that he had confessed and warned him that if he, Brooks, did not do the same he would recant and blame everything on him. Brooks then admitted everything too.

Twenty-seven bodies had been discovered by the time that the police abandoned the search, but both the extra body parts and the frequency of killing indicated that there were probably at least six or seven more. Forty-two boys were missing from the district in all, although some of them may have been genuine runaways.

The trials of Wayne Henley and David Brooks took place in San Antonio, Texas, in June 1974. Their insanity pleas were rejected and Henley was found guilty of nine murders – not including that of Dean Corll – and sentenced to 594 years' imprisonment. Brooks was found guilty of just one count of murder and was given a life sentence.

The Yorkshire Ripper

Peter Sutcliffe, the Yorkshire Ripper, picked up where his namesake, Jack, left off, like him (or her) specialising, in killing prostitutes. By the time that he was caught 20 women had been savagely murdered. During a reign of terror that spanned nearly six years he managed to elude the biggest police squad that has ever been assembled in Britain to date with the aim of capturing one man.

It started on 30 October 1975, when a Leeds milkman on his rounds saw a shapeless bundle lying on a bleak recreation ground. He went over to investigate and found a woman sprawled on the ground, her hair matted with blood and her body exposed. Her jacket and blouse had been torn open, her bra was rucked up and her trousers had been pulled down, below her knees. There were 14 stab wounds in her chest and stomach. The milkman did not see the massive wound on the back of her head that had actually caused her death. Having been attacked from behind, two vicious blows had been delivered with a heavy hammer, smashing her skull; the stab wounds had been inflicted after she was dead.

The body belonged to a twenty-eight-year-old mother of three, Wilma McCann, who had regularly hitchhiked home after spending nights on the town. She had died just 100 yards (91 metres) from her home, a council house in Scott Hall Avenue. Post-mortem blood tests showed that she had consumed 12 to 14 measures of spirits on the night of her death. Although her clothes had been interfered with, her knickers were still in place and she had not been raped. There therefore seemed to have been no overt sexual motive for her murder. Her purse, however, was missing, so in the absence of any other discernible clues the police regarded her murder as a callous by-product of robbery.

This opinion was reassessed, however, when a second killing occurred in Chapeltown (the red-light district of Leeds) three months later. Not all of the women who worked in the area were professional prostitutes: some women sold sex in order to earn extra cash: others, such as the 42-year-old Emily Jackson, were enthusiastic amateurs who sold their bodies primarily for fun. Emily lived with her husband and three children in the respectable Leeds suburb of Churwell. On 20 January 1976 she and her husband went to the Gaiety pub on Roundhay Road, a popular venue with both Chapeltown regulars like Emily and their prospective clients. After leaving her husband in the main lounge she went searching for business. An hour later she was seen in the car park getting into a Land

Rover. At closing time her husband finished his drink and took a taxi home alone; his wife, he assumed, had found a client for the night.

Emily Jackson's body was found the next morning huddled under a coat on open ground. Like Wilma McCann, although her breasts had been exposed she was still wearing her knickers. She, too, had been killed by two massive blows to the head that had been inflicted by a heavy hammer. Her neck, breasts and stomach had been stabbed over 50 times, her back had been gouged with a Phillips screwdriver and the impression of the heavily ribbed sole of a size 7 Wellington boot was stamped on her right thigh (this was the only real clue). The post mortem indicated that Emily had had sex before the attack, although not necessarily with her murderer. Once again, there seemed to be no clear motive for the killing.

Over a year later, on 5 February 1977, the 28-year-old part-time prostitute Irene Richardson left her tawdry rooming house in Chapeltown half an hour before midnight in order to go dancing. On the following morning a jogger running through Soldier's Field, a public playing field a short car ride from Chapeltown, saw a body lying slumped on the ground. It turned out to be that of Irene Richardson. Because she was lying face down the three massive blows that had shattered her skull were obvious. her skirt and tights had been torn off, her coat had been removed and lay neatly across her thighs. Her neck and torso were studded with knife wounds. The post mortem indicated that she had not had sex before her death and that she had died only 30 minutes after leaving her lodgings.

Following the murder of Irene Richardson the police were able to link the three cases: they were plainly the work of a serial killer. Parallels with Jack the Ripper quickly sprang into the public imagination, and the murderer of Wilma McCann, Emily Jackson and Irene

Richardson soon became known as the 'Yorkshire Ripper'.

It was obvious that the Yorkshire Ripper was preying on prostitutes in Leeds, so the working women of Chapeltown moved in droves to Manchester, London and Glasgow, while those who could not afford to travel so far from began plying their trade in nearby Bradford. The Yorkshire Ripper's next victim. Patricia 'Tina' Atkinson, however, was a Bradford girl who lived in Oak Lane, just around the corner from the city's thriving red-light district. On the evening of 23 April 1977 Tina went to her local pub, The Carlisle, for a drink with friends and reeled out shortly before closing time. When nobody saw her the next day it was assumed that she was at home, sleeping off the effects of the previous night.

The following evening some friends visited her flat and found the door unlocked. Inside, they discovered her covered with blankets lying dead on her bed. It seemed that she had been attacked as she had entered the flat. Four hammer blows had smashed in the back of her head and she had then been flung on to the bed, after which her clothes had been pulled off. She had been stabbed in the stomach seven times and the left side of her body had been slashed to ribbons. There was also a size 7 Wellington-boot print on the sheet.

The footprint belonged to Peter Sutcliffe, who believed that he was on a moral crusade to rid the streets of prostitutes. The eldest of John and Kathleen Sutcliffe's six children, he was born in Bingley, a dour-looking town 6 miles (10 kilometres) north of Bradford. A timid child and later an inscrutable young man, he was always regarded as something of an outsider. Being small and weedy he had been bullied at school and clung to his mother's skirts. Although his younger brothers had inherited their father's appetite for life, the opposite sex and the consumption of large quantities of beer, Peter liked none of these things. Despite taking no interest in girls, as an adolescent he spent hours preening himself in front of the bathroom mirror and later took up body-building.

After leaving school at 15 he took a job as a grave-digger at a cemetery in Bingley and regularly joked about having 'thousands of people below me where I work now'. During his three years as a grave-digger he developed a macabre sense of humour. He once pretended to be a corpse, for example, lying down on a slab, throwing a shroud over himself and making moaning noises when his workmates appeared. For their part they called him 'Jesus', because of his biblical-looking beard. At this trial Sutcliffe claimed that he had heard the voice of God while working at the cemetery. He said that he had been digging a grave when he had heard a voice emanating from a cross-shaped headstone telling him to go out on to the streets and to kill prostitutes .

Despite the youthful Sutcliffe's good looks girls were not attracted to him. His first proper girlfriend was Sonia, a 16-year-old schoolgirl whom he had met in his local pub who suffered from the same type of introversion as Sutcliffe. On Sundays they would sit lost in conversation in the front room of her house. She would speak to other members of the Sutcliffe family only when it was absolutely unavoidable.

As a devout Catholic Sutcliffe was devastated when he learned that his mother was having an affair with a neighbour, a local policeman. His father arranged for all of his children – including Sutcliffe, who was accompanied by his bride-to-be, Sonia – to be present at a Bingley hotel to witness a humiliating confrontation with his wife. Having arrived at the bar believing that she was meeting her boyfriend, only to be greeted by her husband and children, Kathleen was then forced to show the family the new nightdress that she had bought for the tryst. This incident was particularly painful for Sutcliffe, who had earlier discovered that Sonia also had a secret boyfriend.

Later in the same year, 1969, Sutcliffe carried out his first-known attack, following a row over a £10 note, hitting a Bradford prostitute over the head with sock containing a stone. Psychiatrists later said that the discovery of his mother's affair had triggered his psychosis.

After a courtship lasting eight years Sutcliffe and Sonia were married. After spending the first three years of their married life living with Sonia's parents they then moved to a large, detached house in Heaton (a middle-class suburb of Bradford), which they kept immaculate.

On the evening of Saturday, 25 June 1977 Sutcliffe gave his wife a lift to the Sherrington nursing home where she worked at nights. With his neighbours, Ronnie and Peter Barker, he then went on a pub crawl around Bradford, ending up at the Dog in the Pound. At closing time they went to get some fish and chips. It was well past midnight when Sutcliffe dropped the Barker brothers at their front door, but instead of parking his white Ford Corsair outside his house Sutcliffe drove off down the main road, towards Leeds. At around 2am, illuminated by the street light s of Chapeltown Road, he saw a young woman wearing a gingham skirt. As she passed the Hayfield pub and turned left, down Reginald Terrace, Sutcliffe parked his car, got out and began to follow her down the quiet side street.

The next morning a girl's body was found lying next to a wall by a group of children on their way to a nearby adventure playground. She had been struck on the back of the head, dragged for 20 yards (18 metres) and then hit twice more. She had also been stabbed once in the back and repeatedly through the chest – the trademarks of the Yorkshire Ripper were unmistakable. But the victim had not been a prostitute: Jayne McDonald was only 16 and had just left school to work in the shoe department of a local supermarket. On the night of her death she had been out with friends in Leeds and was on her way back to her parents' home (which was just a few hundred yards from where her body was found) when she was attacked.

The murder of a teenage girl gave the investigation new impetus. By the September of 1977 the police had interviewed almost 700 local residents and had taken 3,500 statements, many of them from prostitutes who worked in the area.

The investigation's staff was subsequently increased to 304 full-time officers, who had soon interviewed 175,000 people, taken 12,500 statements and checked out 10,000 vehicles. Their main problem was that they had no idea of the type of man for whom they were looking. It is furthermore doubtful whether anyone would have suspected the long-distance lorry driver Peter Sutcliffe. The 31-year-old was a polite and mild-mannered neighbour, a hard-working and trusted employee, a good son and a loyal husband. He was the sort of man who did jobs around the house or tinkered with his car at weekends. Nothing about him suggested that he picked up prostitutes, although that was what he regularly did.

On Saturday, 1 October 1977 Jean Jordan climbed into Sutcliffe's new, red Ford Corsair near her home in Moss Side, Manchester. She took £5 in advance and then directed him to some open land 2 miles (3 kilometres) away that was used by prostitutes when entertaining their clients. They were a few yards from the car when Sutcliffe smashed a hammer on to Jean's skull, hitting her again and again – 11 times in all. He then dragged her body into some bushes, but before he could proceed further another car arrived and he made a quick getaway.

As he drove back to Bradford Sutcliffe realised that he had left a vital clue on his victim's body: the £5 note that he had given Jean was brand new; it had come directly from his wage packet and could therefore link him to the dead woman. He waited nervously for eight long days. During that time, however, nothing appeared in the press about Jean's body having been found, so he risked returning to Moss Side to try to recover the £5 note. Despite a frantic search he could not find Jean's handbag, and in his frustration he started to mutilate her body with a broken pane of glass. He even tried to saw off her head in an attempt to remove his hammer-blow signature, but the glass was not sharp enough to sever her spine. In the end he gave up, kicked the body several times and then drove home.

On the following day an allotment-owner discovered Jean's naked body. The damage to her head had rendered her unrecognisable and there was no evidence among her scattered clothing with which to identify her. (She was eventually identified from a fingerprint on a lemonade bottle that she had handled before leaving home for the last time.) The police did, however, find the £5 note and immediately set about tracing it. Over the next three months they interviewed five-thousand men, one of whom was Sutcliffe, but when the detectives saw Sutcliffe's well-appointed house they discounted him from their inquiries.

Sutcliffe's next victim was the 18-year-old Helen Rytka, who shared a miserable room next to a flyover in Huddersfield with her twin sister, Rita. Both were prostitutes who worked as a pair in the red-light district around Great Northern Street. Because the Yorkshire Ripper's murders had scared them they had devised a system which they hoped would keep them safe. Basing themselves outside a public lavatory, when one sister was picked up separately the other wrote down the number of the client's car; after giving their clients precisely 20 minutes they then returned to the lavatory. Ultimately, however, this system went terribly wrong.

On the snowy night of Tuesday, 31 January 1978 Helen returned to their usual rendezvous five minutes early. At 9.25pm a bearded man in a red Ford Corsair offered her the chance of making a quick £5, which she accepted, thinking that she could perform her services quickly and be back at the rendezvous before Rita returned.

Helen took her client to the nearby Garrard's timber yard. Because two men were already there Sutcliffe could not kill her straightaway and instead had sex with her in the back of the car. By the time that they had finished the men had gone, so as Helen got out of the back seat to return to the front of the car Sutcliffe swung at her with his hammer, but missed, hitting the door of the car. His second blow, however, struck her on the head and he then hit her five more times until the walls of the foreman's shed, which was just a few feet away, were spattered with blood. After that Sutcliffe dragged Helen's body into a woodpile and hid it. Her bra and black, polo-neck pullover had been pushed above her breasts; although she was still wearing her socks the rest of her clothes were scattered over a wide area. Her black-lace knickers were found pinned to the shed door by a lorry driver the next day.

Rita, who had waited for her sister at the lavatory, was desperately worried when she did not appear, but her fear of the police prevented her from reporting Helen's disappearance for three days. It was a police Alsatian that found the hidden body; Helen had been horribly mutilated and there were three gaping wounds in her chest, where she had been repeatedly stabbed.

The Yorkshire Ripper's latest victim had disappeared from a busy street, and the police later traced over a hundred passers-by, eliminating all but three cars and one stocky, fair-haired man from their inquiries. Although they appealed on the radio to any wife, mother or girlfriend who suspected that they were living with the Ripper to come forward no one did.

A few weeks later a passer-by spotted an arm sticking out from under an overturned sofa on wasteland in Bradford's red-light district. After initially thinking that it belonged to a tailor's dummy the putrid aroma that emanated from it sent him rushing to a telephone. The body was that of the 22-year-old Yvonne Pearson, a high-class prostitute who serviced the rich-businessmen trade in most of Britain's cities. She had been murdered two months earlier, ten days before Helen Rytka, and the killing bore all of the hallmarks of the Yorkshire Ripper. A hammer blow to the head had smashed her skull. Her bra and pullover had been pulled up, exposing her breasts, and her chest had been repeatedly jumped on. Her black, flared trousers had been tugged down and some of the sofa's horsehair stuffing had been rammed into her mouth.

Friends reported that Yvonne had spoken of her fear of the Yorkshire Ripper only days before she had disappeared. On the night of her death she had left her two daughters with a neighbour and was seen climbing into a car driven by a bearded man with black, piercing eyes shortly after 9.30pm. Sutcliffe had killed her with a hammer on wasteland in nearby Arthington Street and had then dragged her body to the abandoned sofa, jumping on her corpse until her ribs cracked. Although he had hidden her body the police deduced that the killer had become concerned when it had not been found because he had later returned in order to make it more visible, tucking a copy of the Daily Mirror, dated four weeks after her death, under her arm.

Two months after Yvonne Pearson's body was found the Yorkshire Ripper attacked the 41-year-old Vera Millward. A Spanish-born mother of seven children, Vera had come to England following World War II as a domestic worker. She lived with a Jamaican man and had resorted to prostitution in Manchester's Moss Side in order to earn money to help to support her family. On the night of Tuesday, 16 may 1978 she left home for the Manchester Royal Infirmary to get painkillers to ease her chronic stomach pains. She died in a well-lit part of the hospital grounds, Sutcliffe hitting her three times on the head with a hammer and then slashing her across the stomach. Her corpse was discovered by a gardener the next morning, lying on a rubbish pile in the corner of the car park.

Three months later the police again visited Sutcliffe, this time because his car-registration number had cropped up during checks, carried out in Leeds and Bradford. They subsequently returned to question him about the tyres on his car. (They were looking for treads that matched the tyre tracks found at the scene of Irene Richardson's murder 21 months earlier.) As always, Sutcliffe was helpful and unruffled, giving them absolutely no reason to suspect him. Indeed, they didn't even think it worth asking Sutcliffe what his blood group was – the Yorkshire Ripper's was rare – or for his shoe size, which was unusually small for a man.

Suddenly the Yorkshire Ripper's killing spree stopped: for 11 months there were no more murders. The police speculated that he had committed suicide, taking his identity to the grave with him. It was all eerily similar to the disappearance of Jack the Ripper 90 years earlier.

Sutcliffe was not dead, however, nor could he suppress his desire to murder for much longer. On the night of Wednesday, 4 april 1979 he drove to Halifax, getting out of his car at around midnight and accosting the 19-year-old Josephine Whitaker as she walked across Saville Park playing fields. They spoke briefly, and as they moved away from the street lights he smashed in the back of the head with a hammer and dragged her body into the shadows. Her body was found the next morning.

In common with Jayne McDonald, Josephine Whitaker was not a prostitute. She lived at home with her family and worked as a clerk at the headquarters of the Halifax building society. After her murder no woman felt safe on the streets of Yorkshire after dark.

Two weeks before Josephine Whitaker died a letter arrived at Bradford's police station; it was postmarked Sunderland and dated 23 March 1979. The letter said that the next victim would not be killed in Bradford's Chapeltown district because it was 'too bloody hot there' as a result of the efforts of the 'cursed coppers'. This odd misspelling so closely aped Jack the Ripper's notes that it should have rung warning bells, but the police believed it to be genuine. Handwriting experts confirmed that it had been written by the same person who had sent two previous letters purporting to come from the Yorkshire Ripper. This one furthermore mentioned that Vera Millward had stayed in hospital, information that the police (wrongly) believed could only have been gleaned from Vera herself. On this basis they concluded that the writer of the three letters was indeed the Yorkshire Ripper.

Traces of engineering oil had been found on one of the letters and similar traces were now discovered on Josephine Whitaker's body. Next the police called a press conference asking members of the public to come forward with any information that they might have about anybody who could have been in Sunderland on the days on which the letters were posted. Although the response was overwhelming it ultimately produced merely more useless information that had to be checked, analysed and filed.

Then, on the morning of 18 June 1979, two months after Josephine Whitaker's death, a buff-coloured envelope, addressed in the same handwriting as the previous letters that the Yorkshire Ripper had allegedly sent, arrived at the police station. The envelope contained an audio cassette on to which had been recorded a 257-word message delivered in a broad Geordie accent. A huge publicity campaign was mounted and the public was invited to dial up and listen to the 'Geordie Ripper tape' in the hope that someone might recognise the voice. Within a few days more than 50,000 people had called in. Even though lan-

guage experts had confirmed that the accent was gen-
uinely Wearside and had pinned it down to Castletown
the police could still not find their man – a cruel hoaxer
who had a cast-iron alibi. The identity of the Geordie
Ripper remains a mystery to this day.

In July 1979 Detective Constable Laptew again visited
Sutcliffe, whose car had by now been spotted in the red-
light district of Bradford on 36 separate occasions. Laptew
became increasingly suspicious of Sutcliffe, but because
the police force's attention was focussed on the Geordie
Ripper tape at that time his report was not followed up
and Sutcliffe therefore remained free to return to Bradford
to dispatch his eleventh victim.

On Saturday, 1 September 1979 Sutcliffe was cruising
the streets around Little Horton, a residential area of
Bradford, when, at about 1am, he saw Barbara Leach, a
student, moving away from a group of friends outside the
Manville Arms. He attacked her when she was just 200
yards (183 metres) from the pub, dragging her into a back
yard before stabbing her eight times. He then stuffed her
body into a dustbin and slung an old carpet over it; it was
discovered the following afternoon.

Two high-ranking officers from Scotland Yard were
sent to Yorkshire, but made no progress. Although a police
task force from Manchester reviewed the £5-note inquiry
and narrowed the field down to 270 suspects it, too, could
get no further.

Like everyone else in Yorkshire Sutcliffe spoke to his
family and friends about the Ripper. He made a point of
picking up Sonia from work in order to protect her and
was later reported to have told a workmate 'Whoever is
doing all these murders has a lot to answer for'. On one
occasion his colleagues at the depot even made a bet that
Sutcliffe himself was the Yorkshire Ripper, at which he
laughed, but said nothing.

The Yorkshire Ripper now took another break from

killing, which lasted for nearly a year. Then, on Thursday, 18 August 1980, he struck for the twelfth time. His victim was Marguerite Walls, a 47-year-old civil servant who had been working late at the Department of Education and Science in Leeds that evening, leaving at 10pm to walk home. Her body was discovered two days later, under a mound of grass clippings in the garden of a magistrate's house. She had been bludgeoned and strangled, but because her body had not been mutilated the police did not at first realise that she was another of the Ripper's victims.

Three months later, after he had just finished eating a chicken dinner, Sutcliffe saw Jacqueline Hill, a language student at the University of Leeds, getting off the bus outside a Kentucky Fried Chicken fast-food restaurant. His fingers were still greasy from his supper when he viciously struck her down before dragging her body to some waste ground behind the shops and attacking it savagely. Death had befallen Jacqueline so suddenly that one of her eyes had remained open, and Sutcliffe now stabbed it repeatedly with a rusty Phillips screwdriver that he had sharpened into a fine point.

The Home Office appointed a special squad with which to try solve the case, but only six weeks after Jacqueline Hill's murder it reached the same conclusion as had the West Yorkshire police force – it had no idea of how to crack the case. What it needed was a bit of luck.

On 2 January 1981 Sergeant Robert Ring and Police Constable Robert Hydes started their evening shift by cruising along Melbourne Avenue, in Sheffield's red-light district. On seeing Olivia Reivers climbing into a Rover V8 3500 they decided to investigate. The driver – a bearded man – identified himself as Peter Williams. After saying that he did not want any trouble he scrambled out of the car and asked if he could relieve himself. When the policemen agreed he went over to the bushes that lined the street and dropped a ball-peen hammer and sharp knife from a special pocket in his car coat while pretending to urinate. The policemen did not notice him doing this while Olivia Reivers was remonstrating loudly with them, complaining that they were ruining her livelihood.

By the time the man strolled back to his car, however, the police had discovered that the car's number plates were false. He was accordingly taken to the police station, where he admitted that his name was really Peter William Sutcliffe. During his interview Sutcliffe said that his main concern was that the police would tell his wife that he had been picked up with a prostitute. Otherwise he was calm and forthcoming and readily confessed that he had stolen the number plates from a scrapyard in Dewsbury. He was even allowed to go to the lavatory alone, where he hid a second knife in the cistern.

There was no concrete reason to suspect Sutcliffe of being the Yorkshire Ripper, but the police working on the case had so little to go on that when any man was caught with a prostitute his details had to be forwarded to the West Yorkshire police before he could be released. Sutcliffe was thus locked up for the night before being released, to a Dewsbury police station the next morning.

In Dewsbury Sutcliffe proved himself to be a chatty and eager interviewee. Indeed, he was so full of himself he made two fatal mistakes: in passing, he mentioned that he had been interviewed by the Yorkshire Ripper Squad about the £5 note and that he had also visited Bradford's red-light district.

The Dewsbury police next called the Yorkshire Ripper Squad in Leeds, where Detective Sergeant Des O'Boyle discovered that Sutcliffe's name had come up several times during the course of the investigation. Having driven to Dewsbury, when O'Boyle called his boss, Detective Inspector John Boyle, in Leeds that evening, he told him that Sutcliffe's blood group was B – the rare blood group that the police knew the Ripper shared. Sutcliffe was accordingly locked into his cell for a second night.

Meanwhile, Sergeant Ring had heard one of his colleagues casually mentioning that the man whom he had arrested was being interviewed by detectives from the Yorkshire Ripper Squad. After rushing back to Melbourne Avenue he found the ball-peen hammer and knife that Sutcliffe had hidden in the bushes. Sonia Sutcliffe was furthermore questioned and their house was searched. Early in the afternoon of the next day O'Boyle told Sutcliffe that they had found a hammer and knife in Sheffield, whereupon Sutcliffe, who had been talkative up to this point, fell silent. 'I think you're in trouble, serious trouble', said O'Boyle. Sutcliffe finally spoke: 'I think you are leading up to the Yorkshire Ripper', he said. O'Boyle nodded. 'Well,' said Sutcliffe, 'that's me.'

Sutcliffe's confession took almost 17 hours to complete. He said that he had begun killing after a Bradford prostitute had cheated him out of £10 in 1969. (He mentioned nothing about hearing the voice of God at that stage.)

Sixteen weeks later Sutcliffe stood trial at the Old Bailey. The Crown Prosecution Service's barrister, the defence counsel and the attorney general, Sir Michael Havers, had all agreed that Sutcliffe was mentally ill, and that he was suffering from paranoid schizophrenia. The presiding judge would have none of this, however, and told both counsels that the jury would listen to the evidence and then decide whether Sutcliffe was a murderer or a madman.

Sutcliffe pleaded guilty to manslaughter. During his testimony he remained calm and self-assured, even managing a laugh when he recalled that when he was questioned about the size 7 Wellington boot-print stamped on Emily Jackson's thigh and Tina Atkinson's sheet the policeman who had been interviewing him had not noticed that he was wearing the boots in question. He also claimed that he had been acting on instructions from God to 'clean the streets' of prostitutes.

The jury found Sutcliffe guilty of 13 murders and he was sentenced to life imprisonment, with the recommendation that he should serve at least 30 years.

The Co-ed Killer

One young man's irrepressible sexual appetite – he killed young women and mutilated their bodies for his sexual pleasure – terrorised a small town in the US state of Michigan for more than two years. After he was caught he showed no remorse and was convicted of only one murder, and then only by the flimsiest forensic evidence.

At about 9pm on a warm Sunday in June 1967 Mary Pleszar, an attractive, brunette student, was walking down a street in the small, university town of Ypsilanti when a car pulled over beside her and a young man leaned out to speak to her. An onlooker assumed that he was offering her a lift which she appeared to refuse, whereupon the car drove off. After turning at the next corner, moments later it sped past the girl again and drove into a private driveway. By this time Mary had reached her block of flats and was safe – or so she thought.

On the following day Mary's flatmate phoned her parents to say that Mary had not come home. Concerned, they called the police, who proved unhelpful: Mary was 19 and students often stayed out all night at parties or with boyfriends, they said, to which her parents protested that their daughter was not that sort of girl. On the day after that the police issued a missing-person's report on Mary. Although a witness who responded to it said that he had seen the young man who had offered Mary a lift he was unable to give a detailed description of the youth or of the car that he was driving.

Four weeks later two boys came across a fly-covered mass of rotting meat – which they took to be a deer's carcass – near a secluded lover's lane 2 miles (3 kilometres) north of Ypsilanti. A pathologist subsequently identified it a being human flesh, and more specifically the corpse of a young woman who had been stabbed in the chest more than 30 times. An extensive search of the area failed to uncover the victim's clothes, but the searchers did find one sandal close to the corpse, which Mary's parents identified as belonging to their daughter. Fresh tyre tracks were also found beside the body.

At the funeral home where Mary's body was lying prior to burial the young man was seen again. Having asked the receptionist if he could take a photograph of the body as a memento for his parents the receptionist had replied that that was impossible; it was only when he was going out of the door that she noticed that he was not carrying a camera.

Almost exactly a year later Joan Schell, a 20-year-old art student, left her flat (which was just three streets away from where Mary had once lived) to spend the night with a girlfriend in nearby Ann Arbor. Her flatmate accompanied her to the bus-stop, where they waited for three-quarters of an hour. Then a red car pulled up and a young man, who was wearing an East Michigan University sweatshirt, asked if they wanted a lift. Joan was suspicious at first, but because there were two other men in the back of the car she thought that she would be safe enough. As she climbed into the car she told her flatmate that she would phone her when she arrived in Ann Arbor. She never called.

Five days later Joan's body was discovered rotting in a storm drain. Her blue mini-skirt and whiteslip had been pulled up, round her neck, and she had been raped and then stabbed to death. Although she had been dead for almost a week the pathologist noted that her body had been in the storm drain for less than a day.

Extensive inquiries revealed that Joan had been seen walking with a young man on the evening on which she went missing. The witnesses could not be certain, but thought that the youth was John Norman Collins, a fine football and a baseball player, an honours student and a devout Catholic – in short, a regular, all-American boy. He had a troubled background, however: his father had abandoned his family soon after his son was born and his mother's second marriage had lasted for only a year; her third husband, who adopted John and his older brother and sister, was an alcoholic who beat his wife. Unbeknown to the police, Collins was suspected of stealing $40 from his fraternity house, as well as of other petty thefts. Although he lived directly opposite Joan, when the police interviewed him he claimed that he did not know her.

Ten months later a thirteen-year-old schoolboy saw a suspicious-looking shopping bag in a cemetery. After telling his mother about it she accompanied him to the spot where he had found it, there discovering a girl's body hidden under a yellow raincoat; her skirt had been pulled up and her tights rolled down. The corpse was that of the 23-year-old Jane Mixer, a law student who had been reported missing a few hours earlier. The man whom the press was now calling the 'Co-ed Killer' had struck again.

Four days after that the body of the sixteen-year-old Marilyn Skelton was found lying in a patch of undergrowth. She had been brutally beaten and a tree branch had been jammed into her vagina. The urges that were driving this sexually obsessed serial killer were plainly becoming more urgent, and the police feared that he would soon kill again. Sure enough, three weeks later the corpse of the thirteen-year-old Dawn Basom was discovered lying amongst some weeds. The youngest victim yet, she was wearing only a white blouse and a bra, which had been pushed up around her neck; the rest of her clothes had been strewn over a wide area. She had been strangled with a length of electric flex and her breasts had been repeatedly slashed.

On 9 June 1969 three teenage boys found the body of a girl in her twenties near a disused farmhouse. She had been shot in the head and repeatedly stabbed; her clothes were scattered around her. Pathologists established that she had been dead for less than a day. Although the use of a gun was new, the police were convinced that this killing was the work of the Co-ed Killer. The town was now in a state of panic; a $42,000 reward was offered for information leading to the killer's capture and the police were heavily criticised for not apprehending him. In their defence they argued that they had little to go on.

On 23 July 1969 the 18-year-old Karen Sue Beineman, another student, went missing. She had last been seen in a wig shop buying a $20 hairpiece. There were two foolish things that she had done in her life, she told the shop assistant – one was buying a wig and the other was accepting a lift on a motorbike from the stranger who was waiting for her outside. The assistant agreed that the latter was stupid and took a look at the young man on the motorbike. She had to admit, however, that he looked decent enough.

Four days later a doctor walking near his suburban home stumbled across Karen Sue's naked body, which was lying in a gully. She had been raped and her knickers had been stuffed into her vagina; somewhat strangely, there were hair clippings inside them. The police had already begun to suspect that the murderer returned to the spot where he had dumped each corpse on several occasions, even moving it if he had the chance. Before the news of her death was made public the police therefore replaced Karen Sue's mutilated body with a tailor's dummy and staked out the area. It rained heavily that night, which diminished the visibility, but shortly after midnight an officer nevertheless spotted a man running out of the gully. Although the policeman tried to summon help his radio had been soaked by the rain and failed to work. The man got clean away.

It was then that a young campus policeman put two and two together. The description of the young man on the motorbike that had been circulated reminded him of a member of his fraternity house who had been dropped out of college after having been suspected of stealing. The young man's name was John Collins, and he had already been interviewed by the police. The policeman then showed a photograph of Collins to both the shop assistant from the wig shop and the owner of the shop next door; both identified it as being a picture of the man on the motorbike. After that the policeman went to interview Collins himself, expecting a confession from him; none was forthcoming, however, and Collins was seen by his flatmate emerging from his room and carrying a box that was covered with a blanket. The flatmate caught a glimpse of its contents: a handbag, as well as some women's clothing and shoes.

Police Corporal David Leik had been on holiday with his family and had therefore missed the latest developments in the Co-ed-killer case. After they had returned home his wife had taken some washing to the laundry room in the basement and had noticed that the floor was covered in black spray paint. Only one person had been in the house while they were away: Leik's nephew, John Norman Collins, who had been letting himself in to feed their dog. But why would he paint the basement floor? After receiving an urgent phone call telling him to report to work Leik went to the police station where he was told, to his surprise and disbelief, that Collins was a prime suspect in the Co-ed-killer case.

That evening Leik scraped some of the black paint from the basement floor with a knife; underneath the paint were brown stains, which Leik thought could be blood. Within two hours lab technicians had identified the brown stains as being varnish that Leik had spilled when he had painted some window shutters. A more extensive examination of the basement floor, however, revealed what later proved to be nine tiny blood-stains. Even more significantly, forensic experts discovered some hair clippings lying on the floor next to the washing machine which were subsequently proved to match the clippings that had been found in the knickers that had been stuffed into Karen Sue Beineman's vagina.

Collins was arrested that afternoon. Although he was shaken – and even tearful – he refused to make a confession. A search of his room revealed nothing, his box of gruesome mementos already having been disposed of.

The police knew that Collins ran four motorbikes and funded his activities by means of petty theft. On closer examination, however, it was found that his background was even more disturbed than had first been thought. His sister had become pregnant at the age of 18 and had married the child's father. Although the marriage did not last, when Collins discovered her dating another man he lost control of his temper, beating the man unconscious and hitting his sister repeatedly while screaming that she was a tramp. He furthermore seemed unable to express his sexual feelings in any normal way, and when his girlfriend moved close to him while dancing he chastised her for inciting lustful feelings in him. Later, when his defence attorney was trying to ascertain how well Collins would stand up to cross-examination, he called Collins' mother (who had a new boyfriend, but had not remarried) a 'kept woman', whereupon Collins usually calm demeanour dissolved into uncontrollable rage.

The police case against Collins was still flimsy, so they

began to try to track down Andrew Manuel, Collins' former room-mate, who had committed a number of burglaries with him. Using false names, he and Collins had also once hired a caravan, which they had not returned after their trip – it had been left in Manuel's uncle's back yard in Salinas, California. At around that time the 17-year-old Roxie Ann Philips had vanished from Salinas after telling a friend that she had a date with a man called John, from Michigan, who was staying with a friend in a caravan. Two weeks after her disappearance her body was discovered in a ravine; she had been strangled and her corpse also bore all of the other trademarks of the Co-ed Killer.

Manuel was found in Phoenix, Arizona, and was charged with burglary and stealing the caravan. He knew nothing about the murders, he said, although he did admit to leaving Ypsilanti after he had heard that the police suspected Collins of being the Co-ed Killer. Manuel was sentenced to five year's probation.

Collins went to trial charged only with the murder of Karen Sue Beineman. The prosecution's case centred on the identification of Collins by the wig-shop sales assistant and the hair clippings that were found in Karen Sue's knickers. For his part, the defence counsel questioned the wig-shop assistant's eyesight and contended that the comparison of 61 hairs from the knickers and 59 from the basement floor was insufficient evidence with which to convict a man of murder.

After long deliberation the jury returned a unanimous verdict of guilty and Collins was sentenced to a recommended period of imprisonment of from 20 years to life.

Women Are Doing it For Themselves

Aileen Wuornos never made any secret of the fact that she hated men. When she hung out, drinking and popping pills, in the Last Resort, Hell's Angels' bar in Port Orange, Florida, she would curse all men and boast that she would get even with this rotten, masculine world. For their part, the Hell's Angels put up with her, regarding her as just another outcast – like them – and calling her 'Spiderwoman', on account of the black-leather outfits that she wore.

Wuornos certainly came from a tough background. Her first recollections were of her mother screaming while her alcoholic father administered another brutal beating; when she was five he abandoned his family. Her mother died when she was 14, and by the time that she was 19 she was all alone in the world, her father having died in prison after having been convicted for sex offences and her only brother having died of cancer. Wuornos then took to prostitution and armed robbery. Although she occasionally worked as a barmaid or cleaner, with her love of alcohol and drugs she could never hold down a job for long. More often than not she spent her time hitchhiking around the highways of Florida, sleeping on the beach or at the roadside.

The Last Resort was more of a home to her than anywhere else. She sometimes slept on the porch or in the so-called 'Japanese hanging gardens', from whose trees the Hell's Angels would hang the Japanese motorcycles that they despised. She was known to one and all as a foul-mouthed, ill-tempered drunk.

When Wuornos was 27 she fell in love with the 22-year-

old Tyria Moore. It was a deeply romantic affair and
Wuornos believed that Tyria would put an end to her
loneliness, never abandoning her as all the men in her life
had. She petted and pampered Tyria, stealing in order to
lavish her with luxuries.

In September 1990 Wuornos stole a car for Tyria, but
when the two women took it for a spin down a dirt road
the car went out of control and they subsequently abandoned it. The pair had been spotted, however, and had
been reported to the police. Their descriptions were
entered into the Maion County police computer, which
then linked the two women to six murders that had
occurred in the area. The victims had all been men whose
bodies had been dumped miles from their cars. Each had
been shot exactly nine times and a condom wrapper was
found on the back seat of each of their cars.

Shortly after the incident with the stolen car Tyria left
Wuornos and fled. In January 1991 the police traced her to
Pennsylvania, where they arrested her for car theft. Tyria
then broke down and blamed everything on Wuornos, who,
she said, had enticed Tyria into a life of crime, also murdering and robbing in order to buy expensive gifts for her.

Wuornos was sleeping on the porch of the Last Resort
when she was apprehended. At first she thought that she
was being arrested for a five-year-old firearms' charge,
but when the police dropped the names of the murder victims into the conversation she freely admitted having
killed them.

She explained that she was usually hitchhiking when
her victim stopped his car to offer her a lift, although she
had sometimes pretended that her car had broken down
and that she needed help. Either way, once she had got
into the car she had offered to have sex with the man and
had then asked him to drive to a deserted spot. After having had sex she had then exacted her vengeance on all
mankind, killing her victim and robbing him of his money,

as well as his jewellery.

Even the hardened Hell's Angels were shocked that they had been harbouring a man-slayer in their midst. 'It's scary, man', said Cannonball, the barman at the Last Resort. 'Every one of those guys could have been one of them [Hell's Angels], and we would never have known where it was coming from... Mind you, I sorta think she would not have gone for a biker... we were her only folks... She was a lost soul, like most of us.'

The Night Stalker

On the night of 28 June 1984 the mutilated body of the seventy-nine-year-old Jennie Vincow was found lying spread-eagled on the bed of her one-bedroom flat in the Eagle Rock district of Los Angeles. She had been raped and her throat had been slashed so savagely that she had almost been decapitated; there was blood on the walls of the bedroom and bathroom and her flat had been ransacked. In violent LA, however, it was regarded as just another murder.

Nine months later the killer struck again. Maria Hernandez had just parked her car in her garage in the Rosemeade suburb of Los Angeles and was walking towards her flat when she heard footsteps behind her. On turning around she was confronted by a man holding a gun. Although he aimed the gun at her and pulled the trigger, the bullet miraculously ricocheted off her car keys and dealt her only a glancing blow. Even so, the impact was enough to knock her to the ground, whereupon the gunman stepped over her, giving her a vicious kicking as he did so, and made his way into her flat. Maria then heard a gunshot from inside the flat and staggered to her feet, only to come face to face with the gunman as he ran from the building. 'Please don't shoot me again', she begged, and after freezing momentarily the gunman took to his heels. Inside the flat Maria found her boyfriend, the 34-year-old, Hawaiian-born traffic-manager Dayle Okazaki, lying dead on the kitchen floor. He had been shot through the head.

There was only one clue to the murder: Maria told the police that the gunman was wearing a baseball cap which had the AC/DC logo embroidered on the front of it. AC/DC, an Australian heavy-metal rock band, had recently released an album called *Highway To Hell*, on which a track called 'Night Prowler' appeared. 'Night Prowler' was the *nom d'assassin*, or assassin's name, that Richard Ramirez, the killer responsible for the deaths of Jennie Vincow and Dayle Okazaki, preferred, and he therefore became annoyed when the newspapers insisted on calling him the 'Night Stalker'. Despite having killed Okazaki, his lust for blood was still not satisfied that night, and less than an hour later, when he was on his way home, Ramirez pulled the 30-year-old Tsai Lian Ye, a Taiwanese law student, from her car and shot her repeatedly. She died before the ambulance arrived.

Ten days later Ramirez entered the home of Vincent and Maxine Zazzara, which was half a mile from the San Gabriel motorway. Maxine was a successful lawyer, while Vincent had just fulfilled his lifetime's ambition to open his own pizzeria. Both of them were shot at point-blank range, and Maxine's naked body was mutilated after her death, Ramirez stabbing her repeatedly (the wounds making a pattern resembling a large, ragged 'T') and also gouging out her eyes. The bodies were found by their son, Peter, when he called in at the house on the following day.

On 14 May 1985 Ramirez broke into the home of William and Lillie Doi, shooting the 66-year-old William in the head as he lay sleeping. His wife, the 63-year-old Lillie, who was lying in bed next to William, was beaten repeatedly around the head until she told the intruder where their valuables were hidden. After that Ramirez handcuffed her and ransacked the house before returning to rape her.

A fortnight later Carol Kyle was awoken in her Burbank flat by a torch shining into her eyes, a man pointing a gun at her and dragging her our of bed. Carol's terrified 12-year-old son was handcuffed and locked into a cupboard in the next room before his mother was raped. Despite her ordeal Carol was compassionate towards Ramirez, saying 'You must have had a very unhappy life to have done this to me'. Ramirez, however, shrugged off her compassion, replying 'I don't know why I'm letting you live. I've killed people before.' He then ransacked the flat looking for valuables. Satisfied with the jewellery that he had found, he finally went away, sparing both Carol and her son's life.

At around the same time two elderly women, the 83-year-old Mabel Bell and her 80-year-old sister, Florence Long, an invalid, were attacked in their home in the LA suburb of Monrovia. On 1 June 1985 Carlos Venezuela, a gardener who did chores for the sisters, found Florence lying on her bed in a coma; there was a huge wound over her ear and a blood-stained hammer had been left on the dressing table. The barely conscious Mabel was found lying in a pool of her own blood on her bedroom floor. Both women had been beaten with the hammer, as well as having been cut and tortured – there were even signs that Ramirez had tried to rape the older sister, Mabel. The police concluded that the sister had been attacked two days earlier.

As on previous occasions the culprit had ransacked the house; this time, however, some clues to the attacker's identity were discovered. Along with the hammer, a half-eaten banana was found on the dining table. He had also left what was soon to become his trademark: an inverted pentagram (the encircled, five-pointed star that is used in witchcraft). One was scrawled in lipstick on Mabel's thigh, while another was drawn on Florence's bedroom wall. Tragically, Mabel died six weeks after the attack, but Florence eventually regained consciousness and survived.

Now the Night Stalker's onslaught began in earnest. On the night of 27 June 1985 Ramirez slashed the throat of the 32-year-old Patty Elaine Higgins in her home in Arcadia. The same fate befell Mary Louise Cannon five days afterwards. Three days later, again in Arcadia, Ramirez savagely beat the 16-year-old Whitney Bennett with a crowbar; she survived. On 7 July Ramirez once again turned his attention to Monterey Park (where he had attacked Tsai Lian Yu and the Dois), the 61-year-old Joyce Lucille Nelson being found beaten to death in her home, while the 63-year-old Sophie Dickmann had been raped and robbed in her flat.

On 20 July Ramirez murdered the 66-year-old Maxson Kneiding and his 64-year-old wife, Lela, in their Glendale home before going on to kill the 32-year-old Chainarong Khovananth at his house in Sun Valley. After shooting Chainarong as he lay asleep in his bed Ramirez raped and beat up his 29-year-old wife, Somkid. He furthermore forced Somkid to perform oral sex on him and stole $30,000 in cash and jewellery, before raping her eight-year-old son making her swear in Satan's name that she would not cry out.

Although the police had long ago concluded that they had a serial killer on their hands, their primary problem was that he followed no set *modus operandi*. He killed people with guns, hammers and knives; he raped both children and women – young and old – orally, anally and vaginally; sometimes he mutilated the bodies of his victims after death, but sometimes he didn't.

Some patterns in the Night Stalker's attacks were nevertheless emerging. The killer stalked quiet suburbs away from the city's main centres of crime, where home-owners were less security-conscious, for instance. He also tended to pick houses that were painted in beige or pastel yellow and that were usually close to a motorway. He made his entry through an open window or an unlocked door. Although burglary was clearly one of his motives, he also seemed to enjoy rape and sheer brutality. Pentagrams and other satanic symbols were furthermore commonly left by the killer.

On the night of 5 August 1985 Virginia Peterson, a postal worker, was woken by the sound of an intruder. Sitting up in bed, she cried out 'Who are you? What do you want?', whereupon the burglar laughed and shot her in the face. The bullet entered her cheek, just below her eye, and exited through the back of her head (miraculously, she survived). Her husband, Christopher, who was lying beside her, was woken by the shot and leapt to his wife's defence, which earned him a bullet in the temple. Christopher, who worked as a lorry driver, was, however, a tough guy whom it would have taken more than one small-calibre bullet to subdue. Diving out of bed he chased his attacker. The intruder, who was not prepared for this, panicked and ran.

Like his wife, Christopher Peterson survived the ordeal, although he suffered from partial memory loss thereafter and had to live with a bullet lodged in his brain. For the first time, however, the Night Stalker had been put to flight, although this did not end his violent rampage. Three days later he shot a 35-year-old Asian man and beat up and raped his 28-year-old wife. In common with Somkid Khovananth she was forced to swear by Satan that she would not cry out, but this time he did not molest the couple's two children, apart from tying up their three-year-old son, Amez.

By this time the public state of panic had reached fever pitch in Los Angeles. In the affluent suburbs locksmiths and burglar-alarm outfits were doing a roaring trade, while gun shops quickly sold out of their stock and local residents set up neighbourhood-watch committees. It was now that Ramirez took a holiday and travelled north to San Francisco, where, on the night of 17 August 1985, he shot both the 66-year-old Asian accountant Peter Pan and his 64-year-old wife, Barbara, through the heads in their home in the suburb of Lake Merced. Before leaving the scene of the crime Ramirez drew an inverted pentagram in lipstick on the bedroom wall, underneath it writing 'Jack the knife'. At first the police thought that the Pans' murders were copycat killings, until they discovered that the bullets that had killed the couple matched the small-calibre rounds that had been used in the Los Angeles murders.

A week later Ramirez travelled to the small town of Mission Veigo, south of Los Angeles, where he shot William Carns, a 29-year-old computer engineer, three times in the head before raping his fiancée, Inez Erickson (also 29), twice and ordering her to say 'I love Satan'. 'You know who I am, don't you?' Ramirez tauted. 'I'm the one they're writing about in the newspapers and on TV.' (William Carns survived the shooting, but suffered permanent brain damage. The couple never married.)

Inez had managed to observe Ramirez's rusty, old, orange Toyota leaving the house. James Romero III, a sharp-eyed youth, had also noticed the orange Toyota as it cruised the area and had noted down its licence-plate number. The car would prove to be the vital clue that put an end to the reign of the Night Stalker. After the police had circulated a description, it was found in a car park in LA's Rampart suburb two days later.

Forensic scientists used a radical new technique when examining the car: they put a dab of Superglue on a saucer and sealed the doors and windows before placing the saucer in the car, the theory being that the fumes from the Superglue would react with the moisture contained in any fingerprints in the car and would then turn them white.

The interior of the car was also scanned using a laser beam, which would be able to pick up any fingerprints on the car, including those that the culprit had tried to wipe off. The scan yielded one fingerprint, which a computer matched to a fingerprint belonging the twenty-five-year-old Ramirez, who had been arrested on three previous occasions in El Paso for marijuana possession. Soon afterwards Ramirez's photograph was on the front page of every newspaper in California.

Ramirez was quite unaware of these developments when he stepped off a Greyhound bus at Los Angeles' main bus station. He had been in Phoenix, Arizona, where he had obtained some cocaine, and was now on a high: he had killed 13 people so far and felt good about it – surely, he reasoned, he must be Satan's favourite son.

On going into a shop to buy a Pepsi he saw his face splashed across the Spanish language paper La Opinion that was lying on the counter by the till. He was also recognised by the cashier, as well as by other customers in the shop, causing him to make a run for it. Out on the street someone cried 'It's the Night Stalker' and Ramirez soon heard the wail of police sirens behind him. He knocked on a door, and when Bonnie Navarro opened it he shouted 'Help me' in Spanish. She slammed the door in his face, however. Ramirez tried to pull a woman from her car in the next street, but some bystanders rushed to her rescue. He then jumped over a fence into the garden where Luis Munoz was cooking a barbecue and was hit with Munoz's tongs. In the next garden he was prevented from stealing a red, 1966 Mustang by the 56-year-old Faustin Pinon, who had been working on the car's transmission and now grabbed him in a headlock. Ramirez broke free, but José Burgoin, a 55-year-old construction worker who had heard Pinon's shouts from across the street, picked up a steel rod and hit Ramirez with it. Although Ramirez stumbled away Burgoin soon caught up with him and clubbed him to the ground.

Deputy sheriff Andres Ramirrez pulled up in his patrol car in the nick of time, as far as Ramirez was concerned. 'Save me!' yelled the Night Stalker, commenting as his namesake handcuffed him 'Thank God you came. I am the one you want. Save me before they kill me'. Only the arrival of further police patrol cars stopped the angry mob from taking the law into their own hands, and even outside the police station a crowd soon gathered calling for him to be lynched.

Ramirez showed no contrition for his crimes, explaining to the police:

'I love to kill people. I love watching them die. I would shoot them in the head and they would wriggle and squirm all over the place, and then just stop. Or I would cut them with a knife and watch their faces turn real white. I love all that blood. I told one lady one time to give me all her money. She said no. So I cut her and pulled her eyes out.'

In court he made satanic signs and even appeared with the inverted pentagram scratched into his palm. He told the judge 'You maggots make me sick. Hypocrites one and all. You don't understand me. You are not expected to. You are not capable of it. I am beyond your experience. I am beyond good and evil.'

Ramirez was found guilty of 63 crimes, including 13 murders. He was sentenced to 12 death penalties and over 100 years' imprisonment. When he was on death row many women wrote to him, sending provocative pictures, pledging undying love and even proposing marriage. When Ramirez accepted the proposal of Christine Lee, a divorcee, over that of the nude model Kelly Marquez it made headlines. Christine, a mother of two, bombarded Ramirez with pin-up-style pictures of herself and visited him over 150 times. She was undaunted by the fact that her husband-to-be was a serial killer: 'We really love each other and that's all that matters', she said. 'From the moment I saw him in prison I knew he was special. I couldn't believe he was the evil monster people were calling him. He's always been sweet and kind to me.'

Dr Harold Shipman

Dubbed possibly the most prolific killer of our time, Dr Harold Shipman is currently serving 15 life sentences in Frankland Prison, Durham. The sentences were the result of a highly publicised court case which shocked and horrified Britain.

Dr Harold Shipman began his career in 1974 in Todmorden, West Yorkshire. Three years later, he moved to Hyde in Greater Manchester where he remained until his imprisonment in 2000. In a career spanning 24 years, Shipman is believed to have killed up to 300 'patients'. Although only tried for 15 killings, the lethal doctor is thought to have covered his tracks well. It is only with hindsight that colleagues and police alike are unearthing the awful truth behind his wicked ways.

Shipman seemed to have a 'type' of patient that he would target. They tended to be elderly women who placed their trust in the doctor. Fewer than ten of his victims died in his surgery, the rest were killed at their homes during or after a home-visit by Dr Shipman. He killed his patients by giving them lethal injections and overdoses of drugs, most commonly heroin or morphine. The deaths were quick, simple and easily covered up. At his practices in Todmorden and in Hyde, Shipman's patient death rate was significantly higher than any other practitioner. Although suspicions were raised, no one in the medical fraternity thought it necessary to raise the alarm.

But Shipman's practising irregularities did not go entirely unnoticed. A number of errors on the part of

Shipman were brought to the attention of the police and the General Medical Council (GMC). In 1975, Shipman was made to quit his Yorkshire general practice after stealing, and admitting an addiction to pethidine. He was convicted of fraud and forgery and fined £600 but did not face further disciplinary action; he was permitted to continue his medical career in Hyde. The GMC also decided to take no action when Shipman was reprimanded for bad professionalism in three separate instances of patient cases.

When Shipman established his own practice in 1992, his previous conviction meant that he was not allowed to handle controlled drugs. However, he rapidly developed working relationships with several pharmacies local to his practice; these pharmacies would supply Shipman with any drug he requested if it were done through a prescription form. Shipman was also given drugs such as heroin from the pharmacies if he claimed it was for an emergency case; no one ever checked up afterwards to see if the drugs had been consumed or not.

Harold Shipman was able to continue killing his patients at an alarming rate (his patient death tally was four times a doctor's average) until in March, 1998, a fellow doctor became too suspicious and called the police.

Initial police investigations uncovered evidence of 15 wrongful deaths, and Shipman was duly arrested, tried and convicted of 15 counts of murder. Throughout the legal proceedings, Shipman refused to talk which meant police could only guess at the probable number of patients that he killed.

There are many families who lost loved ones through Shipman's cold killings. If the death tally does stand in the hundreds, there are many more friends and relatives who have unwittingly lost someone at the hands of the lethal doctor.

Leonard Lake and Charles Ng

When a young Chinese man took a vice from a shop without paying for it the sales assistant ran to find a policeman. The officer followed the man to his car, who dumped the vice in the boot before running off when he spotted the policeman. Although the police officer gave chase the youth was too fast for him, and when returned to the car he found a bald, bearded man standing next to it. The man explained that it had all been a mistake: he had now paid for the vice, he explained, and showed the officer the receipt. The policeman was suspicious, however, and examined the car, finding a holdall in the boot containing a .22 pistol, as well as a silencer. (Although it is legal to carry a handgun in the USA adding a silencer is against the law and usually indicates that the gun is likely to be used for some illegal purpose.)

The bearded man's Californian driving licence said that he was called Robin Scott Stapley. He hardly knew the youth who had run away, he told the policeman, but had been about to hire him for a job. Despite his explanation the officer took him to the police station for questioning. once there the man asked for – and received – paper, a pencil and a glass of water. He then scribbled a note to his wife on the paper, which read 'Cricket, I love you. Please forgive me. I forgive you. Please tell Mama, Fern and Patty I'm sorry'. After that he swallowed a cyanide capsule, washing it down with the water. Within seconds he was dead.

The police subsequently discovered that the dead man was not Robin Scott Stapley, who had gone missing five months earlier. A few weeks after his disappearance, however, his camper van, which was being driven by a young Chinese man, had collided with a lorry. Although the young man had begged the lorry driver not to report the accident the latter was driving a company vehicle and therefore had no option but to do so.

It later transpired that the car that the bearded man had driven was registered to a Paul Cosner. When questioned, Cosner's girlfriend said that he had told her that he was selling it to a weird-looking man who had said that he would pay cash for it. Cosner had never returned after he had driven off to deliver the car.

When forensic scientists examined the car they found two bullet holes in the front seat and two spent rounds lodged in the upholstery; there were also bloodstains – human bloodstains – in the car. In the glove compartment they discovered some papers belonging to a Charles Gunnar, of Wilseyville, Calavers County, which was 150 miles (241 kilometres) north of San Francisco.

A call to Wilseyville's sheriff revealed that the Calavers County police already had their eye on Gunnar, as well as his young friend, a Chinese man named Charles Ng. They were suspected of handling stolen goods – videos, television sets, furniture and other household items – and had been selling furniture belonging to Brenda O'Connor and Lonnie Bond. Gunnar had explained to the police that the couple had moved to Los Angeles with their baby and had given Gunnar the furniture in settlement of a debt. There had furthermore been another mysterious disappearance in the area: a young couple had vanished from a camp site at the nearby Schaad Lake, leaving behind their tent, as well as a coffee pot sitting on the stove.

Following a computer check the dead man's fingerprints revealed that his real name was Leonard Lake. Lake had been charged with grand larceny and burglary in Mendocino County and had then jumped bail. It also seemed that he was linked with a number of other disappearances, including that of his younger brother, Donald, who had gone missing two years before, after setting off to visit Lake at a survivalist camp in Humboldt County. Charles Gunnar, the man whose identity Lake was using, had disappeared earlier that year after having acted as best man at Lake's wedding.

The trail inexorably led to the small ranch on Blue Mountain Road where Gunnar – that is, Lake – and Ng lived, and a team of policemen from San Francisco consequently visited it. Set within three acres of wooded grounds, the ranch was an ordinary-looking, two-bedroomed bungalow. Inside, however, it was far from ordinary, for the master bedroom was fitted out like a medieval torture chamber: there were hooks in the ceiling and walls, as well as boxes full of chains and shackles that could be used to immobilise someone who was lying on the bed. There was also a wardrobe full of flimsy nightgowns and sexy underwear, along with expensive video gear. The serial numbers confirmed that the video equipment belonged to Harvey and Deborah Dubbs; following the disappearance of the couple and their 16-month-old baby it had last been seen being carried from their flat by a Chinese removal man.

Lake had been a dedicated survivalist who had built a nuclear-fallout shelter in the garden. Inside the shelter the police found a storeroom containing food, water, candles and guns. Set into the floor was a sinister-looking trapdoor which led to another chamber. This subterranean room was also hung with hooks and chains, and the walls were covered with photographs of frightened-looking girls posing in their underwear. It was clear that all of the pictures had been taken in that very room. Next to this chamber was a tiny cell with a one-way mirror in its wall, which meant that anyone being held inside the room could be subjected to twenty-four-hour surveillance.

The bomb-shelter basement also contained filing cabinets, in which the police found more pictures, as well as a huge collection of video tapes. The first video cassette that they viewed was marked 'Kathy / Brenda'. It began by showing a terrified girl, who was handcuffed to a chair, being menaced by Charles Ng. Then Lake entered the frame and removed the girl's handcuffs, instead shackling her feet, after that ordering the girl to strip. She undressed reluctantly – she could clearly hardly bring herself to remove her knickers, but was forced to do so. 'You'll wash for us,' announced Lake, 'clean for us, fuck for us.' Later she was shown naked, being strapped to the bed and being told by Lake that her boyfriend was dead.

'Brenda' – who was later identified as Brenda O'Connor – also appeared in the video. Shown hand-cuffed to a chair, she entered into a chilling dialogue with Lake while Ng slowly cut her clothes off her. First she asked where the baby was, to which Lake replied that it had been placed with a family in Fresno. 'Why do you guys do this?' she then asked. 'We don't like you. Do you want me to put it in writing?' was the response. 'Don't cut my bra off', she pleaded, to which Lake replied 'Nothing is yours now'. 'Give my baby back to me. I'll do anything you want' Brenda begged, only to be told 'You're going to do anything we want anyway'.

Other videos showed women being shackled, raped, tortured and murdered. They featured all of the missing women of whom the police already knew and others that they recognised from missing-person's reports, along with over 25 more whom they never identified. It was plain that Leonard Lake and Charles Ng had been making 'snuff' movies for two years, for each of the tapes, which were clearly marked 'M Ladies' ('Murdered Ladies'), ended with the death of its reluctant female star.

The police also discovered a bloodstained chainsaw which had been used to cut up the bodies of Lake and Ng's victims; the body parts had then been incinerated and the bones scattered across the hillside at the back of the house. Other bodies were found intact, while in a narrow trench that ran across the garden the police discovered a number of corpses that were too decomposed to identify. Among the latter were the bodies of a man, woman and child, which could have belonged to Bond, O'Connor and their baby, the Dubbs family or, indeed, to any other man, woman and child who had had the misfortune to fall into Lake's gruesome trap. Two weeks of digging produced a total of nine entire bodies and 40 lbs (18 kilogrammes) of human bones. Identifying the corpses themselves was well nigh impossible, but driver's licences and other papers confirmed that Robert Stapley, Paul Conser and the couple from the camping site were all among the victims.

The police found Lake's diary in the files in the basement which indicated that his grisly career of murder had begun long before he moved into the ranch on Blue Mountain Road. Born in San Francisco in 1946, Leonard Lake had been rejected by both parents, being brought up with military discipline by his grandparents. Leonard's brother, Donald, was a sadist who tortured animals and tried to rape his sisters. Leonard protected his sisters, but at a price: they had to perform certain sexual favours for him. He also took nude pictures of his sisters and cousins, later also making pornographic films featuring his wife, 'Cricket' Balazs.

Although he was not the front-line hero that he subsequently claimed to have been, the Vietnam War changed him. Despite disguising his feelings by teaching, becoming a volunteer fire-fighter and doing charity work, he became deeply pessimistic. This pessimism eventually led him to survivalism, as well as to a life financed by petty theft and burglary.

Then Lake's marriage broke up, although his wife still acted as a fence for the credit cards and other items that he stole. After that the idea slowly began to grow in his mind that women were the cause of all his problems. He eventually found the release that he sought by killing his troublesome brother, Donald, whereupon he embarked upon a murder spree. (The police discovered a crude map of California that he had marked with crosses labelled 'buried treasure'. The crosses were believed to represent the graves of his early victims, but the map was too inaccurate for the police to investigate this theory.)

While staying in the isolated village of Miranda, in northern California, Lake came up with the idea for 'Operation Miranda': he planned to stockpile weapons, food, water and kidnapped women in preparation for the nuclear holocaust that he believed was nigh. 'The perfect woman is totally controlled,' he wrote, 'a woman who does exactly what she is told to and nothing else. There is no sexual problem with a submissive woman. There are no frustrations – only pleasure and contentment.' He then put Operation Miranda into practice with the help of Charles Ng.

Ng, the son of a wealthy Hong Kong family, was born in 1961. He was educated at a private school in North Yorkshire before being expelled for theft, thereafter completing his studies in San Francisco. At the age of 18 he was involved in a hit-and-run accident and joined the US Marines in order to escape going to jail. Having been posted to Hawaii, his lifelong kleptomania then reasserted itself and he was arrested for the theft of ammunition and weapons worth over $11,000. After escaping from jail in Hawaii, Ng returned to San Francisco where he met Lake, whom he looked up to. Together they embarked upon a full-time life of crime, later being arrested in Mendocino County for burglary. Ng was imprisoned (also serving time for his earlier theft in Hawaii) and spent some of his sentence at Fort Leavenworth. When he was paroled he joined Lake at the ranch and helped him to transform his paranoid fantasies into brutal reality.

Lake's journal describes how his sex slaves were obtained. Having invited unwitting couples and families to the ranch for dinner the men and children would be murdered straightaway. The women would then be stripped, shackled, sexually abused, humiliated and forced to perform menial chores around the house. Kept in a Spartan cell, they would also be used as the unwilling subjects of sexually sadistic videos. When a woman showed any sign of rebellion against her submissive role – or when her tormentor grew tired of her – Lake and Ng would kill her and film her death.

Psychological studies of Lake showed that he was in the final phase of the serial-murder syndrome when he was arrested: sated with blood, he felt that he had reached the end of a cul de-sac from which there was no way back. Having caused untold misery to others he was now bringing misery upon himself – the only way out was suicide.

Ng escaped to Canada, where he shot a security guard after having been caught shoplifting. He served a four-and-a-half-year sentence for armed robbery before being extradited to California to face charges of mass murder.

Son of Sam

At 1am on 29 July 1976 the 19-year-old Jody Valente and her friend, the 18-year-old Donna Lauria, were sitting in Jody's car outside Donna's home in the Bronx area of New York. It was a hot summer night and they were discussing their boyfriends. Finally Donna said goodnight and opened the car door to get out. As the door opened a young man who was standing a few feet away reached into the brown-paper bag that he was holding, pulled out a gun and dropped into crouching position. 'What does this guy want?' asked the alarmed Donna. The words had just left her mouth when a bullet stuck her in the side of the neck, a second bullet smashing the window in the door and a third shattering her elbow as she raised her hands to protect her face. Fatally wounded, she tumbled out of the car on to the pavement, whereupon her killer shot Jody in the thigh, causing her to fall forward on to the car's horn. As the horn blared the killer made off.

Donna's father, Mike Lauria, who was about to take the dog for a walk, was halfway down the stairs of the family house when he heard the shots. Running outside, he found Jody conscious, though hysterical, and Donna lying collapsed on the ground. In the ambulance he entreated his daughter not to die, but it was too late: when Donna reached the hospital she was pronounced DOA – dead on arrival. Although Jody was treated for hysteria she nevertheless managed to give the police a good description of their assailant: he was a young, white male, about 30 years old, clean shaven, with dark, curly hair. He was not a rejected boyfriend (as the police at first speculated), Jody said – in fact, she had never seen him before. The only other clue to his identity was a yellow car that had been parked near Jody's, but it had gone by the time that the police arrived, and in any case New York is full of yellow cars.

(The car in question actually belonged to David Berkowitz. In the days leading up to the murder he had been looking for a job, but had spent the nights, he later said, 'Looking for a victim, waiting for a signal'. Demonic voices inside his head had told him to kill, he explained. 'I never thought I could kill her', he said of Donna Lauria. 'I just fired the gun, you know, at the car, at the windshield. I never knew she was shot.')

The northern Bronx, where the Laurias lived, is a predominantly Italian area, and the police therefore immediately suspected Mafia involvement in Donna's murder. However, the Mafia are usually scrupulous when it comes to contract killings: women and children are out of bounds. Besides, ballistics tests showed that the murder weapon was a Charter Arms, five-round, .44 Bulldog revolver, which had a powerful recoil and was grossly inaccurate at distances of more than a few yards – hardly a hit man's weapon.

On the other side of the East river from the Bronx lies the Queens area, a comfortable, middle-class district. Twelve weeks after the murder of Donna Lauria, the eighteen-year-old Rosemary Keenan, a student at Queens College, went to a bar in the Flushing of Queens where she met the twenty-year-old record salesman Carl Denaro, who was enjoying his last days of freedom before joining the United Sates Air Force. After having left the bar together in her red Volkswagen, Rosemary and Carl had parked and were talking when a man crept up on them. He may have thought that Carl, who was sitting in the passenger seat, was a woman on account of his long, brown hair. He pulled out the .44 Bulldog handgun that was tucked into his belt and fired through the passenger window five times. His shooting was wildly inaccurate, however, and only one bullet found its mark: as Carl threw himself forward to protect himself from the flying glass the bullet clipped the back of his head, knocking away part of his skull, but not damaging his brain. Although Carl was lucky, in that he recovered completely after a two-month stay in hospital, the metal plate that the surgeons had had to insert into his head ended his air-force career before it had even begun.

On the evening of 27 November 1976 two schoolgirls – the 16-year-old Donna Demasi and her 18-year-old friend, Joanne Lomino – were sitting talking on the front porch of Joanne's home on 262nd Street in Queens. At the end of their conversation Joanne stood up and reached into her handbag for her front-door keys. It was then that the two girls noticed a man walking down the other side of the road. He was acting rather suspiciously: when he saw them he suddenly changed direction. After crossing the street at the corner he came over to them as if he was about to ask for directions, but instead he pulled a gun from his waistband and began firing at them. The two girls ran towards the front door, Joanne frantically search-ing for her keys. The first bullet hit her in the back; the sec-ond lodged in Donna's neck. They stumbled into the bushes as the gunman fired his remaining three shots, all of which missed. He then ran off down 262nd Street and was spotted by a neighbour still holding his gun.

The two wounded girls were rushed to Long Island Jewish Hospital, where Donna was found not to be badly injured (she made a full recovery after three weeks). but Joanne was not so lucky: the bullet had smashed her spinal cord, paralysing her from the waist down, and she would spend the rest of her life in a wheelchair. The neigh-bour who had spotted the gunman making his escape gave the police a description of him: the man had dark curly hair. Strange – because the girls themselves said that he had had long, fair hair. Despite the discrepancy, the description nevertheless linked the shootings of Donna DeMasi and Joanne Lomino to the man who had killed Donna Lauria and wounded Jody Valente.

On 29 January 1977 the 30-year-old John Diel and his 26-year-old girlfriend, Christine Freund, went to see the film *Rocky* in Queens. Afterwards they had dinner at the Wine Gallery, in Austin Street, where they discussed their forthcoming engagement. Soon after midnight the couple walked along several streets to where their Pontiac Firebird was parked. It was cold outside, and once inside the car their breath fogged up the windows. Although they were eager to get home they stopped for a moment to kiss, John then turning the key in the ignition. Before he could pull away, however, he heard the blast of gunfire, whereupon the passenger window shattered and Christine slumped forward, bleeding. She died a few hours later in St John's Hospital of bullet wounds to her right temple and neck. She had never even seen her killer, but he had seen her – and so had the demon within him: Berkowitz later claimed that he had heard a voice commanding him to 'Get her, get her and kill her'. After firing three shots and realising that he had hit her he felt calm again. 'The voices stopped', he said. 'I satisfied the demon's lust.'

After the murder of Christine Freund, Berkowitz surrendered himself completely to his impulse to kill. After all, he reasoned, he was being rewarded by all of the publicity that he was generating: 'I had finally convinced myself that I was good to do it, and that the public wanted me to kill', Berkowitz later explained.

However, the New York Police Department (NYPD) was on his trail. Its ballistics lab had ascertained that the bullet that had killed Christine Freund had come from a .44 Bulldog handgun, which tied it to the murder of Donna Lauria and the shooting of Jody Valente, Carl Denaro, Donna DeMasi and Joanne Lomino. Yet apart from the mention of his dark, curly hair by Jody Valente and the neighbour in the DeMasi-Lomino case the descriptions of the gunman varied so widely that no one in the NYPD had concluded that the shootings were the work of a single individual.

Six weeks later, on 8 March 1977, Virginia Voskerichian, a 19-year-old Armenian student, left Columbia University in Manhattan and set off for her home in Forest Hills, Queens. At around 7.30pm she was nearing her home on Exeter Street when a young man approached her on the pavement. She politely stepped aside, whereupon he pulled out a gun, shoved it into her face and fired. Although Virginia raised her books in a vain attempt to protect herself, the bullet tore through them, entering her body through her upper lip, smashing several teeth and lodging in her brain. She collapsed in the bushes at the side of the street and died instantly. A witness saw a young man running away and later estimated that he was aged about 18 and was 5 feet 8 inches (1.75 metres) tall. No dark, curly hair was noted, however, because the murderer was wearing a Balaclava.

The killer was almost caught that very day. Minutes after Virginia's murder the police put out a 'Code .44' alert and two police officers were assigned to the southern end of the Bronx with orders to stop any car that contained a lone white man. Berkowitz had driven up to the checkpoint with his loaded .44 Bulldog lying in full view of the passenger seat of his Ford Galaxie and was third in line when the police called off the search. He could not believe his luck as he watched the officers walk away.

It was quickly proved that the bullet that had killed Virginia Voskerichian was of a .44 calibre and that the riflings on it matched the marks on the bullet that had killed Christine Freund six weeks before and just a few miles away. Two days later it was established that the same gun was responsible for the shooting of seven people.

On the afternoon of 10 March 1977 a press conference was held at One Police Plaza, the 13-storey, red-stone building that is New York's equivalent of London's New Scotland Yard. As Police Commissioner Mike Codd stood with some trepidation before New York's hard-bitten crime reporters and started to read his carefully prepared statement he had an inkling that he was about to unleash a wave of hysteria that would engulf the city. He began by saying that the murder of Donna Lauria nine months before was linked to the killing of Virginia Voskerichian a mere two days earlier. In both cases, he stated, the killer had used a .44 Bulldog revolver and the same gun had also been used in three other incidents. Worse still, in terms of securing his arrest, the killer apparently chose his victims completely at random. As the reporters pushed for further information Codd revealed that the police were looking for a Caucasian male, about 6 feet (1.83 metres) tall, of medium build, 25 to 30 years old, with dark hair. The .44 killer made the headlines the next day.

The policeman in charge of the investigation was Deputy Inspector Timothy J Dowd. Working under Dowd was Chief of Detectives John Keenan, the father of Rosmary Keenan, who had been in the car with Carl Denaro when he was shot in the head. 'I know he was aiming for her', Keenan subsequently said. 'So let's just say I put a little more than I had to into this case.'

The police realised that their chances of catching a lone, seemingly motiveless, murderer on the streets of New York were remote, so they asked for the help of every New Yorker. As a result, tip-offs jammed the police switch-boards and Dowd and his detectives had to follow up 250 to 300 leads a day. Berkowitz took pity on the police, however, and wrote them a letter, although dropping it into a letter box and letting the postal service deliver it was too mundane an option for him.

On the night of 16 April 1977 another young couple went to a cinema in New York. After the 18-year-old Valentina Suriani and her boyfriend, the 20-year-old Alexander Esau, had seen the film they went on to a party. At around 3am they were sitting in a borrowed Mercury Montego that was parked outside Valentina's block of flats in the northern Bronx, only three streets away from where Donna Lauria had been killed. Valentina was sitting on Alexander's lap, her legs stretched across the passenger seat, enjoying a prolonged series of goodnight kisses when a hail of bullets suddenly shattered the passenger window. Two hit Valentina's head, killing her instantly. Another two struck Alexander on the top of the head as he dived across the seat towards the passenger door; he died two hours later.

When the police arrived they found a white envelope lying in the middle of the road next to the car. It was addressed to Captain Joe Borelli, Dowd's second-in-command. The letter was written in capitals, was full of spelling mistakes and appeared to be the work of a madman. The writer claimed that he had been ordered to kill by his father, who was a vampire. His father's name, the writer said, was Sam (hence the killer's subsequent macabre sobriquet 'Son of Sam'). In the letter he professed to love the people of Queens, but nevertheless stated his intention of killing more of them – particularly the women (he spelt the word as if it rhymed with 'demon'). The writer signed off with a farewell message:

I SAY GOODBYE AND GOODNIGHT. POLICE: LET ME HAUNT YOU WITH THESE WORDS; I'LL BE BACK! I'LL BE BACK!   TO BE INTERPRETED AS – BANG BANG, BANG, BANG, BANG – UGH!! YOURS IN MURDER, MR MONSTER.

By the time that the letter reached the police labs eight policemen had handled it and only tiny traces of the writer's fingerprints remained. He furthermore appeared to have held the letter by the tips of his fingers and there was therefore not enough of a print on the paper with which to identify the sender. Although the police consequently kept the existence of the letter a secret they showed a copy of it to the celebrated New York columnist Jimmy Breslin, who dropped hints about it in his column in the New York Daily News.

On 1 June 1977 Breslin himself received a letter from the .44 killer. It had been posted two days earlier, in Englewood, New Jersey, just across the George Washington Bridge from Manhattan. The New York Daily News, which was then the biggest-selling newspaper in the USA, held back publication of the full letter for six days as speculation about it, and therefore also the newspaper's circulation, mounted. On 3 June the New York Daily News ran the front-page headline: 'THE .44 CAL-

IBER KILLER – NEW NOTE: CAN'T STOP KILLING'. On the next day the headline read: '.44 KILLER: I AM NOT ASLEEP'. In the Sunday edition it said: 'BRESLIN TO .44 KILLER: GIVE UP! IT'S THE ONLY WAY OUT'. This edition had sold out within an hour of going on sale, so the presses kept rolling and by the end of the day the paper had sold 1,116,000 copies – a record that was beaten only on the day on which Berkowitz was arrested.

The paper's editors assumed that public interest in the story had peaked on Sunday and therefore reproduced the letter in full in the Monday edition. Like the first letter that had been received by Borelli it was written entirely in capital letters and showed the same uncertain grasp of basic spelling. The letter was something of an anti-climax to the newspaper's readers as it was as rambling and incoherent as the letter that the .44 killer had sent to the police.

The writer signed off with the words:

NOT KNOWING WHAT THE FUTURE HOLDS I SHALL SAY FAREWELL AND I WILL SEE YOU AT THE NEXT JOB, OR SHOULD I SAY YOU WILL SEE MY HANDIWORK AT THE NEXT JOB? REMEMBER MS LAURIA.
THANK YOU. IN THEIR BLOOD AND FROM THE GUTTER, 'SAM'S CREATION' .44

Then there was a long postscript:

HERE ARE SOME NAMES TO HELP YOU ALONG. FORWARD THEM TO THE INSPECTOR FOR USE BY THE NCIC: 'THE DUKE OF DEATH', THE WICKED KING WICKER', 'THE TWENTY TWO DISCIPLES OF HELL'. JOHN 'WHEATIES' – RAPIST AND SUFFOCATER OF YOUNG GIRLS.
PS: J B PLEASE INFORM ALL THE DETECTIVES WORKING THE SLAYINGS TO REMAIN.

At the police's request this last page was withheld from publication because the police said that they did not want the existence of the NCIC – the National Crime Information Center – to become public knowledge. Yet the .44 killer certainly knew about it. Perhaps the real reason for their request lay in the satanic undertones of the list of pseudonyms that the killer gave: the 'Wicked King Wicker' presumably refers to 'Wicca' (witch-craft), while the 'Twenty Two Disciples of Hell' certainly sounds like a satanic organisation. The name 'Wheaties' was enclosed within inverted commas as if it were the nickname of the John who was supposedly the 'rapist and suffocater of young girls'. When they ran some checks, however, the police could find no trace of him. In fact none of the names given were much help either to the Omega team that was working on the case or the NCIC. Nor were they any use to Breslin, who now began calling the .44 killer the 'Son of Sam'.

The 17-year-old Judy Placido went to the same Bronx school as Valentina Suriani, whose funeral she had attended. On 25 June 1977, three weeks after the publication of the letter that the .44 killer had written to Breslin, Judy celebrated her high-school graduation at Elephas, a discotheque in Queens. There she met a handsome young man called Salvatore Lupo, who worked at a petrol station; they hit it off immediately and soon went outside for some privacy. While sitting in a car Salvatore slipped his arm around Judy's shoulders as they discussed the Son of Sam killings. It was at that precise moment that their lurid speculations turned into murderous reality. A .44 bullet smashed through the passenger window, passing through Salvatore's wrist and into Judy's neck; a second bullet hit her in the head, but miraculously failed to penetrate her skull, while a third entered her right shoulder. The terrified Salvatore threw open the car door and ran into the discotheque to get help, but it was too late: the shooting was over and the attacker had fled. Although she had been hit three times Judy was quite unaware of having been shot and was shocked to see that her face was covered with blood when she glanced into the rear-view mirror. She, too, then jumped out of the car and headed for the discotheque, but only managed to cover a few yards before collapsing. Salvatore nursed a shattered wrist and cuts from the flying glass; in hospital it was ascertained that Judy had been fortunate to escape without serious injury.

The city was now in a state of panic and takings at discotheques and restaurants – particularly in Queens – plummeted. Newspapers' circulation soared: not only did they contain the gory details of the latest shooting, but they also speculated about the next killing. In the Son of Sam's letter to Breslin he had written, 'Tell me Jim, what will you have for July twenty-ninth?' It was noted that 29 July was the date on which he had carried out his first murder. Was he planning to celebrate the killing of Donna Lauria with another?

New York's mayor, Abraham Beame, who was running for re-election, could not afford to wait to find out and quickly announced that even more officers were being seconded to the investigation. Overnight it became the largest single operation in the history of the New York Police Department: 200 men, recruited from every borough of the city, were seconded to the case and the investigation cost more than $90,000 a day to run. Volunteers, like Donna Lauria's father, Mike, furthermore manned special Son of Sam patrols, as well as a hot line, which was receiving 5,000 calls a day by then. For their part, a team of psychiatrists tried to compile a profile of the killer, but the best that they could come up with was that he was 'neurotic, schizophrenic and paranoid'. This description was duly released by the police, but did not help anyone to identify the gunman.

Fortunately 29 July passed without incident and two days later, with a sense of relief, two sisters from Brooklyn, the fifteen-year-old Ricki Moskozitz and the twenty-year-old Stacy, decided to go out. While in a Brooklyn restaurant, they were approached by a handsome young man who introduced himself as Bobby Violante. The next day Bobby and Stacy went to see the film *New York, New York*. Afterwards they went out to dinner before heading off for a quiet place where they could be alone. They drove to a secluded spot on Shore Parkway, near Coney Island, southern Brooklyn, which was used as an urban type of lovers' lane. They felt safe enough there: so far there had been no Son-of-Sam killings in Brooklyn; the nearest shooting had taken place 22 miles(35 kilometres) away, in Queens. What they did not know, however, was that a week beforehand a man claiming to be the Son of Sam phoned the Coney Island police station to say that he would strike in that area next. Extra patrol cars had therefore been assigned to Brooklyn and Coney Island and Shore Parkway was patrolled regularly.

Bobby and Stacy pulled up under a street lamp, the only available parking spot on Shore Parkway. There was a full moon that night and because it was not dark enough for what they had in mind the pair went for a stroll in a nearby park. They walked over a bridge and spent a few minutes playing on the swings. Near the public lavatories they noticed a jeans-wearing man – whom they described as a 'hippie type' – leaning against a wall, but he was no longer there when they returned to the car. They were kissing in the front seat when Stacy suggested that they moved on. Bobby, however, insisted on one more kiss. This was a mistake, for while they were embracing Bobby was hit in the face by two bullets, which blinded him and caused his eardrums to explode. Although he could neither see nor hear he felt Stacy jerk violently in his arms before falling forward. Fearing that she was dead, Bobby threw himself against the car's horn, fumble at the door, called for help and then collapsed on to the pavement.

Tommy Zaino, who was sitting in the car in front, had seen the shooting in his rear-view mirror. He had watched as a man approached the car from behind before pulling out a gun; from a crouching position he had then fired four shots through the open passenger window. When Tommy's girlfriend, Debbie Crescendo, had heard the shooting she had asked 'What's that?' Tommy believed that he knew: 'Get down', he said.' I think it's the Son of Sam.' Tommy had seen the gunman run towards the park and had then looked at his watch: it was exactly 2.35am. (A patrol car was just five streets away at the time.)

Stacy Moskowitz was still conscious when the ambulance arrived. Although one bullet had grazed her scalp the other had lodged in the back of her brain and she died 38 hours later. Bobby Violante survived, but his sight could not be restored.

Tommy Zaino gave a full description of the killer: he was stocky, with stringy, fair hair. This matched the description given by Donna DeMasi and Joanne Lomino, but did not fit the man with the dark, curly hair who had been described by Jody Valente and the neighbour in the DeMasi-Lomino case. The police therefore wondered whether he had been wearing a wig.

There were other witnesses, too. A beautician and her boyfriend had been sitting by the entrance to the park when they had heard the shots. They had then seen a man wearing a denim jacket and what they took to be a nylon wig jump into a light-coloured car and drive off, as if he had just robbed a bank. A young girl who had been riding a bicycle identified the car as being a yellow Volkswagen, while a nurse who had looked out of her window when she had heard the shooting also said that she had seen a yellow VW. It had almost collided with another car at an intersection and the second driver had been so incensed that he had chased the VW, only to lose it a few streets later. The VW's driver, the other motorist said, had had stringy, brown hair.

An even more vital witness took a little longer to come forward, however. She was Cacilia Davis, a 49-year-old widow who had been out with a male friend on the night in question. They had returned to her flat, which was two streets from the park, at around 2am and had then sat in her friend's car and talked for a few minutes, keeping an eye open for other cars as they did so because they had been forced to double-park. Cacilia had noticed a police car a little way ahead, along with two patrolmen, who were writing out parking tickets. Some way behind them was a yellow Ford Galaxie that had been parked by a fire hydrant; a few minutes before a young man with dark hair walk up to the Galaxie and irritably pull the parking ticket from the windscreen. After that she had invited her friend in for coffee, but he had declined, saying that it was late – it was 2.20am by then. At that moment the police car had pulled away, as had the Galaxie shortly thereafter, but because he could not get past her friend's car the Galaxie's driver had impatiently honked his horn. Cacilia had hurriedly got out of the car and her friend had driven off, whereupon the Galaxie had followed and quickly passed him before speeding off after the police car.

Minutes later Cacilia had taken her dog for a walk in the park and had noticed Tommy Zaino and Bobby Violante's cars, as well as a VW van. On her way home she had seen a man with dark hair and a blue-denim jacket striding across the road from the cars. As he glared at her she had observed that he was walking with his right arm held stiffly, as if something was concealed up his sleeve. He also looked rather like the driver of the Ford Galaxie whom she had seen earlier, she thought.

Cacilia did not come forward with this information immediately, however, for she realised that she was in danger if the man whom she had seen was indeed the Son of Sam: he could easily identify her and knew where she lived. It was not until two days after the shootings that she told a couple of close friends what she had seen. Thinking that she might be able to provide a vital clue as to the killer's identity they urged her to call the police, eventually, doing so on her behalf. Although Dectective Joseph Strano visited her and took her statement it caused hardly a ripple of interest among his colleagues, who considered Tommy Zaino to be the best witness to the shooting. Tommy had seen a man with fair, not dark, hair; moreover, the driver of the Ford Galaxie had left the scene of the crime before the shooting began.

By this time, however, Cacilia – who felt that she had risked her life to come forward – was no longer going to be ignored and threatened to go anonymously to the newspapers with her story. In order to humour her, Strano interviewed her again, this time bringing a police artist to make a sketch of the man whom she had seen. He also took her on an expedition to the shops to see if she could pick out a similar denim jacket to the one which the man had been wearing. Yet nothing further was done to investigate her story.

The primary problem with Cacilia's evidence was that the local police said that they had not issued any parking tickets in the area on the night on which the shootings had taken place. The police cars that had been patrolling the area had been seconded from other boroughs, however, and it was thus ten days before four further parking tickets materialised. Three of the four cars that had been penalised were quickly eliminated. The fourth, a yellow Ford Galaxie with the number plates 561-XLB, was found to belong to a David Berkowitz, of 35 Pine Street, Yonkers – a suburban area just north of the Bronx. When Detective James Justus called the Yonkers police headquarters to investigate further, a switchboard operator named Wheat

Carr answered. On explaining that he was working on the Son of Sam case and that he was running a check on David Berkowitz the woman shouted 'Oh, no'.

It turned out that not only did Wheat Carr know David Berkowitz, but that she had suspected that he was the Son of Sam for sometime. It had begun the previous year, when her father, Sam Carr, had started to receive anonymous letters complaining about his dog. In October 1976 a petrol bomb had been thrown through the window of the Carrs' house at 316 Warburton Avenue, Yonkers. A neighbour had also been receiving anonymous letters and abusive phone calls, and on Christmas Eve a number of shots had been fired through their window; their Alsatian had also been killed. Then, on 27 April 1977, someone had entered the Carrs' back yard and had shot their black Labrador, Harvey.

On 10 June 1977 Sam Carr received a phone call from Jack Cassaras, who lived in New Rochelle, on Long Island Sound, who wanted to know why Sam had sent him a get-well card. The card had mentioned that Jack had fallen off a roof, but Jack had claimed that he had not – and, indeed, had never – been on one. Sam who could offer no explanation for the mystery, had invited Jack over to his house to discuss the matter. On Jack's arrival, about 20 minutes later, Sam had examined the card, which had a picture of an Alsatian on it. He had then told Jack about the bizarre things that had been happening.

Jack had driven home feeling even more puzzled, but his son had then told him that he thought that he had the answer to the enigma. In the previous year the Cassarases had rented a room above their garage to a certain David Berkowitz, who had complained about their Alsatian before suddenly leaving a few weeks later without asking for the $200 deposit on his room. Jack's son suspected that Berkowitz might have something to do with the card. When Mrs Cassaras had looked him up in the telephone directory she found that he had moved to 35 Pine Street, Yonkers. She had then called Sam Carr to ask him whether Pine Street was near his house; it was just around the corner from him, Sam had replied. Convinced that Berkowitz was responsible for the harassment that his family had suffered, Sam had therefore gone to the police, but they had explained that they could take the matter no further without more concrete evidence.

Craig Glassman – a police officer who lived in the flat beneath Berkowitz – had also been receiving abusive letters, and when rubbish was piled against his front door and set alight on 6 August 1977 (a week after the Moskowitz murder) he reported it. He also showed detectives two anonymous letters that he had received, which accused Glassman and the Carrs of being members of a black-magic sect that was out to get him, the author alleged. The detective who examined the letters recognised the handwriting to be that of a man whom he was investigating – David Berkowitz.

Berkowitz was not the only suspect in the Son-of-Sam case, however – indeed, New York has a rich supply of potential serial killers. Besides, Berkowitz did not fit the description given by Tommy Zaino, nor did he drive a yellow VW. It was not until 10 August 1977 that detectives John Longo and Ed Zigo went to Yonkers to check out Berkowitz. On their arrival Zigo spotted Berkowitz's Ford Galaxie parked outside the block of flats in Pine Street. On closer investigation they saw that there was a bag on the back seat from which a rifle butt protruded. Although possession of a rifle does not require a licence in New York, Zigo nevertheless forced open the car. Inside he found another, more formidable, weapon: a Commando Mark III semi-automatic. He also discovered a letter in the glove compartment addressed to Deputy Inspector Timothy Dowd – the head of the Son-of-Sam investigation – which said that the next shooting would be in Long Island.

Detective Zigo phoned the police station and told Sergeant James Shea 'I think we've got him'.

Police who had been rapidly ordered to Pine Street from all over the city staked out the car until Berkowitz – a stocky man, with a round, cherubic face and dark hair – turned up six hours later, When he got into the driver's seat he found himself looking down the barrel of a police revolver. 'Freeze!' yelled Detective William Gardella. 'Police!' Berkowitz simply smiled. Detective John Falotico then opened the passenger door, held his .38 to Berkowitz's head and told him to get out. When Berkowitz placed his hands on the roof of the car Falotico asked 'Who are you?' 'I am Sam', replied Berkowitz.

At One Police Plaza, Berkowitz confessed to the shootings, as well as to sending the anonymous letters, furthermore admitting that his crime spree had begun on Christmas Eve in 1975. At about 7pm on that day he had driven to Co-op City in the Bronx, where his adoptive father lived. On seeing a young, Hispanic woman leaving a shop he had followed her before pulling out a knife and stabbing her in the back. Not realising what had happened, she had turned, screamed and grabbed his wrist, whereupon he had run away. On his way home, however, he had stalked the 15-year-old Michelle Forman and had stabbed her in the back and head. When she fell screaming to the pavement Berkowitz had again fled. Michelle had somehow managed to stagger to the block of flats where she lived and her parents had then rushed her to hospital, where it was discovered that she had a collapsed lung. Her other injuries were superficial, however, and she only spent a week in hospital. Berkowitz's first victim had not even reported the attack and was never identified. These early attacks had convinced Berkowitz that he needed a gun, and a friend called Billy Dan Parka had accordingly bought him a .44 Bulldog revolver in Houston, Texas, for $130.

Under interrogation, Berkowitz explained that he had been ordered to commit the murders by Sam Carr, via Carr's demonic dog, Harvey. Other demonic voices had accompanied him when he was staking his victims, he claimed. Berkowitz was so forthcoming that his confession took only half an hour to complete.

Further inquiries revealed that Richard David Berkowitz had been an illegitimate child who had been given up for adoption as a baby. His natural mother, Betty Broder, was Jewish. At the age of 19 she had married the Italian-American Tony Falco, who had left her for another woman six years later. Betty had begun an affair with Joseph Kleinman, a married real-estate agent, in 1947 and had become pregnant by him, but when she told him that she was going to have a child he replied that she had better get rid of it if she wanted to continue seeing him. Their child was born on 1 June 1953 and was immediately adopted by a Jewish couple, Pearl and Nathan Berkowitz, who were unable to have children of their own. They called their new son David. When Pearl succumbed to cancer in 1967 the 14-year-old David was deeply upset by this new loss.

Two years later Nathan decided to move to Co-op City, in the Bronx. It had been a middle-class suburb, but gangs of youths soon began terrorising the neighbourhood. David's school marks plunged and he seemed to lose his sense of direction. A shy boy, he found himself becoming the victim of bullying, although others regarded him as being spoilt and something of a bully himself. He was big for his age, strong and an excellent baseball player, but preferred to play with children who were younger than himself. His biggest problem, however, was with girls (one friend recalled Berkowitz asking him if he wanted to join the 'girl-haters' club'). He only dated one girl in Co-op City: Iris Gerhardt. Although Iris liked his warm and obliging nature the relationship was never consummated, and while Berkowitz remained chaste it seemed to him that almost everyone else was having sex: 'After a while, at Co-op City there wasn't one girl who was a virgin', he said resentfully. In prison, Berkowitz later wrote 'I must slay women for revenge purposes to get back at them for all the suffering they cause me'.

When his friends started smoking marijuana Berkowitz was too inhibited to join in. Things became worse in 1971, when his father remarried, whereupon Berkowitz, who resented his stepmother and stepsister, joined the army (his spell in uniform did not last long, however). By the time that he returned home in 1974 Berkowitz had rejected Judaism and had become a Baptist. Nathan Berkowitz furthermore remembered watching his son standing in front of a mirror while beating his head with his fists. Things became so uncomfortable in the Berkowitz household that David moved out, renting a drab, one-room flat at 2151 Barnes Avenue in the Bronx. By this time Nathan Berkowitz and his new family were moving to Florida. With his adoptive father gone another door to sanity closed on Berkowitz.

Having known since the age of seven that he was adopted, because he was feeling isolated he now tried to trace his natural family. It took a year. Through the Bureau of Records he discovered that his real name was Richard Falco and that he had been born in Brooklyn. With the help of an old telephone directory he managed to locate his mother and an elder sister. A few days after dropping a card into his mother's letterbox she called him and they had an emotional reunion. He also met his 37-year-old sister and became a regular visitor to the house in which she lived with her husband and children. Berkowitz had found his family and was happy at last – or so it seemed.

During the first half of 1976 his visits to his mother and sister became increasingly rare. He complained of headaches. In February he rented the room above the

Cassarases' garage in New Rochelle, but two months later suddenly moved to Pine Street, Yonkers. In July he killed Donna Lauria, marking the start of his year-long killing spree.

Now, however, the police had Berkowitz under lock and key. Judged sane enough to stand trial, Berkowitz pleaded guilty to all of the charges against him and was sentenced to 365 years in prison. Sergeant Joseph Coffey, who had conducted Berkowitz's initial interrogation, commented 'I feel sorry for him. The man is a fucking vegetable'.

Not everyone was satisfied with Berkowitz's conviction; the young, Yonkers-born investigative journalist Maury Terry was one who noted a number of inconsistencies in Berkowitz's story. For example, Berkowitz claimed that he had acted alone, but because descriptions of the killer varied wildly he could have had an accomplice. Terry also noted that some of the Son-of -Sam killings had been performed with ruthless efficiency, while others had been inept and bungled. He eventually concluded that Berkowitz had committed only three of the killings – those of Donna Lauria, Valentina Suriani and Alexander Esau.

Terry believed that Berkowitz was a member of a satanic organisation – the Twenty Two Disciples of Hell mentioned in the letter sent to Jimmy Breslin from the Son of Sam – and that further members of the cult were actually responsible for the other murders (the killer in the Balaclava, Terry speculated, was a woman). However, when he managed to track down some of the cult's members – including Sam Carrs' sons, John 'Wheaties' and Michael – in order to investigate his theory further he learned that they had all died mysteriously.

In February 1979 Berkowitz issued a statement from Attica Correctional Facility, where he was being held, saying that he was indeed involved with a satanic group. Then, on 10 July 1979, he was slashed with a razor by another inmate. The cut ran from the left-hand side of his throat, to the back of his neck; it needed 56 stitches and nearly killed him. Berkowitz claimed that the attack was a warning from the cult that he should keep his mouth shut.

The Hillside Strangler

Between October 1977 and January 1979 the Los Angeles area was plagued by a series of killings. Although these were attributed to the 'Hillside Strangler' they turned out to be the work not of one man, but of two murderous cousins.

It had started as a discussion over a beer, when Kenneth Bianchi had asked his cousin, Angelo Buono Jr, what it would be like to kill someone. This was no drunken banter and they consequently decided to find out exactly how it would feel.

The 25-year-old Bianchi had been raised by foster parents in Rochester, New York State. In 1977 he had moved to Los Angeles, where he stayed with his cousin, Buono, who was 17 years his senior. The intellectually subnormal, yet streetwise, Buono used to bring prostitutes back to his house in Glendale, where he ran an upholstery business. Within months of Bianchi's arrival in California the aforementioned question of murder came up and they accordingly resolved to kill one of the prostitutes whose services Buono used. It would be the beginning of a murder spree that would claim the lives of 12 young women.

Their first victim was the 21-year-old Hollywood prostitutes Elissa Kastin, whose naked body was found on a hillside on Chevy Chase Drive on 6 October 1977. The police believed that she had been murdered elsewhere and that her body had later been dumped there. Indeed, like those that were to follow her, she had been lured to Buono's home, where she had been savagely raped and killed.

By the end of November 1977 five more young women had fallen victim to the putative Hillside Strangler, and a pattern to the killings was beginning to emerge. The bodies of all of the women, who were mainly part-time prostitutes, had been discovered on hillsides around Los Angeles. Their wrists and ankles bore the marks of ropes and they had been stripped naked, raped and sometimes also sodomised. Their corpses had subsequently been carefully cleaned by the killers so that no clues to their own identities remained. From analysing samples of the sperm that had been left inside the women, however, the police knew that two men had been involved, but they kept this information from members of the press, who, presuming that the perpetrator was a single man, had come up with the nickname the 'Hillside Strangler'.

The murderers were clearly enjoying their notoriety, for all of the naked bodies – often arranged in lascivious poses – had been dumped by roadsides, where they were certain to be discovered. Because the corpses had also been left near police stations it was speculated that the killer was taunting the police. In fact, Bianchi had applied for a job with the Los Angeles Police Department (LAPD), and although he had been turned down, police officers had taken him on patrol during the course of the investigation. The killers chose their victims by cruising around Los Angles in Buono's car. When they saw a likely target they would stop and get out. Flashing fake badges, they would claim to be undercover policeman and order the woman to get into what they said was an unmarked police car. The woman would then be driven to Buono's home, where she would be tied up, tortured and abused by both men before being strangled.

Their second victim was the 19-year-old Yolanda Washington, whose corpse was discovered lying beside the Forest Lawn cemetery on the night of 18 October 1977.

Her spread-eagled, naked body had been meticulously cleansed and the only clues to her death that remained were the marks of the ropes that had restrained her during her final hours of torment. Two weeks later the 15-year-old Judith Miller was found dead on a hillside above a Glendale road. Her neck, wrists and ankles all bore rope marks and she had been violently raped before being strangled.

On the night of 20 November 1977 Bianchi and Buono murdered three girls, one of them – Dolores Cepeda – was only 12 years old. Dolores' body was found lying alongside that of the 14-year-old Sonja Johnson in Elysian Park. On the same night the corpse of the 20-year-old Kristina Weckler was discovered on a hillside in Highland Park. Three days later the casually discarded body of the 28-year-old Jane King was found lying on an exit ramp of the Golden State motorway.

Things went quiet for a bit after that, until, on 17 February 1978, the naked body of Cindy Hudspeth was discovered in the boot of a car. Cindy had been registered with a modelling agency which kept a record of their clients' assignments, leading the LAPD to hope that a breakthrough was at last in sight. Although police officers interviewed a security guard named Ken Bianchi, nothing came of it. The killings, however, mysteriously ceased.

Buono's home was filthy and because Bianchi could no longer stand living there he left his cousin's house and moved to Bellingham, in Washington state, where he took a job as a security guard and again applied to join the local police force. For the rest of 1978 there were no more killings and the special murder squad that had been formed in Los Angeles to track down the Hillside Strangler was therefore disbanded.

However, in January 1979 the bodies of two young women were found in the back of a locked car in Bellingham. Diane Wilder and Karen Mandic had been hired by a young man from a security firm to 'house-watch' a luxury residence in Bellingham while the alarm system was being repaired, or so he had said. Their corpses were subsequently discovered near the house and on investigating further detectives learned that there had been nothing wrong with the alarm system. On checking with the Coastal Security Company (for which Bianchi worked) Bianchi's name came up and it was established that he was the security guard who had hired the women to look after the house. The police then found a note of the address of the house, as well as its front-door key, in Bianchi's lorry. A number of blood semen-stained articles of clothing were furthermore discovered in his house, along with Karen Mandic's telephone number. Meanwhile, forensic experts were examining both car and bodies in an attempt to link him to the killings.

Bianchi now claimed to be suffering from multiple-personality disorder and one of his personalities – Steve – was a sex killer. Six Washington-state psychiatrists duly certified him insane, which, according to the law in Washington, saved him from receiving the death penalty (hanging) for the two murders. Bianchi then plea-bargained a deal with the state prosecutors: if he was allowed to serve out his life sentence in California (where he thought the jails to be more comfortable) he would turn state's evidence again Buono in the Hillside-Strangler case.

The Los Angeles prosecutors, however, considered Bianchi's evidence to be worthless – after all, he had been declared insane by six psychiatrists in Washington state. Thereafter the Hillside-Strangler case became one of the longest and most expensive trials in US criminal history. Halfway through it Bianchi even tried to sabotage it by protesting that he was innocent.

More than 400 witnesses were heard before the two men were finally convicted, of whom one of the most important was the 27-year-old daughter of the actor Peter

Lorre. Catherine Lorre identified Bianchi and Buono as the two men who had stopped her in Hollywood claiming to be police officers. Along with her identity card, she had showed them a photograph of herself with her famous father. This had saved her life, for the murderers had decided that killing the daughter of a celebrity would have caused the police to redouble their efforts to catch them.

The trial dragged on from 16 November 1981 to 14 November 1983, and at the end Judge Ronald George told the pair 'I am sure, Mr Buona and Mr Bianchi, that you will only get your thrills by reliving over and over the tortures and murders of your victims, being incapable as I believe you to be, of ever feeling any remorse'. Bianchi – who was considered to have broken the terms of his plea bargain – was transferred to Washington state to serve his sentence of life imprisonment in Walla Walla Prison, while Buono, who was also sentenced to life,was sent to Folsom Prison in California.

The Backpacker Killer

After meeting in Australia in 1992, two British backpackers, Caroline Clarke and Joanne Walters, teamed up together to hitchhike around the south of the country, leaving a hostel in Sydney in April and then heading south. In September a jogger found their remains in a shallow grave at a place called Executioner's Drop in the Belanglo Forest. In the October of the following year, 1993, two more corpses were discovered in the same area. They belonged to James Gibson and Deborah Everist, both of whom were 19 and from Melbourne, who had disappeared in 1989.

It was soon begun to be feared that a serial killer was at work and an intensive search of the region was therefore set in motion. On 1 November 1993 the body of the 23-year-old Simone Schmidl, from Germany, was unearthed nearby; she had last been seen in January 1991. On the following day the skeletons of the 21-year-old Gabor Neugebauer and his 20-year-old girlfriend, Anja Habschied – two more German backpackers, who had disappeared two years previously – were found. Both victims had died from multiple stab wounds and Anja had also been beheaded.

Over 300 police officers were then ordered to comb a vast area of remote woodland and scrub for clues and other graves. It was the biggest murder hunt in Australia's history. One clue was identified: cartridges from a .22 Ruger were found near the grave of the 22-year-old Caroline Clarke which matched some spent cartridges that had been discovered at an isolated farmhouse.

After searching their records the New South Wales police thought that they had identified the serial killer's eighth victim. In 1991 the body of a 29-year-old Australian mother, Diane Pennacchio, had been found in a wood; last seen leaving a bar near Canberra, she had been stabbed to death sometime thereafter. Although her body have been found more than 100 miles (161 kilometres) from the others, she had been buried in the same, distinctive way. All eight had been found lying face downwards, with their hands behind their backs, alongside a fallen tree trunk; a small wigwam of sticks and ferns had been constructed over each body.

By the beginning of 1994 the 'Backpacker Killer' was making the headlines world-wide. Then a 24-year-old British woman came forward and told the police that she had been hitchhiking in the Belanglo Forest in January 1990 when she had been picked up by a lorry driver. When he had started acting strangely she had leapt out of the vehicle and had run into the woods. As she fled the driver had fired a gun at her, but had missed. Another

British backpacker, the 25-year-old Paul Onion, also told the police that he had been hitchhiking in the same area in 1990 when he had accepted a lift from a man who had later pulled a gun out of the glove compartment. As Paul was fleeing the man had shot at him, thankfully missing his intended victim. Paul was able to identify the driver's car, as well as picking out his photo from the New South Wales police's collection of mug shots.

Following a dawn raid on 22 may 1994 a 49-year-old lorry driver and gun fanatic named Ivan Milat was arrested. Parts of a rare, .22-calibre, Ruger rifle were found hidden in his bungalow and ballistics tests later link it to cartridge cases that had been picked up at the scenes of two of the killings. It was also identified as the weapon that had been used to kill Caroline Clarke, Milat's fingerprints furthermore being found on the gun.

Ivan Robert Marko Milat was consequently charged with the deaths of seven backpackers. Although he pleaded not guilty he was accordingly sentenced to life imprisonment.

The Gay Slayer

Colin Ireland, London's 'Gay Slayer', wanted to achieve notoriety as a serial killer. He revelled in the fact that the details of his hideous murders were reported week by week by a fascinated press and furthermore telephoned police detectives to taunt them: 'I've got the book', he would say (meaning the FBI Handbook). 'I know how many you have to do.' After he had murdered his fifth victim – which officially classed him as a serial killer – he phoned up and boasted 'I've done another one'.

There is no doubt that Ireland was a deranged character. The illegitimate son of a newsagent's assistant in Dartford, Kent, he never knew his father. His mother remarried when he was 12 and he did not get on with his stepfather, who beat the boy for the slightest reason. Always something of a loner, he then became 'difficult' and was sent to a school for maladjusted children. After having been expelled for arson he began a life of petty crime, which took him firstly to borstal and eventually to prison. At the same time he became obsessed with both uniforms and the newly fashionable cult of survivalism, moreover making it plain to his friends that he hated 'queers'.

In 1990, at the age of 35, the 6 feet (183 metre) tall Ireland, who now weighed 15 stones (95 kilogrammes), married the landlady of a pub in Newton Abbot. He dumped her on their honeymoon, however, before returning to the pub, plundering it and then making off in her car. By the end of 1992 he had two failed marriages behind him and was working at a night shelter for the homeless in Southend. Shortly before Christmas he had a violent row with a gay man at the shelter and upon being sacked set about taking his revenge on all homosexuals. He began frequenting the Coleherne, a pub in the Earl's Court district of London that was popular with homosexual men who were into sado-masochism (S & M). Ireland later told detectives: 'I had gone there with the idea that if someone approached me something would happen. It would be some sort of trigger – a stepping over the line in a way.

On 8 March 1993 Peter Walker, a 45-year-old theatre director, stepped over that line when he accidentally spilled some water on Ireland's jacket and begged Ireland to punish him for it by beating him. They then took a taxi to Walker's flat in Battersea for a sado-masochistic sex session, Ireland having come equipped with a cord, knife and pair of gloves. Walker eagerly submitted to being tied to the bed. 'Once I had tied him up I knew my intentions were different from his', Ireland said later. 'I'm not sure if I really set out to kill him, but it went from there... In the end I killed him with a plastic bag. I put it over his head.' Two days later he called the Samaritans, and a newspaper, asking them to visit the flat to take care of Walker's dogs.

On 28 May 1993 Ireland returned to the Coleherne and fell into conversation with Christopher Dunn, a 37-year-old librarian. Like Peter Walker, Dunn was a masochist who was into bondage – perfect for Ireland's purposes. The two men went back to Dunn's flat in Wealdstone, where Ireland handcuffed the willing Dunn to his bed. Dunn's pleasure quickly turned to dismay, however, as he watched Ireland rifle through his wallet and pull out the money that it contained, along with his cash-point card. When Dunn refused to tell Ireland his PIN (personal identification number) Ireland burnt Dunn's testicles with a cigarette lighter until he complied, then strangling him with a length of cord.

Ireland's third victim was Perry Bradley III, a 35-year-old sales director from Sulphur Springs, Texas, whose father was a congressman. The bisexual Bradley was another habitué of the Coleherne, where, on 4 June 1993, he met Ireland, shortly thereafter taking him to his smart, Kensington flat. Although Bradley was not really into S & M, Ireland eventually persuaded him to let Ireland tie him up, going through his wallet once Bradley was trussed up and helpless. 'At one point I was thinking of letting him go', Ireland said in his statement to the police. 'Then I thought it's easier to kill him rather than walk the streets alone while it was dark.' He therefore settled down to listen to the radio until morning, wiping away his fingerprints after dawn and then leaving the flat.

Andrew Collier, the 33-year-old warden of a block of sheltered-accommodation flats in east London, was another Coleherne regular. After having been picked up by Ireland on 7 June 1993 Collier took him to his flat in Dalston. While the two men were having a drink they heard an altercation on the street and went to the window to see what was happening, Ireland leaning out of the window accidentally leaving a fingerprint on the outside of the window frame. Afterwards Collier consented to Ireland tying him up and once he was helpless Ireland strangled him with a noose. Ireland was then inspecting the contents of Collier's wallet when he found some medical papers: 'I was going through his documentation and I became aware he had AIDS', Ireland said. 'He didn't warn me... I went fucking crazy. I burnt certain areas of his body. He loved his cat, that was his life – so I did the cat with a noose, draped it over the body.' The cat was actually arranged so that its mouth was around Collier's penis, its tail having been stuffed into his mouth. Ireland later told the police 'I wanted him to have no dignity in death. It was a way of saying to the police "What do you think of that?" It was like a signature to let them know I'd been there. I was reaching a point where I was just accelerating. It was just speeding up, getting far worse.'

After Collier's killing, Ireland phoned the police and asked them whether they were still investigating the murder of Peter Walker. He taunted them, saying 'I will do another. I have always dreamed of doing the perfect murder'. Then Ireland laughed about killing Collier's cat – following the call that he made about Peter Walker's dogs the press had been speculating that the killer was an animal lover.

On 13 June 1993 Ireland killed for the fifth, and last, time. His victim was the 42-year-old, Maltese-born chef, Emanuel Spiteri. 'I'd seen him a couple of times at the Coleherne', said Ireland. 'He was obviously the leather type.' Having accompanied Spiteri to his flat in south London, Ireland then tied him up and tortured him in an attempt to make him reveal the PIN for his cash-point card. Spiteri, however, resisted, screaming 'You will just have to kill me'. 'He was a very brave man, but I couldn't allow him to stick around', explained Ireland, continuing 'I killed him with a noose.'

It was at this point that Ireland telephoned the police

and bragged that he had now taken five lives, which, he claimed, made him a real serial killer and hence 'famous'. What Ireland did not know, however, was that when he and Spiteri had passed through Charing Cross station on their way to Spiteri's home in Hither Green they had been filmed by the station's security cameras. A description of the man whom the police wanted to question was first issued to the public and then the British Transport Police's video of Spiteri with his killer was shown on television.

On 20 July 1993 Ireland walked into a solicitor's office in Southend and revealed that he was the man who had been filmed with Spiteri, whereupon the solicitor advised him to go to the police. Having done so, Ireland told police officers at New Scotland Yard that although he had indeed gone to Spiteri's flat with him he had left shortly afterwards; a third man had also been present, he claimed. The police quickly demolished Ireland's story, however: one of his fingerprints was found to match that left on the frame of Collier's window and the police also recognised Ireland's voice from his anonymous phone calls. Realising that the game was up Ireland confessed to all five murders en route to the magistrates's court.

At the Old Bailey Ireland pleaded to five counts of murder. On sentencing him to serve five life sentences Mr Justice Sachs said.

By any standards you are an exceptionally frightening and dangerous man. In cold blood and with great deliberation you killed five of your fellow human beings in grotesque and cruel circumstances. The fear, brutality and indignity to which you subjected your victims are almost unspeakable. To take one human life is outrageous. To take five is carnage. You expressed your desire to be regarded as a serial killer – that must be matched by your detention for life. In my view it is absolutely clear you should never be released.

The Monster of Florence

In 1968 Antonio Io Bianci was making love to Barbara Locci in the front seat of his car when they were both shot dead, Barbara's husband being subsequently arrested and convicted of the murders. It would be six years before Signor Locci could prove his innocence and establish that the double murder was the first atrocity committed by a serial killer who preyed on courting couples in Tuscany who later became known as the 'Monster of Florence'.

While Signor Locci was languishing in jail another courting couple was killed in a car. The police established that they had been shot with the same .22-calibre Beretta pistol that had been used in the Bianchi and Locci murders; the female victim had furthermore been mutilated. During the course of the next year two more people were killed in a similar manner. Although a German couple was murdered, too, neither of them was mutilated (they were homosexuals and their killing was probably a mistake).

Upon Signor Locci's release the Monster of Florence appeared to suspend his activities. He struck again in 1981, however, stabbing his female victim some 300 times. Four months later, in October 1981, another woman was murdered and mutilated. The Monster of Florence continued to wage his campaign of murder over the next four years. The slayings followed a rigid pattern: all of the men were shot through the driver's window before the women were killed, their bodies then being dragged from the car and mutilated with a knife (their left breasts were generally hacked off). Ballistics tests revealed that all of the 67 bullets that were fired in a total of 16 murders came from the same gun, all also being marked with the letter 'H'. The Monster of Florence's final attack, in 1985, differed slightly from the rest, however. He slaughtered his last victims – a French couple – in their tent, cutting off a section of the woman's genitalia (which he later posted to the police) during his grisly mutilation of her body.

The Florence police handled the case badly. Numerous false accusations were made and one man who had been named as the killer committed suicide by cutting his throat. Another five were jailed for the killings, three of whom were released when the Monster struck again while they were behind bars; because there was no evidence against a fourth a judge released him, while the fifth man remained the subject of controversy.

During the course of the Monster of Florence's bloody reign of terror the police received scores of anonymous notes identifying Petro Pacciani as the killer. Pacciani was a peasant farmer who had been convicted of murder in 1951 and jailed for 13 years for killing a rival in love. (Pacciani had followed his 16-year-old fiancée upon seeing her going into the woods with another man; when he could no longer stand the sight of them making love he had stabbed the man 19 times before raping the terrified girl next to the mutilated corpse.) The police speculated that if he was indeed the Monster of Florence the embittered Pacciani had sought to avenge himself on other couples. Key to their thinking was the theory that it had been the sight of his fiancée's exposed left breast during her seduction that had triggered Pacciani's initial attack and that this was also why the Monster usually amputated the left breasts of his female victims. Pacciani had again come to the police's attention in 1987, subsequently being convicted of molesting his two daughters and accordingly being jailed.

His name was fed into a computer, along with those of more than 100,000 people who had the opportunity of carrying out the Monster of Florence's crimes. The computer identified just one suspect, however: Pacciani. Convinced that Pacciani was the perpetrator of the murders, the police searched his farm in minute detail for evidence, but nothing was found. They were on the point of giving up when a bullet was unearthed which was later found to match those that had been used in the murders.

Although a weapon was never recovered Pacciani was charged with murder. His trial dragged on for six months before the jury finally convicted him, whereupon he was jailed for life in 1994. Subsequently, however, a judicial review reassessed the flimsy evidence against him and after its ruling that his conviction was unsafe Pacciani was released from prison in 1996. As far as anyone knows the Monster of Florence is still at large.

The Rostov Ripper

Following the collapse of the Soviet Union during the early 1990s the rest of the world – as well as its own people – discovered that Russia, along with the other former Soviet republics, could produce serial killers that were more than a match for any found in the West.

The first such notable case was that of Nikolai Dzhumagaliev, the killer cannibal who was known as 'Metal Fang' because of his white-metal, false teeth. Dzhumagaliev operated in Kazakhstan during 1980, picking up tall, attractive women in the capital , Alma-Ata, before taking them for a walk along the river bank, where he raped them and then hacked them to death with an axe. On the night following each murder he would invite friends to dinner and serve them roast meat, his reign of terror coming to an end when two of his guests found a woman's head and entrails in his fridge. Charged with seven murders, Dzhumagaliev was found to be insane and was sent to psychiatric hospital in Tashkent. He escaped in 1989, however, and after trying to pick up women in Moscow fled to Uzbekistan, where he was eventually captured. Yet terrible as his crimes undoubtedly were, Metal Fang's reputation as a serial killer would soon be eclipsed by that of the 'Rostov Ripper'.

At first sight Andrei Romanovich Chikatilo, a former schoolteacher, was a mild-mannered grandfather. He was also an apparently happily married man – if slightly henpecked – although some thought his habit of sleeping in the bathroom a little odd. Those who were closer to him, however, knew that he was haunted by the memory of a cousin who had been killed and his body subjected to cannibalism during the 1934 Ukrainian famine. Even so, no one who knew Chikatilo would have believed that he had tortured, murdered, raped, mutilated and eaten as many as 53 victims, many of them children, between 1978 and 1990. (There may have been more: because Chiktilo's victims were loners and strays some disappearances may have gone unreported.) During the course of the 12-year murder investigation 500,000 people were questioned; Chikatilo himself was arrested and interrogated twice, but was released on both occasions.

It was Chikatilo's sexual problems that sparked his murder spree. His wife, Fayina, later admitted that her husband had not been able to make love to her properly. He had therefore turned to prostitutes and had bought a shack to which he would take them for sex. This strategy ultimately proved unsuccessful, too, however and his inability to perform sexually seems to have enraged him.

His first victim was a pretty nine-year-old named Lena Zakotno. In December 1978 he lured her to rape her; having failed to do so, he then murdered her. It was then that he discovered that he was only able to have sex with someone when they were dead. Afterwards he disposed of Lena's body in a river. Chikatilo was suspected of being involved in Lena's death after neighbours reported seeing a light burning in the shack during the night on which

Lena had vanished. He was interviewed nine times about the murder before suspicion fell on another man who lived nearby. The man confessed, was found guilty and executed.

Chikatilo then embarked upon a career of prolific murder – 11 bodies were found in 1984 alone. With the sixth sense of the natural predator he would pick out the weak and vulnerable, hanging around bus stops and railway stations looking for prostitutes and runaways. He would also stalk potential victims on buses and trains or target them in the street. His favourite targets were homeless drifters who were unlikely to missed, or else solitary children on their way to school. A lone child could be tempted by a packet of chewing gum, while a drifter would jump at the offer of a meal or a chance to watch a video. After all, Chikatilo looked for all the world like a kindly grandfather.

'As soon as I saw a lonely person I would have to drag them off to the woods', he later told the police. 'I paid no attention to age or sex. We would walk for a couple of miles or so through the woods and then I would be possessed by a terrible shaking sensation.' He then murdered his victims before raping and mutilating their corpses. Sometimes he disembowelled them and cut out or bit off their organs; fearing their deathly gaze, he would usually pluck out their eyes, and would furthermore bite off their nipples in a sexual frenzy.

The police found themselves out of their depth: 'We just couldn't imagine what sort of person we were dealing with', said Lieutenant Colonel Viktor Burakov, who led the murder hunt. 'This was the height of sadism, the like of which we had never seen.' At the height of the murders the police mounted a regular surveillance of the woods around Rostov. Although Chikatilo himself was stopped in an isolated, wooded area in 1979, he persuaded the police that he was an innocent hiker and after noting down his name and address they let him go.

Chikatilo's wife and friends were baffled when he gave up his teaching job of ten years in 1981 for the position of a lowly supply clerk in a locomotive-repair shop in Rostov. His new job gave him the opportunity to travel, however, and he extended his murderous activities to St Petersburg, the Ukraine and Uzbekistan. The manhunt, which was led by detectives seconded from Moscow, now stretched to Siberia.

In 1983 he was arrested close to the scene of one of the murders, the police finding a length of rope and a knife in his briefcase. A sample of his blood was taken, but because it proved to belong to a different group to that of the semen samples that had been recovered from the victims' bodies Chikatilo was released. (At that time the Soviet police did not know that in extremely rare cases secretions from various parts of the body can have different serological groupings; Chikatilo was one of those rare cases.)

During the summer of 1984 Chikatilo was forced to take a break from murder when he was arrested and jailed for three months for the theft of three rolls of linoleum. Over the month following his release Chikatilo relieved his pent-up frustration by slaughtering eight people.

Chikatilo's murderous campaign was only halted because the police had a stroke of luck. In November 1990 a policeman stopped Chikatilo in the street after spotting bloodstains on his face. When the body of his final victim, a young boy, was later discovered nearby witnesses reported having seen a middle-aged man hanging around the railway station while the boy bought a ticket. Having run a check on 25,000 possible suspects detectives put Chikatilo under heavy surveillance on reading the police report pertaining to his having been stopped while covered with blood. Six-hundred policemen were drafted in to cover the station and adjoining woods and some were watching on 20 November 1990 when Chikatilo approached a teenage boy at the railway station. He was immediately arrested.

Under interrogation Chikatilo readily confessed to murdering 11 boys and 42 women and girls during his reign of terror, although he claimed that 'there may be more'. Of his known victims the youngest was Igor Gudkov, a seven-year-old who had strayed from his home; the oldest was the 44-year-old prostitute Marta Ryabyenko. Upon realising that her husband was the Rostov Ripper Chikatilo's wife, as well as his two grown-children, went into hiding.

Chikatilo was 56 when he went on trial in Rostov on 14 April 1992. Throughout the proceedings, he sat in chains within an iron cage that had been built around the dock. On the first day of the trial proceedings were delayed for half an hour while the hysterical crowd bayed for his blood, Chiktilo merely rolling his eyes and waving pornographic magazines to inflame the audience further as first-aiders administered sedatives to the families of his victims. The two-volume indictment listed thirty-five child victims and eighteen women. The facts of the case were not contested and Chikatilo was sane; experts from Moscow's Serbsky Institute, Russia's leading institute of psychiatry, testified that he was.

It took Judge Leonid Akabzhanov an hour and a half to read the verdict on 15 October 1992, during which he concluded that 52 of the 53 murders had been proven. He expressed fierce criticism of the police, however: 'If they had done their job in 1978 after the first killing 52 lives could have been saved', he said, continuing: 'Or if they had not released him after questioning in 1984 at least 20 people would not have died'. Of the accused he said: 'He ruthlessly and cold-bloodedly dismembered his victims, pulling them apart while they were still alive'. The judge then sentenced him to death, outraging Chikatilo: 'I fought in Afghanistan', he ranted. 'I was a partisan who defended the barricades; I fought for a free Russia.' The courtroom was in pandemonium when he was finally taken from the iron cage for the last time.

On 14 February 1994 Andrei Chikatilo, whom the press was now calling the 'world's most sadistic and perverted killer', was executed by means of a single bullet to the back of the head after President Boris Yeltsin had rejected his appeal for clemency.

The Terminator

The Ukrainian serial killer Anatoly Onoprienko was sentenced to death in 1999 after having been convicted of murdering fifty-two people, including ten children in villages across Ukraine, most of them during a three-month killing spree. The former sailor, who had become known as 'The Terminator', admitted the killings, saying that he had been driven by a higher force.

In its eagerness to join the European Union (EU) the Ukraine had in the meantime complied with EU requirements in suspending its death sentence, however, and in 1999 Onoprienko was therefore still being held in a tiny, 9-by-5-feet (2.7-by 1.5-metre) cell at the nineteenth-century prison in Zhitornir, 8 miles (13 kilometres) west of Kiev, while his fate was being decided. Because Onoprienko relished killing even the toughest guards on death row took no chances with him.

'The first time I killed I shot down a deer in the woods', he later reminisced. 'I was in my early twenties and I had done it, and I felt sorry for it. I never had that feeling again.' Onoprienko's first human victims were a couple whom he had seen standing by their Lada car on a motorway. 'I just shot them', he said. 'It's not that it gave me pleasure, but I felt this urge. From then on it was almost like some game from outer space.'

After that he terrorised the Ukraine for months, slaughtering men, women and children alike, wiping out entire families in cold blood, battering children and raping one woman after having shot her in the face. 'To me killing people was like ripping up a duvet', he explained. 'Men, women, old people, children – they are all the same. I have never felt sorry for those I killed. No love, no hatred, just blind indifference. I don't see them as individuals, but just as masses.' On one occasion he had killed a young girl who was praying, having just seen him kill both of her parents. 'Seconds before I smashed her head in, I ordered her to show me where they kept their money', he said. 'She looked at me with an angry, defiant stare and said "No, I won't". That strength was incredible. But I still felt nothing.'

The Ukraine had been plunged into panic when Onoprienko's savagery reached its climax in early 1996, when he committed about forty murders in three months. The determined force that he used was almost unbelievable: he blew the doors off homes on the edges of villages, gunned down adults and beat children with metal cudgels, stealing money, jewellery, stereo equipment and other valuable items before burning down his victims' homes. 'To me it was like hunting. Hunting people down', he explained. 'I would be sitting, bored, with nothing to do. And then suddenly this idea would get into my head. I would do everything to get it out of my mind, but I couldn't. It was stronger than me. So I would get in the car or catch a train and go out to kill.'

Although he took pleasure in the 'professionalism' of his crimes, Onoprienko claimed that he had derived no pleasure from killing. 'Corpses are ugly', he confided. 'They stink and send out bad vibes. Once I killed five people and then sat in the car with their bodies for two hours not knowing what to do with them. The smell was unbearable.' Investigators feared that his final tally of victims was higher than 52 – with some justification, for there appeared to have been a long gap between murders when he roamed illegally around other European countries.

After weeks of tests and interviews a commission consisting of the Ukraine's top psychiatrists and psychologists concluded that Onoprienko was not mentally ill, rather that his main motivation for murder appeared to have been money: he killed to steal. The fact that he had grown up without parents and had been sent to an orphanage by his elder brother may have explained why he had slaughtered entire families, they speculated. Indeed, his most frenzied killing spree had occurred after he had moved in with a woman (who said that he had always been very loving) and her children. The couple had intended to marry, Onoprienko having proposed to his girlfriend with a ring that he had forcibly removed from the finger of one of his victims only a few hours earlier.

For his part, Onoprienko – who claimed that he was a good-natured person and a sensitive music-lover – maintained that he was possessed. 'I'm not a maniac', he said.

'It's not that simple. I have been taken over by a higher force, something telepathic or cosmic, which drove me. For instance, I wanted to kill my brother's first wife, because I hated her. I really wanted to kill her, but I couldn't because I had not received the order. I waited for it all the time, but it did not come... I am like rabbit in a laboratory, part of an experiment to prove that man is capable of murdering and learning to live with his crimes. To show that I can cope, that I can stand anything, [I] forget everything.'

Onoprienko was finally caught after the Ukraine had staged its biggest manhunt, which involved 2,000 police officers and more than 3,000 troops. He was eventually arrested in April 1996 at his girlfriend's house, near the

Polish border, as the result of an anonymous tip-off.

During his trial, which took place in his hometown of Zhytomyr, Onoprienko stood locked within a metal cage in the courtroom. He described himself as 'the devil' and boasted about being the world's greatest serial killer. he expressed no remorse for his crimes, continuing to claim that a higher force had driven him to commit them. 'He is driven by extreme cruelty', disagreed Dmytro Lypsky, the presiding judge at his trial. 'He doesn't care about anything, only about himself. He is egocentric and has a very high opinion of himself.'

Five judges, including Lypsky, sat in judgement on Onoprienko during his four-month trial. It took three hours to read out their verdict, after which Lypsky told the court: 'In line with the Ukraine's criminal code Onoprienko is sentenced to death by shooting'. In March 1997, however, the Ukraine was admitted to the Council of Europe, and in compliance with EU rules the Ukraine's president, Leonid Kuchma, announced a moratorium on capital punishment. Yet Onoprienko's crimes had caused such revulsion in the Ukraine that commuting the serial killer's death sentence to 20 years in jail accused outrage. Even Onoprienko himself refused to ask for his sentence to be commuted, instead insisting that he should be executed and warning:

'If I am ever let out I will start killing again. But this time it will be worse, ten times worse. The urge is there. Seize this chance because I am being groomed by Satan. After what I have learnt out there I have no competitors in my field. And if I am not killed I will escape from this jail and the first thing I'll do is find Kuchma and hang him from a tree by his testicles.'